Studies in Interdisciplinary History

Patterns of Social Capital

izens, work
vic culture.
d by volun-
ocial capital

pital across
oluntary as-
ortant indi-

ocial capital
the authors
capital will
ation as we
y about the
d how these

erdisciplinary
and adjunct
onflict at the
. He is the
ia, and the
frica (1965),
*Rhodes and
r Democracy*

Patterns
of
Social Capital

Stability and Change in Historical Perspective

Edited by
Robert I. Rotberg

Contributors:
Gene Brucker
Elisabeth S. Clemens
Gerald R. Gamm
Claudia Goldin
Jack P. Greene
Raymond Grew
Myron P. Gutmann
Lawrence F. Katz
Marjorie K. McIntosh
Edward Muir
Sara M. Pullum
Robert D. Putnam
Lucian W. Pye
Leonard N. Rosenband
Robert I. Rotberg
Mary P. Ryan
Reed Ueda

CAMBRIDGE
UNIVERSITY PRESS

PUBLISHED BY THE PRESS SYNDICATE OF THE UNIVERSITY OF CAMBRIDGE
The Pitt Building, Trumpington Street, Cambridge, United Kingdom

CAMBRIDGE UNIVERSITY PRESS
The Edinburgh Building, Cambridge CB2 2RU, UK
40 West 20th Street, New York, NY 10011-4211, USA
10 Stamford Road, Oakleigh, VIC 3166, Australia
Ruiz de Alarcón 13, 28014 Madrid, Spain
Dock House, The Waterfront, Cape Town 8001, South Africa

http://www.cambridge.org

First published 2001

This book is derived from articles published in two special issues of *The Journal of Interdisciplinary History*, XXIX (1999), 3 & 4.

Printed in the United States of America

This book was typeset in Bembo using Corel Ventura 8   [Wellington Graphics]

A catalog record for this book is available from the British Library.

Library of Congress Cataloging in Publication Data

Patterns of social capital : stability and change in historical perspective / edited by Robert I. Rotberg ; contributors, Gene Brucker . . . [et al.].
    p. cm. – (Studies in interdisciplinary history)
    Includes bibliographical references.
    ISBN 0-521-78086-1–ISBN 0-521-78575-8 (pb)
    1. Social participation–Cross-cultural studies.   2. Community life–Cross-cultural studies.   3. Social networks–Cross-cultural studies.   4. Social groups–Cross-cultural studies.   I. Rotberg, Robert I.   II. Series.

HM771 P38 2000
302'.14–dc21   00-059878

ISBN 0 521 78086 1   hardback ✓
ISBN 0 521 78575 8   paperback

Contents

Robert I. Rotberg

Social Capital and Political Culture in Africa, America, Australasia, and Europe

Societies work best, and have always worked best, where citizens trust their fellow citizens, work cooperatively with them for common goals, and thus share a civic culture. A civic community is marked, in Putnam's words, "by an active, public-spirited citizenry, by egalitarian political relations, [and] by a social fabric of trust and cooperation." Vibrant networks and norms of civic engagement are essential for such a community. In societies where distrust is prevalent and horizontal ties of mutual involvement are replaced by hierarchical politics, social capital is absent, and little civic engagement exists. Indeed, the dilemmas of collective action at almost any level can best be solved through networks of reciprocal trust, a key component of social capital and a essential ingredient of democracy. For political stability and government effectiveness, Putnam says, "social capital may be even more important than physical or human capital."[1]

The accumulation of reciprocal trust, as demonstrated by a variety and combination of voluntary efforts for the creation of common goods, helps to build social capital and contributes to effective government. Societies with high levels of social capital function with greater, rather than lesser, participation of citizens. Social capital contributes to the making of civil society. A civic culture exists because citizens have accumulated large amounts of social capital. Although *political culture* is the term that describes how a society and a collection of leaders and citizens chooses, and has long chosen, to approach national political decisions, high levels of social capital contribute to the creation of a political

Robert I. Rotberg is co-editor of *The Journal of Interdisciplinary History,* President of the World Peace Foundation, and Adjunct Professor and Director of the Program on Intrastate Conflict at the Kennedy School of Government, Harvard University. He is the author/editor of numerous books about Africa, Asia, and the Caribbean, including *A Political History of Tropical Africa* (New York, 1965); *Haiti: The Politics of Squalor* (Boston, 1971); *The Founder: Cecil Rhodes and the Pursuit of Power* (New York, 1988); *Burma: Prospects for Democracy* (Cambridge, Mass., 1998).

1   Robert D. Putnam, with Roberto Leonardi and Raffaella Y. Nanetti, *Making Democracy Work: Civic Traditions in Modern Italy* (Princeton, 1993), 15, 170–183.

culture that is open, pluralistic, deliberative, tolerant, and democratic.

These are propositions advanced to explain why countries or
regions within countries display high levels of civic engagement
and democratic performance over years and decades, and why
other countries and regions do not. Conversely, these propositions
imply that without healthy levels of volunteerism, civic engagement, reciprocal trust, and citizen involvement in politics, civil
society will not flourish. Nor will plural democracy. In countries
or regions where, for whatever reason, citizens volunteer less and
less, help each other less and less, and disengage from civic life
more and more (as measured by a number of not uncontroversial
indices), plural democracy will suffer. Moreover, under these
circumstances, a political culture that is plurally democratic will
lose some of its key attributes of participation and cohesion.

Social scientists have used measurements of civility, cohesion,
and participation to explain why similar cultures might produce
divergent political outcomes, why democracy has taken root
where it has, and why even a single country might have regions
with different levels of civic engagement. What generalizations
follow about the creation of, or failure to create, civic consciousness? Putnam, in attempting to answer this and additional questions for Italy, advanced a theory of social capital to distinguish
the experiences of Italy's North and South: The development of
attitudes of reciprocal trust, derived from a tradition of face-to-face
relations, permitted democratic norms to flourish in the North,
and not in the South (caught up as it was in a tangled web of
amoral familism).[2]

Trust and reciprocity in human endeavor provide the basis
for effective group action. A dearth of social capital in a society
hinders social mobilization as well as political and economic
growth. High levels of social capital, reflecting reciprocal bonds
of trust, cut horizontally across classes and ethnicities and encourage cooperation for the commonweal. Low levels, reflecting predominantly hierarchical (vertical) ties between patrons and clients
or rulers and the ruled, indicate a government often more concerned with private than public good—a recipe for corruption.

2 *Ibid.*, 163–185. For amoral familiasm, see Edward C. Banfield, *The Moral Basis of a
Backward Society* (Chicago, 1958), 17, 33.

Putnam returned social capital as an explanatory bundle of variables to the United States, and to other democracies. In a series of influential articles, he hypothesized, as Tocqueville had noted at the beginning of the nineteenth century, that volunteerism provided the bedrock for the accumulation of social capital in the United States, and elsewhere. Likewise, in the years after World War II, especially after the Vietnam War, lower levels of volunteerism signalled civic disengagement and the fraying of democracy, even in as well-established a democratic society as the United States.[3] Putnam's essay in this volume, in collaboration with Gerald Gamm, measures voluntary participation past and present to examine such hypotheses. Putnam and Gamm's contribution complements other articles in this volume about comparable phenomena, globally, by Mary P. Ryan and Elisabeth S. Clemens.

Before Putnam modernized and refined social capital as an analytical tool capable of explaining the roots of civic engagement, social scientists had developed a theory of political culture—the sum of the values within a society, or a part of a society, that influences how rulers govern and citizens exercise their civic responsibilities and opportunities. For Almond and Verba, political culture was the "particular distribution of patterns of orientation toward political objects"—in other words, the sum of a society's political attitudes and orientations, or its political system "as internalized in the cognitions, feelings, and evaluations" of its people. Pye explicated political culture as the collection of "attitudes, sentiments, and cognitions" that govern political behavior, representing "coherent patterns which fit together and are mutually reinforcing." Political culture, moreover, gives "meaning, predictability, and form" to a nation's political process. Since each generation within a society receives its politics from the previous one, political culture embraces the traditions of a society, the spirit of its public institutions, the passions and collective reasoning of its citizens, and the "style and operating codes" of its leaders; it is a collective history of institutions and individuals. According to Verba, political culture is the "system of empirical beliefs, expres-

3 Putnam, "The Prosperous Community: Social Capital and Public Life," *The American Prospect*, 13 (Spring 1993), 35–42; *idem*, "The Strange Disappearance of Civic America," *ibid.*, 24 (Winter, 1996), 34–48. Alexis de Tocqueville (ed. J. P. Mayer; trans. George Lawrence), *Democracy in America* (Garden City, 1969; orig. pub. 1835–1840).

sive symbols, and values" that define political action. It denotes each citizen's identification with his fellow citizens and his nation, and it shapes each's citizen's expectations about the legitimacy and output of his/her government.[4]

Political culture was/is hardly static; the feedback loop is natural and continuous. The behavior of citizen is influenced by the operations of government, and the attitudes and responses of governments are influenced by the shifting values, orientations, and approaches of its citizens. There is no one global political culture, but many. Political culture, however, has been regressing for some time toward a mean. As the opening essays in this collection by Gene Brucker and Edward Muir about early republican Italy—a complicated and fluid era—make abundantly clear, the varieties of political culture have been steadily dwindling. Despite a hypothesized clash of civilizations, there has been a convergence of political culture, particularly in the aftermath of communism's collapse.[5] The political orientations and values that theory suggests are now more widely accepted than ever, and it is possible to generalize about them more easily than in earlier times.

Lucian W. Pye's essay—"Civility, Social Capital, and Civil Society: Three Powerful Concepts for Explaining Asia"—employs the overlapping constructs of social science theory explicitly to rethink the nature of social relations, and therefore the underlying firmament of political culture in Asia. Every society, he reminds readers, "has its rules of *civility* that ensure social order." A strong and well-respected civility betokens an integrated and coherent society. Moreover, a society's level of civility determines how democratic is its political culture. Pluralistic democracy—the most taxing variety of democracy—requires the highest degree of civility. Pye suggests that social capital (constructed on bases different from that of the West, as he explains in detail) builds upon norms of civility and contributes to a democratic ethos. The

4 Gabriel A. Almond and Sidney Verba, *The Civic Culture: Political Attitudes and Democracy in Five Nations* (Princeton, 1963), 14–15; Lucian W. Pye, "Political Culture and Political Development," and Verba, "Comparative Political Culture," in Pye and Verba (eds.), *Political Culture and Political Development* (Princeton, 1963), 6–10, 513; Almond, "The Intellectual History of the Civic Culture Concept," in Almond and Verba (eds.), *The Civic Culture Revisited* (Boston, 1980), 26–32.
5 Samuel P. Huntington, *The Clash of Civilizations and the Remaking of World Order* (New York, 1996), 126–179.

creation of civil society—"diverse autonomous interest groups that can exert pressure on the state"—is necessary for effective democracy. Civil society articulates and aggregates interests that support pluralistic democracy.

Asia is hardly lacking in civility. The citizens of its nations have accumulated considerable social capital and produced elaborate civil societies. But they have combined these elements in a manner that differs from the Western pattern. To Pye, the Asian way of dealing with persons outside the inner circle of familiars, in the impersonal realm, is precisely what makes their democracies and their national democratic performances unlike those in the West. Asians have a particularistic outlook, not a universalistic one. Pye concludes that although Asians focus on community, they do not equate community with the state, as so many of their leaders would have us believe. The state falsifies Asian values, he says, when it asserts itself as the only legitimate community and, under that cover, deprives citizens of their rights as individuals.

Pye deftly employs and reinterprets the propositions of social science that purport to explain how citizens come to engage civically and amass the kinds of social capital, and other values and interests, that are manifested in particular governmental outcomes. Nonetheless, Pye's view on how trust is engendered differs from Putnam's. His analysis of Asian society and government adapts Putnam's social capital for his own explanatory purposes. Social capital, in Pye's hands, is a concept of constructive value (alongside civility) for the understanding of society, and especially for an appreciation of why certain societies embrace democratic values and others do not.

Other contributors to this volume are not so hospitable to social science and to the propositions that Putnam and his predecessors have advanced. Although only a few explicitly reject the way in which the hypotheses of social capital and political culture have been formulated, many either implicitly reject the validity of those hypotheses or employ substitute formulations that are less precise and less tested. Some prefer to employ social capital and political culture as metaphors, not as theoretical propositions, or to describe empirical realities rather than directly to use or refute the available theory.

Although several of the historians contributing to this volume are reluctant to borrow theory from social science to test it against their own materials and periods, Brucker and Muir, historians of Renaissance and early modern Italy, take social capital and its origins seriously. They disagree openly with Putnam, however, over what northern Italian city-states were like before the Risorgimento. They squarely criticize Putnam's assumptions about how northern Italy came to accumulate much more social capital than did southern Italy.

Putnam argued that the civic engagement that was apparent in modern Italy stemmed from, or at least had its roots in, the postfeudal communes of central and northern Italy after the twelfth and through the fifteenth century. Those republican regimes celebrated cooperation and exhibited mutual trust; their egalitation ethos flowed from successful horizontal bonds. The hierarchical parts of Italy, still dominated by a monarchy, followed a different model. But Brucker terms this too idealized a reading: Republican communes were rife with factionalism, brutality, and authoritarianism. The oligarchies that ran them demanded strong, intrusive government that could curb violence. They trusted regulation, not each other. Likewise, Muir maintains that the first communes were certainly not democracies. Some succumbed to petty tyrants; others were absorbed by warring neighbors. Yet, courtly manners spread throughout the larger urban entities of northern Italy. Civility, as Pye indicates, had its uses. As Brucker shows, Florentines organized themselves along interest-group lines; they balanced rights and duties, accepted taxation that was fair, and administered justice equitably.

Unfortunately for generalizations about the accumulation of social capital and the evolution of political culture, Brucker argues that the Medici grand dukes eradicated civil society, as did others in other communes. Absolutism, not republicanism, was the rule even for the city-states of northern Italy until the Risorgimento. Indeed, in this respect, Brucker sees no important differences between southern Italy (and Sicily) and northern Italy. He argues that postrevolutionary Italy inherited autocracy, not civic engagement and civic humanism, from earlier eras. Throughout Italy, the order was vertical, not horizontal. Religious dissent was stifled; so was political participation. Submission and obedience were common. Brucker also finds little evidence of voluntary associations in prerevolutionary Italy.

Civil society arrived in Italy only with the nineteenth-century revolution, and it arrived painfully slowly. Muir echoes Brucker's conclusion, to the extent that courtly manners and evasiveness about intent were the critical factors of continuity. Whereas Putnam relied on the older historians of northern Italian republicanism, and their views of its enduring influence over time, the new revisionists observe discord and disruption, and seek other explanations.

Raymond Grew, who also focuses on Italy in his article, holds that the ennobling public works of the eighteenth century appealed to a civic spirit that "was assumed to be present already." High culture had its civic uses as the Enlightenment spread onto the peninsula. So had sanctified memories of a connection to a glorious past and its relevance for, say, good government. Grew views the new governing bodies and bureaucracies during this era—in kingdoms, cities, religious orders, and the Church—as useful training centers for thousands of civic functionaries. The many consultative bodies—the parliaments and councils—were further examples for Grew of the development of a kind of social capital (his broad definition includes cultural capital) that stood Italians in good stead when they were overwhelmed by Napoleon and Napoleonic ideas.

Grew's cultural capital was evident in eighteenth-century festivals, cafes, and theaters—in Italy's active public sphere. Promenades and piazzas, with their displays of elites and lesser lights, played their part in building cultural capital. Indeed, the relevance of public arenas was well recognized, especially as such spaces facilitated civic engagement and celebrated personal liberty. On the eve of the French onslaught, an Italian culture existed despite the absence of a national state. The lessons of the past were instantiated in a strong legal tradition and a vigorous bureaucratic enterprise. Public affairs were debated alongside public displays throughout all of what would become Italy. A political culture with the air of continuity might well have been developed.

The French came sooner, and stayed longer, in the North, but, confounding Putnam, France's influence in Italy made North and South more alike. Their institutions and legal systems became common. Yet, within a half century (by 1865), North and South would bifurcate along the fissures noted by Banfield, Putnam, and others. Grew suggests that history did little to preserve social capital in Italy. To preserve it would have required the "continuity of recurrent use" and the establishment of acknowledged ways of utilizing social capital for public purposes.

European journeymen formed associations—craft guilds—in prerevolutionary times to assert their rights against their masters. Putnam suggests that craft guilds, as examples of horizontal reciprocal trust, were incubators of social capital from medieval times onward. Leonard N. Rosenband, like Brucker and Muir, argues that such generalizations stretch the facts too far: The guilds of medieval and early modern Europe were rife with conflict and division. The rise of industrialization may have exacerbated those tensions, but for centuries, associations of craft workers were typified more by disorderly disequilibrium than by any inexorable progression from a protean state of tentative cooperation to one in which artisans assembled strong bonds stretching across guilds and onto, or at least toward, national political centers.

Guild life was as much hierarchical and formal as it was voluntary, as much discriminatory as levelled. Fraternity was often honored in the breach. Mutuality there was, Rosenband agrees, but horizontal collaboration rarely involved whole trades or tradesmen. Yet, journeymen evinced an undeniable solidarity, whether coerced by their fellows or expressed in open appreciation of individual self-interest. As opposed to their masters, they helped each other in times of need and agitated together for higher real wages and improved conditions. Their concerted action was like that of militant modern trade unions; it created seedbeds of political action. In certain crafts and in selected European countries, the workers were threatening and powerful. Even as industrialization overcame their control of the value-added techniques of particular pursuits—like hatmaking or papermaking—they could spend a store of accumulated social capital in other political arenas, not least those of the tentative democracies of Europe.

Brucker, Muir, Grew, and Rosenband test generalizations, as most historians do, against empirical details over longer or shorter episodes of time. So does Marjorie K. McIntosh, who examines networks of trust in village England during the late Middle Ages (with a suggestive glance at more modern Nigeria). These English proto-associations were organized formally at the village level by men of locally respectable wealth and status; they generated social capital that was transportable and convertible. Their variety produced social capital capable of being utilized by their own members as well as the broader community. Local secular courts, parish church bodies, voluntary religious groups, and local charitable institutions, even though they were constituted officially or formally, generated social capital. Volunteerism, McIntosh asserts, is not the only route to the creation of social capital.

Parallel to these formal English entities were loosely defined linkages of neighborliness and assistance, focused mainly on women. They produced reciprocal social credit that protected members against the vicissitudes of a hard and unpredictable life. In that manner, women of middle or lower rank provided a modicum of security for themselves. They shared food, loaned goods for money, assisted those who were ill, or took in relatives or orphans. McIntosh relates how women interacted socially to produce social capital, and then shows how the comparative freedoms of the late medieval era were constrained during the early modern centuries. She accepts, too, that the women's networks may not have had an impact beyond their villages, and may not have resulted in much public good. Further, McIntosh agrees with Brucker that "externally beneficial social capital" of the modern period cannot necessarily, or easily, be traced back to a point of origin in earlier times. What was relevant for men and women in a simpler England need not have produced modern civil society, a free market economy, or democratic political institutions.

Jack P. Greene's contribution to this collection takes English human, social, and cultural capital overseas to the American colonies. His essay explicitly "liberates" social capital from its usage in modern social science, which he deems "too narrow, too instrumental, too whiggish, and too Western." Like Grew, he widens social capital to include an entire range of "institutions, practices, devices, and learned behaviors" that permit individuals and groups to "render physical spaces productive and social and cultural spaces agreeable."

The social and cultural capital that the English settlers brought to the Western Hemisphere assisted them in the colonizing process. Included were McIntosh's transferability (which enabled social/cultural capital to combine with labor and investment capital and thereby to transform Amerindian settings); adaptability; partibility (settlers could select their most useful assets to help construct their new surroundings); and enhancibility (adaptation, imitation, and invention). To Greene, the human capital of individuals with specialized skills effectively translated into social capital.

The explosive expansion of Britain's North American colonies during the eighteenth century occurred demographically, economically, culturally, and territorially. It accompanied, and built upon, a formidable accumulation of social, cultural, and human capital. The result, Greene asserts, was the establishment of a European-style civil society that existed well before the American Revolution; indeed, it was a precondition for that revolt. The colonizers were engaged, sometimes consciously, in a large-scale civilizing project that brought great swaths of land and indigenous persons under their thrall. This process was repeated with each westward assault on the frontier, as social, cultural, and human capital, along with investment capital, came into play to expand the limits of civil society. The British-Americans in the colonies believed that the legal traditions, governmental approaches, and constitutions that they had taken with them to the New World, and elaborated, existed to promote civil society.

Greene argues that the American Revolution was the colonists' attempt to "perpetuate and improve" a civil society that already existed and to preserve the social and cultural capital on which it was predicated. Colonial American social sensibilities thus had a profoundly formative bearing on the civil society and government that emerged from the second founding of American civil society and government after the Revolution. It was of a piece, Greene says, with the first, and the contingencies that arose within the radical civil societies that had been constructed in North America between 1607 and 1776.

From the eighteenth century onward, Gamm and Putnam report, Americans were joiners. As Tocqueville so perceptively noted, Americans of all ages and all stations were "forever forming associations."[6] Such associational activity is a cornerstone of the theory of social capital, contributing as it does to the forging of horizontal networks of reciprocal trust. Without such reciprocal trust, it is difficult to sustain civic engagement and strong support for the democratic process. Indeed, Putnam has elsewhere connected falling levels of trust and political involvement in the United States, according to many measures, to the rise of individualism—to "bowling alone" rather than in groups, to smaller numbers of church and union memberships, to the abandonment

6 Tocqueville, *Democracy in America*, 513.

of Parent–Teacher Associations, and to the shrinking size of a vast array of voluntary associations.[7]

Do Americans join less? Have they joined with decreasing intensity since World War II, when associations began their now steep decline? Or has Americans' penchant for associational life since Tocqueville been cyclical rather than sloping steadily (or abruptly) downward? Those are among the questions that Gamm and Putnam answer, and that the other essays in this volume also attempt to answer, although less longitudinally than Gamm and Putnam.

Because a quantitative assessment of the density of associational life involves thousands of cities and towns and hundreds of thousands of well-known and obscure institutions, a systematic analysis depends upon the manipulation of vast arrays of data. Gamm and Putnam used directories for twenty-six cities and towns by ten-year intervals from 1840 to 1940, finding that numbers of associations grew rapidly between 1850 and 1900, and more slowly to 1910. Associations grew hardly at all, or declined, from 1910 to 1940. The number of members of associations largely followed suit, especially in the explosive phase of associational activity during the last third of the nineteenth century. They also found that associational activity was strongest in the small cities and towns beyond major urban centers, and more in the Midwest and West than in the East, where Tocqueville had noticed so much joining. Associational activity was at its lowest ebb in the large cities that had grown rapidly and at its peak in small cities of about 5,000 inhabitants. Homogeneity may have influenced the proliferation of joiners in the small hinterland centers; Gamm and Putnam analyze the competing explanations. The strength of civic engagement in those nineteenth-century settings may help to assess the prospects for the United States' faltering civil society at the end of the twentieth century.

Mary P. Ryan's study of associations in nineteenth-century America focuses on three rapidly growing port cities, New York, New Orleans, and San Francisco. Though she, too, starts with city directories, she also consults the contemporary daily press. Like Gamm and Putnam, she notes the proliferation of associations after 1830 and 1840 in New York and New Orleans, as well as

---

7   Putnam, "Bowling Alone: America's Declining Social Capital," *Journal of Democracy,* VI (1995), 65–78.

during the 1850s, 1860s, and thereafter in San Francisco. However, the earliest religious and benevolent societies were hardly egalitarian, being founded by and for patricians. Later ones—fraternal encampments—"dissolved class differences" and stressed mutual care and the provision of social safety nets for their members. These mutual-benefit societies sprung up in all three cities during the last third of the century. Indeed, Ryan sees them as marks of urban social diversity. Voluntary associations, she says, should not be construed entirely as examples of "a small town mentality forever lost."

Although Ryan rejects Putnam's definition of social capital as "discordant" and "economistic," she claims that as a metaphor, social capital aptly describes the associations in her cities; they accumulated material and cultural resources according to class, ethnic, religious, and gender affiliations. But measurements of social capital cannot, she says, capture the vitality of democratic politics in America. Civic engagement flourished; it was passionate, contentious, and not always civil. Nor did it always depend on voluntary associations. Citizens also attended public meetings to discuss plans of action or to mobilize others to implement those plans. Participants in these meetings were not just joiners; they were "alert citizens." The public meetings were urban-political phenomena. By contrast, associations were parochial. They rarely created social meaning in the way that social movements focusing on single issues, or sets of issues, did. More complex than social capital, the combination of associations, public meetings, political parties, and social movements had, by mid-century, empowered citizens and helped support the growth of democracy.

For Elisabeth S. Clemens, few efforts to employ social capital effectively for political ends match the accomplishments of the "woman movement." She argues that social capital is generated and destroyed in the course of collective action and political contests. The deployment of social capital in politics depends on its distribution across different kinds of associations. According to Clemens' expanded definition, social capital refers either "to the skills and capacities of individuals for social action or to the web of ties among individuals." Informal networks of trust may or may not coincide with formal memberships. The "genius" of nineteenth-century voluntary associations, she says, was their development of rules that facilitated collective action and their creation of national organizations from a web of local arrays of trust. Thus, women could avail themselves of social capital at secondary and tertiary levels, within the interpretive frames of particular institutions and associations.

Women's clubs proliferated in the United States during the second half of the nineteenth century. They helped to shape regional and national political culture and social policy in the decades before World War I. In order to understand patterns of associational activity within this realm, Clemens focused on a sample of ninety women from four states, looking for multiple affiliations with formal organizations under the assumption that they would parallel an array of individual-level ties. What she found was an abundance of bridging social capital (especially among elite women). The civic lives of Clemens' women reveal how membership in voluntary associations and political participation went hand in hand. Club life was the school for citizenship. It led to rich cross-affiliations of women in voluntary associations and the suffrage movement. But it also led, as Clemens demonstrates, to intergenerational, class, and partisan conflict.

The case of the woman movement, Clemens concludes, suggests the importance of moving beyond counting participants and interactions to mapping the distribution of social capital across formal organizations and various civic pursuits. She also doubts that regional patterns of social capital endure for long periods; networks of associational life ebb and flow over decades, not centuries.

Reed Ueda analyzes the bridging social capital developed by second-generation immigrant communities that facilitated their entry into local, regional, and national political life. Secondary education and settlement houses were structures of civic acculturation that nurtured social capital. Ueda closely examines a high school in Honolulu attended by Japanese-Americans and a settlement house in Boston frequented by Russian Jews. Both institutions, he says, exemplified high degrees of voluntary initiative.

Japanese-Americans were Oahu's most numerous immigrants. They preferred, and received, an assimilationist, Americanized curriculum that was aimed at exposing Nisei to liberal democracy. McKinley High School's newspaper reflected this approach throughout the 1920s and 1930s, espousing patriotism and citizenship both inside and outside the classroom. It favored complete linguistic assimilation over a kind of Hawaiian pidgin, celebrated the American flag, promoted the Reserve Officers' Training Corps, and emphasized a pantheon of mainland heroes, like Presidents Washington and Lincoln. The newspaper also favored racial egalitarianism and Christian morality. Japanese-American high school students were determined to be "true Americans."

The Boston West End House was a boys' club that provided sports and cultural programs for neighborhood youth within a context of mutal assistance. Its larger goal was to prepare its members to be productive citizens, and to find them jobs when they were ready. Hence, it emphasized teamwork, self-help, and the arts of civic advocacy. In a different era, the behavior of the house's members was influenced by debates and lectures, by uplifting essays in its newsletter, and by the daily actions of individual leaders and staff workers. The strong civic bonds forged at the house were later strengthened by an active alumni association and an employment referral network.

Ueda believes that the deepening of democratic social awareness among Japanese-Americans in Honolulu and Russian Jews in Boston, through the two vigorous settings that he describes, extended civic engagement beyond ethnic-group boundaries. The networks of trust that their acculturational activities created heightened levels of voluntarism and activism, and a collaborative approach to public life that weakened parochial divisions and "made group relations more open and permeable."

In the United States, at least in Iowa and the heartland education belt of middle America that Claudia Goldin and Lawrence Katz examine—social capital was "the handmaiden" of human capital. Goldin and Katz's finding that it was more accessible in small towns and villages than in larger urban centers fits squarely with Gamm and Putnam's conclusions. So might their finding that an index of social capital in the 1990s correlates better with per capita wealth before World War I than with income in 1994. High school graduation rates in 1928 also correlate well with social capital today, as well as with a current educational performance index. According to Goldin and Katz's research, social capital has endured, surviving changes in the economy and society.

Goldin and Katz rely on the unusual Iowa census for 1915 to determine why the high school movement flourished so much

and politics. The imposing thread that unites this collection is political culture, and the contribution to it of social capital.

Plural democracy certainly was fed and supported by voluntary associations and by the civic engagement that the authors have analyzed in each of their societies and eras. An important conclusion, along the way, is that social capital may not be continuous, or endure. Several of the authors, Putnam among them, wonder if the accumulation of social capital, and its diminution, will prove cyclical. Or has there been a societal deterioration as the joiners of Tocqueville's time have gradually and forever become the television watchers and solitary bowlers of a more anonymous age? This collection is ultimately about the pattern of social and civic interactions in past times, and how these patterns may no longer exist.

Gene Brucker

Civic Traditions in Premodern Italy
In the fifth chapter of *Making Democracy Work,* Putnam argues that the origins of civic society in modern Italy can be traced back to the age of the communes (twelfth to fifteenth centuries) in its northern and central regions. The distinctive features of those republican regimes were a high degree of cooperation and collaboration among their members, an atmosphere of mutual trust essential for their survival and the achievement of common goals, and an egalitarian ethos based upon horizontal social bonds. The associative impulse that led to the establishment of the communes also inspired the creation of other civic organizations: tower societies; guilds, Guelf and Ghibelline "parties"; and confraternities. The contrast between the political and social structures of the feudal world, from which these associations emerged, was dramatic. In those parts of the peninsula that were not intensely urbanized—Piedmont and the Appennine region—or dominated by a strong, centralized monarchy—like the towns in the south—a social structure based upon vertical relationships survived intact.[1]

Putnam admits that the civic ethos of the communal world was weakened in the decades following the Black Death, and particularly after the foreign invasions and the hegemony established in the sixteenth century by Hapsburg Spain. Still, he insists that the values and ideals of the communal era survived into the modern age of the Risorgimento and unification: "In the North, norms of reciprocity and networks of civic engagement have been embodied in tower societies, guilds, mutual aid societies, cooperatives, unions and even soccer clubs and literary societies." "Mutual aid societies were built on the razed foundations of the old guilds, and cooperatives and mass political parties on the experience of mutual aid societies."[2]

Gene Brucker is Shepard Professor of History, Emeritus, University of California, Berkeley. He is the author of *The Civic World of Early Renaissance Florence* (Princeton, 1977); *Renaissance Florence: Society, Culture, and Religion* (Goldbach, 1994).

1 Robert Putnam, with Roberto Leonardi and Raffaella Y. Nanetti, *Making Democracy Work: Civic Traditions in Modern Italy* (Cambridge, Mass., 1993), 121–162.
2 *Ibid.,* 181, 174.

The scenario developed by Putnam can stand some revisions, first and most fundamentally, his view on the civic culture of communal Italy. He presents too idealized a picture of that culture, with its communitarian and egalitarian components; his view neglects the darker side of that world—its factionalism, its violence and brutality, and its coercive and authoritarian dimensions. A second problem is Putnam's argument that the civic values of the communal age survived centuries of invasion, foreign domination, absolutist government, and a hierarchical social order—to be revived and rejuvenated in the twentieth century—as the key to Italy's modernization. For Putnam, that revival of a civil society in north and central Italy, and its absence in the south, is the primary explanation for the gulf still dividing the two Italies—the one civic, dynamic, progressive, and "modern" and the other "feudal," reactionary, backward, and depressed. To focus so exclusively on the "civic" theme in explaining the divergent paths of the two regions since unification is to simplify and distort a complex historical reality.

The character of Italy's communal experience, and its role in its historical evolution, has been one of the most controversial themes in recent historiography. The traditional interpretation, formulated initially by the chroniclers and historians of Italian towns and accepted by (among others) Jacob Burckhardt in his classic work, *The Civilization of the Renaissance in Italy* (New York, 1929), stressed the progressive, innovative and "modern" qualities of that civic world. The institutions and values fostered by those urban governments were seen as the solvent that destroyed the old feudal system, with its hierarchical social structure, its land-based economy, and its fragmented political order. The towns were the dynamic engines that created a new capitalist economy; a social order based on wealth; a political system that stressed cooperation, equality, and freedom; and a culture that embodied secular rather than religious values.

Lane, the distinguished historian of Venice, articulated this vision: "My thesis here is that republicanism . . . is the most distinctive and significant aspect of these Italian city-states, that republicanism gave to the civilization of Italy its distinctive quality . . . and contributed mightily to its triumph later in modern nations and primarily in our own."[3]

---

3 Frederic C. Lane, *Venice and History* (Baltimore, 1966), 520.

Since World War II, however, this view of the communes and their historical significance has been challenged by scholars who have emphasized the weaknesses, limitations, and failures of these urban regimes. Some critics have stressed their instability, their failure to overcome factional discord, and their tendency to rely upon powerful lords (*signori*) from feudal backgrounds to resolve their recurrent crises. By the end of the thirteenth century, independent communal regimes had been replaced by *signorie* in those regions of northern Italy where feudal nobilities were powerful. Communal regimes in Lombardy, the Veneto, and Emilia-Romagna were viewed as aberrant phenomena with brief life spans in a world that remained overwhelmingly feudal. Independent communes did survive longer in central Italy—Tuscany and Umbria—where rural nobilities were weaker, but these regions witnessed the gradual demise of these republics, which were either absorbed by their more powerful neighbors, like Florence, or (like Siena and Perugia) were taken over by local *signori*.[4]

Since World War II, an international cadre of scholars has studied the history of Florentine republicanism intensively, particularly its mature phase in the fifteenth century, and its demise in the sixteenth. Florence's past is too exceptional and idiosyncratic to serve as a model for the Italian city-state experience, but no Italian city has left a richer documentary record, nor a more fully articulated civic ideology. In his treatise on Florence's constitution, written c. 1440, Bruni, the civic humanist, focused on the exercise of public power by the magistrates, and the limits imposed on their authority by the statutes. The executive bodies (the Signoria and their two advisory colleges) could initiate legislation, but their proposals had to be ratified by a two-thirds vote of the councils of the *popolo* and the Commune. To prevent an excessive concentration of authority in the hands of a few, the tenure of all civic offices was brief (between two and six months), and eligibility to those positions was carefully regulated.[5]

4 Daniel Waley, *The Italian City-Republics* (London, 1969), 221–239; Philip Jones, "Economia e società nell'Italia medievale: la leggenda della borghesia," in Ruggiero Romano and Corrado Vivanti (eds), *Einaudi Storia d'Italia* (Turin, 1978), I, 185–372; Romano, "Una tipologia economia," and Vivanti, "Lacerazioni e contrasti," in *idem* (eds.), *Einaudi Storia d'Italia* (Turin, 1973), I, 253–304, 867–948, respectively.
5   For recent surveys of the literature, see Brucker, *The Civic World of Early Renaissance Florence* (Princeton, 1977), 3–13; John Najemy, "Linguaggi storiografici sulla Firenze rinascimentale," *Rivista storica italiana*, XCVII (1985), 102–159. Leonardo Bruni, "On The

Florence's constitution was a mixture of the aristocratic and the democratic. In Bruni's world, those citizens (magnates) "with too great a power of numbers and of force at their command" were excluded from the chief executive offices, while "mechanics and members of the lowest class" were not allowed any role in the state. "Thus, avoiding the extremes, the city look[ed] to the mean, or rather to the best and the wealthy but not over-powerful." That middling mass of politically active citizens comprised artisans and shopkeepers from the lower guilds and merchants, cloth manufacturers, bankers, and professionals (lawyers, notaries, physicians) from the greater guilds.[6]

Every year, more than a thousand citizens participated directly in the political process as members of the supreme executive and as officials who staffed the forty-odd commissions responsible for the administration of the dominion, the collection of taxes, and the enforcement of sumptuary laws. More than a thousand citizens assembled regularly each year as members of the legislative councils. They also participated in the administration of their guilds, as consuls and councillors. They attended meetings of their electoral districts (*gonfaloni*) and assemblies of their parish churches.

Thousands of Florentines also participated in the meetings and rituals of their confraternities and in the processions that commemorated civic and religious holidays. The anniversary (June 24) of John the Baptist, the city's patron saint, was celebrated by a procession that included the secular and religious authorities, representatives of subject communities, and a large contingent of guildsmen. This annual ritual symbolized most dramatically the civic community and the bonds that united its members.[7]

The political agenda of this large and heterogenous mass of middling Florentines, which constituted the *popolo,* was quite straightforward. These citizens wanted their traditional place and voice in the government, based upon their guild memberships. The essence of republicanism for these men was its corporate and collegiate quality, in which decisions were made and policies formulated by citizens chosen to represent the whole community.

Florentine Constitution," in Gordon Griffiths, James Hankins, and David Thompson (eds.), *The Humanism of Leonardo Bruni* (Binghamton, 1987), 171–174.
6 Bruni, "Florentine Constitution," 171.
7 Gregorio Dati, *Istoria di Firenze dall'anno MCCCLXXX all'anno MCCCCV* (Florence, 1735), in Brucker (ed.), *The Society of Renaissance Florence* (New York, 1971), 75–78.

As Najemy wrote, they believed in the principles "of consent and representation as the foundation of legitimate republican government, of officeholding as a public trust, of the supremacy of law, and of the delegated quality of all formal power." They felt that the common good (*ben comune*) was best served by the firm and equitable administration of justice, which would protect their persons and their property, regulate their business affairs, and adjudicate their private disputes. They also favored rigorous scrutiny of the conduct of civic officials and severe punishment for malfeasance.[8]

In the interest of a fiscal system that was fair, they supported the famous law of the *catasto* (1427), which allocated the tax burden according to the declared wealth of individual households. Appended to their tax returns were statements that articulated with clarity and eloquence their perception of an ideal civic polity. Giovanni Corbinelli informed the catasto officials that he prayed to God "to give [them] grace to do justice to each [taxpayer], and if [they did] so, [they would give] health to this city in perpetuity and . . . be the instrument to maintain this *popolo* in liberty forever." Giovanni Vettori wrote, "If you act according to your honor, you will maintain and strengthen this glorious city in triumph and virtue." A belt maker named Luca di Cino appended to his tax report, "I, Luca, have compiled this document with my own hand, and I believe that what I have declared is the whole truth. . . . So that the commune will have what it is owed, and you will have done your duty and [preserved] your honor, and we will be treated fairly, may Christ keep you in peace."[9]

The tenor of these statements reveals another dimension of the popolo's agenda: the desire for strong, active, and even intrusive government. These citizens were convinced that their turbulent and violence-prone society required a heavy measure of discipline and regulation. This was not a community that trusted its members to live together in peace and harmony (*vivere civile*) without coercion. Florentines had no conception of a private realm immune from public scrutiny and intervention. No

8 Najemy, "The Dialogue of Power in Florentine Politics," in Anthony Molho, Kurt Raaflaub, and Julia Emlen (eds.), *City States in Classical Antiquity and Medieval Italy* (Stuttgart, 1991), 278.
9 Catasto, 17, fol., 749r; 18, fol, 806r; 21, fol. 88r, Archivio di Stato di Firenze (hereinafter ASF).

intimation is evident in either public or private records that the citizenry resented this close surveillance and regulation of their private lives.

By large majorities, they voted in favor of special magistracies to regulate (among other matters) their weddings and funerals, their clothing and jewelry, their relations with the Jewish community, and their sexual behavior. These officials hired informers to spy on their fellow citizens, and they established boxes (*tamburi*) into which secret denunciations could be deposited. Florentine statutory law gave broad powers to the Signoria and its colleges to elect certain officials, to cancel or alter judicial penalties, to issue safe conducts and grants of immunity from persecution, and to force individuals and corporate bodies to obey their decrees. These magistrates did not hesitate to intervene in private affairs— for example, to prohibit a mother described as "quarrelsome and prone to scandalous behavior" from living with her two nubile daughters.[10]

Two cases will illustrate the extent of this arbitrary executive authority. In April 1429, on the occasion of a tournament in honor of a visiting member of the Portuguese royal family, the Signoria issued an executive order that a penalty of 1,000 florins would be levied against five citizens unless they appeared with horses and armor to participate in the joust. Eleven years later, the Signoria threatened to impose a fine of 1,000 florins on Uguccione de' Ricci unless he could persuade his cousin, the archbishop of Pisa, to abandon a judicial process against an alleged usurer in his ecclesiastical court.[11]

Within this republican polity, that men from the city's most prominent wealthy lineages wielded more power and influence than did citizens of lesser rank was a perennial fact of political life, as valid for the fifteenth century as for that pristine age when Dante's ancestor, Cacciaguida, lived. These men of high social status (*ottomati*) viewed their political system from a somewhat different perspective than did the popolo. They, too, favored a strong, activist government, accepting the principle that the general welfare of the community took precedence over private

10   For examples of regulatory legislation and its enforcement, see Brucker (ed.), *Society of Renaissance Florence,* 179–212. Deliberazioni dei Signori e Collegi (ordinaria autorità), 99, unpaginated, February 25, 1498, ASF.
11   Giudice degli Appelli, 75, fols. 201r–201v, 80, fol. 282r, ASF.

interests. But they resented the political role of the popolo in the regime, and after the Ciompi revolution, they succeeded in limiting their access to civic office, and their influence on policy.

Even though the ottomati had gained a dominant role in the regime by the early fifteenth century, they were unable to control the bitter rivalries and factional quarrels that periodically threatened the stability of the regime. The primary source of these partisan conflicts was not political or ideological but personal and familial—the struggle among individuals and families for civic office, and the benefits and perquisites that accrued to those who held it. These conflicts intensified during times of crisis, particularly during the years of warfare (1391 to 1402, 1411 to 1414, and 1423 to 1431) that drained the city's wealth, sparked widespread unrest in Florence and throughout the dominion, and inspired bitter quarrels and recriminations within the leadership. An especially intense crisis in the early 1430s culminated in the emergence of one family, the Medici, which was able to create a party or faction composed of kinfolk, neighbors, friends, and clients that governed Florence for sixty years (1434 to 1494).[12]

The ability of the Medici to seize and maintain control of the republic was due not only to their political skills but also to the vast wealth that they could use to buy allegiance. They immobilized their rivals by exiling them and by excluding the rank and file from office, while restoring the political rights of old magnate families. They preserved many of the republican institutions inherited from the past, though they did replace the old legislative councils (in which the influence of the popolo was strong) by smaller and more tractable bodies of their adherents.

When the regime was threatened by internal discord and popular unrest, it created commissions (*balie*) with extraordinary powers to reform the state. The Medici developed complex electoral strategies to ensure that their allies would control the major electoral offices, while excluding any current or potential rivals. They gradually dismantled the old judicial system administered by foreign (and supposedly impartial) judges, substituting magistracies staffed by citizens from the ranks of their partisans. Even though the statutes guaranteed the right "of citizens to be free to give

---

12 The main themes in this paragraph, and the one preceding, are discussed in detail in Brucker, *Civic World,* 248–507; Dale Kent, *The Rise of the Medici: Faction in Florence 1426–1434* (Oxford, 1978).

counsel and to judge public affairs," the regime was prepared to silence its critics by accusing them of fomenting discord and engaging in treasonous activity. As had been true throughout the republic's history, the distinction between legitimate criticism and sedition was always a fine line.[13]

To the more equitable system of tax assessments embodied in the catasto, they favored the older method of *arbitrio,* by which tax commissions in each electoral district decided levies to be imposed on their neighbors. As the Medici had long recognized, this was a powerful weapon for rewarding friends and punishing enemies.

The Medicean system of government reached its apogee under Lorenzo, who, following in his grandfather Cosimo's footsteps, built a polity that retained its formal republican facade while enabling its *maestro* to control the levers of power. Lorenzo's authority derived primarily from the elaborate network of patron–client relations that Cosimo had developed and that he and his father Piero had fostered and expanded. Lorenzo's network extended from the city throughout the dominion, even beyond Florentine territory to include the whole Italian peninsula.[14]

Lorenzo was the supreme patron of the Florentine state, and letters came to him from individuals, corporations, ecclesiastical foundations, and political authorities inside and outside the state's territorial boundaries. Petitioners appealed to Lorenzo for support and favor—for civic office, ecclesiastical benefices, tax exemptions, cancellation of criminal sentences, arranging marriages, and letters of recommendation. Lorenzo's influence was considered to be decisive in the operations of the Florentine government, and personal appeals for his help more useful than requests to the civic magistracies.

Writing to Lorenzo in 1478, Giovanni Capponi noted that Medicean support for his family "[was] the reason why . . . we

---

13 On Medicean electoral strategies, see Nicolai Rubinstein, *The Government of Florence Under the Medici 1434–1494* (Oxford, 1966); on the fisc, Elio Conti, *L'imposta diretta a Firenze nel Quattrocento 1427–1494* (Rome, 1984); on the judicial system, Lauro Martines, *Lawyers and Statecraft in Renaissance Florence* (Princeton, 1968), 387–404; on the issue of "free speech," Rubinstein, *Government of Florence,* 156–157.

14 For descriptions of Lorenzo's network, see Lorenzo de' Medici (ed. Riccardo Fubini et al), *Lettere* (Florence, 1977–), 6 v. to date. For a succinct summary, see Francis W. Kent, "Patron–Client Networks in Renaissance Florence and the Emergence of Lorenzo as 'Maestro della Bottega,'" in Bernard Toscani (ed.), *Lorenzo de' Medici: New Perspectives* (New York, 1993), 279–313.

have with assurance had recourse to you and to your ancestors, by whom graciously we have been exalted." In 1488, Piero Buondelmonti wrote to a close associate of Lorenzo "that everything proceeds from God by the virtue, merits and dignity of our God on earth, the Magnificent Lorenzo, to whom I beg you to recommend me as his creature."[15]

Friends in high places were critical in this highly competitive and agonistic society. Giovanni Rucellai, the wealthy merchant, once wrote that he needed a large circle of *amici* to protect himself from his enemies. Alberti commented that "there is really nothing more difficult in the world than distinguishing true friends amid the obscurity of so many lies, the darkness of people's motives and the shadowy errors and vices that lie about us on all sides." Even close friends were capable of betrayal; discord within families over inheritances, marriages, and business transactions were common. Florence was a veritable cauldron of suspicion, mistrust, and envy, fuelled by the struggle for wealth, status, and reputation, which in concrete terms signified the ability to obtain civic office and to arrange honorable marriages for daughters and lucrative careers for sons.[16]

In this "paradise inhabited by devils," the achievement of these objectives was an arduous enterprise. The attainment of high civic office could be thwarted by the machinations of one's enemies. A family's prosperity could be destroyed by business failures or confiscatory taxation. The competition for appropriate marriage partners led to the escalation of dowries and the inability of impoverished fathers from prominent lineages to contract "honorable" liaisons. The penalties exacted upon these losers included imprisonment for debt, withdrawal from the city to a marginal life in the *contado,* and unemployable sons and unmarriageable daughters.[17]

15 *Idem, Household and Lineage in Renaissance Florence* (Princeton, 1977), 212; *idem,* "Lorenzo and Oligarchy," in Gian Carlo Garfagnini (ed.), *Lorenzo il Magnifico e il suo mondo* (Florence, 1994), 46.

16 Alessandro Perosa (ed.), *Giovanni Rucellai ed il suo Zibaldone* (London, 1960), 9. Leon Battista Alberti, quoted in Ronald Weissman, *Ritual Brotherhood in Renaissance Florence* (New York, 1982), 29. Weissman's first chapter, "Judas the Florentine," 1–41, describes the agonistic character of Florentine society.

17 F. W. Kent, "Un paradiso habitato da diavoli": Ties of Loyalty and Patronage in the Society of Medicean Florence," in Anna Benvenuti (ed.), *Le radici cristiane di Firenze* (Florence, 1994), 198; Brucker, "Florentine Voices from the *Catasto," I Tatti Studies,* V (1993), 22–32.

These unpalatable scenarios explain the desperate tone of the appeals to Lorenzo and other prominent figures in the regime— for instance, that of Bernardo di Nicola, who pleaded for a reduction of his tax bill, which would be "the cause of [his] coming again to life," and that of Bernardo Cambini, who, seeking to obtain a seat in the Signoria that his ancestors had occupied, "did not wish by comparison [with them] to appear 'a wooden man.'" Cambini added that his selection to the supreme executive "would be useful in enabling [him] to marry [his] daughters."[18]

In addition to manipulating the political system and promoting a city-wide network of patron–client bonds, Lorenzo also developed a strategy to limit the autonomy of the city's corporate bodies and make them more responsive to the regime's agenda. Florence's major guilds—Lana, Calimala, and Cambio—had long since been taken over by Medici partisans, as had been the Merchant's Court (*Mercanzia*), which regulated commercial and financial affairs. Lorenzo's influence within the Florentine church was solidified by the appointment of Rinaldo Orsini, his brother-in-law, as archbishop. He intervened directly in the administration of San Lorenzo, his family's parish church, and in monastic and conventual foundations that had been subsidized by Medici largesse. The Medici also funded and governed the city's charitable foundations—hospitals, foundling homes, and hostels for plague victims.

Confraternities—approximately 100 of them—constituted one of the most important segments of the city's associative life. These societies were an obvious target for Medicean penetration. Since their memberships comprised as much as one-fifth of the adult male population, they were potential sources of either support for or resistance to the regime. By joining these sodalities, Lorenzo was able to control their ritual and charitable activities and to exert a decisive influence on their internal administrations. After becoming a member of the confraternity of Sant' Agnese, for example, Lorenzo was recognized as its chief benefactor and patron. He also supervised the society's transformation from an egalitarian association of neighbors into "a more aristocratic organization, whose councils promoted Medicean political interests

---

18 F. W. Kent, *Household and Lineage,* 83; *idem,* "Patron–Client Networks," 294.

and whose rituals worshipped and magnified the aura surrounding the lineage."[19]

The Florentines never wholly accepted Medicean hegemony. Opposition to the regime came initially from those families whose members had been exiled, excluded from office, and penalized by the judicial and fiscal systems. But even the Medicis' close allies and associates came to resent the dominant and often domineering roles of first Cosimo and, later, Piero and Lorenzo. Playing subversive roles in the crises of 1458 and 1466, which threatened the regime's stability, they adopted republican slogans, calling for the restoration of "liberty," "freedom," and "good government" and the abolition of the Medici's self-aggrandizing electoral and fiscal strategies. Echoes of these sentiments are found in council debates throughout the 1450s and 1460s, testifying to the tenacious survival of republican ideology in the city.

No public criticism of Lorenzo and his authoritarian regime, however, was ever voiced; it would have invited "immediate imprisonment, exile or even death." Opposition took the form of conspiracies, which were inevitably crushed; of anonymous placards posted in the city squares; of negative gossip and rumors that circulated in public places; and of critical comments recorded in private diaries and account books. Although many of Lorenzo's detractors were motivated by a sense of personal mistreatment, they justified their opposition by appealing to the republican tradition, which (so they claimed) the Medici had destroyed. When Lorenzo died in 1492, the entire city participated in his funeral rites with expressions of grief and loss. Yet, according to one witness, many of these mourners "instead rejoiced, thinking that the republic would recover its liberty and they would escape from servitude."[20]

Two years after Lorenzo's death, a French invasion precipitated the expulsion of the Medici, and the city was given the opportunity to "recover its liberty." A makeshift republican regime restored most of the institutional structures that the Medici had dismantled. One significant innovation was the creation of

19 Weissman, *Ritual Brotherhood;* John Henderson, *Piety and Charity in Late Medieval Florence* (Oxford, 1994); Nicholas Eckstein, *The District of the Green Dragon: Neighborhood Life and Social Change in Renaissance Florence* (Florence, 1995), 217.
20 Alison Brown, "Lorenzo and Public Opinion in Florence," in Garfagnini (ed.), *Lorenzo il Magnifico e il suo mondo*, 61–85.

the Great Council, whose members included all of the citizens whose fathers and/or grandfathers had qualified for the highest executive offices—the Signoria and its two colleges. The Great Council voted on all legislative proposals and selected the officials who filled the civic magistracies and those who governed the dominion. This "fundamental law of the republican period" shifted the balance of power from the elite back to the popolo. Given the large number of citizens newly integrated into the government, the reformers expected this revived commitment to the *vivere popolare* (republican government) to enable the regime to survive and prosper.[21]

The establishment of this republican polity could not have occurred at a more difficult time than in the wake of the French invasion. By maintaining its traditional alliance with the French monarchy, the republic incurred the enmity of those states and interests (Venice, Naples, and the papacy) that had fought to keep the French out. The arduous military effort to rescue the rebel city of Pisa drained hundreds of thousands of florins from the city's treasury, and imposed heavy burdens upon the citizenry. These fiscal problems were compounded by a series of poor harvests that threatened the urban poor with starvation, and by the disruption of trade routes that resulted in unemployment among the workers in the cloth industry.

These crises exacerbated the deep and pervasive divisions within the government. A hard core of Medici supporters sought to weaken the new regime and to prepare for the Medici's resumption of power. Furthermore, the conflict that had resulted from Savonarola's brief and tumultuous career as a religious leader with a political agenda still persisted after his execution in 1498. But the issue that ultimately doomed the republic concerned the balance of power between the elite and the popolo. Members of the old and prominent lineages attempted to monopolize the major offices and to formulate civic policy by curtailing the authority of the Great Council, with its guild constituency, and enacting institutional reforms that would give them a greater voice in fiscal matters and foreign policy. The popolo strongly resisted these efforts, consistently voting against proposals to levy taxes for

---

21   Felix Gilbert, *Machiavelli and Guicciardini* (Princeton, 1965), 19. The phrase, *vivere popolare,* was commonly used by contemporaries, for example, Luca Landucci, *Diario fiorentino dal 1450 al 1516* (Florence, 1883), 97, 110.

military operations. During this period, the regime was peri-odically threatened by Medicean conspiracies, rebellions in the dominion, and military incursions by foreign troops. Instead of uniting the citizenry in defense of the regime, these perils inten-sified the factional quarrels and divisions.[22]

The republican regime that governed Florence from 1494 to 1512 was the city's most "democratic" polity since the late four-teenth century. Some 3,000 citizens—one-fourth of the adult male population—belonged to the Great Council. Not since the 1460s were Florentines so free to express their opinions in council deliberations. But this unaccustomed freedom to discuss the *res publica* did not result in coherent and constructive policies, but, rather, in lengthy and inconclusive debates that revealed the deep fissures within the city and the regime's inability to respond effectively to crises.

The civic mood throughout these years was one of pervasive anxiety: "We are in such a state that our demise appears to be imminent. . . . To live in this manner is the height of insanity. . . . It is not necessary to describe the dangers and disorders that confront the city; they are so great that one can speak of chaos." Speakers repeatedly criticized every facet of government—the fisc, the administration of justice, the selection of officials, and the conduct of military affairs and foreign policy. They also speculated about the sources of "disorder" and the failure of the citizenry to unite in defense of the liberty that their ancestors "had acquired with so much bloodshed." One popular explanation was that private interest had become more important than the general welfare. An ominous sign of civic alienation was the frequent absence of a quorum at sessions of the Great Council, leading to the postponement of legislative action and a halt to the selection of magistrates.[23]

Civic debates exposed all of the systemic weaknesses of re-publican government throughout the communal era. From city to city, the scenario varied only in the details: beleaguered regimes plagued by internal divisions, weak and indecisive leadership, the erosion of civic institutions and values, and the transfer of power

22   Gilbert, *Machiavelli and Guicciardini*, 7–104; Humfrey Butters, *Governors and Government in Early Sixteenth Century Florence 1502–1519* (Oxford, 1985), 1–165.
23   The quotations in this paragraph are from Denis Fachard (ed.), *Consulte e pratiche della Republica fiorentini 1498–1505* (Geneva, 1993), 1–9.

from the community to an individual or a family. In Florence, this process was more prolonged than elsewhere; republican ideals there were stronger and more deeply rooted in the urban culture. The Medici were finally successful in regaining control of the state, with the assistance of their two popes, Leo X (1513–1521) and Clement VII (1523–1534). The transformation was solidified with the selection of Cosimo de' Medici as Duke of Florence in 1537, establishing a dynasty that ruled the city and its territory for two centuries.

The Florentine elite accepted the Medicean *principato,* in exchange for the recognition of its privileged position in government and in society. Francesco Guicciardini, a historian and a prominent figure among the ottomati, preferred that the regime be controlled by the city's leading families, but he accepted a high office under the Medici that brought him *onore e utile,* honor and profit.

The educational process by which upper-class Florentines were converted from citizens to courtiers was described by Alamanni, a Medici partisan, in 1516:

> Florentines are not accustomed to be deferential to anyone except their magistrates and then only with some pressure and effort. They felt that it was beneath their dignity to doff their hats, and this ancient practice became embedded in their customs. . . . The older generation will never abandon this habit, but being wise, these men will not revolt (*non fanno mai novità*). But the younger generation is more flexible, more malleable, and the prince can win their support and loyalty by inviting them to join his court, and by granting them offices and benefits.[24]

The construction of an authoritarian government and a hierarchical social order, begun by the Medici in the fifteenth century, was completed in the sixteenth. The popolo were too weakened and demoralized by successive crises (plagues, famines, the depredations of military forces, heavy taxation, and conspiracies) to challenge their exclusion from the polity. Under the Medici, the *popolani* (citizenry) had become accustomed to a political and social order based on patronage and clientage, which offered them

---

24 Lodovico Alamanni, quoted in Rudolf von Albertini, *Das Florentinische Staatsbewusstsein im Übergang von der Republik zum Prinzipat* (Bern, 1955), 370.

more support than did their civic institutions and their guilds. After the expulsion of the Medici in 1494, a merchant named Piero Vaglienti expressed the view of many citizens of middling rank: "Now one does not know to whom to turn for help. . . . With a prince [signore] there is only one [leader], but now in Florence there are a hundred, and some pull you in one direction, and others in another."[25]

Within the ranks of the popolo, too, were hundreds, perhaps thousands, who had benefitted from Medicean favors and welcomed their return to power. In the dominion, the peasantry, which comprised some 70 percent of the total population, were largely indifferent; they could not distinguish between rulers and exploiters, whether republican or Medicean. As for the residents in the subject towns, who were governed by officials sent from Florence, the words "liberty" and "freedom," so often articulated in council deliberations, had little meaning for them.[26]

The demise of the republic at the hands of Medici rule did not signal a revolutionary change in the lives of the Florentine populace. It brought no abatement to the plagues, famines, and marauding armies that afflicted every urban community in Italy at the time. Nonetheless, the establishment of the principato produced a degree of political stability that the city had not experienced for decades. Medici princes continued the tradition of a strong and intrusive government. The implementation of its policy was the task of the granducal bureaucracy, the upper echelons of which were recruited from the city's elite families. To bolster their status and reinforce the principle of hierarchy, members of these lineages also received titles of nobility when they enrolled in the exclusive knightly order of Santo Stefano. The Medici also utilized the city's traditional rites and ceremonies, both secular and religious, to enhance their reputation and curry favor with the populace.[27]

25   F. W. Kent, "Patron–Client Networks," 302.
26   George Bull (trans.), *The Autobiography of Benvenuto Cellini* (Baltimore, 1956; orig. pub. 1538–1562), 21–22.
27   The impact of a devastating plague in the early 1630s is described by Giulia Calvi, *Histories of a Plague Year* (Berkeley, 1989). Political stability ensued not only in the city but also in the territory: See Giorgio Spini, *Cosimo I de' Medici e la indipendenza del principato mediceo* (Florence, 1945), 178–187. The elaborate celebration of a Medici marriage is described by James Saslow, *The Medici Wedding of 1589: Florentine Festival as Theatrum Mundi* (New Haven, 1996).

The Medici grand dukes gradually eradicated all traces of the vivere popolare and civil society. Although Cosimo I once asserted that he was bound "by the laws, the order and the magistrates of our city," in reality he was the sole fount of power. "Our advice is our will," he once wrote to a councillor, "and we consider as adversaries all those who oppose it." Varchi, the historian, told his readers not to marvel "that [he spoke] only of Cosimo, and never of the state nor the magistracies, since . . . Cosimo alone govern[ed] everything, and nothing [was] said or done, however great or small, concerning which he [did not say] either 'yes' or 'no.'" Early in his rule, Cosimo had published a decree that prohibited "any kind of assembly, congregation or conventicle," since such gatherings were viewed as potential sources of dissent and conspiracy.[28]

Under the Medici grand dukes, guilds lost their autonomy and became state agencies for the regulation of commerce, industry, the retail trades, and the crafts. The confraternities were also radically transformed:

> In contrast to traditional confraternities of republican Florence, sixteenth-century confraternities reveal major departures in ideology, ritual and social organization, introducing principles of hierarchy into confraternal membership, localizing new confraternities in parishes, bringing city-wide confraternities under the control of the duke, stressing a new ethic of obedience, and replacing older rituals that emphasized community, equality and the suspension of social differentiation and hierarchy with ritual celebrations of status, honor and rank.

For example, when a group of Florentine intellectuals spontaneously formed a cultural society in the early 1540s, Cosimo first disbanded and then reconstituted the association as the Academia Florentina, its membership and its constitution strictly controlled by the prince.[29]

The establishment of the Medici principato brought Florence and its territory into the larger Italian world dominated by

28 Eric Cochrane, *Florence in the Forgotten Centuries* (Chicago, 1973), 43, 64; Benedetto Varchi, quoted in Furio Diaz, *Il Granducato di Toscana: I Medici* (Turin, 1987), 74; Cochrane, *Florence,* 40.

29 Weissman, *Ritual Brotherhood,* 198. See also Konrad Eisenbichler, "Italian Scholarship on Pre-Modern Confraternities in Italy," *Renaissance Quarterly,* L (1997), 567–580. Diaz, *Granducato,* 201.

autocratic rulers and landed nobles, in which, as Machiavelli asserted, "no republics nor any *vivere politico* had ever existed, since those men are totally hostile to civic life." Members of Florence's leading families adapted easily to this milieu, changing their mode of dress to conform to courtly fashion, and intermarrying with noble lineages from other Italian provinces. Some acquired fiefs in Tuscany and elsewhere; those with military training found employment in the armies of Italian and foreign princes. The church provided career opportunities for the younger sons of these families, and convents became a convenient depository for their unmarried sisters.[30]

The Medici recruited substantial numbers of aristocrats into their bureaucracy; the economic benefits of state service were an important source of revenue for these noble houses. The ottomati, whose ancestors had once proudly governed their free city and its territory, had become loyal subjects and servants of the prince, competing with their rivals for his favor and largesse.[31]

Certain distinctive features of post-invasion Italy were inherited from city-state republics. The concept of individual rights and liberties, and of a private realm immune from state intervention, had never been a part of the communal legacy. Nor did it emerge, either in theory or practice, during this age of autocratic government. The impulse toward scrutiny, surveillance, and control was no less present in republican than in despotic regimes, or, for that matter, than in the feudal governments of Piedmont and Sicily. This intrusive and invasive mentality was manifest in the flood of legislation emanating from these governments, and in the publication of edicts (*bandi*), the repetition of which testified to their limited efficacy.[32]

30   Niccolò Machiavelli, *Discorsi*, I, chap. 55, in Guido Mazzoni and Mario Casella (eds.), *Tutte le opere di Niccolò Machiavelli* (Florence, 1929), 127. Machiavelli mistakenly included Lombardy and the papal states in his catalogue of regions that had never experienced republican government. Landucci, *Diario fiorentino*, 371: "Si cominciò a lasciare la portatura de' capucci, e nel 1532 non se ne vedeva pure uno, che fu spenta l'usanza, e scanbio di capuccio si porta berrette e cappegli . . . e or cominciossi a portare la barba" ([Florentines] no longer wore hoods on their cloaks, and by 1532, there were none to be seen. Instead of hoods, they wore caps, and they also began to grow beards).

31   The definitive study of these ottomati is Burr Litchfield, *Emergence of a Bureaucracy: The Florentine Patricians, 1530–1790* (Princeton, 1986).

32   Diaz, *Granducato*, 3: "La libertà civile, in quanto tutela dei diritti individuali, è sempre state . . . ignorata dalle 'democrazie' communali" (civil liberty, in the sense of protecting individual rights, had always been ignored by communal "democracies"). For the legislation

The responsibility for enforcing this thicket of legislation was entrusted to a large, expensive, and burdensome bureaucracy, which was trained to execute the ruler's will, and to regard his subjects with suspicion and condescension. For example, to implement Cosimo I's prohibition against the export of grain from the duchy, the Medici government employed a veritable army of "functionaries, agents, rectors, notaries, police officials, spies and informers." These officials inspected all goods in transit at the borders; they examined the account books and the storage facilities of grain merchants; and they invaded the cottages of villagers and peasants to search for hidden food supplies. Their methods were as arbitrary and ruthless as those of the tax officials who collected the gabelles and the levies that subsidized the regimes' administrative and military structures.[33]

These tactics, employed by every regime from Sicily to Piedmont to enforce obedience and raise revenue, created a pernicious legacy for the future—a pervasive and deeply rooted distrust of, and hostility to, the state, its institutions, its operations, and its personnel. Subjects did not perceive the state as a protector and defender but as an exploiter and predator. It is as true today, as it was in the seventeenth and eighteenth centuries, that "by and large, the state bureaucracy has oppressed rather than served the Italian citizen. . . . Far from exercising over time a pedagogic role in Italian society, the state has rather itself been shaped by those patron–client and kinship relations which are so deeply rooted in Mediterranean culture." From the highest to the lowest level of the bureaucracy, officials were commonly viewed as arrogant, inefficient, and corrupt.[34]

An Austrian diplomat in the 1730s sent this report on the Tuscan bureaucracy back to his master in Vienna: "Theft is everywhere in the military and civil administration, in the finances; there is no tribunal, no receivership where the prince is not deceived and the people oppressed. . . . [The officials] all *eat*, to use the local term, they eat off everything, off the vilest things,

---

that flooded granducal Tuscany, see *Legislazione toscana raccolta e illustrata da Lorenzo Cantini* (Florence, 1800–1807), 30v.

33 Diaz, *Granducato*, 133.

34 Paul Ginsborg, "The Italian Republic in the Face of the Future," *Italian History and Culture* (Florence, 1966), II, 4.

off the most miserable people." Since the state was not a reliable source of protection and justice, the majority of Italians instead depended upon kinship ties and the support of powerful patrons. As Delille has noted, the truly poor in early modern society "are not those who have nothing whatsoever, but those who are outside any network of solidarity."[35]

The post-Tridentine Catholic church supported the efforts of secular rulers to discipline and control their recalcitrant subjects. The church's ideology was, in most respects, identical to that of Italy's princes, and it defended the principle of hierarchical organization, which it exemplified, as it applied to Italy's "society of orders." While insisting upon its own autonomy, and its immunity from secular control, the church advocated the doctrine of submission to both lay and ecclesiastical authority, developing strategies to instruct the laity in doctrinal matters and to persuade laymen to perform their Christian obligations.[36]

Priests were required to keep records of their parishioners' vital statistics (births, marriages, and deaths) and to threaten those who violated the church's rules with excommunication. More effectively than in the past, the parish clergy established tighter controls over marriage, sexual behavior, and social life and brought the confraternities under their surveillance. The clergy also tried to weaken kinship ties in their communities, but with only limited success.[37]

Behind all of these strategies were the revitalized coercive powers of the Roman church: excommunication, the Index, and the Inquisition. The Medici grand dukes were more receptive to the operation of these mechanisms than were most other Italian rulers. Civic life in the Tuscan duchy was vitiated by Cosimo's subservience to the Roman papacy: "The persecutions of the

---

35 Jean Claude Waquet (trans. Linda McCall), *Corruption: Ethics and Power in Florence, 1600–1770* (University Park, 1991), 17. Gerard Delille, quoted in Domenico Sella, *Italy in the Seventeenth Century* (New York, 1997), 83.

36 Sella, *Italy in the Seventeenth Century,* 80–81.

37 John Bossy, "The Counter-Reformation and the People of Catholic Europe," *Past & Present,* 47 (1970), 51–70; William Hudon, "Religion and Society in Early Modern Italy—Old Questions, New Insights," *American Historical Review,* CI (1996), 783–804. The plight of confraternities is a major theme in Bossy's seminal article, "Counter-Reformation," 54–59, but his statement that confraternities were no longer an obstacle to uniform parochial observance "because they ceased to exist" is too extreme. See Sella, *Italy in the Seventeenth Century,* 137–142.

Inquisition . . . against any citizen suspected of heresy, the vigilance of the clergy in scrutinizing the behavior and thoughts of Tuscans . . . created a climate of heavy, bigoted conformism."[38]

The most potent and influential legacy received by postrevolutionary Italy was not a civic tradition inherited from the communal era but the structures and patterns developed during the "age of absolutism"—authoritarian government, both secular and religious, and a hierarchical social order in which patron–client networks flourished, in both the north and the south. Only a few urban communities—Venice, Genoa, Lucca, and San Marino—retained some degree of political autonomy. The primary objective of urban elites in those cities was the preservation of their privileged status. In towns governed by princes or viceroys, elites (both secular and ecclesiastical) were able to minimize their tax burdens and maintain their property and influence in the countryside.[39]

No associations of any kind could be established without the approval of secular and religious authorities. Unlike the European authorities across the Alps, those in Italy effectively stifled religious dissent in their territories, with the sole exception of the Waldensian community in Piedmont. The absence of any serious challenge to religious orthodoxy was, and long remained, a significant deterrent to the revival of civic values and traditions. The popularity of Italy's most celebrated novel—Alessandro Manzoni's *I promessi sposi* (Milan, 1827)—was due primarily to the familiarity of nineteenth-, and even twentieth-century Italians with its depiction of seventeenth-century Lombardy as overwhelmingly "feudal," with its lawless and arrogant nobles and their *bravi* (hired thugs), its dependent and deferential lower orders, its autocratic but fundamentally weak government, and its religious culture of submission and obedience.[40]

---

38 Diaz, *Granducato*, 194.

39 Sella, *Italy in the Seventeenth Century*, 52–62; Stuart Woolf, *A History of Italy 1700–1860: The Social Constraints of Political Change* (New York, 1991), 21–26.

40 Sella, *Italy in the Seventeenth Century*, 154–155. An illustration of the survival of this mentality in the nineteenth century involved Bettino Ricasoli, the "enlightened" Tuscan statesman and landowner:

> Whenever there was the least hesitant attempt to change customary relationships, with the peasants hinting at the existence of wishes diverging from those of their master, Ricasoli reacted swiftly, conveying to his factor [steward or manager] at Brolio that he was the master, that the property was his, that he alone could decide how to manage

If the definition of *civil society* includes as a central feature "a complex tissue of voluntary associations which occupy a public space and have a public voice," then it is difficult to find evidence for this phenomenon in prerevolutionary Italy. The academies and fledgling masonic lodges that were formed in the eighteenth century did not have a political agenda, nor any significant influence on princes and their administrators. Italy's elites were united only in their determination to preserve their traditional privileges.[41]

Not until the revolutionary era, which witnessed the radical overhaul of Italy's political and socioeconomic structures, were conditions ripe for the first tentative efforts to establish a civil society. This process was painfully slow and halting in a country whose citizens viewed the state as "a hostile presence . . . not merely in terms of the identification of the state with the land-owner, the tax-collector, and the *carabiniere,* but because of the paucity of intermediary strata attached to the values of the state." Even though the associations established before and after unification helped to contribute to this fledgling form of civil society, the assumption of "any simple correlation among voluntary associations, civil society and liberal democracy" is hardly warranted. As Nolan recently suggested, scholars "should pay less attention to quantifying civil society and more to understanding the qualitatively different meanings of associational life in different contexts. Societies can be, and since the nineteenth century have been, bourgeois without necessarily being liberal."[42]

---

it, and the first peasant that dared to speak ill of him would be dismissed. (Federico Chabod [trans. William McCuaig], *Italian Foreign Policy. The Statecraft of the Founders* [Princeton, 1996], 293).

41 Raymond Carr, *Times Literary Supplement,* 15 Oct. 1993, 4. See also Ernest Gellner, *Civil Society and Its Rivals* (New York, 1996). Woolf, *History of Italy,* 69–74, 95–111; Aldo Mola, *La massoneria nella storia d'Italia* (Rome, 1981), 21–57; Cochrane, *Tradition and Enlightenment in the Tuscan Academies, 1690–1800* (Chicago, 1961), 3–47.

42 Woolf, *History of Italy,* 476; Mary Nolan, "Against Exceptionalism," *American Historical Review,* CII (1997), 772–773.

Edward Muir

The Sources of Civil Society in Italy
Putnam explains the successful democratic performance of regional governments in northern and central Italy since 1970, as opposed to the poor record of those in the South, as the product of an abiding tenacity of civic traditions. His analysis presupposes some fundamental historical questions:

> "Why did the North and South get started on such divergent paths in the eleventh century?" The hierarchical Norman regime in the South is perhaps readily explained as the consequence of conquest by an unusually effective force of foreign mercenaries. More problematical and potentially more interesting are the origins of the communal republics. How did the inhabitants of north-central Italy first come to seek collaborative solutions to their Hobbesian dilemmas? The response to that question must await further research, not least because historians report that the answer seems lost in the mists of the Dark Ages. Our interpretation, however, highlights the unique importance of trying to pierce those mists.[1]

This essay is an attempt to grope through the historical mists. Although the vast cultural chasm between us and the early Middle Ages makes it difficult to ask modernist questions of a decidedly archaic society, the so-called Dark Ages are not a cipher. A great deal can be discovered about the process of building civil societies in northern Italy. Even more important, the construction of civil society—as Putnam posits in his more recent work on social capital—was not so much an event as a process, the inner dynamics of which is clearly discernable in later periods, and the process was not always evolutionary. It was punctuated by dramatic moments of rapid political change.

Edward Muir is the Clarence L. Ver Steeg Professor in the Arts and Sciences at Northwestern University. He is the author of *Mad Blood Stirring: Vendetta and Factions in Friuli during the Renaissance* (Baltimore, 1993; reader's ed. 1998); *Ritual in Early Modern Europe* (Cambridge, 1997).

1   Robert D. Putnam, with Roberto Leonardi and Raffaella Y. Nanetti, *Making Democracy Work: Civic Traditions in Modern Italy* (Princeton, 1993), 180.

It is certainly true that northern Italy has enjoyed an unparalleled continuity of community institutions and traditions stretching back to the formation of the communes or city-republics in the eleventh and twelfth centuries. The difficult question, however, is, Does this continuity have anything to do with the success or failure of contemporary democratic institutions in Italy or elsewhere? Putnam's approach, which looks to the communal experience of medieval Italy as somehow salient for the origins of modern democracy, betrays a peculiarly American reconstruction of Italian history that prizes the Italian past only insofar as it can be shown to lead to the triumph of republican institutions and democratic practices. Since, for the past century, this approach has dominated the American historiography of Italy, it is hardly surprising that a political scientist borrowing from the work of historians, such as Putnam, would pick it up. Yet, the reconstruction of a foreign country's past in terms created by the American present has little to recommend it as a historical method.[2]

Nevertheless, Putnam's concern to discover the sources of social capital, which he argues is a crucial precondition for effective democracy, has led him to an eloquent analysis of medieval and early modern Italy, which certainly produced one of the earliest examples of a civil society. The processes that generated it, however, probably do not have much to do with contemporary Italian and even less with American political life. The first communes, hardly more than mutual defense pacts drawn up by a group of neighbors, were certainly not democracies. Most of them collapsed in distrust and violence, were absorbed by more powerful cities, or succumbed to petty tyrants. Moreover, our knowledge of the communes' early history suffers a great deal from the ex post facto elaborations of subsequent centuries, when jurists, chroniclers, and local historians fabricated the ideological foundations of their town's civic identity in order to reinforce community cohesion.[3]

2 On the American historiography of Italy, see Muir, "The Italian Renaissance in America," *American Historical Review*, C (1995), 1095–1118.
3 For an analysis of politics in Italy before and during the rise of the communes, see Chris Wickham, *Early Medieval Italy: Central Power and Local Society, 400–1600* (Ann Arbor, 1981); Giovanni Tabacco, *The Struggle for Power in Medieval Italy: Structures of Political Rule* (New York, 1989); George W. Dameron, *Episcopal Power and Florentine Society, 1000–1320* (Cambridge, Mass., 1991). Cf. the crucial work by Carol Lansing, *The Florentine Magnates: Lineage and Faction in a Medieval Commune* (Princeton, 1991).

The best way to begin to discover the sources of civil society in Italy might be to ask, What were the Italian communes supposed to do? To contemporaries the answer was obvious—to keep families and factions under control. Banfield's "amoral familism," which Putnam establishes as the antithesis of civil society, represents a social system that medieval Italians would have understood almost instinctively. The autonomy of powerful families in an era of weak central authority bred patron–clientelist social relations. The politics of such a society coalesced around factions composed of allied families and networks of clients. Factions habitually interacted through the violence of feuding. In fact, the social ethics produced by medieval conceptions of aristocratic honor, the persistence of vendetta as a form of conflict resolution, and the modern Mafia code of silence all required powerful men to engage in periodic acts of demonstrative violence. As usual, Machiavelli went straight to the nub of the matter: "Men do injury through either fear or hate . . . such injury produces more fear; fear seeks for defense; for defense partisans are obtained; from partisans rise parties in states; from parties their ruin." Lurking within this portrait is an almost Hobbesian vision of the dilemmas of a social world impoverished by inadequate supplies of social capital, a world in which cycles of fear prevented the construction of civil society.[4]

Putnam's crucial question—"How did the inhabitants of north-central Italy first come to seek collaborative solutions to their Hobbesian dilemmas?"—can be explored, if not answered, from the historical record by reformulating it slightly: "How did the inhabitants of north-central Italy employ collaborative solutions to eliminate the political violence of families and factions in their communities?" Hobbesian dilemmas do not leave traces in the historical record; acts of political violence do. Moreover, even if the historical origins of a particular institution could be discovered, we would learn little from that fact about how it performed through history or how it could be duplicated in another society. What we are searching for are not so much origins but the elements of a feedback process that reinforced civic culture at

---

4   Edward C. Banfield, *The Moral Basis of a Backward Society* (Chicago, 1958). Cf. Putnam, *Making Democracy Work,* 177. Quotations from *Machiavelli: The Chief Works and Others* (trans. Allan Gilbert) (Durham, 1965), I, 34, 212.

many different levels and that had the cumulative effect of creating social capital.

In northern Italy, creating collaborative, rather than coercive, solutions to political violence owed a great deal to three characteristic forms of control that can be seen loosely as deriving from civic religion, judicial practice, and the mores of refined manners. The religious life of northern Italy, especially in contrast to the kingdom of Naples, was decidedly civic, in the sense that crucial institutions were subject to lay control, that patron saints served as the foci of civic cults, and that the ideal of communal cooperation was repeatedly modelled and reinforced through civic rituals—mainly processions. Civic religion in medieval Italy, however, was compromised by a necessary attachment to civic politics, which excluded everyone from political privileges except the members of a small oligarchy and created a lofty political rhetoric that was noticeably distant from the normal operations of government. The fatal flaw of this civic solution to factional violence was that it could not be easily exported beyond the town walls to the countryside.

The long-term success of civil society depended on two additional complementary processes that were less exclusive and more easily exportable—one based on juridical procedures and the other on the spread of courtly manners. The juridical culture that permeated northern Italy through the ubiquitous presence of notaries brought some element of due process and regularized procedure to even the most obscure backwater villages. Furthermore, extremely influential models of personal comportment contributed to what Elias labelled the "civilizing process," in which northern Italians were decidedly precocious, if for no other reason than the fact that literate culture was more widespread there than anywhere else before modern times. These cultural forms found institutional expressions, but, most important, cultural practices and institutions reinforced one another, creating ways of behaving in institutional settings that made collaboration against divisive violence possible.[5]

Shifting the focus away from the origins of formal institutions to cultural processes helps to resolve some of the striking historical

5 Norbert Elias (trans. Edmund Jephcott), *The History of Manners. I. The Civilizing Process* (New York, 1978). On the dissemination of "civilizing texts," see Peter Burke, *The Fortunes of the Courtier: The European Perception of Castiglione's Cortegiano* (University Park, 1996).

anomalies in Putnam's analysis of Italian regions. Several of the post-1970 regions that score highest on his civic community index completely lack the deep institutional roots of civism that he argues are crucial for institutional success in contemporary Italy. For example, Piedmont coalesced as a region not around a city-state (as did Lombardy, Veneto, or Tuscany) but around an absolutist prince, who, long after the heyday of city-republics, established his capital in Turin as a military bastion of coercion. Liguria formed around Genoa, which, though a city-republic, was hardly a model of civic virtue—a city with such a frail civic identity (try to find, for example, the town square of Genoa) that its long history of aristocratic and factional violence produced chronic political instability. Strangest of all is Friuli, a region high on the contemporary civic community index, even though not one of its more than 800 towns and villages was ever a city-republic. Friuli long endured the rule of a feuding, arrogant, irresponsible aristocracy; for centuries the region was crushed under the weight of inefficient and corrupt political institutions. Between 1945 and 1954, it suffered a bloody civil war that prefigured the Bosnian War of the 1990s in its brutality. If Friuli could become a successful civic community, as it most certainly has, then practically any place can. Its example offers a challenge to Putnam's somewhat guarded conclusion that "most institutional history moves slowly." In Friuli, as elsewhere, the transformation of the mores of political elites, combined with abrupt and widespread social change, can force institutional history to move very quickly.[6]

CIVIC RELIGION   The late medieval and renaissance Italian city-states provide a kind of historical laboratory for the study of the most rudimentary forms of reciprocal violence—factional, or what we now call gang violence. The first communes in this nesting ground of civil society were conceived to eliminate, or at least limit, such violence. The city-republics created *res publicae* of elected rather than hereditary officials and a culture of citizenship that required, in principle, the subordination of personal, familial,

6   For the civic-community index, see Putnam, *Making Democracy Work,* Table 4.4, 96, and Figure 4.4, 97; 184 for quotation. On Piedmont, see Geoffrey Symcox, *Victor Amadeus II: Absolutism in the Savoyard State, 1675–1730* (Berkeley, 1983); on Genoa, Steven A. Epstein, *Genoa & the Genoese, 958–1528* (Chapel Hill, 1996).

and factional interests for the public good. All of the city-republics struggled to find a way to inculcate this ideal in its citizens. By almost universal acknowledgment, the most successful in this respect was Venice, which may have been the first political regime in Europe to have eradicated violent methods as a common path for achieving political power.

By the thirteenth century, the Venetian republic supplanted the feuds of its own magnate clans with a system of elections and the distribution of preferments or graft. The early political history of Venice was certainly violent enough. If the chronicles can be trusted, between 697 and 1172, five doges (the "dukes" of Venice) were forced to abdicate, nine exiled or deposed, five blinded, and five murdered. The early doges and their families were famous for their involvement in conspiracies and vendettas. In the late twelfth and thirteenth centuries, however, new families who had made fortunes in trade with the Levant seized the dogeship and transformed the institutions of Venice to serve their interests, encapsulated in the belief that domestic political violence was bad for business. Moreover, as Lane argued, generations of experience at sea, where a ship's captain had nearly absolute power and where the fastest ship in a convoy had to accommodate itself to the slowest, created habits of collective obedience that resulted in a distinct form of political behavior. To Lane's ideas about this collective discipline of seafaring should be added Becker's insights into the subjective conditions necessary for marketplace transactions: The abstract trust needed to sustain trade in early capitalism was a necessary precondition for civil society. The problem with both of these theories is that there were plenty of seafaring and protocapitalist societies—Genoa for one—that neither eliminated political violence nor developed a lasting civil society.[7]

During the thirteenth century, the hegemonic families in Venice accepted the rule of law over most aspects of life, building a political consensus that supplanted the feuding of the past. There were still significant internal enmities—especially those between the factions headed by the Tiepolo and Dandolo families, which might have been rooted in class—but quarrels neither threatened

7 On the early doges, see Pompeo Molmenti, "I bandi e i banditi della repubblica veneta," *Nuova Antologia*, XVIL (1893), 126–129. Frederic C. Lane, *Venice: A Maritime Republic* (Baltimore, 1973), 91–95; Marvin B. Becker, *Medieval Italy: Constraints and Creativity* (Bloomington, 1981); idem, *Civility and Society in Western Europe, 1300–1600* (Bloomington, 1988).

the electoral system nor produced a tyrant as they did in so many mainland cities.[8]

Although new social groups rose to political influence when Venetian law was codified in 1242, those living outside of the Rialto city, even the inhabitants of the lagoon settlements, lost their right to be consulted about their own affairs. That they had to accept the rule of a podestà sent out from the capital city reveals one of the weaknesses of the civic solution to factional violence. The civic model, wherever it was found, was highly exclusive about who could enjoy political privileges, always entailing some sort of property qualification: Women, young men, and priests never could hold office; privileged families often proscribed their enemies and guaranteed their hegemony through legislation; and citizenship did not extend beyond the city walls. Hence, despite the reduction of violent factionalism, the history of the Italian city-republics—such as Venice, Florence, and Siena—from the late thirteenth to the sixteenth century is one of oligarchic domination. However, even though these oligarchies tended to contract over time (so much for the social mobility of republics), they generated a certain measure of political stability, reduced political violence, and encouraged a system of preferments that offered many groups outside the ruling circle at least a modest stake in the regime.[9]

Venetian oligarchs became so concerned about the danger of vendetta in their city that they systematically attacked the social customs associated with factional identity. A law in 1266 banned all displays of the armorial insignia of the magnate families. After the defeat of the conspiracy of Marco Querini and Baiamonte Tiepolo in 1310, the city prohibited the bearing of the blazons of either family for more than a century. Because large banquets,

---

8 On the Dandolo and Tiepolo, see Giorgio Cracco, *Società e stato nel medioevo veneziano (secoli XII–XIV)* (Florence, 1967), 89–173.

9 The Venetian republic seems to have been particularly effective in creating loyalty among those excluded from formal political power. For the excluded professional and propertied classes, see Brian Pullan, *Rich and Poor in Renaissance Venice: The Social Institutions of a Catholic State, to 1620* (Oxford, 1971). For artisans in Venice, see Richard T. Rapp, *Industry and Economic Decline in Seventeenth-Century Venice* (Cambridge, Mass., 1976); Robert C. Davis, *Shipbuilders of the Venetian Arsenal: Workers and Workplace in the Preindustrial City* (Baltimore, 1991); idem, *The War of the Fists: Popular Culture and Public Violence in Late Renaissance Venice* (New York, 1994); Richard Mackenney, *Tradesmen and Traders: The World of the Guilds in Venice and Europe, c. 1250–c. 1650* (London, 1987).

ideal for the building of factional alliances, were deemed especially dangerous, the law limited guest lists to immediate kinsmen, even for weddings. Godparentage placed children under the protection of a godfather and solidified his relationship to the parents. Some children had as many as 150 godparents until a 1505 law prohibited nobles from serving as the godparents of other nobles' children in an attempt to prevent the creation of factional alliances within the ruling class. Insulting words, gestures, pictures, and writings that could lead to vendettas came to be seen as highly subversive. The solution was to silence all personal insults. Laws protecting the doge and his counselors—the personification of government honor—from insults, were more readily enforced than those against more physically violent personal crimes such as rape. For example, a man who drew offensive caricatures of the doge and other officials in 1464 had his right hand cut off. As Ruggiero has shown, Venice remained a crime-ridden city, but Venetian nobles found it more useful to exact vengeance through the courts or the political process than to assault enemies or hire assassins. The values of Venetian nobles assumed a particularly civic cast that prized their collective honor as civilized men over the visceral protection of personal honor. In their light, the chivalrous fantasies of the rural nobility began to look increasingly absurd.[10]

By the fifteenth century, the most characteristic feature of the Venetian civic ideal became unanimity (*unimitas*)—"the convergence of a multitude of wants and aspirations into a single will"—as King has defined it. This ideal permeated the writings of Venetian humanists, influencing how they understood their own politics and depriving all dissenters of legitimacy. The principle inspired the most important Venetian treatise on the subject of factions—Bishop Pietro Barozzi's *On the Extirpation of Factions and*

---

10 On the criminalization of vendetta in Venice, see Guido Ruggiero, *Violence in Early Renaissance Venice* (New Brunswick, 1980), 125–155; *idem, The Boundaries of Eros: Sex Crime and Sexuality in Renaissance Venice* (Oxford, 1985), 89–108; Jacques Heers (trans. Barry Herbert), *Family Clans in the Middle Ages: A Study of Political and Social Structures in Urban Areas* (Amsterdam, 1977), 103; Donald Queller, *The Venetian Patriciate: Reality versus Myth* (Urbana, 1986), 75–84, 234–239; Stanley Chojnacki, "Crime, Punishment, and the Trecento Venetian State," and John Kenneth Hyde, "Contemporary Views on Faction and Civil Strife in 13th- and 14th-Century Italy," in Lauro Martines (ed.), *Violence and Civil Disorder in Italian Cities, 1200–1500* (Berkeley, 1972), 184–228 and 273–307, respectively; Elisabeth Crouzet-Pavan, "Violence, société et pouvour à Venise (XIVe–XVe siècles): Forme et évolution de rituels urbains," *Mélanges de l'École française de Rome: Moyen Age—temps modernes,* XVIC (1984), 903–936.

Recalling and Compelling the Citizens to Obedience (1489), written as advice to Bernardo Bembo, who had been elected podestà of strife-torn Bergamo. Although Barozzi had ample practical experience and understood the historical causes, he chose to diagnose the disease of factionalism in moral terms: "Certainly there has been in Italy, as long as men can remember, no plague more pernicious," a plague caused by the greed of the poor, the pride of the rich, and the envy of the mediocre. From these deadly vices derived nine ordinary and eleven extraordinary causes of factionalism, which could be checked by the secular and ecclesiastical authorities' effective employment of the virtues of liberality, humility and charity, beneath which lay the principle of the consensus of all parties (*consensus partium*)—the ideal of the city as a balanced organism found in Aristotle's *Politics*.[11]

Even though humanist ideals created a powerful model of behavior, the humanist analysis of factionalism had little prescriptive value for a Venetian, or any other, governor who was faced with the intractable problem of factional violence. In fact, the humanist ideals of civic unity led, most often, to a dangerous cleavage between the operations of civic government and the political rhetoric about it, creating the second weakness of civism, the non-referentiality of Italian political thought to Italian political practice, especially after the suppression of Machiavelli's works in the late sixteenth century. Despite the widespread influence of Cicero, much in the humanist curriculum worked against the elimination of factionalism in government. A now forgotten classic study written in the 1930s by Maugain, but never much discussed, demonstrated how easily humanism could serve violent impulses. Maugain supplies numerous examples of what he calls "revenge humanism"—that is, one humanist scholar murdering another because of some minor point of philology and justifying the deed with learned citations about ancient tyrannicides.[12]

Although the protocapitalist mores of sailors or marketplace traders and the ethics of humanist pedagogues certainly had an effect, the most successful cultural element of the civic model for

---

11   Margaret L. King, *Venetian Humanism in an Age of Patrician Dominance* (Princeton, 1986), 92 (first quotation), 150–157 (second quotation from 151 is her translation), 333–335.
12   On the success of the humanist curriculum in Italian education, see Paul F. Grendler, *Schooling in Renaissance Italy: Literacy and Learning, 1300–1600* (Baltimore, 1989). On revenge humanism, see Gabriel Maugain, *Moeures italiennes de la Renaissance: La vengeance* (Paris, 1935).

suppressing factional violence might well have derived from civic religion, particularly the vast panoply of religious rituals that city governments deployed to refashion the behavior of citizens.[13]

Beginning in 1450, the republic of Venice charged a patrician from each neighborhood with responsibility for erecting and protecting images of the Virgin Mary and other saints set up in *capitelli* on the outside walls of a house or church. The relevant legislation made it clear that these images were to be a prophylactic against blasphemy and street violence. Presumably, a Virgin on every street corner would inhibit potential combatants from committing mayhem, or at least impair their fighting ability, since they would have to genuflect in front of every image as they chased each other through the alleys of the city. Needless to say, the strategy did not always work, but it does afford an insight into how Italian officials conceptualized behavior modification. The erection of these miniature shrines is reminiscent of the tradition in which priests managed to calm riotous crowds by carrying sacred objects through the city. The ability of processions and public displays of religious objects to create order depended on a belief that they inherently evoked certain kinds of behavior. Demonstrative reverence for statues of the Virgin was proper Christian social behavior; behind it was the idea that the Virgin was somehow present in the image.

The erection of sacred images throughout the city might be seen as an attempt to make the civic procession a permanent feature of daily life. Saints had to be honored on a regular basis, usually with an annual procession displaying relics or images. In Siena, icons of the Virgin were carried in processions on her feast days until 1308 when the city government commissioned Duccio di Buoninsegna to paint a more elaborate panel—the famous

---

13 On civic religion, see Donald Weinstein, "Critical Issues in the Study of Civic Religion in Renaissance Florence," in Charles Trinkaus with Heiko A. Oberman (eds.), *The Pursuit of Holiness in Late Medieval and Renaissance Religion* (Leiden, 1974), 265–270. On civic rituals, see Richard Trexler, *Public Life in Renaissance Florence* (New York, 1980); Muir, *Civic Ritual in Renaissance Venice* (Princeton, 1981); *idem,* "The Virgin on the Street Corner: The Place of the Sacred in Italian Cities," in Steven Ozment (ed.), *Religion and Culture in the Renaissance and Reformation* (Kirksville, 1989), 25–40; Ronald F. E. Weissman, *Ritual Brotherhood in Renaissance Florence* (New York, 1982); Sharon T. Strocchia, *Death and Ritual in Renaissance Florence* (Baltimore, 1992); Angelo Torre, *Il consumo di devozioni: Religione e comunità nelle campagne dell'Ancien Régime* (Venice, 1995); Matteo Casini, *I gesti del principe: La festa politica a Firenze e Venezi in età rinascimentale* (Venice, 1996).

Maestà—which became the central altarpiece in the cathedral, making more flamboyant representations possible. Henceforth, instead of church and city officials carrying an image of the Madonna through the city, all of the citizens filed past the dazzling painting, especially on the Assumption. Legislation made participation compulsory in Siena and its subject towns, and everyone except criminals and other malefactors had to make offerings of candles. Those who violated the civic order were deprived both of the Virgin's protection and of the privileges of citizenship. The civic procession had such deep resonances with the symbolism of authority that, as Partridge and Starn have noted, the painted walls of the council chambers where officials gathered created the illusion that viewers were walking in a procession. To be an official, in effect, was to be *present* in a procession.[14]

Ex-votos clustered around a reliquary or a miracle-working image revealed the desire to gain proximity to the holy, and pilgrimages testified to belief in the efficacy of obtaining direct access to sacred objects. Pious laymen and women often seem to have considered images as signs that indicated the presence of the saint rather than as symbols that brought the saint's spiritual qualities to mind, despite the insistence of clerics to the contrary. The impulse to decorate and embellish churches (especially altars) may have come, in part, from an underlying anxiety about the mobility of the sacred. A saint who was ill-treated or forced to dwell in shabby surroundings might allow his or her body to be "translated" elsewhere.[15]

Related to the notion that an icon indicated the presence of whomever it depicted was the assumption that the very act of seeing a sacred object brought viewers under its power. The extromission theory of vision at the time posited that objects acted directly upon viewers' eyes through "species" or "rays." Leonardo da Vinci explained the theory concisely by an analogy to the

---

14   Brian Kempers, "Icons, Altarpieces, and Civic Ritual in Siena Cathedral, 1100–1530," in Barbara A. Hanawalt and Kathryn L. Reyerson (eds.), *City and Spectacle in Medieval Europe* (Minneapolis, 1994), 89–136. Cf. Daniel Waley, *Siena and the Sienese in the Thirteenth Century* (Cambridge, 1991). Loren Partridge and Randolph Starn, "Triumphalism and the Sala Regia in the Vatican," in Barbara Wisch and Susan Scott Munshower (eds.), *"All the World's a Stage . . .": Art and Pageantry in the Renaissance and Baroque* (University Park, 1990), 22–81; idem, *Arts of Power: Three Halls of State in Italy, 1300–1600* (Berkeley, 1992).

15   Hans Conrad Peyer, *Stadt und Stadtpatron im mittelalterlichen Italien* (Zurich, 1955); Patrick J. Geary, *Furta Sacra: Thefts of Relics in the Central Middle Ages* (Princeton, 1978).

rippling effect that a stone flung into water creates: Any object placed in a luminous atmosphere diffuses images of itself outward in circles through the medium of air.[16]

The invisible emanations from street processions and capitelli created a series of spiritually "hot" zones that made a city's social life sacred by turning the walls of the churches inside out—that is, by bringing the sacred into the profane and making civic government possible. Some kind of sacred presence was absolutely crucial to the task of urban pacification.

The most consistent such presence was that of the patron saints who were thought to favor particular cities and to watch over them. One of the chief ritual tasks of citizens was to guarantee the patron saint's good graces through propitiation and supplication. Although the tradition of patron saints existed all across Christian Europe, the cults of patron saints were most fully elaborated in northern and central Italy where the independent city-states faced the necessity of strengthening civic identities to diminish obstinate internal strife and to withstand threats from neighbors and invaders. Peyer argued that the "state miracle" of these cults offered divine sanction to the established political order of the Italian city-states, particularly the republics that lacked a charismatic prince or figure-head.[17]

The contrasts between the culture of saints' cults in the North and that in the South is telling. Naples exhibited a remarkable instability of the sacred, especially in contrast to republican cities such as Florence or Venice. Naples and its environs hosted a stunning number of saints' cults, in which the sudden liquification of the saints' dried blood foretold disasters. That of St. Januarius in Naples became the most famous, stimulating popular enthusiasms and disturbances three times each year. The relics of St. Januarius, however, arrived late (1497) and remained solely in the bishop's possession to the exclusion of the civic authorities. Since the cult flourished while Naples was under foreign control, unable to develop new civic institutions, it failed to stimulate the kind of communal solidarity that patron-saint cults in the North were

16 Lee Palmer Wandel, "The Reform of the Images: New Visualizations of the Christian Community at Zürich," *Archiv für Reformationsgeschichte*, LXXX (1989), 106–109; David D. Lindberg, *Theories of Vision from Al-Kindi to Kepler* (Chicago, 1976), 147–177; quotation on 161.

17 Peyer, *Stadt und Stadtpatron*.

able to establish. The Neapolitan situation is in marked contrast with that of Venice where St. Mark's body was in the possession of the doge, St. Mark's basilica became a state church, and the bishop or patriarch participated in civic rituals only as an invited guest.[18]

Unlike in the northern Italian towns where bishops were often at the mercy of the laity to enforce the church's will, in the kingdom of Naples during the fifteenth century, the plethora of bishops kept the church financially impoverished, hard-pressed to deliver spiritual services to the laity, and indifferent to local affairs because of chronic episcopal absenteeism. Before the Catholic Reformation, the South also lacked the North's vibrant tradition of lay confraternities, which, by the fourteenth century, had become not only the principal source of public charity but also, through egalitarian rituals of flagellation and processions, a training venue for participation in other kinds of cooperative organizations. It would hardly be an exaggeration to suggest that the lay confraternities provided the single most important lesson about cooperation of any Italian civic institution.[19]

The northern city-states tried to unite the capital city with the towns and villages of the surrounding countryside by requiring subjects to join civic processions in the capital city or to emulate them at home: Regional dominion was built upon the exportation of civic cults, which tended to diminish in effectiveness with distance from the capital. One of the most common forms of rural resistance to urban domination was to reject these ceremonial obligations. In the late thirteenth century, the mountain peoples of the Garfagnana region severed the right hand of a notary from a local village who had taken a candle to the festival of Santa

18 See Muir, "Virgin on the Street Corner," 36–37.
19 The pattern in Naples was even more dramatic in the hinterlands of the kingdom where the organization of local churches guaranteed domination by entrenched local elites who treated church benefices as family sinecures. The systematic evangelization of the populace came late, during the seventeenth and eighteenth centuries, when the Jesuits launched missions in the South. See David Gentilcore, *From Bishop to Witch: The System of the Sacred in Early Modern Terra d'Otranto* (Manchester, 1992). On confraternities and charity, see Weissman, *Ritual Brotherhood*; Pullan, *Rich and Poor*; Philip Gavitt, *Charity and Children in Renaissance Florence: The Ospedale degli Innocenti, 1410–1536* (Ann Arbor, 1990); Carol Bresnahan Menning, *Charity and State in Late Renaissance Italy: The Monte di Pietà of Florence* (Ithaca, 1993); John Henderson, *Piety and Charity in Late Medieval Florence* (Oxford, 1994).

Croce in Lucca; this act of symbolic subjugation offended his neighbors.[20]

A third weakness of the civic model in the face of factional violence—besides social exclusivity and hollow political rhetoric—was its inability to work outside the capital cities themselves. The civic solution to internecine violence was to transform the city into a *corpus mysticum,* a place that derived its authority from the relics of a powerful saint (St. Mark for Venice, St. John the Baptist for Florence, and the Virgin Mary for Siena). It was too much a product of a particular city to be applicable to the countryside, the breeding ground of feuds and factions. The Venetian pattern of erecting images of the lion of St. Mark in provincial cities only underlined the futility of applying the civic model of Venice beyond its local context.

JUDICIAL PRACTICE   The three weaknesses of early civism became evident primarily during the fifteenth century and thereafter, when the large city-states began the long process of consolidating subject territories into regional states. During the sixteenth and seventeenth centuries, Venetian magistrates gradually created an alternative to civism for rural pacification that was largely collaborative; they supplemented it with coercion only in the most extreme cases. Their system, which might be called continuous litigation, gave provincials access to appellate courts that bound up local tyrants in the formalities of judicial practice. It gave rural communities an arena for dodging and maneuvering against feudal privilege by pitting the top and bottom of the political system against the bull-headed violence of honor-bound aristocrats—the most dangerous group in any early modern state. The continuous-litigation model of community pacification did not require republican institutions as much as a culture of procedural regularity created and sustained by notaries who had a rudimentary legal education and who could be found virtually everywhere. Nevertheless, notaries in republics may have been more likely than those in principalities to litigate against aristocratic factions.[21]

20   Giorgio Chittolini, "Civic Religion and the Countryside in Late Medieval Italy," in Trevor Dean and Wickham (eds.), *City and Countryside in Late Medieval and Renaissance Italy: Essays Presented to Philip Jones* (London, 1990), 69–80.
21   Continuous litigation might be imagined as a form of resistance. According to James C. Scott, the transcript of a litigation was not as "hidden" as it might have been in other forms of resistance practiced in situations of extreme domination, but the public transcript of court cases hid the actual political issues behind the litigation to some degree (*Weapons of the Weak:*

The consolidation of the regional states of northern Italy in the fifteenth and sixteenth centuries might have been even more important to the development of civil society than the establishment of the first communes in the eleventh. It was certainly a crucial stage in the creation of the cultural and political identities of the regions, and they, not the communes, were the unit of analysis in Putnam's *Making Democracy Work*. The formation of the regional states integrated networks of communes together and, for the first time, began to control political violence in the countryside and the great walled cities, as well as in lagoon-protected Venice. Since the establishment of the regional governments in 1970, a growing number of Italian historians have turned their attention toward the evolution of the regions from the fifteenth to the eighteenth century, and their research has associated the strengthening of civil society with regionalization.[22]

When Venice or Milan conquered new cities, their habitual respect for the local statutes and customs (*statuti e consuetudine*) in theory affirmed local autonomy by allowing the selection of local officials by traditional means, but it also left undecided how the various ruling cities were to exercise the privileges of *dominio* over their territories; none of these cities had elected the Venetians or Milanese to uphold the common good. The communes had been conquered or absorbed by a more powerful regime. The Venetian

---

Everyday Forms of Peasant Resistance [New Haven, 1985]; *Domination and the Arts of Resistance: Hidden Transcripts* [New Haven, 1990]). On continuous litigation, see Muir, "Was There Republicanism in the Renaissance Republics? Venice after Agnadello," in John Martin and Dennis Romano (eds.), *Venice Reconsidered: Venetian History and Civilization, 1297–1797* (Baltimore, 1999). For parallel examples of the salutary social consequences of continuous litigation in other cultures, see David T. Konig, *Law and Society in Puritan Massachusetts: Essex County, 1629–1692* (Chapel Hill, 1979); Melissa Macauley, *Litigation Masters in Late Imperial China: Social Empowerment and Chinese Legal Culture, 1723–1919* (Stanford, 1998).

22 The leader of this move toward regional history has been Chittolini, *La formazione dello Stato regionale e le istituzioni del contado* (Turin, 1979); *idem*, "Stati padani, 'Stati del Rinascimento': Problemi di ricerca," in Giovanni Tocci (ed.), *Persistenze feudali e autonomie communitative in stati padani fra Cinque e Seicento* (Bologna, 1988), 9–29; *idem*, "The 'Private,' the 'Public,' the State," *Journal of Modern History,* LXVII, supplement about "The Origins of the State in Italy, 1300–1600" (1995), S34–61. This last article provides the best introduction to the historical research about the regional states in the late medieval and early modern periods. It has been separately published in Julius Kirshner (ed.), *The Origins of the State in Italy, 1300–1600* (Chicago, 1996), 34–61. Paolo Prodi, brother of the recent prime minister of Italy, is one of the most influential regional historians: See Prodi (trans. Susan Haskins), *The Papal Prince: One Body and Two Souls: The Papal Monarchy in Early Modern Europe* (Cambridge, 1987); *idem, Il sacramento del potere: Il giuramento politico nella storia costituzionale dell'Occidente* (Bologna, 1992).

system is particularly revealing because it pitted its own republican institutions against provincial ones, which were communal or feudal in origin but typically controlled by local aristocratic or citizen elites.

The northern Italian regional states hardly resembled Max Weber's conception of a modern state administered by trained officials who carried out their duties in a routine, legal, and impartial manner. Lacking a professional bureaucracy, administrative centralization, and uniform procedures, these states can best be understood as a network of diarchies in which the patrician families and institutions from the capital established bilateral relationships with the dominant families and institutions in the subject cities. The semi-autonomous groups that composed these asymmetrical diarchies were called *corpi e ceti*—literally "bodies and classes." They consisted of such territorial organizations as the parliament of Friuli; cities, towns, and villages incorporated as communes; and aristocratic jurisdictions. Governing these regional states required a process of continuous negotiation, or continuous litigation—between the dominant city on the one hand and these various corporate groups and privileged families, on the other. Venice and Genoa might represent the extreme forms of indirect government that prevailed among the regional states of northern Italy. The decentralized government of Venice was completely unsystematic: The jurisdictions and responsibilities of its various councils overlapped or conflicted, and Venetian law was more "oracular" than guided by statute or precedent.[23]

---

23   On the inapplicability of Weber's model of the modern state, see Kirshner, "Introduction: The State is 'Back In,'" *Journal of Modern History,* LXVII, supplement about "The Origins of the State in Italy, 1300–1600" (1995), S1–2. On the Venetian territorial state, see Marino Berengo, *La società veneta alla fine del Settecento: Ricerche storiche* (Florence, 1956); for the concept of "diarchy," Angelo Ventura, *Nobiltà e popolo nella società veneta del Quattrocento e Cinquecento* (Milan, 1993; 2d ed.); on cultural differences throughout the *terraferma,* Gaetano Cozzi, "Ambiente veneziano, ambiente veneto," in Stefano Rosso-Mazzinghi (ed.), *L'uomo e il suo ambiente* (Florence, 1973), 93–146; *idem,* "Considerazioni sull'amministrazione della giustizia nella Repubblica di Venezia (secc. XV–XVI)," in Sergio Bertelli, Nicolai Rubinstein, and Craig Hugh Smyth (eds.), *Florence and Venice: Comparisons and Relations. I. Quattrocento* (Florence, 1979), 101–133; *idem* (ed.), *Stato, società e giustizia nella Repubblica Veneta (sec. XV–XVIII)* (Rome, 1980, 1985), 2v.; *idem,* "Politica, società, istituzioni," in *idem* and Michael Knapton (eds.), *La Repubblica di Venezia nell'età moderna* (Turin, 1986), 3–252; Muir, *Mad Blood Stirring: Vendetta and Factions in Friuli during the Renaissance* (Baltimore, 1993), 49–67; Furio Bianco, *1511: La "Crudel Zobia Grassa": Rivolte contadine e faide nobiliari in Friuli tra '400 e '500* (Pordenone, 1995); Marco Bellabarba, *La giustizia ai confini: Il principato vescovile di Trento agli inizi dell'età moderna* (Bologna, 1966). See also the excellent synthesis of work on the

Venetian law was never brought into conformity with Roman law principles as was that of the *terraferma* cities, most of which had revised their own statutes on the basis of Roman law and hired bureaucrats trained in jurisprudence at Padua. The judges in Venetian courts were politicians who lacked legal training, and their limited terms in office prevented them from relying on past experience and knowledge of precedents. The Venetian system was well suited to guarantee the domination of the patrician class. It made the law courts a mechanism of patronage, the famous *broglio*—the systematic distribution of bribes and favors in exchange for political support. In this sense, the Venetian regional state functioned through informal and highly adaptable political organizations—such as networks of cognatic and agnatic kin or alliances among lineages. Since these structures worked sufficiently well to sustain a successful regional state, they ought not be dismissed as archaic or dysfunctional, as they would be from a Weberian perspective. Moreover, a government based on patronage ties was not entirely incompatible with civil society. Throughout northern Italy, civil societies functioned atop a grid of patron–client relationships, through what looks suspiciously like corruption.[24]

The Venetian case isolates the conundrum of civil society's exportability. How can civic institutions be imitated or imposed

Veneto, Alfredo Viggiano, *Governanti e governati: Legittimità del potere ed esercizio dell'autorità sovrana nello Stato veneto della prima età moderna* (Treviso, 1993).

On "indirect government" in the Genoese state, see Osvaldo Raggio, *Faide e parentele: Lo stato genovese visto dalla Fontanabuona* (Turin, 1990), xiv. Cf. Maurice Aymard, "La transizione dal feudalismo al capitalismo," in *Storia d'Italia. Annali. I. Dal feudalismo al capitalismo* (Turin, 1978), 1131–1192. One comparative historian of Mediterranean empires has described the Genoese empire in terms of the "'absence' of the state": Felipe Fernández-Armesto, *Before Columbus: Exploration and Colonization from the Mediterranean to the Atlantic, 1229–1492* (Philadelphia, 1987), 96–120. The best synthetic study of the Genoese state is Epstein, *Genoa & the Genoese.*

24 This view of Venetian legal administration derives from the work of Cozzi and his students in *Stato, società, e giustizia nella Republica Veneta,* summarized in Viggiano, *Governanti e governati.* On corruption among Venetian governors and judges, see Queller, *Venetian Patriciate.* See Muir, *Mad Blood Stirring,* for an analysis of the most prominent case of politics pursued through informal factions. For an argument that clientelism and feuding should not be viewed as antimodern but as ways of consolidating states during the early modern period, see Chittolini, "The 'Private,' the 'Public,' the State." On patronage and corruption in Florence, see Andrea Zorzi, "The Florentines and Their Public Offices in the Early Fifteenth Century: Competition, Abuses of Power, and Unlawful Acts," in Muir and Ruggiero (eds.), *History from Crime* (Baltimore, 1994), 110–134; Jean Claude Waquet (trans. Linda McCall), *Corruption: Ethics and Power in Florence, 1600–1770* (University Park, 1992).

and at the same time respect local laws and practices? Unlike ancient Rome or Renaissance Siena and Florence, where many notables from provincial towns were given citizenship, Venice rarely granted membership in the governing patriciate to non-Venetians and never extended political privileges to Venetian commoners, Venetian patrician women, and resident foreigners. This failure to incorporate provincial elites into the ruling class sustained the diarchic character of the regime and maintained asymmetries in favor of the Venetian patriciate.[25]

Written culture was more common in northern Italy than elsewhere in Europe, playing a great role in daily life there, even though only a minority were literate. The professionals who made writing so important were notaries, trained specialists who helped to construct familial, corporate, and communal memories through a disciplined, rule-laden form of written legal procedure. They registered virtually every human transaction: the contents of a trousseau, marriage contracts, wills, real-estate deals, the terms of tenancy or apprenticeship, and business partnerships. The literate culture of notaries probably permeated Italian life more than the literate culture of priests, especially in rural areas where educated priests were rare. There were about 8 notaries per 1,000 people in the Florence of 1427 and the Verona of 1605. Even isolated villages that might not have been able to afford a priest still needed at least the occasional services of a notary. Itinerant notaries travelled from village to village, for a small fee laying out their parchment and pen on the wall of a well or pigsty, carefully recording the linens, sheets, and utensils in a peasant bride's dowry

---

25 The legal status of *cittadino* was available to provincials and commoners of substantial property who were resident in Venice, but it granted only trading privileges, access to technical and clerical jobs in Venetian government, and the opportunity to join certain charitable institutions, such as the Scuole Grandi. It did not carry any political privileges. Cf. Pullan, *Rich and Poor*. Little is known about the *cittadini* as a class, but James Grubb is currently working on a comprehensive study. Before the seventeenth century, only a small number of provincials received membership in the patriciate, usually because of military services. On the suicidal reluctance of the Venetian patriciate to recruit new members, see James C. Davis, *The Decline of the Venetian Nobility as a Ruling Class* (Baltimore, 1962); Volker Hunecke, *Der venezianische Adel am ende der Republik, 1646–1797* (Tübingen, 1995).

On the structural history of the Italian states, see Federico Chabod, *Scritti sul Rinascimento* (Turin, 1981); idem, *Lo Stato e la vita religiosa a Milano nell'epoca di Carlo V* (Turin, 1977). On the Tuscan grand ducal state, see Elena Fasano Guarini (ed.), *Potere e società negli Stati regionali italiani del '500 e '600* (Bologna, 1978); idem, "Center and Periphery," *Journal of Modern History*, LXVII, supplement about "The Origins of the State in Italy, 1300–1600" (1995), S74–96.

chest, or describing a plot of land that was for sale. The cultural power of notaries meant that even illiterates had an appreciation for the value of written records.[26]

In the villages of northern Italy, notaries safeguarded and interpreted the laws, customs, and practices of the community. Most rural localities had some kind of assembly (*vicinia*) for heads of families, which followed traditional norms that had been passed down orally from father to son. In many cases, the common law of tradition was transformed into the civil law of statute under the influence of notaries trained in Roman law. These written statutes, most of which were drawn up between the eleventh and fifteenth centuries, constituted the legal basis for communal government.[27]

In serving the public good of a commune, the principal task of the village notary and other notables was to manage carefully the relations of the community with external authorities, usually a local feudal lord or a provincial town with superior jurisdiction or a distant capital city—Venice, Milan, Florence, or Genoa. The precise definition of communal powers in communal statutes did not prevent infringements of autonomy or abuses of power by the local lords, but it did provide communes with a juridical basis for resistance.

26 Burke, *The Historical Anthropology of Early Modern Italy: Essays on Perception and Communication* (Cambridge, 1987), on the importance of literate culture, 130, on notary statistics, 128. For an account of the career of a notary who specialized in peasant clients in the Padovano, see Berengo, "Africo Clementi, agronomo padovano del Cinquecento," in *Miscellanea Augusto Campana* (Padua, 1981), I, 27–69. An illiterate Sienese peasant in the fifteenth century found writing so alluring that he had various people keep a diary for him: Duccio Balestracci, *La zappa e la retorica: Memoire familiari di un contadino toscano del Quattrocento* (Florence, 1984); English version (trans. Paolo Squatriti and Betsy Merideth), *The Renaissance in the Fields: Family Memoirs of a Fifteenth-Century Tuscan Peasant* (University Park, 1999).
27 Since the medieval statutes have long played a crucial role in forming communal identities, they have received a great deal of attention by local historians, and many of them are published. For a list of the published statutes for Friuli alone, see Gaetano Perusini, "Gli statuti di una vicinia rurale Friulana del Cinquecento," *Memorie storico forogiuliesi*, XIIIL (1958–1959), 213n. A recent example is the superb critical study and edition of the statutes of Rovereto in the Trentino: Federica Parcianello (ed.), *Statuti di Rovereto del 1425* (Venice, 1991). On the role of statutes in communal life, see Chittolini and Dietmar Willoweit, *Statuti, città, territori in Italia e Germania tra medioevo ed età moderna* (Bologna, 1991); idem, *L'organizzazione del territorio in Italia e Germania: Secoli XIII–XIV* (Bologna, 1994). On notarial practice in general, see Claudio Povolo, "Aspetti e problemi dell'amministrazione della giustizia penale nella repubblica di Venezia, secoli XVI–XVII," in Cozzi (ed.), *Stato, società e giustizia nella Repubblica Veneta (sec. XV–XVIII)*, I, 153–258.

The village of Buia in central Friuli saw virtually continuous litigation by local notaries on behalf of the commune from the fifteenth to the eighteenth century. Buia's suits were typically attempts to outflank its Savorgnan lords through appeals to Venice on the basis of Buia's statutory privileges. Specific disputes concentrated on feudal obligations and access to local resources, particularly the citizens' desire to irrigate their fields with water from the Ledra River, which conflicted with the Savorgnans' intent to maintain a high water level to move timber rafts. The most contentious cases arose from the nearby Savorgnan fortress of Osoppo, which subjected peasants in the vicinity to such extraordinary obligations as special levies, work details, and guard duty, especially during times of war. Since statutory exemption from these feudal dues and duties was at the heart of Buia's self-conception as a commune, the notaries of Buia apparently never hesitated to petition the Venetian courts to enforce the distinction between a commune and a fief.[28]

This complex litigation demonstrates how conflicting jurisdictions and competing powers created a space for a rural community legally to resist local oligarchs and feudal lords. The ground for this resistance was not some imagined religious utopia but the statutes of a commune. The leaders were neither millenarian prophets nor reform-minded priests but notaries willing and able to employ the requisite legal procedures. The consequence was hardly ever a firm resolution but a semipermanent state of litigation that subjected clashing privileges to continuous negotiation through the court system, thereby minimizing the possibilities of violence or coercion.[29]

The liberty of the commune of Buia and other rural communities did not rely on a concept of rights or even a Venetian guarantee to respect local statutes, which were regularly ignored or abrogated by powerful oligarchs; it was preserved through

---

28 Muir, "Was There Republicanism?"

29 For the contrasting German model that connected communal ideology and Protestant leadership during the German revolts of 1525, see Peter Blickle (trans. Thomas A. Brady and H. C. Erik Midelfort), *The Revolution of 1525: The German Peasants' War from a New Perspective* (Baltimore, 1981); *idem* (trans. Thomas Dunlap), *Communal Reformation: The Quest for Salvation in Sixteenth-Century Germany* (Atlantic Highlands, N.J., 1992). For the radical millenarian phase led by Michael Gaismair, which spilled over into the northern Veneto, see Giorgio Politi, *Gli statuti impossibili: La rivoluzione tirolese del 1525 e il "programma" di Michael Gaismair* (Turin, 1995).

community resistance, based mainly on custom, which had to be constantly asserted and vigilantly defended through litigation. What from the Weberian point of view appear to be the contradictions, inefficiencies, and ineptitude of Venetian justice were the very features that made communal government possible. The Venetian legal system did not render justice for rural communities so much as create room for maneuver and negotiation—a form of social capital that might further differentiate northern and southern Italy. In effect, the Venetian legal system, rather than its political system, mediated factional and class conflict, and the institutionalization of class conflict was the very principle that Machiavelli argued to be essential for a free republic: "In every republic there are two opposed factions, that of the people and that of the rich, and . . . all the laws made in favor of liberty result from their discord."[30]

The ways in which judicial culture assisted the accumulation of social capital depended considerably on local contexts. The case of Orgiano—a small town near Vicenza that Povolo studied—illustrates the process differently than that of Buia. In the early seventeenth century, Venice's abrogation of the communal statutes that gave authority to feudal lords served to reinforce community cohesion in Orgiano. The precipitating event was the trial in 1605 of Paolo Orgiano, a scion of the dominant aristocratic family, on multiple charges of raping and sodomizing young peasant women of the town. Povolo's analysis of the trial turns on two "contexts": First, the community of Orgiano was in a state of virulent social conflict as a result of profound changes that had begun more than two decades before. The struggle took the form of a feud about the usual rural issues between the members of the local aristocratic consorteria and the small proprietors who had traditionally held communal offices. Second, during this same period, Venice began to outlaw such traditional forms of conflict resolution among rural aristocrats as vendetta and the employment of bravos. Contrary to Venice's promise in the fifteenth century to respect the jurisdictional autonomy of rural communities, the criminalization of aristocratic feuding inserted Venetian law into local power disputes to the advantage of the small proprietors. The alliance

---

30 Machiavelli, *Discourses,* 1.4. Quotation from *Machiavelli: The Chief Works and Others,* II, 203.

between Venetian capital, Venetian jurisprudence, and the local non-noble citizen elite cost rural aristocrats their political legitimacy; the image of the aristocratic tyrant replaced the traditional one of aristocratic honor.[31]

Probably what distinguished these cases in the Veneto from many similar examples of aristocratic abuse in the kingdom of Naples was the judicial character of this alliance between the top and the bottom of the political order. The implication is not that the South lacked a comparable legal system—Naples has long been a principal center of Italian jurisprudence and legal studies—but that it lacked a cadre of local provincial elites who were schooled in the notarial sciences and who understood how to bypass aristocratic jurisdictions to obtain redress in the royal court. Differing strategies of rule also came into play: The kings of Naples (and later of the Two Sicilies) ruled through the aristocracy, and they had no independent means of direct contact with their provincial commoner subjects. Northern regimes, especially beginning in the sixteenth century, attempted to control the aristocracy by reaching out to the rural communities through a system of judicial appeals. This strategy appealed not just to the republics—such as Venice, Florence, and Siena—but also to the principalities—such as Milan and Ferrara. Thus did the northern regional states make civil society possible, even in places such as the Venetian parts of Friuli that had not gone through the communal revolution of the eleventh century.

MANNERS   To reiterate, the origins of Italian civil society can be found in the centuries-long struggle between aristocratic families and factions, on the one hand, and communities, on the other, that began in the eleventh century with the founding of the first communes. The identities of communities, their collective solidarity, and their ability to eliminate their own internal political violence interconnected with a peculiarly civic religiosity, institutionalized primarily through civic rituals.

The limitations of the communal solution to factional violence became evident during the fifteenth and sixteenth centuries, as the regional states were cobbled together. The exclusivity of

---

31 Povolo, *L'intrigo dell'Onore: Poteri e istituzioni nella Repubblica di Venezia tra Cinque e Seicento* (Verona, 1997). Cf. Dean and K.J.P. Lowe (eds.), *Crime, Society and the Law in Renaissance Italy* (Cambridge, 1994).

these communities hindered their ability to export their collective identity and solidarity beyond the walls of the capital city. The regional states of northern Italy came to depend on various diarchic arrangements that were institutionalized through a culture of judicial and notarial procedures that arrested aristocratic violence through continuous litigation and the criminalization of aristocratic feuding.

The class and factional conflicts that drove this process led to a peculiar paradox: The rural aristocracy was neither defeated nor eliminated, and all communal political regimes were governed by oligarchies that usually had aristocratic pretensions, if not aristocratic titles. Somehow the aristocratic and oligarchic elites adapted to, and even championed, civil society. The resolution of this paradox lies in the sixteenth-century revolution in social mores, the "civilizing process," which inculcated habits of internalized behavior control through the adoption of civilized or courtly manners outside any threat or reality of physical coercion.

Republics by definition value the principles of equality and liberty, whereas principalities esteem exclusivity and privilege. In Venice, however, membership in the political class of the republic was hereditary; it was more exclusive than almost any feudal aristocracy ever studied. As Molho has recently shown, the ruling elite of the Florentine republic, although less legally circumscribed than the Venetian patriciate, also maintained its class domination for centuries despite numerous dramatic political upheavals, including the various periods of Medici hegemony. Republics restricted the privilege of civic duties to a few who managed to maintain their position through legal definitions of citizenship or endogamous intermarriage.[32]

Although princely courts were also highly exclusive political bodies and at least formally limited to aristocrats, citizenship was not a prerequisite. In this special sense, princely courts were oddly more "democratic" than republics. A parvenu in a princely court needed only be of a certain stamp, a creature of courtesy who had a service to offer the prince. If such service were valuable enough, it could turn a commoner into an aristocrat. In fact, only when Florence became a principality during the sixteenth century did

---

32   On Venice, see James C. Davis, *Decline of the Venetian Nobility*. On Florence, see Anthony Molho, *Marriage Alliance in Late Medieval Florence* (Cambridge, Mass., 1994).

substantial numbers of provincial elites find positions of influence in the capital city. Provincial aristocrats and ambitious young gentlemen and ladies in the Veneto were more likely to find a place of influence in a foreign court, such as Mantua, Milan, or Ferrara, than in Venice itself. Because princely courts were extensions of the family household, they were also less gendered polities than republics: Courts were the only places where women's public speech and action had political force.

The patronage of a prince enlisted courtiers in a voluntary association that subordinated the needs of its constituent members to those of the prince. After all, private vendettas could injure princely authority. Through its etiquette, the court incorporated its members into a new social body that had its own values, separate and distinct from the traditional family-centered values of the aristocracy and its factional alignments. In response to the injured or insulted gentleman's dilemma of desiring revenge but not wanting to challenge the authority of his patron-prince, the princely courts developed the elaborate compensatory measures of the duel. Although the society of the princely courts needed such a mechanism, at best they could only wink at what was technically illegal. At least in its early phases in Italy, the duel had a civilizing effect, to follow Elias' famous formula; it markedly reduced levels of reciprocal violence.[33]

The Renaissance revival of courtly values shared with medieval versions of the courtly ethic Cicero's *De Officiis* as the principal source of inspiration, but the sixteenth-century movement, which was inspired by Desiderius Erasmus' *Manners for Children* and Baldassare Castiglione's *The Book of the Courtier*— both widely available in numerous printed editions in the vernacular—had a far broader and more lasting influence.[34]

The influence of these new values is clear, for example, in a short treatise about family management written by Mario Savorgnan in 1561. He belonged to a Friulan family that had long been embroiled in an intractable vendetta. His treatise took the form of a reply to Alvise Cornaro's widely read *Discourses on the Sober Life,* which presented Cornaro as a paragon of humanist moderation and temperance—virtues that had given him a long and healthful life. Savorgnan asserted that his family shared Cor-

---

33 Elias, *History of Manners; idem, The Court Society* (New York, 1983).
34 Burke, *Fortunes of the Courtier.*

naro's principles, referring to five brothers "whom we have made into one alone and that one has made us all." This virtue of family unanimity had required a strategy: By common consent, the brothers had chosen Marc'Antonio, the fourth eldest among them, as the head of the family and hence the only one entitled to marry. At the time of Mario's writing, Marc'Antonio's wife had given birth to six sons, each named after their father or one of his brothers, including even their dead brother. Mario hoped that by following the precepts in Cornaro's book, the brothers would live long enough to see themselves reproduced—if only in name—a second and even third time.[35]

In the "fraternal society or small republic" of their brotherhood, the Savorgnans practiced a form of restricted marriage—the bestowal of their property to the offspring of the only married brother. Such a plan prevented the extreme subdivision of property in each generation, leaving the Savorgnans with a large, undivided estate and preventing the competition over patrimonies that often poisoned family relationships and led young men to seek their fortunes elsewhere by joining a factional gang.[36]

Mario saw the family obligation toward his nephews as a process that would free them from the rude manners of the rural aristocracy and engage them in pursuits that taught the new values of masculine honor. Despite the recent spate of murders that the Savorgnan family had suffered, Mario never discussed any obligations to retaliate. Instead of preparing for local vendettas, the boys were raised in accord with the didactic recommendations of Erasmus' *Manners for Children* and sent abroad at an early age to avoid local feuds, to learn foreign languages, and to adapt themselves to the manners of princely courts. By the 1560s, even the older generation of Savorgnans, under the influence of relatives who had spent time in foreign courts, had turned entirely to duelling to resolve personal disputes.[37]

35 Alvise Cornaro, *Discorsi intorno alla vita sobria,* in Giuseppe Fiocco, *Alvise Cornaro: Il suo tempo e le sue opere* (Vicenza, 1965), 171–190; Mario Savorgnano, *Del governo della sua famiglia: Lettera a Luigi Cornaro* (Udine, 1862), 10.

36 Savorgnano, *Del governo,* 12–13. On restricted marriage, see the useful discussion of the Venetian practice in James C. Davis, *A Venetian Family and Its Fortune, 1500–1900: The Donà and the Conservation of Their Wealth* (Philadelphia, 1975), 93–112.

37 Ernesto Degani, *I partiti in Friuli nel 1500 e la storia di un famoso duello* (Udine, 1900), 79–116. On the murder of Antonio Savorgnan in 1552 and a mass attack on the Savorgnan family in 1561, see Archivio di Stato, Venice, Consiglio dei Dieci, Parti criminali, reg. 8, fols. 50, 60, 67v, 148v–150, 236; reg. 9, fols. 62v–64v. For the murder of Francesco Savorgnan in 1560, see Soldoniero di Strassoldo (ed. Degani), *Cronaca dal 1509 al 1603* (Udine, 1895), 48.

The new values adopted by the upper levels of the provincial aristocracy—the group most commonly imitated by others—subjected violent behavior to an elaborate set of social rules, which required the sublimation of negative emotions. The courtesy books compared good manners to the wearing of fine clothes. As Erasmus saw it, such clothing revealed much more than a superficial exercise of taste; it was "in a sense the body of the body," which put on view the character of the wearer's soul. Gestures, facial expressions, bodily movements, and, above all, speech were evidence of a person's qualities. Although this notion was a Platonic commonplace, the courtesy books of the sixteenth century transmuted the obscure abstractions of Neoplatonism into practical rules of behavior that abhorred excess of any kind, especially the angry kind. The new courtesy constituted a theory of the relationship between communication and behavior.[38]

Giovanni Della Casa's *Galateo* (1552–1555)—probably the source most responsible for the spread of refined manners among aristocrats in northern Italy—uses the charming device of an ignorant old man as narrator, the better to engage the simple gentleman who aspired to emulate those in the highest aristocratic circles. *Galateo* not only refashioned conduct but made unmentionable whole realms of human experience: Polite people never alluded to another's wrath, gluttony, lust, avarice, or other unseemly desires, "in as much as these appetites are not evident in their manners of behaviour or in their speech, but elsewhere." In other words, those traits not manifest through the accepted forms of gentle conduct and refined speech had no place in the mind of a gentleman or a lady.[39]

The proliferation of new formalities—such as the spread of the polite pronoun *Lei,* ever-more elaborate modes of address, bowing, the doffing of hats, and moving with measured gravity—provoked considerable comment during the last half of the sixteenth century. Rough traditionalists saw the trend as unmanly—an incipient feminization of public life. Among the more

38 Erasmus is quoted in Elias, *History of Manners,* 78–79. On the new courtesy as a form of communication theory, see Muir, "The Double Binds of Manly Revenge in Renaissance Italy," in Richard C. Trexler (ed.), *Gender Rhetorics: Postures of Dominance and Submission in History* (Binghamton, 1994), 65–82.
39 Giovanna Della Casa (trans. Konrad Eisenbichler and Kenneth R. Bartlett), *Galateo* (Toronto, 1986), xi–xiii, xxi–xxii, 10–11, 19–24. On the success of *Galateo,* see Elias, *History of Manners,* 81–82.

thoughtful, the sense that the formalities promoted social stability and prevented violence coexisted with the understanding that truth, in all its unmannerly harshness, had been sacrificed. Even those who were not courtiers had to cultivate the virtue of honest dissimulation, the trait that required silence or at least discretion in the expression of thought and feeling. Honesty became discourteous. As a result, the language of the princely court and of many other social settings avoided meaningful discourse. To be caught in a lie did not so much mean a loss of personal dignity, or even credibility, as a loss of honor for the failure to manage impressions properly. The upshot was a dramatic decline in vendettas among aristocrats (although not other forms of criminal violence) not unlike the decline of factional violence in the city-republics that was reinforced by the criminalization of aristocratic feuding during the late sixteenth and seventeenth centuries.[40]

Civil society succeeded in eliminating the most endemic forms of political violence through a combination of collective policy and self-restraint: Social controls had deeply religious roots, primarily in their connection with the urban adaptation of the late medieval cult of the saints. Eventually, the juridical-notarial culture extended civil society beyond the walls of the cities by facilitating an alliance between the ruling urban elites and the bottom of the political order in the countryside. Finally, the rural aristocracy joined civil society not by accepting civic solutions but by assimilating the mores of princely courts.

The accumulation of social capital in northern Italy, however, came at the expense of the long-term capacity of public discourse to represent political practices and social conflicts accurately. That cost was a political culture that prized dissimulation or, worse,

---

40 On the new formalities, see Burke, *Historical Anthropology*, 90–92; Frederic Robertson Bryson, *The Point of Honor in Sixteenth-Century Italy: An Aspect of the Life of the Gentleman* (New York, 1935), 15–17. On the spread of courtesies in France, see Orest Ranum, "Courtesy, Absolutism, and the Rise of the French State, 1630–1660," *Journal of Modern History*, LII (1980), 426–451. On the theme of honest dissimulation, see Perez Zagorin, *Ways of Lying: Dissimulation, Persecution, and Conformity in Early Modern Europe* (Cambridge, Mass., 1990); Pietro Redondi (trans. Raymond Rosenthal), *Galileo Heretic* (Princeton, 1987), 24. Cf. the rather different approach in Martin, "Inventing Sincerity, Refashioning Prudence: The Discovery of the Individual in Renaissance Europe," *American Historical Review*, CII (1997), 1309–1342.

silence about vital concerns. When Alvise Mocenigo, a Venetian patrician, imposed a peace on the feuding factions of Friuli in 1568, his solution sentenced the parties to a mutual silence: "We attest and declare by the authority conceded to us that both sides must desire that everything said or written be nullified, as if nothing had ever been [said] or written on this subject."[41]

Mocenigo exemplified a lasting tendency. When the civil war in Trieste finally abated in 1954, another kind of collective amnesia fell over the city, creating taboos only a few historians have dared to break. The imposed silences have attempted to prevent past grievances from disturbing the public order, but underneath the transient ideologies and circumstances of the moment lurk memories of ancient injuries that periodically threaten to destroy the carefully accumulated social capital of centuries. The silences have helped to perpetuate an enormous gulf between the grubby practices of political life and the elevated rhetoric of political discourse. Northern Italy has been able to maintain civil society, in part, by failing to wash clean the dirty hands of its politics.[42]

41 For the Mocenigo quotation, see Archivio di Stato, Venice, Consiglio dei Dieci, Parti comuni, register for 1567–68, fol. 110.
42 On amnesia about massacres during the Triestine civil war, see Chris Hedges, "In Trieste, Investigation of Brutal Era Is Blocked," *New York Times,* 20 Apr. 1997.

Raymond Grew

Finding Social Capital: The French Revolution in Italy

> *[History] should be explored, not for scenes of carnage, but for instruction in the government of mankind.*
>
> J. C. L. Sismondi de Sismondi, *A History of the Italian Republics*

If *social capital* were sharply defined, the term would be less usefully suggestive. It seems to refer to those social practices, customs, groups, and institutions that strengthen civil society. In a sense, the concept is always retrospective. We acknowledge the presence of "social capital" whenever we attribute collective (essentially political) behavior more to established patterns of social behavior than to immediate requirements, interests, or tactical calculations. The term is temptingly residual, a signifier for social behaviors not simply selfish, and it tends to be used in notably judgmental ways, treating as social capital those practices considered beneficial to society's smooth functioning. Logically, this usage seems somewhat circular and historically rather deterministic.

I propose to make this loose term looser, by expanding it to include cultural capital. By cultural capital, I mean the customs of public behavior (a part of culture in the anthropological sense) and the content of shared values (as communicated through the literature and arts of high culture). This definition extends the idea of social capital as used by Putnam and his associates. They measured social capital primarily in terms of voluntary organizations, on the grounds that associational life may, as Tocqueville thought it did, build habits of cooperation and trust that facilitate effective, democratic government. Thinking in the broader terms of cultural capital invites attention to less institutionalized habits of association that may also be important, especially when gov-

Raymond Grew is Professor of History, University of Michigan. He is the author of "On Seeking the Cultural Context of Fundamentalism," in Martin E. Marty and R. Scott Appleby (eds.), *Religion, Ethnicity, and Self-identity: Nations in Turmoil* (Hanover, N.H., 1997), 19–34; "Liberty and the Catholic Church in Nineteenth-Century Europe," in Richard Helmstadter (ed.), *Freedom and Religion in the Nineteenth Century* (Stanford, 1997), 196–232.

ernments restrict organized activity. Perhaps patterns of social connection and modes of thought constitute cultural capital that has the potential to affect collective action. Social capital is said to be greater or weaker depending on the vigor of associational life and the degree of satisfaction with government. Cultural capital is even harder to quantify. All societies have cultures; cultural capital can be deduced only from the tests that history provides. To explore the possible utility of including culture as part of social capital, I focus on a particular historical problem, why Italy adapted so readily to the French Revolution, both in its initial and its later Napoleonic forms.[1]

On the whole, Italy received the French with remarkable warmth in 1796; the elites of northern Italy set about immediately, and enthusiastically, to write constitutions for the Cispadane and Cisalpine republics. Their energetic participation in creating new political structures and reforming civil society spread with surprising ease (and French arms) to Rome—where the effort to establish civil authorities independent of church or aristocracy was widely welcomed—and then to Naples, even if the republic there lasted only six months. Subsequently, despite the dampening effect of Napoleonic rule, the constrictions that accompanied continual warfare, and the exactions required to support it, the new institutions took root in their Napoleonic forms so strongly that across the peninsula, the restoration governments of 1815 kept the administrative, judicial, military, fiscal, and educational systems that the French had introduced and Italians were operating. The lasting social effects of this vast political and social transformation were essential to Italy's Risorgimento in the next century. A case can be made that no European society outside France more readily accepted, or was more permanently affected by, the French Revolution and Napoleon.[2]

It is not obvious why Italy should have responded in this way. A leading theorist of nationalism has suggested that intellectuals often lead in resisting the cultural effects of industrialization

1   Robert D. Putnam, with Roberto Leonardi and Raffaella Nanetti, *Making Democracy Work: Civic Traditions in Modern Italy* (Princeton, 1993), 163–185; Alexis de Toqueville (ed. J. P. Mayer; trans. George Lawrence) *Democracy in America* (Garden City, 1969; orig. pub 1835–1840).
2   On Rome, see Fiorella Bartoccini, *Roma nell'Ottocento* (Rome, 1971) I, 75–78.

when an economically backward society confronts an "exogenous scientific-industrial culture." Thus, Italian leaders might be expected to have resisted the political and economic impact of the French Revolution. They did not. Movements opposing the Revolution and French influence greatly affected the subsequent history of Spain and Germany, but had much less impact in Italy. Perhaps Italy had varieties of social capital that facilitated adaptation to the revolution from across the Alps.[3]

Politically, there was no Italy in the eighteenth century, and so the widespread assumption of an Italian nation in eighteenth-century discourse deserves to be noted as an instance of cultural capital. Geography helped. In 1800, Lomonaco wrote,

> Italy divided neither by large rivers nor mountains, enjoying everywhere the same beautiful climate and, more or less, the same fertility of soil, contains within itself all human resources. Bathed by the Mediterranean, the Ionian, and the Adriatic, separated from other peoples by a chain of inaccessible mountains, Italy seems by nature destined to form a single unified power. Its inhabitants, who speak the same language, who have the same marks of passion and character . . . are made to be members of the same family.[4]

But cultural cohesion was more important than geographical identity. In a peninsula of small polities with limited autonomy or power, a shared cultural core provided a sense of immediate ties to past glories. Yet, this culture could also be experienced as local; hundreds of towns, North and South, remembered an event, a famous person, or some work of art as their contribution to a larger Italian achievement. By 1600, Italian culture had acquired a national identity, reinforced by the continuous movement across the peninsula—from the Middle Ages through the Risorgimento—of Italy's intellectuals and artists, princes and merchants, and priests and nuns. Weaving cultural bonds as they went, they sustained the vision of a living, changing culture. The styles of different eras and changing genres, from commedia dell'arte and

3   Ernst Gellner, *Nations and Nationalism* (Oxford, 1983), 57–61.
4   Francesco Lomonaco, *Colpo d'occhio su l'Italia,* cited by David LoRomer in "The Geography of Italian Nationalism," unpub. paper (East Lansing, 1993).

lyric opera to the scientific experiments of Evangilista Torricelli, were understood to be part of a larger, Italian, culture.[5]

Burckhardt insisted on the importance of culture in the politics of the Renaissance city-state, and attention to that connection remains a fruitful line of research. Burckhardt's emphasis, however, was on cultural display as an expression of civic pride and on patronage as a source of legitimacy for princes who had handcrafted the thrones on which they sat. By the sixteenth and seventeenth centuries, the situation had changed: Communal governments gave way to principalities; foreign armies kept the peace; local rulers required the favor of foreign (mainly Spanish) sovereigns; and the Counter-Reformation narrowed the range of permitted expression. Still, a public culture of high art, music, and letters remained important, not merely as patronage but as part of the social fabric of life among the elites.

Cultural capital also had political import. The republics of Venice and Genoa, the Grand Duchy of Tuscany, the papacy, and the Kingdom of the Two Sicilies systematically put culture on exhibit and sought to appeal to men of letters. In an era of stable regimes, the glory that redounded to the credit of the princely, senatorial, or noble patron also reflected on the state, its elites, and the creators of cultural goods. Monuments, paintings, operas, and statues were more than mere display. They engaged notables and intellectuals in common projects that required the support of state and society, creating the cultural equivalent of political participation and, in a limited way, bridging distinctions of social rank, occupation, and region. These forms of cultural expression employed a rhetoric of universality that connected minor states and individual towns through Italian culture to Christianity and European civilization.

Italian governments had a long tradition of using public works, especially monumental buildings, to appeal to civic pride and represent a beneficent regime. This use of culture may also have helped to drown out issues of liberty or public policy, but

5 Eric Cochrane, *Italy, 1530–1630* (London, 1988), 250–259, makes this point about identity, noting that Italy had come to refer to those regions where the literary language was Tuscan; where the works of Dante, Petrarch, Ariosto, and Tasso were recognized as classics of poetry; where the works of Baldassare Castiglione and Francesco Guicciardini were the classics of prose; where the works of Raphael, Michelangelo, and the Carracci "were normative in art"; and where Tridentine Catholicism was the only true religion.

the social and political significance of official culture could change. In the sixteenth and seventeenth centuries, the governments of Italy were nearly all more or less new and more or less imposed by outside force. Their assertions of legitimacy—in statues, coins, ceremonies, and rhetoric—thus made heavy use of symbols of state that evoked memory and culture. In a regime still justifying itself, the Tuscan grand duke could be credited with having brought "all the sciences and arts [once again] to take up residence" in Florence. On a larger scale, Italy could be declared "the most beautiful part of the world. It has the greatest number of villages, towns, and cities with the greatest abundance of inhabitants; and its inhabitants are valorous and prudent in the letters and arts, excellent in architecture, sculpture and painting as well; trained and learned in the other liberal arts, diligent and expert in agriculture."[6]

Such praise from fawning clients at the turn of the sixteenth century tended to become a call to civic spirit and national pride at the turn of the eighteenth. By then, the colonades of the Uffizi palace, which had stood empty for nearly three centuries, had been lined with statues of the great men of Florentine history, mainly artists and intellectuals, and the cathedrals of Milan and Florence at last got marble facades over their bare bricks, according to designs chosen in public competitions. Such works—examples of which were numerous throughout Italy on the eve of the French Revolution—now served a different purpose. They were not so much acts of patronage or praiseworthy proclamations of official values as conscious attempts by governments to appeal to a civic spirit that was assumed to be present already.

Nor was it just governments that sought civic uses of high culture. Authors used their customary, cultivated rhetoric and classical references in writing about political reform, a tendency probably strengthened in Italy by the absence of any strong interest in folk culture as an alternative expression of Italian values. When dilettantes called themselves Arcadians, they were not just engaged in a literary movement or making exaggerated claims for the primacy of Etruscan over Greek civilization. They were opening the way to visions of political change. All educated Italians were

6 Scipione Ammirato, Jr., preface to *Delle famiglie nobili fiorentine* (Florence, 1615) and Lorenzo Capelloni's dedication to Duke Emmanuel Philibert of Savoy in *Ragionamenti varii* (Genoa, 1576), both cited in Cochrane, *Italy, 1530–1630, 250.*

aware of connections to a glorious past; ancient (especially republican) Rome, the medieval communes, and the Renaissance were
said to have lessons for the present. The past was becoming a call
to future action. Muratori's still-admired *Annales,* a multi-volume
monument to eighteenth-century historical erudition, made that
past a plea for good government, rather like Ambroglio Loren-
zetti's depiction of good and bad government in Siena's town hall
five centuries earlier. To mobilize memory had become part of a
process that used cultural capital for social and political purposes.[7]

In his *Consiglio politico,* published in the Veneto in 1734, the
historian and essayist Scipione Maffei expressed a characteristic
moral view of what good government required. But his praise of
the ancient Romans for rising above private interests in favor of
the *utile pubblico* and his rejection of the despotism of Louis XIV
became more programmatic when he praised the English system
of government. England, he argued, had evolved a way to combine freedom and concern for the common interest; and he
considered the electoral system a crucial step. Although believing
that each society should conduct elections "according to its rites
and customs," he did not hesitate to propose specific reforms for
Venice on the basis of his comparison of England, the Netherlands, Sweden, and Poland.[8]

By mid-century, Enlightenment ideas were well known and
widely shared in Italy. If there was a note of pride whenever Italian
writers such as Antonio Genovese or Cesare Beccaria were admired in Paris, there was little hesitance or embarrassment about
receiving ideas from abroad, especially from England or France.
Participation in the European-wide intellectual currents of the day
and confidence in Italy's traditional humanist culture contributed
to the easy engagement with radical ideas from across the Alps.

Italian publications also reported on the American Revolution, readily drawing conclusions about its meaning for Italy that,
as in the description of President George Washington standing

7 Emiliana Noether, *Seeds of Nationalism, 1700–1815* (New York, 1951). Some see Etruscan
influences in contemporary Italy even today. See Nancy Thomson de Grummond, "Etruscan
Italy Today," in John F. Hall (ed.), *Etruscan Italy: Etruscan Influences in the Civilization of Italy
from Antiquity to the Modern* Era (Provo, 1996), 317–365. The full title of Ludovico Antonio
Muratori's work was *Annali d'Italia dal Principio dell'Era Volgare sino all'Anno MDCCXLIX*
(Modena, 1752–1754), 12v.
8 Eluggero Pii, *Immagini dell'Inghilterra politica nella cultural italiana del primo Settecento*
(Florence, 1984), 109–119.

before Congress and smashing the crown proffered him, depended more on the Italian context than on the news from overseas. Soon events in France would be followed even more closely. Enlightenment thought in Italy was always closely tied to practical programs. The reforms of Joseph II in Lombardy and, especially, of Leopold in Tuscany attracted much praise in Italy and elsewhere. Even though less was accomplished in the Kingdom of the Two Sicilies, talk of reform and essays spelling out the changes needed were sufficiently widespread to assure that in the *mezzogiorno,* too, much of what revolutionaries later proposed would have a familiar ring.[9]

Social practice firmly rooted in Italian culture also facilitated Italy's adaptation to the new ways brought by the French. Multiple governments meant that Italy already had multiple bureaucracies, and Italy's many cities added another layer of governance, as well as sociability. So did its hierarchical church, which had bishops in every town of note, its own courts where permitted, and scores of religious orders. The point is not that these institutions operated efficiently but merely that they existed, literally training thousands and thousands of functionaries. In addition, Italy's many universities, produced an unusually large number of lawyers, the majority of whom found employment in offices and courts that relied on a heavy and awkward proceduralism. Thousands of Italians were experienced in how to make legal formulae fit immediate pressures, how to collect data, and how to keep records. Many of them would take with ease to a more open political system that preserved, and even enhanced, their status, while increasing the importance and effectiveness of what they did.

Italian institutions sustained a great many consultative bodies, for Italy's old regime was full of talk. Everywhere residues remained of former parliaments and councils, and everywhere (but especially in Naples) constitutional treatises were a favorite genre, spelling out the importance of the law and of different forms of representation, attaching the principles of a strong legal tradition to memories of different regimes and the great revolt of 1647–1648. In eighteenth-century Naples, as Croce noted, "Life in the law courts represented what, in different conditions in other times,

9 Franco Venturi, *Settecento riformatore.* IV. *La caduta dell'Antico Regime (1776–1789)* (Turin, 1984), 46–95, 970–1039.

was political life, because [that is where] issues between church and state, between holders of feudal rights and civil society were argued out and the new arrangements devised that advances in public economy and related theories made necessary." These traditions would show their value as social capital in the ease as well as the enthusiasm with which new constitutions were written once the French armies arrived.[10]

Certain institutions had provided the structure for a fairly extensive associational life among Italian elites. Nearly every city had one or more academy. Frequently sponsored, or at least recognized, by the local state, academies sometimes had important duties, as did the Tuscan Accademia della Crusca, responsible for the Italian dictionary. Many of those founded in the seventeenth century focused on science. Later ones (the Georgofili in Florence being the most famous) stressed practical matters or discussed the arts and sciences more generally. Composed of local people who knew each other well, the academies were much like the salons of eighteenth-century France, though only a few became important centers of intellectual activity and influential association. Most remained mere gentlemen's clubs until they quietly decayed—a reminder, perhaps, that creating social capital requires a particular kind of well-protected civil society.[11]

The literary and learned journals of the eighteenth century circulated Enlightenment ideas and news of progress to a small but influential audience, almost as if they were committees of correspondence. Important agents of new knowledge and ideas, they were themselves builders of literary networks across Italy. Although they could not engage in the kind of controversies that flourished in the journals of England, the Netherlands, and France, their diverse subject matter, well-placed subscribers, and number suggest their importance (in 1730, Venice had thirteen such periodicals, nearly as many as all of France). Their readers were well aware of who other readers were. By the time the French arrived,

10 Benedetto Croce, *Una famiglia di patrioti* (Bari, 1919), 3–4, cited in Pasquale Villani, *Mezzogiorno tra riforme e rivoluzione* (Bari, 1962), 272.
11 The Accademia dei Lincei in Rome included well-known mathematicians and physicists, such as Evangelista Torricelli. The Accademia del Cimento was founded in Florence in 1657; the Accademia degli Investigatori in Naples dated from 1663; the Accademia dei Georgofili was established in Florence in 1753.

Italian elites knew in stimulating detail about the changes in France.[12]

Nowhere is this elision of cultural into social capital more demonstrable than in the case of theater. Important in nearly every Italian town, theaters (especially lyric opera) played to audiences of all classes. They were the home of social satire (in commedia dell'arte and the plays of Carlo Goldoni), and a locus of aristocratic social life, a kind of civic center. The fact that theaters would become sites of political demonstration and mobilization is hardly surprising, but it reflects an important element of Italy's cultural capital. Because the world of city-states had been too small to permit the aristocracy to form an exclusive caste, elites maintained a practice of association that reached across classes, ideologies, and changes of regime and that facilitated acceptance of such new entrants as the condottieri, the recently ennobled, successful merchants, upper clergy, artists, and intellectuals.[13]

Such people were constantly on display, not only in ceremonies and festivals but also in the daily *passeggiata,* or promenade. Gibbon found the parade of carriages in Turin and Naples remarkable (and boring) but did not sense its importance as social cement. In fact, much of urban life was lived in the street. The poor were on display, too, in famous quarters, such as those of the poverty-stricken *lazzaroni* of Naples or of the workers in Rome's *trastevere* area. Among the observers and celebrants in seasonal festivals, living in tight quarters, and fodder for collective action, they responded readily to rumors and orators. In times of political turmoil, links across social classes could be quickly formed.[14]

---

12   Brendan Maurice Dooley, "Science, Politics, and Society in Eighteenth Century Italy," unpub. Ph.D diss. (Univ. of Chicago, 1986). Dooley's study of the *Giornale de'letterati d'Italia* establishes an impressive list of subscribers and connections to other journals (1–2, 87–145, 342–345, 349–383). In 1789/1790, two new journals in Tuscany—the *Giornale dell'Assemblea generale della Francia* and the *Giorgnale istorico politico dell'Assemblea di Parigi*—were devoted to reporting events in the French Assembly. See Giovanni Luseroni, "Gli echi del 1789 francesi nei giornali del granducato di Toscana," in Ivan Tognarini (ed.), *La Toscana e la Rivoluzione francese* (Naples, 1994), 516–517.

13   Among important theaters opened to the public in the eighteenth century were Bologna's Teatro Communale, Florence's Teatro della Pergola, Mantua's Teatro Scientifico, Milan's Teatro alla Scala, Naples' Teatro San Carlo, Parma's Teatro Farnese, Turin's Teatro Regio, and Venice's Teatro La Fenice.

14   Gibbon did notice the beautiful women, cited in Christopher Hibbert, *The Grand Tour* (London, 1974), 99, 156–157. Lauro Martines, *Violence and Civil Disorder in Italian Cities* (Berkeley, 1972), 344, comments on the spaces. Messina offers an interesting example of links

Formal culture intersected with daily life and, when permitted, with politics in Italy's urban public spaces. For religious and secular authorities, these were places of cooperation or contestation; for society as a whole, they balanced the representation of order (in hierarchical parades and official ceremonies) with varied forms of participation (observing, shouting, and demonstrating) that stopped short of the right to vote. This theme of the observer–participant recurs often in Italian paintings and in commedia dell'arte, in which public and private spaces overlap. Figures looking from the towers and windows become part of the action, much as piazza ceremonies naturally included social actors officially left out. The informality, which made such expansion easy, avoided issues of where power lay and preserved the individual's freedom to disengage.[15]

Piazzas themselves remained ambiguous spaces, stages for events not altogether predictable, where the lines between ritual and collective action were never tightly drawn and where observers were hard to distinguish from participants and plotters. To an eighteenth-century French magistrate, Italy seemed "a great festival of enjoyment (*une grande fête de jouissance*), of sensuality, and of personal liberty." Such freedom was always dangerous. Italy's Spanish rulers, by making rituals more formal and giving them greater pomp and galantry, had constrained the dangers that such freedom fostered; but public rituals remained "a form of communication by action which is public, stereotyped, and symbolic." As such, they allowed opportunities for changing, even forbidden, meanings. Through repetition and symbol, public festivals also connected local tensions and immediate issues to regional and national conflicts, an important form of politicization. The value placed on spectacle in Italy foreshadowed modern, mass society in its capacity to create shared experience outside explicit social ties.[16]

---

that cut across class. See Salvo Carmen, *Giurati, feudatari, mercanti: l'elite urbana à Messina tra medio evo e età moderna* (Rome, 1955), 121–153.

15 Most of these points are taken directly from Jane Tylus, "Women in the Windows," unpub. paper (Madison, 1996).

16 Hermann Harder, *Le Président de Brosses et le voyage en Italie au dix-huitième siècle* (Geneva, 1981), 437. Croce, *La Spagna nella vita italiana durante la Rinascenza* (Bari, 1949), 181–209, notes the change in ritual under Spanish rule. On festivals, see Peter Burke, *The Historical Anthropology of Early Modern Italy: Essays on Perception and Communication* (Cambridge, 1987), 225.

In this system, central, public spaces were critical. There, community became visible while its boundaries remained permeable. Distinctions between public and private were constantly shifting; poverty and wealth, anger and hope, and the fact of having a job or plans for marriage could become as public as the evening passegiata. This fluid transition between private and public accomplished something of what voluntary associations do more stably, connecting personal interests and civic action. Public architecture contributed to social capital by creating a ritual stage surrounded by buildings that associated present concerns with past grandeur, power with culture. The piazza, familiar meeting ground and symbolic center of patriotic feeling, was also the place of temporary participation, where ritual recurrence bestowed a sense of order without the discipline of formal rules. The alliances and policies presented in public were understood, however, to rest on arrangements concluded behind closed doors.

By the eighteenth-century, Italian society had nurtured a strong public sphere of talk and festivals, cafes and theaters, academies and newspapers, despite limited public politics. Nevertheless, the interest in law and in talk sustained a lively civic sense that, starting with local pride and familiar ritual, could be extended to a vision of civic education and a transformed civil society.

The looseness of the connection between reform and a vibrant urban life of promenades, parades, cafes, and ceremonies did not undermine the belief that they went together. In 1796, a famous competition offered a prize for the best treatise on the form of government most suitable for Lombardy. The winning essay declared that a good constitution would foster a society in which the rich and the poor mixed in balls, theaters, and festivals, and public ceremonies in piazzas and theaters would instill a sense of communal purpose. The Neapolitan constitution of 1799 called for theaters, national festivals, and public schools to provide civic training. In effect, statements about social capital, these programs—so attentive to custom and civic virtue—continued to avoid questions of power or social conflict.[17]

This rising commitment to civic values is evident in the funerary inscriptions lining the walls of even the smallest Italian

17 Armando Saitta (ed.), *Allo origini del Risorgimento: I testi di un "celebre" concorso* (Rome, 1964; orig. pub. 1796), 105. A. Aquarone, M. d'Addio, and G. Negri (eds.), *Le Costitutuzioni Italiane* (Milan, 1958), 295.

churches and cloisters. Previously in Latin, by the eighteenth century these inscriptions were more often written in lapidary Italian. Miniature lessons in emulation, they listed not merely the honorable offices that a prominent figure had held but also the civic virtues that he had displayed while holding them. Similar values would later echo from the public platforms of every revolutionary republic (and be repeated throughout the Risorgimento). In a world of face-to-face relations, such commitments could be compelling as a basis for institutional reform. Antonio Genovesi, an eighteenth-century Neapolitan intellectual much admired in France, as well as Italy, for his concrete and detailed proposals for economic reform, built his philosophy around *fede pubblica*. When one of Grand Duke Peter Leopold's councillors restated the case for granting Tuscany a constitution, he talked about civic freedom (*onestà libertà civile*). Vincenzo Cuoco, now remembered as the most penetrating critic of the Revolution in Naples' naive adoption of French abstractions, held throughout his life to the idea of "libertà civile" that he had absorbed from eighteenth-century writers.[18]

Such was the cultural capital available to those who supported revolution in Italy at the end of the eighteenth century—a conviction that an Italian culture existed despite the absence of a national state; belief in a glorious past; the political and public importance of high culture; active engagement with Enlightenment thought; a strong legal tradition with many lawyers; multiple administrations and bureaucracies; academies and gazettes at the heart of intellectual and social networks that reached across the peninsula; theaters and festivals where people of all classes encountered each other; and piazzas where townspeople occasionally

18 "Civil courage is not inferior to military valor," d'Azeglio declared, explaining that the majority of Italians were moved only by material needs because they lacked *"educazione civile."* See Massimo d'Azeglio, "Degli ultimi casi di Romagna," in Marcus de Rubris (ed.), *Scritti e Discorsi Politici* (Florence, 1931; orig. pub 1846), I, 9, 15. Sandra Cavallo, *Charity and Power in Early Modern Italy: Benefactors and Their Motives in Turin, 1541–1789* (Cambridge, 1995), 253. Giannone's essay, first published in 1723, was one of the most famous and influential; by civil history he principally meant secular and legal history rather than ecclesiastical: Pietro Giannone (ed. Sergio Bertelli), *Istorie civile del Regno di Napoli* (Turin, 1978), 5. Only *onesta libertà civile*, Leopold's advisor said, would avoid the dangers of misery and unhappiness that despotism generated, obviously alluding to events in France. Memorandum of Francesco Maria Gianni to Peter Leopold, written in 1790 (he had first presented his project in 1782), reprinted in Gabriele Turi, *"Viva Maria," La reazione alle riforme leopoldine (1790–1799)* (Florence, 1969), 305–306, 98–99. Villani, *Mezzogiorno*, 53.

performed civic or religious rituals, frequently met to discuss public affairs, and sometimes demonstrated their views to those in power.

Revolutionary events in France evoked a good deal of spontaneous enthusiasm in much of Italy from 1790 onward, including significant conspiratorial activity after 1794. In 1794–1795, there were revolutionary attempts in Piedmont, Bologna, Palermo, and Sardinia, frightening governments everywhere. In the sclerotic old republic of Lucca, fear of the dynamic new one in France increased as word spread of changes occurring as nearby as Corsica. Authorities hastened to arrest Vincenzo Gherardi, an artisan, for declaring that a universal judgment that would make everyone equal was imminent. From 1796 to 1799, a distinctive Italian Jacobinism, mild by French standards, came to the fore, as revolutionary regimes were established under French aegis.[19]

The Italian experience of revolution was different from that of the French. Revolutionary ideology in Italy only rarely and briefly developed with the autonomous momentum and open contestation of Girondins and Jacobins. Italians experienced much of France's revolutionary program, after Thermidor and in a different environment, without the violent tensions from which it had grown. The revolution in Italy was less insistently anticlerical (in Tuscany, especially, Jansenist priests were prominent among supporters of the revolution), sustained no systematic Reign of Terror, and was less divisive and less violent than its French model, making it easier for many Italians to hold a rather positive view of revolution as a way to effect change.[20]

19   Giorgio Tori, "Il Movimento giacobino lucchese e l'attegiamento delle popolazioni della campagna al tempo della repubblica democratica del 1799," and Tognarini, "La Repubblica negata! La Toscana e la rivoluzione francese," in *idem* (ed.), *La Toscana e la Rivoluzione francese,* xvii–xviii, 330–331.
20   There is an Italian pattern of truncated ideologies. Italian Jansenism, less focused on theology than the French original, became a widespread and influential movement for ecclesiastical reform. Later, Italian liberalism similarly stopped short of the impassioned consistency of the Manchester School, and Marxism in Italy maintained softer edges than in Germany. All students of the revolution in Tuscany have been struck by the active role of Jansenist clergy. See Turi, *"Viva Maria,"* 192–198, 218–247, 297. The positive connotations of revolution are discussed somewhat more fully in Grew, "The Paradoxes of Italy's Nineteenth-Century Political Culture," in Isser Woloch (ed.), *Revolutions and the Meanings of Freedom in the Nineteenth Century* (Stanford, 1996), 212–245.

Diluted by distance, the Italian revolutions occurred in the presence of French armies that prevented the opponents of revolution from effectively fighting back (another reason for limited violence). Because the Italian revolutions remained closely tied to French arms, they occurred in two distinct phases. In the first, French forces were welcomed by support that had been bubbling up before their arrival. This period, which began with considerable excitement and spontaneity, was notable for the rapid spread of revolutionary symbols and rhetoric, the writing of constitutions, and the effective establishment of a new style of government. Disillusionment followed before long, however, as the French authorities revealed themselves to be much more concerned with their military strength and with extracting money and men from Italy than with fostering democracy. This initial phase, which ended in 1799 when allied armies drove the French from the peninsula, lasted from about three years in Lombardy to only a few months in most of Italy.

From the Veneto to Naples, the retreating French armies were subjected to popular uprisings against the new order, all of which had several qualities in common. These were movements largely of peasants and the urban poor; religion played a central part; and they were often very violent. Sometimes led and supported by outsiders (the insurrection led by Cardinal Fabrizio Ruffo in Naples is the most famous and bloodiest example), these revolts were also economic protests (against high prices, scarce food, and unemployment, as well as against French exactions), and often culminated in looting and pillaging.

In these respects, the Viva Maria riots in Tuscany were fairly typical. The French had occupied all of Tuscany for only three months when word began to spread of French military defeats and the return of the Austrians. The rumors were accompanied by an increase in reports of religious miracles and by more forceful collective action, as peasants crowded into towns. The violence that followed had all the elements of old-regime grain riots. But angry desperation mixed with religious passions as the poor who turned to the Church for hope and charity associated their current suffering with past moral lapses and associated war, requisitions, and foreign rule with the disrespect for religion attributed to foreigners and revolutionaries. The clergy often took the lead in these local movements, encouraging the crowds, for example, to cut down and burn liberty trees. Although many of the uprisings petered out after a few days of violence, some grew into armed mobs—like the peasant army that took charge of Arezzo and then plundered its way across the Val di Chiana to Siena, burning some Jacobins and Jews in the Campo, Siena's central square.[21]

In Italy, the counterrevolutionary outbursts were bloodier than revolution had been, whether led by the aristocracy in Genoa and Lucca immediately after revolution first broke out or, especially, those of 1799 involving the clergy, peasantry, and the lower classes as in Tuscany and Naples. Neither aristocracy nor clergy would be eager in the future to risk using popular anger as a weapon, a hesitance that weakened opposition to Napoleon's return and to the revolutions of the nineteenth century.[22]

The second phase of Italy's experience of the French Revolution was very different. This was revolution as reshaped by Napoleon's increasingly conservative policies. Institutionally and socially still a major transformation, it took place in a regime of order rather than radical democracy. Once again, the French were generally welcomed but now in the name of stability, and with the realization that exactions under the restored regimes had been no less great and repression much more brutal than under the French. Upon their return to Tuscany in the fall of 1800, some of the nobility and clergy, concerned for order, joined in the cheering. Although the French would not get back to Naples until 1806, their reception was impressive there, too (as was the failure to mount any heroic resistance against them). Before 1800, the conflict between radicals and moderates had been a critical problem for republicans everywhere, and that split may have been the principal reason for the short life of the republic established in Naples. Now, there was no room for radicals; and the issue that had divided Neapolitan republicans most sharply, the abolition of feudalism, was resolved by its elimination under Joachim Murat. The Neapolitan middle class at least found that the Napoleonic regimes suited them very well.[23]

---

21 The Leopoldine reforms on occasion had led to similar outbreaks of popular opposition. See Tognarini, "La Repubblica negata!" xxi–xxiii.

22 Peasant agitation took place against the French in the Veneto in 1796. The rural risings against Bonapartist rule in the South were less a counter-revolution than a guerrilla war. Crushed once British support was withdrawn, they anticipated the war against France in the Spanish peninsula a few years later and the "brigandage" following Italian unification.

23 Villani, *Mezzogiorno*, 54–55, 59–61; Turi, *"Viva Maria,"* 257, 278–287; Angelantonio Spagnoletti, *Storia del Regno delle Due Sicilie* (Bologna, 1997), 33.

The concept of social capital is helpful for an understanding of how these two waves of revolutionary change took root. Once established institutions and practices had been disrupted (by revolution and the arrival of the French), a series of local and specific events fostered political mobilization around groups, ideas, and behaviors that realized more of the social capital already visible under the old regimes than had been possible when those held sway. Much that was characteristic of the new regimes can be described in terms of their selective use of this social capital.[24]

Much of Enlightenment discourse in Italy (both inherently and of necessity) was only weakly attached to any particular government, or even any specific form of government. This political agnosticism, which has been much criticized by commentators, facilitated the installation of the revolutionary regimes. The universalistic rhetoric of the Enlightenment and the French Revolution did not sound strange or alien in Italy. Napoleon's call to the nation—like the neoclassical style that he brought with him—struck a note long familiar in a land accustomed to accepting foreigners.

Official French declarations and the proclamations and constitutions written by Italians regularly referred to the "nation" while preserving the term's useful ambiguity. Recourse to the nation meant opposition to old privileges of church and aristocracy, and it meant the inclusion of the people in political affairs—a basis for legitimacy that remained radical even under the Napoleonic empire. It also meant efficient administration of the commonweal. Territorially, it could apply to the Cisalpine Republic, Tuscany, the Two Sicilies, or the whole peninsula (with an elasticity much like that in earlier discussions of Italian culture). In reality, revolution unleashed municipal patriotism, perhaps the strongest political loyalty of all in Italy. The restiveness—of Modena against Bologna; Arezzo, Siena, and Pisa against Florence; Vicenza and Padua against Venice; and the provinces and cities of the mezzogiorno against Naples—was a crucial dynamic in the replacement of the old regimes. Italians had many reasons for

24 Recently, a lively interest has developed in the "event" as a central element in social theory. See William H. Sewell, Jr., "Historical Events as Transformations of Structures: Inventing Revolution at the Bastille," *Theory and Society,* XXV (1996), 841–881; Sidney Tarrow, "Contentious Event Analysis: Eventful History, Event Histories, and Events in History," unpub. paper (Ithaca, 1995).

rallying to the tricolor and welcoming common measures, coins, and tariffs.

That Italian and French officials readily acknowledged the continuity between the new institutions and laws and those created, or at least described, in earlier reform programs undoubtedly helped to win the participation of a significant proportion of the ablest administrators and magistrates from the old regimes. Many Milanese nobles accepted public office and fought in the Napoleonic armies. The priest who had served as the Bourbon regime's chief censor became the minister of the interior of the revolutionary republican government (and was tortured and executed when it fell). One of ablest officials of the Bourbon government, long an advocate of reform, ended up serving under the Napoleonic governments. Cuoco, who criticized the revolution in Naples as "passive" and its republic for failing to build a popular base, nevertheless went north after the fall of the Neapolitan republic to become editor of the *Giornale Italiano,* published in Milan under Napoleon.[25]

Even when their authority was circumscribed, a remarkable number of men of capacity and standing were willing to serve the new governments. In the spring of 1799, the French belatedly called for the establishment of municipal councils in eleven Tuscan towns. Although these councils had little power (their main responsibility was the formation of a national guard), prominent local lawyers, professors, doctors, and cultural figures sat in them alongside a few students, members of the clergy, and even some nobles. In a place like commercial Prato, where the revolution had been warmly received, a new political class of entrepreneurs, forged in these years, would lead the city into the Risorgimento.[26]

25 Continuity was claimed especially for the reforms of Joseph II in Lombardy and Peter Leopold in Tuscany but was also noted of the reforms, more described than attempted, in the Kingdom of the Two Sicilies. The point has resulted in a somewhat fruitless debate about the degrees of continuity and change in the revolutionary era. See Turi, *"Viva Maria,"* 189–190, and note the report of Karl Friedrich Reinhard, the French Republic's official in Tuscany, to Talleyrand March 22, 1799, in Tognarini, "La Revoluzione negata!" xlv–xlix. Guido Bezzola, *La vita quotidiana a Milano ai tempi di Stendhal* (Milan, 1981), 71. See Villani's essays, "Contributo alla storia del anticurialismo napoletano: L'Opera di G.F. Conforti" and "Giuseppe Zurlo e la crisi dell'Antico Regime nel Regno di Napoli," in idem *Mezzogiorno,* 185–370.
26 Turi, *"Viva Maria,"* 151–162; Stefano Trinca, "Il 1799 a Prato," in Tognarini (ed.), *La Toscana e la Rivoluzione francese,"* 200–201.

These are the sorts of people who spent months writing detailed constitutions, and in their affectionate descriptions of electoral procedures and their confident consignment of decision making to parliament, one can sense the eagerness of authors who imagined themselves on the rostrums that they were creating. They believed in the importance of the new chairs in constitutional law established at the universities of Bologna, Pavia, and Ferrara in 1797/1798, and they were equally serious about instructing the people.[27]

All of the new constitutions stressed education, and scores of patriotic societies took it upon themselves to instruct ordinary citizens on civic responsibility. In Florence, the society "of true friends of the patria" convened at the Accademia degli Armonici in Florence and agreed to meet every evening in order to educate the public, carefully changing moderators every ten days. The society, which published a monthly bulletin of public instruction, enjoyed important connections. Some of its leaders were clergymen, and it developed ties to older societies like the Georgofili. The Circolo d'Istruzione pubblica in Livorno met three times a week. The doctors and professors who formed a similar group in Siena added attention to charitable activities as well. The scores of newly founded newspapers declared that they fulfilled a similar responsibility. Theaters, which had flourished in the old regime, especially in Milan under Maria Theresa, reached a new peak after the revolution and continued to thrive under Napoleon (although Milan's Teatro Patriottico changed its name to the more generic Teatro dei Filodrammatici).[28]

Revolutions, almost by definition, know how to make propaganda, and serious commitment is unmistakable in the symbol-laden letterheads printed for the newly established offices of government. The woodcuts of the period cannot be taken as what

27 On the long tradition of Italian parliaments, see Antonio Marongiu, *Il parlamento in Italia nel medio evo e nell'età moderna* (Milan, 1962). On the case for the long-term significance of this constitution-making, see Grew, "Paradoxes," 221–231.
28 The first moderator of the Florentine society was Reginaldo Tanzini, a well-known Jansenist abbot (and editor of the works of Machiavelli). The society's *Biblioteca mensuale di pubblica istruzione* was edited by Francesco Fontana, the priest who was director of Riccardiana library. Florence added three newspapers to the two that already existed. These new papers circulated throughout Tuscany. Many other cities and towns had papers of their own that treated a broad range of issues and from a variety of perspectives. See Turi, *"Viva Maria,"* 166–169, 172–178; Bezzola, *Milano ai tempi di Stendhal,* 188–190.

actually happened; but if the scenes of people from all classes (including clergy) cheering the entry of French soldiers into a city and celebrating around liberty trees seem too good to be true, they do capture the revolutionaries' pedagogical seriousness and their sense of theater in public spaces. The depictions of golden books of nobility discarded, of noble escutcheons crumbling, and of figures from commedia dell'arte suffering (old Pantaleone, for example, as the dying Venetian republic) all speak to the ways in which the revolution connected with Italian society and culture.[29]

In this sense, the triumphal arches, liberty trees, and symbols of aristocracy shattered deserve to be taken seriously, whatever proportion of public opinion they are thought to represent. As liberty trees were planted in the central squares of cities and towns, the accompanying rituals—speeches by prominant citizens, including priests; bands playing; and dancing—were familiar social capital with which to baptize a new order.[30]

The revolutionaries continued something of the old ceremonial system, with public rites in assigned spaces, but celebrating revolutionary holidays, both French and local. These ceremonies underscored important changes: Old hierarchies were not maintained, and the aristocracy was largely absent from public affairs; the clergy were present to lend legitimacy to these occasions but were not their sponsors. Officials appeared less ex officio and more as representatives. These ceremonies remained visible expressions of community, but more a political act and less simply a matter of social custom. Whereas the old regime demonstrated power and hierarchy, while leaving decision making behind closed doors, the revolutionary governments intended their ceremonies to give the impression that power had a popular base and that political decisions were arrived at through public procedures.

These changes enlarged opportunities for the expression of opinion (including distrust and disagreement), and they gave greater and more explicit meaning to participation. Piazzas and markets were the natural sites for popular political expression,

---

29 Christian-Marc Bosseno, Christophe Dhoyen, and Michelle Vovelle, *Immagini della libertà: L'Italia in rivoluzione, 1789–1799* (Rome, 1988), 256–263.

30 Turi, *"Viva Maria,"* 176–201, treats Tuscany. See also the articles in Tognarini (ed.), *La Toscana e la Rivoluzione francese,* which discuss these events (and subsequent antirevolutionary activity) in seventeen different towns. By rushing to cut down these trees, the counterrevolutionary rioters of 1799 acknowledged their significance.

whether spontaneous or planned (radicals believed that the nobles used market days to mobilize their sharecroppers against the republic). As political activity became more familiar and associational networks spread, patriots used shops, cafes, and pharmacies as sites for mobilizing support. Once in power, they would tend to seek more institutional, public settings.[31]

The revolutionary experience widened the political horizon in terms of the issues addressed and the vocabulary used. Following the example from France, the governments established in Italy gave new incentives for certain kinds of activity and associations, provided rules within which civil society could function, and stimulated more focused public activities. Local interests and conflicts became more directly tied to national politics, broadening engagement in political life. As the government reached more deeply and more directly into society, the state became the focus of expectations and resentments that gave politics greater immediacy and significance. The networks, associations, exchanges, and collective action that constitute social capital increased with the stimulus of revolutionary activity, gaining importance as more and more issues and interests became politically charged. These activities expanded further with the opportunities provided by the institutions and policies of the revolutionary regimes, despite the restrictions on political freedom.[32]

In many respects, Italy's social capital was greater in 1815 than it had been twenty years earlier. The experience of the French Revolution in Italy left behind a more sharply defined, and circumscribed, civil society. It created an enlarged public sphere formally freed of aristocratic and clerical rights to guide, restrict, or censure. Confusion between the spheres of public authority and of private influence has been a consistent problem in Italy, especially in the mezzogiorno. That differentiation was much more clearly drawn under the governments of Joseph Bonaparte and Murat. No change was more fundamental than the abolition of feudalism in Naples, which made way for enhanced social capital both by redefining "relations between public and private [and] by reasserting the absolute sovereignty of public power." It

31 Tognarini, "La Revoluzione negata!" lxxxvi.
32 Gian Bruno Ravenni, "Poveri, giacobini e sanfedisti: l'insorgenza del 5 maggio a San Giovanni Valdarno," in Tognarini (ed.), *La Toscana e la Rivoluzione francese,* 73–74.

goes far to explain the powerful appeal of the French Revolution to southern intellectuals and members of the middle class.[33]

In all of Italy, access to the public sphere was enlarged and made more important by increased freedom of association (despite significant limitations), by the emphasis on public opinion (accompanied by propaganda, programs for education, and social rituals), and by the new opportunities for public action created by new policies and institutions. By recruiting officials from among those who had acquired status within and through civil society, the new governments added to the prestige of civil society itself. At the same time, emphasis on status through professional achievement restricted further access to a public sphere that was increasingly constrained by systematic restrictions on public expression. French arms left little space for political enemies or mass spontaneity. In the short term, rather like protective tariffs nurturing infant industries, these restrictions may have encouraged cautious members of the middle class to participate in civil society.

Revolutionary governments gave new meaning to politics, first by bringing efficacy to political action and, second, by expanding the realm of politics. Matters not always seen as political in the past, and certainly not as matters of public politics—relations with the Church, issues of equality, class differences, and education—would ever after be understood to be political issues. Decision making, the means of mobilizing support, and the subtler uses of power had been largely masked in the old regimes. The idea that political decisions should be open to public scrutiny would not be forgotten, even when it functioned only as one more criticism of government.

In practice, however, the paradoxical effect of the revolutionary years was to reinforce the tendency to treat procedures with the kind of legalistic (and cautious) respect that had been sustained by royal favor and social pressure before the French arrived and by the policies and personnel of suspicious Restoration regimes after the French were driven out. Carefully maintained

33 Spagnoletti, *Regno delle Due Sicilie,* 31–38. The point about the abolition of feudalism is true even if the "precocious . . . collapse of paternalism and deference" left a society more vunerable than before to corruption and violence, with little to substitute for old constraints. See John A. Davis, "Changing Perspectives on Italy's Southern Problem," in Carlo Levy (ed.), *Italian Regionalism: History, Identity and Politics* (Oxford, 1996), 63.

procedural protections offered more security than deliberative bodies did.

Much as the revolutionary and Napoleonic governments bequeathed a more efficient administrative system and an improved infrastructure of better roads, they left an array of public institutions that strengthened the public sphere and increased the vitality of civil society. Valuable in themselves, new lycées (and the Scuola Normale in Pisa modelled on France's Ecole Normale), music conservatories, theaters, and public art galleries were the manufactories of social capital. They nourished an expanding professional elite and reinvigorated bourgeois culture. As part of the state's responsibility rather than the accident of princely gift and as important elements of the public sphere, they would continue to fulfill this role (usually in handsome properties that revolutionary regimes had commandeered from the Church) through the next century.

Whereas continuity of personnel helped revolutionary governments to take root, the generation of administrators, magistrates, and military officers who served in the Napoleonic regimes would play a far greater part in the development of civil society during and after the years of French rule. Prominent in civil affairs, especially in Milan and Naples, their efforts and, eventually, their frustrations with the rigidity and inefficiency of the Restoration regimes would be important to the Risorgimento, beginning with the carbonari uprisings of the 1820s, in which so many of them took part.

The revolutionary years strengthened forms of social capital less dependent on the state. Books, newspapers, and other periodicals circulated more widely, and the habit of meeting and talking—in clubs, circles, cafes, and bookstores—became more entrenched. This transformation of Italian associational life went further beyond intellectual elites and particular occupations than ever before, fostering important networks of opinion and interest and broadening the sets of issues that concerned them. Much of this activity was repressed, or at least made risky, under the Restoration regimes, but its traces were evident throughout the next fifty years in private correspondence and clandestine publications and in the conspiracies, secret societies, and political sects for which others upbraided Italian radicals.[34]

34 Spagnoletti, *Regno delle Due Sicilie,* 41–55, 90–102, 182–206.

Thinking in terms of social capital, which helps to explain the impact of the French Revolution in Italy, also points to potential social capital that the revolutionary governments did not realize. They did not effectively engage the peasantry, despite the social capital represented by peasant networks, by their face-to-face relations with city people, their market connections, and ties to landowners. With regard to the Church, probably Italy's greatest locus of social capital, the revolutionaries were barely able to accomplish more than to win its hesitant neutrality.

Nearly every commentator has noted the limited role of Italy's peasants during the French Revolution (and the Risorgimento). Sismondi's description, not long after Napoleon's defeat, is typical:

> The lower orders in the cities of Lombardy preserved no other memory of the period of liberty than that impressed on the imagination by some ruin, which their forefathers pointed out as monuments of ancient battles or of ancient violence. The peasantry, having never enjoyed any political right, feared nothing but the scourge of war; and prized a government in proportion only to its pacific disposition.[35]

But more than peasant ignorance and middle-class fears of a threat to property restricted the political role of the peasants. Italy's loose forms of participation in council and piazza—an important asset to the revolutionary and Napoleonic regimes, especially at first—had marked limitations. The techniques that worked for reaching the large urban minority (among the largest proportions in Europe) only occasionally extended to peasants. Even during prior centuries, city-states had only irregular and inconsistent relations with the land around them, and the later monarchical regimes tended to leave rural authority in the hands of nobles, who stood as buffers between peasants and the state. Only sporadic participants in civic affairs before the Revolution, peasants were feared by both radicals and conservatives alike, when they recognized them as a potential political force at all. The revolutionary governments largely ignored them, too, offering peasants few tangible benefits and irritating them through conscription and attacks on religion in a society focused on cities rather than rural

35 J. C. L. Sismondi de Sismondi, *A History of the Italian Republics: Being a View of the Origin, Progress, and Fall of Italian Freedom* (Gloucester, Mass., 1970; orig. pub 1832), 257.

life and on high culture rather than folk tradition. Nor did the urban practices that failed to reach the peasantry consistently give an effective voice to the very poor. The social ties, such as they were, of these more marginal groups, had to pass through aristocratic landlords, parish clergy, and Catholic charity. For reasons of structure as well as ideology, the revolutionary regimes did not reach effectively beyond these intermediaries or across the spaces separating town and country.

No issue, institution, or interest was a greater source of division during the French Revolution than religion. Italian revolutionaries, however, were not the passionate anticlericals that Jacobins were, and by the time the French got to Italy, they were pursuing the milder religious policies of the Directory or the still more accommodating ones of Napoleon. Significantly, popes and many Italian bishops were less intransigant in their response to those who carried the revolution into Italy than most of the French hierarchy was to the Revolution there. Despite this restraint on both sides and despite the fact that many priests were sympathetic to the new order (a fact that created important divisions within the clergy), the great potential of Catholic organizations as social capital in parishes, bishoprics, confraternities, volunteer associations, charities, and communal festivals was never realized. The revolutionaries did not recruit within these associations, and the clergy did not encourage their participation in civil affairs. This failure made it easier for the famous uprisings of 1799—hardly contributions to civil society—to leave behind a memory of Catholic opposition to the revolution that became a kind of ideological assumption that reached deep into Italian life. Cartoons printed in Italy at the end of the Napoleonic wars used the style of Counter-Reformation religious paintings to show St. Antony or the Madonna directing from the sky the victorious counter-revolutionary armies below.[36]

There were also structural constraints on Italy's increased social capital. The clergy were now more tied to conservative government and less free to campaign for reform of church or state. In 1815, urban reformers were more disconnected from peasants and from most of the clergy than in the old regime. The abolition of feudalism in the South had broken, or at least weak-

---

36   Bosseno, Dhoyen, and Vovelle, *Immagini della libertà, passim.*

ened, the ties between landlords and peasants, and fewer of the nobility were interested in reform. Everywhere property owners and reformers had new reason to fear peasant violence and little desire to mobilize peasant interests for any cause.[37]

Although the experience of revolutionary change was different in the North, where French forces arrived sooner and stayed longer, than in the South, one of the most important outcomes of the era was to make northern and southern Italy more alike. In addition to the common institutions and the Napoleonic Code—the importance of which historians have long noted—Italy's increased (and geographically more comparable) social capital deserves mention, too. Institutionally more similar in 1815 than ever before, North and South would develop differently in the next fifty years. The associational life and civil society that Italy's enhanced social capital foreshadowed would not be allowed to develop in the South as it did in the North.[38]

Applying the idea of social capital to the history of the French Revolution in Italy invites some reflection about social capital itself, and that leads me to make four points. First, in this case at least, social capital should include patterns of behavior rooted in culture as well as in institutions. The importance of high culture, the role of law and lawyers, the acceptance of things foreign, and the use of distinctive public spaces as centers of community, exchange, and demonstration were more than passive elements of a long tradition. They affected political life and did so differently as politics changed.

Second, tradition and memory do matter in the formation of social capital. In the eighteenth and nineteenth centuries, Italian leaders occasionally evoked the civic example of the medieval

37 Turi, *"Viva Maria,"* 299–300, while stressing the revolutionary regime's failure to address peasant concerns about private property, 205–210, argues that in Tuscany, class division had already grown with the Leopoldine reforms.

38 The different effect of the British presence on Sicily underscores the impact of Napoleonic rule across the peninsula. But as one leading expert has commented, the real problem of Italian regionalism is why there is so little of it. See Adrian Lyttleton, "Shifting Identities: Nation, Region, and City," in Levy (ed.), *Italian Regionalism,* 33–52. In the nineteenth century, too, "in Italy, at least, the opposite of civic politics is not *no* politics but rather a quasi-feudal patron-client politics." See Putnam, Leonardi, Nanetti, and Franco Pavoncello, "Explaining Institutional Success: The Case of Italian Regional Government," *American Political Science Review,* LXXVII (1983), 66.

communes. After 1815, the most effective governments in Italy were in states that had begun major reforms before 1799. The revolutionary regimes left a heritage, too. The institutions that they bequeathed were generally preserved, and so was the recollection of constitutional participation and open discussion (which on occasion even the most conservative governments had to promise to allow). Continuity also included changes in behavior that, for example, made aristocrats and bourgeois appear more alike and the bureaucracies of the different states function more similarly.

Third, social capital is vulnerable to power. Many practices that had once constituted social capital either disappeared or became largely commemorative under (mainly foreign) absolute monarchs during the centuries between the Renaissance and the French Revolution. Repeated evidence that external military force was decisive in Italian politics was bound not merely to discourage confidence in political action but also to disconnect associational life from politics. Similarly, much of the social capital inherent in the social networks fostered during the revolutionary period was undermined by, or only surreptitiously invoked under, the repressive policies of the Restoration regimes. Official institutions preserved greater continuity in social capital, because they had some protection in their formal structures and proved more adaptable to the requirements of successive governments. Beyond the tolerance of authorities, a vigorous associational life may also require some resonance between the organizational structure of voluntary associations and the way in which political power is exercised.[39]

Fourth, discontinuities can seriously effect social capital. Revolution provided training in how to mobilize public sentiment and build networks, which undoubtedly increased social capital. But the fact of sudden and radical political changes had a contrary impact. Political changes accompanied by bloodshed, turmoil, repression, and ideological division weakened the public sphere. If trust is the ultimate measure of social capital, then that capital must have been diminished with each change of regime. We do not know how many Tuscans were scheduled for trial,

---

39 Michael W. Foley and Bob Edwards, "The Paradox of Civil Society," *Journal of Democracy,* VII, 38–49 (1992), make a series of related points and cite Tocqueville on the importance of free political associations to the development of all other associations.

imprisonment, or execution because of their participation in the revolutionary wave of 1799; we cannot begin to know because the lists of names and charges drawn up after the Austrians came back were hastily destroyed when the French armies returned. Frightened neighbors, whether potential victims or seekers of revenge, must have learned cynical caution and bitter distrust—a kind of negative social capital.[40]

Social capital is like potential energy. Its transformation into kinetic energy lies in conjunctures and events, which may reduce the value of some forms of social capital while increasing that of others. Gramsci's well-known distinction between civil and political society and his emphasis on the power of cultural hegemony encapsulate much of Italian experience by emphasizing the ways in which Italy's social capital had been used most effectively throughout history. Historical change alters social capital, making some of it more accessible and powerful and some of it irrelevant, but history does little to preserve social capital. Preservation requires the continuity of recurrent use, a set of habits that makes certain kinds of responses seem natural and predictable and penalizes others, establishing customary ways of realizing social capital for public purposes.[41]

Readers may notice that this effort to use ideas of social capital for understanding Italy's response to the French Revolution differs in many respects from Putnam's influential discussion of social capital, also about Italy. The divergence, which may be conceptual, methodological, or merely chronological, illustrates the stimulating malleability of the term. Calling attention to unnoticed relationships between social and political behavior, it can lead to fresh understandings of both. The proof of the presence of social capital in any polity lies in political practice, and that invites the kind of hindsight with which historians are comfortable.

40   Tognarini, "La repubblica negata!" xx.
41   Antonio Gramsci's use of these ideas to interpret Italian history run through his *Quaderni del carcere* (ed. Valentino Gerratane) (Turin, 1975), 4v.

Leonard N. Rosenband

Social Capital in the Early Industrial Revolution

"The first rule" of France's paperworkers was "to be the despotic masters of their bosses." Journeymen across early modern Europe forged associations to control hours, output, and the identity of their shopmates. Short-lived or venerable, these combinations turned the world of production upside down. An anonymous *mémoire* from France raged that "the master [papermakers] are like slaves of the journeymen and workers." In 1771, an alarmed observer recast this levelling in political terms: "The journeymen paperworkers form a sort of little republican state in the midst of the monarchy." This muscular republic had deposed the hierarchy formally inscribed in the craft. The state was concerned, too. Writing in 1772, a provincial official in the Auvergne worried about "a republic of inferior workers, accustomed to laying down the law to the masters." He knew that the paperworkers' association defined their social responsibilities and shaped their patterns of mutual assistance. It was the journeymen's civic body, and the persistent measure of more than one civic tradition in the trade. Master papermakers and journeymen did not perceive themselves as members of a craft community with a single set of interests.[1]

For Putnam, medieval craft guilds were distant nurseries of effective political reform in modern Italy. More precisely, in his influential study, *Making Democracy Work,* Putnam contends that the craft communities were incubators of social capital. As he understands it, social capital amounts to the "norms of reciprocity and networks of civic engagement" at the base of responsive, democratic government. These connections, he argues, were egalitarian in texture and operation. Implicitly, Putnam's norms

Leonard N. Rosenband is Associate Professor of History, Utah State University. He is the author of "Jean-Baptiste Réveillon: A Man on the Make in Old Regime France," *French Historical Studies,* XX (1997), 481–510; co-editor, with Thomas Max Safley, of *The Workplace before the Factory: Artisans and Proletarians, 1500–1800* (Ithaca, 1993).

1 Quoted passages in Alexandre Nicolaï, *Histoire des moulins à papier du Sud-Ouest de la France, 1300–1800* (Bordeaux, 1935), I, 63 (L. Lescourre), 60 (anonymous *mémoire*), 64 (Lescourre); Mignot quoted in Charles-Moïse Briquet, "Associations et grèves des ouvriers papetiers en France aux XVIIe et XVIIIe siècles," *Revue internationale de sociologie,* V (1897), 178.

and networks yielded craft communities with unified interests, but the guilds of early modern Europe were actually honeycombed with internal divisions and enduring conflicts.[2]

This essay examines the role and manipulation of social capital within guilds and the wider orbit of manufacture, primarily on the eve of large-scale mechanization. It suggests that production, whether in the fourteenth or the eighteenth century, was an unsettled realm composed mainly of "eager and apprehensive men of small property." The formal distinctions between these masters and journeymen and the obligations of each, etched in guild regulations, provoked more discord than harmony. The unpredictable play of markets, the weather, and dissolute teamsters amplified these tensions. So did the arrival of new technologies, although shifts in the organization of production probably touched more journeymen. Yet, the horizons of most masters and men did not change appreciably in the centuries before Josiah Wedgwood and Pierre Montgolfier. Accordingly, early modern European production was governed by expectations rooted in interest, experience, and the particular needs and knowledge of each trade community. These expectations provided the crafts with a disorderly equilibrium, a balance that was continually reconfigured in the shops, on tramping trails, and in the noisy, joyous transmission of skill. Here social capital was made and remade, less a system and more a reservoir of resources and loyalties in the enduring contest for advantage between master craftsmen and their journeymen. The marshalling and spending of social capital constituted the warp and woof of this struggle. Consequently, this article questions whether the historical norms and networks of social capital that Putnam locates beneath successful, modern institutions were so distant from the culture of mistrust and hierarchical structures that he finds at the root of contemporary political despair.

Pre-Revolutionary Europe consisted of societies divided into distinct orders, in which certain ranks enjoyed rights and privileges denied to others. Within this great chain, cities, bishops, and kings all possessed the authority to charter guilds. These communities of craftsmen received the exclusive right to produce a particular

2 Robert Putnam, with Roberto Leonardi and Raffaella Y. Nanetti, *Making Democracy Work: Civic Traditions in Modern Italy* (Princeton, 1993), 125–126, 167, 181.

item, determine technique and set standards of quality, as well as recruit, train, and discipline their members. The range of their monopolies generally coincided with the borders of towns. From a twentieth-century perspective, the guilds' entitlements and responsibilities conflated public and private functions. This blurring helps explain the craft communities' distinctive idiom. First, however, the guildsmen's notion of community needs strict definition. Above all, it meant that a group of producers belonged together and shared a commitment to their art, whether tooling gold or cutting meat. Each guild, therefore, had a built-in source of cohesion; its members had common interests, knowledge, and assumptions about their work and lives.[3]

Although the sons of masters were treated differently than outsiders, and real gaps existed between rich and poor guildsmen, the corporate idiom of solidarity (as well as ceaseless struggle with neighboring guilds) worked against potential dissonance. Membership in a craft community gave a man an *état*, a certain dignity and standing. He swore an oath of fealty to his art and its brotherhood, and became the spiritual son of its patron saint. He shared in the bawdy and the solemn rituals of his fellows. Much social capital was surely minted by all these trappings—but not necessarily warm relations. As Kaplan shrewdly observed, "[g]uild life was characterized by a relentless tension between the representation of equality and the practice of hierarchy and discrimination."[4]

---

3 On the place and functions of the guilds, see Emile Coornaert, *Les Corporations en France avant 1789* (Paris, 1941); Steven Epstein, *Wage Labor and Guilds in Medieval Europe* (Chapel Hill, 1991); Steven Kaplan, "The Character and Implications of Strife Among the Masters Inside the Guilds of Eighteenth-Century Paris," *Journal of Social History*, XIX (1986), 631–647; idem (trans. John Merriman), "Guilds, 'False Workers,' and the Faubourg Saint-Antoine," in James McClain, Merriman, and Ugawa Kaoru (eds.), *Edo and Paris: Urban Life and the State in the Early Modern Era* (Ithaca, 1994), 355–383; idem, "The Luxury Guilds in Paris in the Eighteenth Century," *Francia*, IX (1981), 257–298; idem, "Réflexions sur la police du monde du travail, 1700–1815," *Revue historique*, CCLXI (1979), 17–77; Etienne Martin Saint-Léon, *Histoire des corporations de métiers, depuis leurs origines jusqu'à leur suppression en 1791* (Paris, 1909); Gervase Rosser, "Crafts, Guilds and the Negotiation of Work in the Medieval Town," *Past & Present*, 154 (1997), 3–31; Thomas Max Safley and Rosenband (eds.), *The Workplace before the Factory: Artisans and Proletarians, 1500–1800* (Ithaca, 1993); William Sewell, Jr., *Work and Revolution in France: The Language of Labor from the Old Regime to 1848* (Cambridge, 1980); Michael Sonenscher, *The Hatters of Eighteenth-Century France* (Berkeley, 1987); idem, *Work and Wages: Natural Law, Politics, and the Eighteenth-Century French Trades* (Cambridge, 1989).
4 Sewell, *Work and Revolution*, 25–39; Kaplan, "Character," 632.

The craft communities in the eighteenth century were often termed the *maîtrises*. Technically, the masters alone filled the ranks of the guilds; journeymen and apprentices remained in filial subordination to the men who had made a masterpiece and sworn an oath. Not surprisingly, the journeymen, who were mostly transient wage workers, chafed under the powers and pretensions of their masters. But many guildsmen, masters themselves, were equally angry. (Occasionally, these dissident masters even broke rank and joined the journeymen in their conflicts with guild officials.) Although mastership conferred status and distinction, it had not placed every master on the same practical footing. Many guilds were in the hands of a self-interested elite, "a kind of self-perpetuating corporation within the corporation." Lesser guildsmen, the young and those without deep connections of family and place, endured a sort of second-class mastership. They were absent from guild assemblies, if any were held, when the big men made policy. They had to rely on their own resources in litigation, while the better-placed turned to the guild treasury. They had no say when the guild grandees decided to indulge the transgressions of some masters while prosecuting others. They were not consulted when certain masters received favorable access to labor and raw materials. Their frequent opposition movements within the craft communities revealed just how frayed the rhetorical cloak of craft brotherhood had always been.[5]

Disparities of wealth, ambition, and opportunity eroded fraternity in many guilds. Only one in five hatters in eighteenth-century Rouen actually manufactured hats. The other four, restricted to the retail trade or the repair of damaged goods, lacked the credit and capital necessary to secure workers or beaver pelts. In 1785, the syndics of the Parisian company of bakers began legal proceedings against six of their fellow guildsmen who had collected funds without the permission of the wardens to cover the costs of petitioning the Council of State. They received a favorable hearing, and the tax on the wood that fuelled their ovens was reduced. Perhaps the syndics were embarrassed by the success of their lesser brethren; doubtless, they intended to put the six in their place. Finally, within the guild of linen thread merchant–manufacturers of Lille, several insurgent masters proposed that no

5 Kaplan, "Character," passim.

man's holdings should exceed two mills. But the larger, more enterprising producers rejected this scheme. For the good of all, the big men claimed, each master must bask in *"une grande liberté."* No restrictions were imposed.[6]

Particularism within the craft communities was more than matched by competitiveness along their borders. By 1300, the masons and millstone makers in Orvieto belonged to separate guilds. Isaac Gribelin, painter in enamel and goldsmith in seventeenth-century Blois, had twenty-seven watches confiscated by an official of the Crown, who searched his home in the company of two members of the clockmakers' guild. In the eighteenth century, the Parisian guild of gold-and-silversmiths squabbled with the casters, engravers, watchmakers, and a host of other craft communities. When the Parlement approved the statutes of the Parisian guild of carpenters and cabinetmakers in 1743, thirteen neighboring guilds complained that their rights had been violated.[7]

If guildsmen in separate *corporations* found common ground, reciprocal interests generally fertilized the soil. A bewildering array of artisans were linked in production networks, in which their particular refinements accounted for only one aspect of the final product. Consider the various trades involved in the production and profits of saddle making in fourteenth-century London: The saddlers supervised the work of joiners, who crafted the saddle-trees; lorimers, who fashioned the harness; and painters, who provided the decoration. In Schwarz's vivid description of subcontracting webs in Georgian London, "an assembly-line ran through the street." But even these networks had their hierarchies, since the craftsmen with access to credit and raw materials wielded the whip hand.[8]

Much production in early modern Europe took place beyond the reach of the guilds. The craft communities condemned as shoddy, and even dangerous, both the legal and illicit manufacture that eluded their control. Meanwhile, they pressured the state to

6 Sonenscher, *Hatters,* 43; idem, *Work and Wages,* 63; Gail Bossenga, *The Politics of Privilege: Old Regime and Revolution in Lille* (Cambridge, 1991), 152–154.

7 Richard Goldthwaite, *The Building of Renaissance Florence: An Economic and Social History* (Baltimore, 1980), 245; David Landes, *Revolution in Time: Clocks and the Making of the Modern World* (Cambridge, Mass., 1983), 216; Kaplan, "Luxury," 277–278.

8 Sonenscher, *Work and Wages,* 130–133, 147–149; Rosser, "Crafts, Guilds," 14; L. D. Schwarz, *London in the Age of Industrialisation: Entrepreneurs, Labour Force and Living Conditions, 1700–1850* (Cambridge, 1992), 33.

disband the barely hidden brigades of chamberers, *Bohnhasen,* and *faux ouvriers* (false, or non-guilded, workers). As early as 1421, the spur makers of London railed to the mayor about the "chamberer" who "sels such fals work in greate disceite hynderynge of all the comyn people." Yet, guildsmen themselves were often implicated in the underground employment of false workers. Three centuries after the spur makers, the Parisian gold-and-silversmiths lamented that masters and their widows "let themselves be seduced [into protecting the faux ouvriers] by a recompense as derisory as it is illegal." Equally dangerous, the guild wardens believed, were privileged enclaves like the faubourg Saint-Antoine of Paris, where men and women pursued the crafts of their choice without guild affiliation. In fact, the connections among unlicensed work, privileged territory, and grasping guildsmen received a delightful twist in the apparent hypocrisy of the Parisian mercers. While they loudly denounced those who carried out "their commerce secretly" in the faubourg, the stockingers and producers of gilt- and silver-edged cloth complained that the same mercers fattened on the great number of guild-exempt hands that they employed in this free quarter. Too often, the guild *gardes* might have said, social capital was sacrificed for the real thing.[9]

Laissez-faire and the "[w]inds of change" that swirled about the French Revolution, Putnam claims, swept away the guilds and other old forms of "organized sociability." A more apt metaphor might have been a firestorm, since Putnam places the craft communities within a general, "moldering social underbrush." Here he echoes the Enlightenment, which portrayed the guilds as closed communities of obscurantists fighting rearguard actions against the natural forces of talent, the market, and technological progress. But recent work on the bakers' and locksmiths' guilds in Paris suggests that access to the trades was not as limited as the physiocrats maintained. Only 34 percent (116 of 346) of the men newly admitted to the Parisian company of locksmiths between 1742 and 1776 were the sons of masters. These craftsmen entered a vital world of the unsentimental pursuit of self-interest. The market was not a revelation to Old Regime guildsmen; they found

9 Sylvia Thrupp, "The Gilds," in Michael M. Postan, Edwin E. Rich, and Edward Miller (eds.), *The Cambridge Economic History of Europe: Economic Organization and Policies in the Middle Ages* (Cambridge, 1963), III, 255; Kaplan, "Luxury," 261 (brackets in original); *idem,* "Guilds, 'False Workers'," 369.

a place in production networks, turned state privileges to their own account, and went it alone. Their interest-based, rough-shouldered legacy suited the changing economies and politics of nineteenth-century Europe far better than would a revival of civic humanism.[10]

Whether sustaining or burying an indigent brother, most guilds provided assistance to their vulnerable members. Funerals, saints' days, and processions reflected the public harmony of the craft communities, although it would be interesting to know what passed through the minds of lesser guildsmen as they marched behind their betters. The masters, however, were usually of a single mind when they faced insubordinate journeymen. The guildsmen believed that the journeymen's social capital was counterfeit and, like any false coin, its use was illegal. In fact, the social capital amassed by journeymen and workers took shape amid workbenches and on dusty expeditions in search of an easy foreman. It was expressed in counter-communities, custom, and riot. It conserved the social wisdom distilled from common tasks, passages, and interests, and mirrored the mistrust that so often separated masters and men. The journeymen's associations and "Clubs," wrote an advocate of the workers' cause in 1750, "are the grand Obstacle to Oppression and Tyranny."[11]

In 1303, Putnam notes, a guild statute from Verona spoke of "[f]raternal assistance in necessity of whatever kind," and "hospitality towards strangers, when passing through the town." Were journeymen in desperate straits or simply on the move entitled to this aid? Put another way, were these provisions the measure of borders and stratification, as well as the mutuality Putnam finds in them? Whole trades rarely figured in such "horizontal collaboration," as he terms it. Instead, by the time the Veronese code was drafted, journeymen bakers, cobblers, skinners, and tanners—to name a few—plotted and agitated for better conditions and increased wages. Masters of their arts but not masters in name, they nevertheless deserved elevated rewards. As some sixteenth-

10 Putnam, *Making Democracy Work,* 137. On the bakers, see Kaplan, *The Bakers of Paris and the Bread Question, 1700–1775* (Ithaca, 1996), 278–283; on the locksmiths, Sonenscher, *Work and Wages,* 107.

11 Robert Malcolmson, "Workers' Combinations in Eighteenth-Century England," in Margaret Jacob and James Jacob (eds.), *The Origins of Anglo-American Radicalism* (Atlantic Highlands, N.J., 1991; orig. pub. 1984), 178.

century journeymen said, "the name Printer should truly be reserved for [us, since we] perform the greatest part of printing."[12]

Whether in the age of Petrarch or Voltaire, skill was the basis of the mechanical arts. As the apprentice, and then journeyman, mastered his craft, he also learned the expectations and code of conduct of his fellow workers. The journeymen metalworkers of Frankfurt took a vow of mutual support in 1402, and had their oath written out fifteen years later. Every skilled trade, and even certain unskilled work, was shrouded in "mystery," that is, custom, experience, and know-how. This mystery was absorbed through long hours in the shops, such as the standard fourteen-hour days in the construction trades of seventeenth-century Amsterdam or the sixteen-hour marathons expected of the journeymen bookbinders of pre-Revolutionary Paris. The journeyman baker was a "veritable troglodyte" who spent his nights in the company of a hot oven and his brother journeymen; small wonder that these men likened themselves to "bats." Indeed, the journeyman baker and his wife often retained separate residences. In these trades and many others, such marital distance was the converse of the strong emotional bonds generated by endless hours with endpapers or in bakers' caverns.[13]

The collective nature of much artisanal work enhanced these emotional links, as well as the journeymen's powers. The withdrawal of one member of the vat crew halted the making of paper. Of course, an idle vat full of fermented rag filaments, the perishable raw material of papermaking, was an effective way to bring a stubborn master to his knees. When new skills widened the division of labor, the bottleneck tightened. The Calder Iron Works could not meet a filemaker's order because their tilter had a fever, and the whole of Scotland lacked a competent tilter to replace him. Common or rare, the journeymen's skills translated

12 Putnam, *Making Democracy Work,* 124–125; Natalie Z. Davis, "A Trade Union in Sixteenth-Century France," *Economic History Review,* XIX (1966), 48, 53. See also Catharina Lis and Hugo Soly, "'An Irresistible Phalanx': Journeymen Associations in Western Europe, 1300–1800," *International Review of Social History,* XXXIX, supplement 2 (1994), 21, 35.
13 Rosser, "Crafts, Guilds," 13. On the construction trades, see Jan de Vries, "An Employer's Guide to Wages and Working Conditions in the Netherlands, 1450–1850," in Carol Leonard and Boris N. Mironov (eds.), *Hours of Work and Means of Payment: The Evolution of Conventions in Pre-Industrial Europe* (Milan, 1994), 47–48; on the bookbinders, Sonenscher, *Work and Wages,* 95. See Kaplan, *Bakers,* 227–228, 255, for a powerful discussion of the journeymen bakers' miseries.

into a certain authority over production, and constituted a permanent counterpoint to the formal hierarchy of the trades. Consequently, the journeymen glaziers of eighteenth-century Paris dared to form "factions," hold "clandestine" assemblies, and set their own piece rates, which they tried to impose on the masters.[14]

Both collective work and the pursuit of a less segmented craft on, say, butchers' row or goldsmiths' lane, produced shared identities, often expressed in ritual. The Company of the Griffarins, the association of journeymen printers in sixteenth-century Lyons, held elaborate banquets for the initiation of newcomers. There the freshly minted journeyman learned passwords and complex greetings, complete with a bite on the ear. He also swore never to work for wages below those set by the Griffarins, never to labor in place of a man who had been unjustly sacked, and never to toil for a boss while a brother journeyman had an unresolved dispute with him. Thus was the tyro taught that he had joined the Company of the Griffarins, rather than a trade unified by the masters' interests.[15]

In the nineteenth century, it was said that "no man knows his own ability or what he is worth until he has worked in more towns than one." Tramping was the journeyman's response to the seasonal and irregular unemployment produced by economies that lacked integration and elasticity. Every craft had its particular hurdles. The manufacture of paper was stopped by floods and droughts, shortages of rags and alum, cracked vats and frozen millwheels. Since tramping was a routine passage in the journeyman's life, it was larded with ritual that reminded him that he should trust his craft brothers, not his betters. Wandering German journeymen counted on the handicraft's gift (*Handwerksgeschenk*) on arrival or departure. Consider, moreover, the custom that French paperworkers knew as *les rentes*. A journeyman on the move would pass through the mill gates and demand his subsidy of wine, which was replenished time and again by his mates and his boss. When the jug ran dry, the new man picked up the tools of his trade. After a ream or two piled up, the millmaster inspected the work and, if pleased, offered the itinerant a job and a wage. To Jean-Baptiste Serve, a petty producer in the Auvergne, the

14 Sidney Pollard, *The Genesis of Modern Management: A Study of the Industrial Revolution in Great Britain* (Cambridge, Mass., 1965), 167; Sonenscher, *Work and Wages,* 23.
15 Davis, "Trade Union," 60–61.

purpose of this ritual was devastatingly clear. The tramping man avoided the humiliation of asking for work; instead, the boss humbled himself by making "proposals" to the journeyman. Consequently, the itinerant compelled the manufacturer to validate his skills. Moreover, the easy access that strolling men had to most workshops reminded the masters of how tenuous was their mastery over tools and men.[16]

In the German states, the travel-worn journeyman first displayed his worthiness by offering the proper greeting. He then served a fortnight's probation, in which he demonstrated his mastery of the raw materials and the custom of his craft. Both ensured the journeyman's survival. At the English dockyards, workers were entitled to chips, the scraps left by the work of axes and adzes on ship timbers. In 1702, the hands at the Deptford Yard claimed the right to carry off chips three times a day. In fact, the men believed they were free to enlist their families in this task. The results were visible in the housing near Portsmouth Yard, where each chip was restricted to less than three feet: "Stairs were just under three feet wide; doors, shutters, cupboards, and so forth were formed of wood in pieces just under three feet long." Even more remarkably, "only a sixth of the timber entering Deptford Yard left it afloat."[17]

Ironically, elite idioms and practices also provided journeymen with models for the defense of their interests. Like the masters, the journeymen struggled mightily to maintain their monopolies over the exercise of their skills. They drew on guild statutes that limited the masters to one or two apprentices in order to restrict the supply of labor. They tried to weed out "illegal" and "irregular" workers, that is, men who had not served an apprenticeship. They attempted to run off "dishonorable" masters, those who violated the dignity of the craft or met the journeymen with their elbows out. They sought to impose mutual respect

16   Eric J. Hobsbawm, *Labouring Men: Studies in the History of Labour* (New York, 1964), 37; Hans-Ulrich Thamer, "On the Use and Abuse of Handicraft: Journeyman Culture and Enlightened Public Opinion in Eighteenth- and Nineteenth-Century Germany," in Kaplan (ed.), *Understanding Popular Culture: Europe from the Middle Ages to the Nineteenth Century* (Berlin, 1984), 288; Jean-Baptiste Serve, "Mémoire adressé à Son Excellence le Ministre des Manufactures et du Commerce," F[12] 2368, Archives nationales (henceforth AN).

17   Thamer, "Use and Abuse," 288; Peter Linebaugh, *The London Hanged: Crime and Civil Society in the Eighteenth Century* (Cambridge, 1992), 378–380.

between masters and men—but on their own terms. Witness the blend of defiance and conciliation in a poem composed by the London silk weavers in 1773, just after a strike:

> And may no treacherous, base, designing men
> E'er make encroachments on our rights again;
> May upright masters still augment their treasure,
> And journeymen pursue their work with pleasure.[18]

For Putnam, covenants and contracts were distinctive features of the medieval Italian communes rich in social capital. These instruments were alternatives to "force and family," and elevated collective life. But to journeymen and masters, the "contract" often bore the signature of muscle. In 1738, "above a thousand Nailers [in Hales-Owen, Worcestershire] got together, and went to all the Ironmongers in and near that Place and Birmingham, and oblig'd them to sign a Paper to give them an advance Price for Nails . . . and threaten'd to come again in a Month's Time to see it comply'd with." Not surprisingly, one outcome of the London tailors' strike of 1720 was an act of Parliament that annulled all "contracts, covenants or agreements" reached by the journeymen to raise wages or restrict hours. Tailors who entered into such an arrangement risked two months' imprisonment, at least on paper.[19]

Workers also managed to reverse the measures that states enacted to assist the masters' police of their trades. From the middle of the eighteenth century, French journeymen were expected to carry *certificats de congé,* discharge documents signed by their former masters. According to the government's reasoning, these written credentials would permit producers to fish only docile, assiduous men from the stream of itinerants. By forging their papers or carrying an extra passport or two, French journeymen skirted the regulations. Their English brothers, at least in papermaking, went further. They issued their own "cards of

---

18   Lis and Soly, "Irresistible," 22, 50; John Rule, "The Property of Skill in the Period of Manufacture," in Patrick Joyce (ed.), *The Historical Meanings of Work* (Cambridge, 1987), 109.
19   Putnam, *Making Democracy Work,* 126–127; Malcolmson, "Workers' Combinations," 175; John Orth, "English Combination Acts of the Eighteenth Century," *Law and History Review,* V (1987), 181–182.

freedom," which were meant to ensure that only men immersed in their ways toiled beside them.[20]

Often, journeymen took "innocent" forms and recast their purposes. The journeymen's "Clubs," an English commentator charged in 1749, "were at first formed for the Support of [their] Members in Sickness or old Age, but are now become the great Sources of Tumult and Sedition, of Rage and Riots." Within the craft communities, the confraternity, or religious association, was responsible for dispensing charity and even pensions to the masters. By the fourteenth century, parallel and distinct *confréries* were organized by journeymen bakers, fullers, furriers, shoemakers, smiths, tailors, and weavers. They, too, were expected to practice "devotion and charity," and some enjoyed acceptance by the clergy, who permitted the journeymen to establish chapels devoted to their patron saints in churches and the sanctuaries of religious orders. But these brotherhoods had secular causes as well. The religious association of the journeymen weavers and wool beaters of fourteenth-century Freiburg discussed wages. The *confréries* of sixteenth- and seventeenth-century Paris, fumed the authorities who tried to shut them down, had degenerated into "conspiracies." In eighteenth-century Turin, gatherings of journeymen to venerate their saints and collect funds for indigent brothers were condemned as occasions for "disorder and incitement," "driving one another to change masters," and the "rise of a factious and independent spirit." As the wardens of the Parisian guild of gold-and-silversmiths put it, "behind [their] pretended pious association . . . [the journeymen] met and plotted practices contrary to the good of the business of the Masters." Whenever journeymen appropriated the institutions and idioms of their betters, they did so to enhance their own social capital rather than promote the unity of their trades.[21]

The emergence of journeyman associations by no means required the presence of guilds. As early as 1285, the journeymen

20 Kaplan, "Réflexions," 48–56; *idem,* "La Lutte pour le contrôle du marché du travail à Paris au XVIIIe siècle," *Revue d'histoire moderne et contemporaine,* XXXVI (1989), 373–387; *British Parliamentary Papers,* IV (1825), 555; Donald C. Coleman, "Combinations of Capital and of Labour in the English Paper Industry, 1789–1825," *Economica,* XXI (1954), 43.

21 Malcolmson, "Workers' Combinations," 176; Lis and Soly, "Irresistible," 24–25; Rosser, "Crafts, Guilds," 26; Sewell, *Work and Revolution,* 32–37, 40–42; Kaplan, "Luxury," 296–297; Sandra Cavallo, "Conceptions of Poverty and Poor-Relief in Turin in the Second Half of

weavers of Rouen who gathered in the squares set aside for hiring were accused of affiliating. Wherever there are workers, there is "esprit de cabale," wrote a French commentator in the early eighteenth century. The journeymen's policing of their brothers reminded opportunists and rate busters of the virtues of solidarity. Benjamin Franklin was not the only overachieving compositor to have his type mixed by the "chapel ghost." The journeyman shipwright in Liverpool who engrossed more than his share of work was "drilled," or boycotted, by his fellow hands; as a result, he could not work at all. Paperworkers fined and beat wayward brothers, and composed circular letters to exclude those men who violated their standards. For journeymen in a wide variety of crafts, social solvency—their reputation and material security—turned on the defense of these expectations. In one set of trades, the rights and duties took the form of chips, in others, the maintenance of a venerable piece rate, and in yet another, a seat at the table of a master who did not tuck in his napkin until the journeymen joined him. Excluded from the formal craft communities, the journeymen fought for respect—a voice of their own in the determination of compensation and conditions. In England, journeymen petitioned Parliament and local magistrates because the Elizabethan Statute of Artificers granted justices in the counties the authority to establish wages. The journeymen tailors of London, for example, turned to the Middlesex justices in 1764 and gained a small concession. When their claims fell on deaf ears, journeymen usually relied on the noise and numbers of assembly, whether peaceful or riotous.[22]

Riot in the name of standards took many forms. Clothiers protested to Parliament in 1718 and 1724 about weavers who "threatened to pull down their houses and burn their work unless they would agree with their terms." In 1724, a petition to the House of Commons complained of "several riotous and tumultuous Clubs and Societies of Workmen" in Exeter. The "riotous"

---

the Eighteenth Century," in Stuart Woolf (ed.), *Domestic Strategies: Work and Family in France and Italy, 1600–1800* (Cambridge, 1991), 194.

22   Rosser, "Crafts, Guilds," 26; Kaplan, "Luxury," 293; Rule, "Property," 112; Rosenband, "Hiring and Firing at the Montgolfier Paper Mill," in Safley and Rosenband (eds.), *Workplace,* 229; George Rudé, *The Crowd in History: A Study of Popular Disturbances in France and England 1730–1848* (New York, 1964), 67.

men had set a wage for work in the woollen manufacture, and "hinder[ed]" any who dared to toil for less. The ritual hanging of effigies of stiff-necked masters was common. Sometimes indignant journeymen hoisted more than effigies: In 1763, the journeymen coopers of Liverpool hauled an unfortunate master around the city on a pole. Earlier, in Tiverton, exasperated woollen workers "carried several of the Masters on Poles, in a sort of mock Triumph." Such rough justice frequently accompanied the renewal of annual contracts or sudden changes in hours and rewards. Thus the Luddites' cry of "full fashioned work at the old fashioned price."[23]

When the fortunes of the whole trade were threatened, masters and journeymen temporarily linked arms in the streets. The defeat of a bill in 1765 to protect silk weaving from French competition brought the entire craft into London's alleys. They marched to Parliament under black flags and besieged Bedford House, the home of the duke who had blocked the bill. Still, this was a momentary alliance in a trade marked by bitter wage disputes: Two years earlier, 2,000 journeymen had smashed looms and burned a master in effigy. Similarly, in 259 strikes, mainly from 1780 to 1805, the master craftsmen from six German cities generally stayed apart from their protesting journeymen. Despite common trade interests, only 16 percent of these actions involved both masters and men.[24]

Masters and men did join in a different sort of crowd action, the food riot. Sparked by thin harvests, high prices, hoarding (or the popular impression of hoarding), these incidents entailed the seizure of flour and unmilled grain, their distribution at a just (traditional) price, and the pulling down of the mills and country houses of engrossers. Following an immemorial script, the crowd claimed not only the right to survive, but the right to perform tasks, such as the setting of a fair price, that the authorities had abandoned. In these heady hours, the divisions that separated large guildsmen and small, or masters and journeymen, disappeared. Vertical structures briefly dissolved into horizontal collaboration,

---

23 Hobsbawm, *Labouring Men*, 7–8; Malcolmson, "Workers' Combinations," 174–175; Rudé, *Crowd*, 69; Rule, "Property," 109.

24 Rudé, *Crowd*, 72–73; Jürgen Kocka, "Craft Traditions and the Labour Movement in Nineteenth-Century Germany," in Pat Thane, Geoffrey Crossick, and Roderick Floud (eds.), *The Power of the Past: Essays for Eric Hobsbawm* (Cambridge, 1984), 110–112.

but once the four-pound loaf was again affordable, masters and journeymen resumed their negotiations across a chasm of mistrust and contested meaning.[25]

In 1751, the proprietors, tenants, and journeymen of the royal manufactory of paper in Angoumois reached a collective agreement. Despite the elevated title of the linked mills that formed the *manufacture royale,* the local industry had fallen on hard times. During the previous eighty years, more than sixty mills had slipped into "total ruin." To ensure the survival of the remaining enterprises, masters and workers came to an elaborate accord about hours, output, recruitment, and above all, the nourishment of the men. In light of the deep differences that separated them, nothing could be left to chance.[26]

Capital-intensive and dependent on a centuries-old division of labor, papermaking had never been organized in craft communities. Still, the trade's idiom and social classification resembled those of the guilded crafts. The bosses denounced the journeymen's conventions as "abuses," and the journeymen struggled to maintain their social capital and material solvency. Perhaps the masters of Angoumois assumed that a period of "forced unemployment," due primarily to the scarcity of raw materials, had broken the journeymen's resolve. They pressed for concessions across a broad range of "practices and usages." In response, the workers headed to the hamlet of La Couronne and the cabaret of the widow Jeanne Barrière, where they waited out the bosses. Four months later, a compact was signed. It reflected the vibrant associational life of the shopfloor, and the norms and reciprocities that divided journeymen and masters.[27]

Ritual and symbolic capital figured in the bargaining, but largely as adjuncts to meat-and-potatoes issues. In exchange for "fat wages," the bosses would no longer feed the journeymen.

25 The literature about bread riots is enormous. Some useful entry points are John Bohstedt, *Riots and Community Politics in England and Wales, 1790–1810* (Cambridge, Mass., 1983); Cynthia Bouton, *The Flour War: Gender, Class, and Community in Late Ancien Régime French Society* (University Park, 1993); Rudé, *Crowd*, 108–122; Edward P. Thompson, *Customs in Common* (New York, 1991), 185–258; Louise Tilly, "The Food Riot as a Form of Political Conflict in France," *Journal of Interdisciplinary History*, II (1971), 23–57.
26 Alexandre Nicolaï, "La Papeterie en Angoumois au XVIIIe siècle: Pierre Vantongeren et la grève des ouvriers compagnons papetiers de 1751," in *Contribution à l'histoire de la papeterie en France* (Grenoble, 1945), X, 12–22.
27 *Ibid.*, 13, 15.

The traditional banquets that celebrated a move up the ladder of skill, an apprentice's arrival at the journeymen's table, or the death of a paperworker were reduced to toasts. Rather than the upwardly mobile apprentice or journeyman contributing the princely sum of 150 livres to the workers' treasury, he would now offer the meager fee of 10 livres. Or so the masters wished to believe.[28]

The journeymen allowed their bosses to select apprentices without roots in the craft's worker dynasties. But ceding control over recruitment did not end the journeymen's mastery of shop culture. Apprentices had to reward the veteran hands each month for their time and pains as teachers. Time mattered in this art, so the compact reaffirmed the traditional formulas for daily output and *bâtards,* or overtime work. For their part, the bosses retained their customary right to penalize the journeyman who "quit work for debauchery, caprice or otherwise." Moreover, the masters pledged to avoid pressing the journeymen by cutting the price of their wares. This accord, ostensibly rich in concession and collaboration, in reality permitted both sides to conserve essential symbols and ties, and hence their social capital.[29]

For many masters, negotiation with journeymen implied an unacceptable equality, a levelling that erased proper distinctions. To offset their dependency on the workers' skill and labor power, the masters formed counter-combinations—informal associations among themselves to reduce wages and effectively subordinate the journeymen. In the late fourteenth century, the tailors' guilds of twenty-eight towns along the Upper Rhine banded together to set wages and blackball any journeyman who had abandoned his former boss. By 1383, the smiths of several German towns and cities had "reached an agreement to cope with the demands of their journeymen." Three centuries later, the master clothiers of nine Dutch cities affiliated to standardize wages and exclude subversive hands. Finally, the hatters of Mechelen, in the Austrian Netherlands, endorsed a plan in 1764 to cease poaching journeymen with high wages, and to hire only those itinerants who possessed written discharges.[30]

---

28 *Ibid.,* 16–17, 19–20.
29 *Ibid.,* 17–18, 22.
30 Lis and Soly, "Irresistible," 40, 42–43.

Maintaining such unity among the masters, however, proved difficult. Attentive to their immediate interests, large and small producers clashed over appropriate wage rates and the distribution of journeymen. As John Fielding explained in 1760, London's master tailors had "repeatedly endeavoured to break and suppress the combinations of their journeymen." But a wage dispute provided the most substantial tailors with a chance to expand their shops at the expense of the lesser masters. The big employers "complied" with the journeymen's "exorbitant demands . . . while many other masters have had a total stop put to their business." The defeat of the master tailors' counter-combination, Fielding reasoned, was "due to the infidelity of the masters themselves to each other." With even their informal affiliations hobbled by internal division and conflicting interests, masters in many crafts turned to the state to subordinate the ungovernable journeymen.[31]

In 1298, London's carpenters agreed among themselves to disregard a city ordinance that reduced their wages. According to a regulation proclaimed in the Holy Roman Empire in 1530, journeymen were not to administer justice to their brothers or decamp from workshops en masse. Such attempts to domesticate journeymen and restrict their wages frequently followed petitions by their employers, who linked "excessive" wages with social disorder and economic decadence. Consequently, in 1424, the English Parliament outlawed "congregations and confederacies" of masons that threatened to subvert the "good course and effect of the statutes of labourers." In a society of orders, the journeymen's proper station mixed sweat and obedience. When they dared to spend or shore up their social capital, to voice their concerns or act collectively, they encountered a rash of ordinances, statutes, and prescriptions. From 1721 through 1792, seven anti-combination acts banned association in twenty English trades. But the journeymen usually found ways to maintain their standards. For example, in 1721 Parliament proscribed combinations among the tailors of London and Westminster. Almost half a century later, however, the House of Commons had to enact a second statute aimed at the "many subtil devices" that enabled the tailors to evade the regulations.[32]

---

31 *Ibid.,* 45.
32 *Ibid.,* 27, 35; Orth, "English Combination Acts," 179, 180 (table), 184.

The Combination Acts revealed the complicity of the state in the masters' designs, and the limit of the government's capacity to aid producers dependent on their journeymen's skill. In 1837, a Parliamentary committee heard the testimony of James Low, a paper manufacturer, who was asked if he was "formerly a good deal at the mercy of [his] men." Low replied that before the machine transformed his trade, the bosses "were very much at the mercy of the men, because they had a very powerful club, and were in fact the masters." In 1796, an English Parliament terrified by the French Revolution learned that "frequent Conspiracies" among the journeymen paperworkers dated from 1789. The petitioners warned that the paperworkers aggressively pursued "a general Increase of their Wages" and prevented the "Employment of *North Britons*," who willingly toiled for less. The results of a wage hike, said the aggrieved manufacturers, would be disastrous: "[A]n Advance in the Price of Paper . . . would most effectually injure the Exportation of that Article to Foreign Parts." It was almost as if the master papermakers were reciting a mantra: Combinations among the workers yielded high wages, diminished trade, and fomented insubordination, now with a revolutionary edge. The journeymen's association had to be broken.[33]

The key to the workers' power was their general fund—hard capital in support of social. Once all the journeymen at a particular mill deserted, "the other Journeymen [were] prohibited from applying for Work at that Mill till the Master [was] brought to Compliance." Of course, the men who had "thrown themselves out of Employ" drew sustenance from the general fund. If the master brought charges, the striking workers fled, and "it would be at least Nine or Twelve Months before they could be brought to Trial." Exhausted, the manufacturers clamored for a law to divest the journeymen of their capacity to organize.[34]

The statute was enacted in 1796, and served as the inspiration for the act of 1799 that barred combinations in all crafts. The legislators complained that the paperworkers, like the tailors seventy-five years earlier, had inscribed their norms and reciprocities in their own "contracts, covenants, and agreements." Whether these compacts were "in writing or not in writing," the state

33 "Report from the Select Committee on Fourdrinier's Patent," *British Parliamentary Papers,* XX (1837), 12; "Petition," *Journals of the House of Commons,* LI (1796), April 19, 1796, 585.
34 "Petition," April 19, 1796, 585.

declared them all null and void. It outlawed worker accords to increase wages, shorten hours, reduce output, exclude (uninitiated) men from the mills, or coerce veteran hands to quit a particular master. The journeyman who summoned his fellows to assemble risked imprisonment; so did the man who collected funds for the workers' hoard. To ensure that the journeymen put in a full day, this ode to individualism reached back for a mercantilist theme and prescribed precise quotas. Trials of offenders were to be held within a month of the master's complaint. The justices of the peace were empowered to try the accused in their absence and free from penalty any journeyman who bore witness against his brother. Civic engagement by journeymen paperworkers, at least in institutions of their own, was unwelcome by the governors of fin-de-siècle England. Through the centuries, the question always was whose social capital, applied to what ends, against which forces and ideologies of resistance.[35]

Despite the Combination Act, the paperworkers' society continued to aid the journeymen who abandoned their masters "for wages or customs." In 1801, the journeymen secured a general increase in pay. In response, twenty-three manufacturers joined forces as "The Society of Master Paper-Makers of the Counties of Kent and Surrey, associated for the Purpose of resisting the illegal Combinations amongst the Journeymen Paper-Makers." Their counter-combination was no more legal than the workers' association, but these men of the market had tired of the journeymen's "*adoption* of a *regular system* of *constant encroachment* on the *fair* and *established* customs and usages of the trade."[36]

In 1803, the manufacturers extended their alliance across Great Britain, but conflicting interests splintered their unity. Accused of raising the wages of their own hands, two Hampshire employers vowed to avoid "all meetings whatsoever [of the manufacturers] thinking it the surest Mode of being on the best of terms with the trade." Meanwhile, the Kentish masters established company unions, in the form of funds at each mill for the relief of journeymen burdened by sickness, misfortune, or the rigors of tramping. But this strategy had the same limited prospects as the anti-combination acts. When asked about his journeymen's reac-

35   36 Geo. III, c. 3 (May 18, 1796). See Danby Pickering (ed.), *The Statutes at Large* (Cambridge), XL, 813–816.
36   Coleman, "Capital and Labour," 44 (italics in original).

tion to the repeal of the general Combination Act in 1824, one paper manufacturer answered, "I think upon the whole they knew very little about the laws; I never heard any thing said of them."[37]

Across the Channel, the French Republic issued a fresh decree concerning its insubordinate paperworkers. Despite the different political setting, the edict of 16 Fructidor, year IV (September 2, 1796), mirrored the Combination Act of the same year. Once again, the paperworkers' custom was associated with commercial distress, wage pressure, and general unruliness. To "liberate commerce, industry, and the right of property" from the workers' "malevolence," the French state intended "to suppress" the journeyman's coterie. It barred coalitions among the journeymen of several mills, circular letters, and placards that menaced "foreign" (unknown) workers, as well as the convocations at which paperworkers set minimum wages. Manufacturers were henceforth free to choose the apprentices and veterans that they desired in the numbers that they needed, without interference by the workers. Fines levied by the journeymen against their mates or bosses would be treated as "common theft." As a result, practices "contrary to public order," such as the "absolute cessation" of work, would cease. Wages were to be negotiated on the basis of the "actual workday" rather than stale "customs," said the draftsmen of the decree. But these customs reflected shared skills and expectations, cold nights on the road, and the warmth of a welcoming inn. That they had hardened into transnational patterns of mutuality and self-sufficiency partially explains the similarity of the English and French anti-combination acts. The rest can be accounted for by the rulers' (and masters') common assumptions about journeymen and the need to domesticate them. Accordingly, the journeymen's accumulation of social capital did not integrate them into any polity other than their own. Small wonder that they defended their little republics so tenaciously in Revolutionary France, as in William Pitt's England.[38]

Establishing proper discipline in their shops was not enough for the improving manufacturers of the eighteenth century. They wanted more than steady, assiduous men; they longed for malleable hands. They intended to overthrow the rule of thumb with

37 Ibid., 47; testimony of Thomas Gardner, British Parliamentary Papers, IV (1825), 599.
38 "Arrêté du Directoire exécutif, contenant règlement pour la police des papeteries," F[12] 2278, AN.

rationalized, even scientized, systems of production. Such reform entailed much more than acquainting journeymen with a new rhythm of work or a new bundle of incentives. Rather, men like Wedgwood dreamed of controlling and demystifying skill, thereby ending the transfer of the workers' culture from father to son, journeyman to apprentice, and tramping artisan to settled employees. As a leading French papermaker put it, "vicious routine" was at the heart of the journeymen's *"esprit de corps."* Hence, he and his family, the Montgolfiers, refused to tolerate the journeymen's custom and thereby provoked a strike, locked out the veterans, and, in 1781, had a mill teeming with fresh, young faces. Cut off from the conventions of their craft and assigned carefully engineered tasks, these youngsters would mature, the masters imagined, into a novel sort of disciplined worker. Vertical loyalties and a new probity would replace horizontal links. This program would have impressed the collusive master papermakers of Kent, who believed that "the preservation of their existence as Manufacturers" turned on their access to raw, unspoiled men.[39]

Samuel Bentham, the designer of the panopticon, applied similar principles in England's dockyards. Appointed inspector general of the Naval Works in 1795, he redefined both the tasks and culture of shipbuilding. According to his widow, Bentham "began by classing the several *operations* requisite in the shaping and working up of materials of whatever kind, wholly disregarding the customary artificial arrangement according to trades." He transformed both the machinery and organization of production "without regard to the popular divisions of trades." He proposed to deepen the pool of apprentices to drown the journeymen's association: "It is well known," he argued, "that an increase of the number of workpeople in any business is the most effectual bar to combinations." In 1801, he introduced a modest premium in place of chips, reducing custom and symbolic capital to a few pence. He and improvers like him were even less hospitable to

---

39 Sewell, "Visions of Labor: Illustrations of the Mechanical Arts before, in, and after Diderot's *Encyclopédie,*" in Kaplan and Cynthia Koepp (eds.), *Work in France: Representations, Meaning, Organization, and Practice* (Ithaca, 1986), 268–279; C 143, document 55, Archives départementales de l'Ardèche. Etienne Montgolfier's claim was a familiar theme in the upper reaches of late eighteenth-century French manufacturing. Rosenband, "Hiring," 231–232; Thomas Balston, *William Balston: Paper Maker, 1759–1849* (London, 1954), 161.

the journeymen's conventions than the traditional masters who longed for nothing more than docile workers.[40]

Not every trade, however, offered prospects for thoroughgoing reform. Sometimes tools and techniques were too intricate, or journeymen proved too guileful or resolute. For Nicolas-Louis Robert, a foreman in an important French paper mill, the answer lay in machinery. He had grown "impatient with the irascibility and ill temper of the workers." Robert's papermaking machine, patented in 1799, was spurred more by a desire to end "this constant wrangling and discord" than by the need for cheap, abundant paper. The device certainly shifted the balance between masters and men. When Low was asked in 1837 if the machine "has in a great measure done away with the means of combination," he answered, "Yes, in the machine mills it has done away with it; but the old system still exists in the other mills." Social capital had given way to fixed, enduring only at the margin of the industry, like the journeymen it bound together.[41]

At the close of the eighteenth century, however, most manufacture still depended on the sweat, skill, and culture of masters and journeymen. Revelry and speeches spiced the entry of a compositor into the company of journeymen printers in Old Regime Paris. He learned that his trade was "a free and republican territory in which everything is permitted; live as you like but be an *honnête homme,* no hypocrisy." An *honnête homme* observed the wage rate and never betrayed his mates. It was this "system of independence" among the journeymen, explained the master bakers and hatters of Paris, that made the reforms of Anne-Robert-Jacques Turgot so dangerous. In 1776, Turgot used his office as controller general to abolish the guilds in France. He hoped to usher in a natural order of production, in which artificial privilege vanished and talent received its just rewards. To the guildsmen, this edict was simply another source of turmoil. The dyers feared that the journeymen would grasp the opportunity "to abandon their masters in order to become masters themselves." Others worried that the journeyman would become a "cruel usurper," or that the workers would cabal in "tumultuous and seditious assemblies." In fact, Turgot's reform was repealed within the year, but

---

40 Linebaugh, *London Hanged,* 396–400.
41 Dard Hunter, *Papermaking: The History and Technique of an Ancient Craft* (New York, 1978; 2d ed.), 343; "Fourdrinier's Patent," *British Parliamentary Papers,* XX (1837), 12.

the masters' anxieties underscored their sense of the interests that divided each of the crafts, the same lesson that the printers' ritual instilled in their new mates.[42]

To further their interests, the masters formed craft communities and counter-combinations, while the journeymen formed combinations and counter-communities. Large guildsmen exploited lesser masters and journeymen, and journeymen exploited the breaches between the masters. Aggressive and vulnerable at once, masters and journeymen looked after their interests in unstable yet inelastic economies. Presumed legacies of collaboration mattered less than current prospects or alliances. Interest and rank overlapped imperfectly, sometimes splintering craft communities or the solidarity of journeymen. Still, in an early modern Europe of orders and closely defined status, conflict between men of separate ranks outweighed collaboration. Journeymen turned to magistrates to enforce their rights, but they remained apart from the states and municipalities that generally sided with their masters. They trusted bonds forged among themselves to preserve and extend their norms and prerogatives, and to block and domesticate their masters' initiatives. Thus, they prepared the ground for both the trade unions and informal collective actions of succeeding generations. The politically efficacious legacy that their nineteenth-century heirs seized was a rough-and-ready, nondeferential pursuit of their own interests. They did so through inherited ties and fresh associations of their own making. They combined self-sufficiency and mutual assistance in ways that alarmed their betters and the state, thereby attracting the attention of both. Not until the extinction of formal orders and privilege, the repeal of such inequities as the Combination Acts, and socioeconomic reform, would journeymen and workers entrust much of their social solvency to the state, if they ever did.

42 Robert Darnton, *The Literary Underground of the Old Regime* (Cambridge, Mass., 1982), 161; Kaplan, "Social Classification and Representation in the Corporate World of Eighteenth-Century France: Turgot's 'Carnival,'" in Kaplan and Koepp (eds.), *Work in France*, 188–190.

Marjorie K. McIntosh

The Diversity of Social Capital in English Communities, 1300–1640 (with a Glance at Modern Nigeria)

Social capital was produced by many types of human interaction in the villages and market centers of later medieval and early modern England. Each of these communities contained at least a few formal organizations that performed legal, economic, religious, and/or charitable functions. Their activities were shaped by locally influential people, mainly men, who possessed no great wealth or status when viewed from the national level but were economically self-sufficient—working from 20 to 100 acres of land or operating as craftspeople—and respected by their neighbors. The social capital generated by these organizations was of benefit not only to their own members but also externally. It was transportable and convertible, able to be carried from one group or setting to another, and it contributed to the growth of the lateral and vertical ties (both institutional and ideological) that were necessary to the emergence of a national state. Although most of these bodies were not voluntary organizations, they, and the social capital that they created, were similar to the associations studied in most of the other essays in this volume, including their implicit emphasis on men. This resemblance emphasizes that the history of community institutions that produced beneficial social capital must be traced far beyond the emergence of civil society in the eighteenth century and beyond even the Renaissance Italian city-states.[1]

A different form of social capital was generated by the completely informal and loosely defined networks of friendship,

Marjorie K. McIntosh is Professor of History, University of Colorado, Boulder. She is the author of *A Community Transformed: The Manor and Liberty of Havering, 1500–1620* (Cambridge, 1991); *Controlling Misbehavior in England, 1370–1600* (Cambridge, 1998).

The author would like to thank Peter Temin for his comments about the initial version of this article, given at the conference, "Patterns of Social Capital: Stability and Change in Comparative Perspective," Harvard University, December 4–6, 1997, and for his thoughtful suggestions about the revised version. The author is also grateful to her colleagues, Chidiebere Nwaubani and Adeleke Adeeko, for invaluable advice.

1 The working definition of *social capital* in this essay follows Robert D. Putnam's emphasis on features like the "trust, norms, and networks" produced by social organization in *Making Democracy Work: Civil Traditions in Modern Italy* (Princeton, 1993), 167.

neighborliness, and assistance that operated alongside these organizations. In the unstructured reciprocal systems, people attempted to provide some form of insurance for themselves by sharing information with their friends and neighbors, contributing their own time and labor to their needs, and giving or loaning goods or money. In so doing, they built up a pool of social (and implicitly economic) credit upon which they could draw in the future if they ran into hard times. Networks like these, which rested upon the idea that extra wealth should be distributed socially among the group as an investment for the future rather than used in more specifically economic terms for individual profit, are found in diverse historical periods and contexts. They are, however, difficult to study since they have left few historical records, and the problem is exacerbated when we look at women's experience.

The study of female social networks requires a broader analysis of social capital than usual in several respects. In considering how the social capital produced by organizations affects the wider community, traditional forms of assessment based upon male organizations have concentrated upon how social capital contributed directly to political and economic growth through facilitating shared ideas and interactions at a higher or public level. Reference to those standards alone when examining women's informal credit systems would force the conclusion that although the social capital produced by these groups had great value for their own members, it had only limited external benefit and, in some cases, worked to restrict political or economic development. Yet, consideration of women's roles within the household, especially their impact upon the attitudes of the next generation, suggests other ways of assessing the impact of social capital. In parallel terms, an anthropologically derived definition of social capital proves a more useful analytical tool than one shaped by the concerns of sociology and political science when exploring female social credit systems.

To illustrate the diversity of social capital, this article first examines the two types of social interaction and their resulting capital, as they operated in England between 1300 and 1640—a period of transition from medieval to early modern forms of political, economic, social, cultural, and religious activity. We then take a brief look at southern Nigerian market women between

1900 and 1960, as an example of cross-cultural similarities in female networks of social credit. The central questions throughout this investigation are, How is social capital produced and by whom? How is it affected by changes in the wider economy and society? What utility does it have for the participants in associations and for the broader community? and How can we best analyze it? In the case of informal social networks, because altered conditions of material life and altered gender definitions created tension between the traditional distributive/collective ethic that supported group interactions and newer profit-oriented, individualistic values, we must examine the ideological expectations and cultural mechanisms—including accusations of witchcraft—that reinforced or challenged female credit systems in England and Nigeria.

FORMAL ORGANIZATIONS AND SOCIAL CAPITAL IN ENGLISH LOCAL COMMUNITIES   In English villages and market centers—places with fewer than 3,000 inhabitants—a variety of institutions brought together some of the residents on a regular basis to address problems of common concern. Although these associations operated within different contexts and had different specific goals, they all generated social capital that was of use not only to their own members but also to the broader community. At the highest level, their interactions contributed to the growth of shared legal/political institutions and a common ideology across the country as a whole, despite the fact that considerable social pressure was created during the period from 1300 to 1640 by rapid demographic change, the early stages of agrarian and mercantile capitalism, and religious and political controversy. These institutions and the social capital that they generated closely resemble the patterns described in other settings, with the exception that most English organizations were public and nonvoluntary: Participation was required of men who had been elected to office. It is not clear why political scientists have placed such emphasis upon voluntary organizations in their study of social capital; the connection seems by no means necessary. We must recognize, moreover, that many people who were actively involved in groups working toward broader community goals also manifested a strong sense of individual identity and considerable economic competitiveness. There was no inherent contradiction in early modern England—or elsewhere—between personal autonomy and cooperation based on common values.[2]

Local secular courts performed a range of legal, administrative, economic, and social functions. The residents of villages and many market centers participated in manor courts, and some smaller towns had their own borough courts. These bodies, which met at least three times per year and usually more often, had three main duties: to provide a forum in which disputes between local people could be resolved; to enforce the rights of the lord of the manor or the borough's government, requiring its members to accept or, at least, accommodate themselves to the concept of authority; and to address issues of wider concern to the community, such as people's tendency to let their animals onto the common fields beyond the permitted seasons.[3]

Some local courts, those with "leet" jurisdiction, had additional obligations. Operating through juries of responsible men who reported problems that threatened the public good, they maintained order, punishing those who broke the peace through assaults, robberies, or other violent offenses. They performed economic functions as well, supervising the production of food and drink and ensuring that these items were of proper quality, size, and cost. In some periods and settings, the jurors exceeded their formal authority to address social problems as well. They reported people who disrupted local tranquillity by spreading malicious gossip, wandering around at night without cause, or listening to their neighbors' private conversations while hidden under the eaves of their houses. They might be troubled by such

---

2 Although urbanization was increasing by the latter part of this period, England remained an overwhelmingly rural country into the eighteenth century. Only thirty-two towns had populations of more than 3,000 or so, and only London contained more than 25,000 between 1300 and 1700, although there were thousands of villages (by c. 1600, England and Wales contained c. 9,000 parishes, each of which normally served one village or smaller town), and c. 715 communities had markets. See McIntosh, *Controlling Misbehavior in England, 1370–1600* (Cambridge, 1998), 25. For competition and individualism, see, for example, *idem, Autonomy and Community: The Royal Manor of Havering, 1200–1500* (Cambridge, 1986); for the same combination in northern Italy and among the Igbo in Nigeria, see Putnam, *Making Democracy Work,* and Simon Ottenberg, "Ibo Receptivity to Change," in William R. Bascom and Melville J. Herskovits (eds.), *Continuity and Change in African Cultures* (Chicago, 1959), 130–143. All three settings were characterized by large amounts of social capital.

3 For this paragraph and the two following, see McIntosh, *Controlling Misbehavior,* esp. 34–41, 54–107.

violations of good order, control, and discipline as sexual misbehavior, rowdy drinking, or excessive betting at alehouses, and they
sometimes addressed the problems associated with poverty—taking wood from the common hedges for use as fuel, or adding to
the number of people who qualified for poor relief by allowing
vagrants or other newcomers to live as subtenants in someone's
cottage.

Participation in these courts bound together the dominant
local families who defined standards of conduct and decided
whom and what to report; the surprisingly low level of objection
on the part of those accused of misbehavior suggests that most
people subject to the courts' jurisdiction were willing to accept
their authority. All of the functions of these courts were present,
and indeed magnified, in the larger towns, where the power of
more formal governmental bodies was commonly reinforced by
economically based craft or merchant guilds. By the later medieval
period, English people were long accustomed to the rule of law
and order, imposed, to a large extent, by the leading members of
their own communities.

Another set of organizations operated within a religious
sphere. Most villages and market centers shared boundaries with
a parish, in which elected lay officials carried out a range of
spiritual and social functions. The churchwardens and sidesmen
were responsible for the physical maintenance of the laity's portion
of the parish church. To raise the necessary funds, which might
be considerable if the church needed major repair or if an expansion or modernization were planned, parish officials prior to the
Reformation employed diverse techniques: putting on "church
ales," in which ale was produced gratis in large quantities and then
sold at a communal drinking session for the benefit of the church;
allowing wealthier members of the congregation to be buried
within the church itself, rather than in the graveyard, in return
for a contribution to parish funds; soliciting large donations from
local lords, gentlemen, or prosperous merchants; or, if all else
failed, imposing a church rate or tax upon the parishioners. In
some pre-Reformation parishes, the churchwardens also hired
secondary priests and/or parish clerks to supplement the duties
performed by the official incumbent, including teaching local
children. At least once each year, the churchwardens and sidesmen
were required to submit a report to the church courts held by

their bishop or his representative. In their statement they had to list any offenses committed by their priest/minister or by other members of the congregation in spiritual and many social areas, including working on Sunday or holy days, misbehaving sexually, and living apart from one's spouse. The church courts also heard private suits dealing with such issues as marriages that had been promised but not completed, defamation, and disputed wills. Since the people chosen as parish officials were likely to serve as jurors or officers in the local secular courts too, their experience in one setting was readily applicable to the other.[4]

Up until the Reformation, many communities contained voluntary religious organizations as well. Some had lay fraternities or guilds devoted to the worship of a particular saint. In these fraternities, the members paid small sums to support candles or other forms of respect before an image of their saint in the church; wealthier groups might build a side chapel onto the parish church in his/her honor. They normally held a procession and grand feast on their saint's day each year, and, in some cases, they provided assistance to their own members who fell into need during an emergency or old age. The religious fraternities were usually open to women as well as men, and some parts of the country had separate guilds exclusively for women. Most of the larger, more powerful fraternities attempted to limit conflict between their members by insisting that disputes be arbitrated within the guild itself, and a number of them insisted upon appropriate social conduct by their members. In another pattern, some parishes, especially in the south and southwest of England, had guilds organized by gender and marital status or age that raised money for their church, sometimes through dramatic performances. The unmarried women's guild might present the Maid Marian play on May Day, the young men's guild the Robin Hood play, and the senior men's guild the Saint George and the Dragon play.[5]

4 See, for example, Beat A. Kümin, *The Shaping of a Community: The Rise and Reformation of the English Parish, c. 1400–1560* (Brookfield, Vt., 1996); Richard M. Wunderli, *London Church Courts and Society on the Eve of the Reformation* (Cambridge, Mass., 1981); Martin Ingram, *Church Courts, Sex and Marriage in England, 1570–1640* (Cambridge, 1987); for a local example, McIntosh, *A Community Transformed*, 219–257.
5 See, for example, Barbara A. Hanawalt, "Keepers of the Lights: Late Medieval Parish Gilds," *Journal of Medieval and Renaissance Studies*, XIV (1984), 21–37; Ben R. McRee, "Religious Gilds and Regulation of Behavior in Late Medieval Towns," in Joel Rosenthal

A final category of institution filled charitable functions, either on a voluntary basis or as mandated by the law. Throughout these centuries, a body of men functioning as private trustees could hold property for philanthropical purposes, such as a hospital or almshouse for the elderly poor or a school for local boys. Villages or towns located at the point where a major road crossed a large river might have bridgewardens, who used the income from a stock of land and animals donated over time to pay for the maintence of the bridge, which was essential to local trade and communication. From the 1550s onward, communities began to experiment with publicly supported systems of poor relief, financed by compulsory taxes imposed upon more prosperous members of the parish. In 1598 and 1601, Parliament extended these efforts to all parishes in the country, which, henceforth, were required to tax themselves in order to provide basic food, clothing, and shelter to those people unable to labor for their own support. The collectors and overseers of the poor who gathered and distributed this money were often men active in the secular courts and parish groups.[6]

The members of these local organizations were linked to their counterparts in other communities and to higher authorities through the meetings of legal and religious institutions at the county or diocesan level. The sessions of the peace, held every three months by the justices of the peace, required each area to send a jury of local men to report on certain kinds of problems. The assize justices who travelled from the capital to preside over felony trials summoned witnesses and assembled county-wide juries to reach judgment. The bishop, or his dean or subdean, moved in circuit through the larger communities in their dioceses, calling upon lay parish officials to deliver their reports and holding sessions of their ecclesiastical courts. At all of these gatherings, local leaders met their peers from other places and interacted with representatives of the state and church. In ideological terms, they

and Colin Richmond (eds.), *People, Politics and Community in the Later Middle Ages* (Gloucester, 1987), 108–122; Katherine L. French, "'To Free Them from Binding': Women in the Late Medieval English Parish," *Journal of Interdisciplinary History*, XXVII (1997), 387–412; Joanna Mattingly, "The Medieval Parish Guilds of Cornwall," *Journal of the Royal Institution of Cornwall*, X (1989), 290–329; David Wiles, *The Early Plays of Robin Hood* (Cambridge, 1981).
6   McIntosh, *Controlling Misbehavior*, 134–135; idem, "Local Responses to the Poor in Late Medieval and Tudor England," *Continuity and Change*, III (1988), 209–245.

were exposed to rhetorical statements about secular and religious problems and goals prepared by Parliament, the Crown or Privy Council, and the leading bishops.[7]

The formal institutions active within England's smaller communities generated considerable social capital, regardless of whether participation in them was obligatory or voluntary. The internal returns—the benefits accruing to the participants themselves—included the creation of personal networks based upon respect, trust, and shared experience that comprised people beyond their own families, immediate neighbors, and personal friends. Thus, participants had numerous contacts to whom they could turn for advice, assistance, or partnership when needed, regardless of the specific issue at hand. Members of local organizations also gained information about their community and area that might assist them economically or legally. Experience with large financial issues, such as the maintenance of a parish church or a bridge, could prove valuable personally, as could social/legal skills acquired through dealing with people of all ranks and statuses.

Such organizations also produced external benefits for their villages and towns. Men who served as jurors or officers in the secular courts or in religious or charitable bodies learned to work cooperatively as leaders, developing public mechanisms through which disagreement could be handled: They both punished violence and encouraged their neighbors to use the courts for private suits. Their discussion of local problems promoted shared norms and a conception of the public good, as evident, for instance, in the idea that since individual economic and social transgressions might harm the whole community, they could legitimately be punished by the courts. Further, since the social capital acquired in one context could be applied to other local institutions, it was convertible and transportable. All of these forms of social capital helped communities to function more effectively at an official level.

Local institutions built more far-reaching social, institutional, and ideological bridges as well. Although the inhabitants of a given region of England might appear similar to outsiders, suggesting that it would be easy to develop close ties between them, com-

7 McIntosh, *Controlling Misbehavior*, 23–45, 127–136, 186–208.

munities were often sharply divided from their neighbors on the basis of historically divergent patterns of settlement and local traditions. Hence, social capital that created trust and a sense of common identity among them was of great value. Such benefits were produced when local leaders met with people from other places and found that they faced the same kinds of problems; discussion of public issues, in turn, promoted the formation and articulation of shared norms.

Likewise, the social/cultural gap between local leaders and people of higher status that formed an obstacle to vertical integration was lessened by the social capital generated through cooperation in institutions at the county or diocesan level. Villagers and townsmen who came before those bodies were increasingly encouraged to align their own values with those expressed by the government and church as part of a broader English ideology. Thus, locally generated social capital contributed to the growth of an English national state in two ways: by promoting lateral interactions and common values between communities and regions, and by integrating the middling and upper strata of society vertically into a more cohesive unit with common institutions and a shared definition of themselves as a nation.[8]

Although this account has emphasized the benefits of the social capital produced by locally dominant families, a more negative component was present as well. Premodern English towns and villages were not uniform and integrated bodies, but rather comprised a range of overlapping sub-communities. Considerable tension could exist between the economically comfortable and generally respectable men who controlled local institutions and those people placed into subordinate roles because they were poor, young, female, recently immigrated, or disorderly. When local leaders operated within formal organizations, it was unlikely that the social capital that they produced would extend beyond their own membership to those excluded from power. To the contrary, the actions of authority figures and the personal advantages that they gained from their positions might well be resented by others. Analysis of social capital must pay closer attention to its limited ability to spread between the various groupings within a given

8   See McIntosh, "Response," in the symposium about McIntosh, *Controlling Misbehavior*, in *Journal of British Studies*, XXXVII (1998), 291–305, which includes a fuller discussion of the development of a national state.

community, recognizing that the functioning of institutions can promote hostility and division, as well as social integration.

A different type of social capital was produced by the loosely defined networks of reciprocal social credit that flourished in these same communities. Found at all levels of society, such systems were especially important to groups that lacked access to institutionalized power, serving as a means of protecting their members against unexpected difficulty. By establishing a wide range of positive contacts, individuals could create what has been described as a "problem-anchored helping network," permitting them to turn to others within their systems of reciprocal exchange for advice or assistance. Networks of mutual obligation varied in size, and those included had diverse relationships to each other. Most commonly the contacts were lateral, involving family or kin, neighbors, co-workers, or friends; vertically defined relationships might be involved as well, such as those with landlords or employers. In early modern Europe, such networks of self-help and mutual support played a key role in the lives of the laboring poor; members were able "to maintain independence and to avoid becoming a burden on others by accumulating enough 'social capital' which could be exchanged for instrumental help or advice."[9]

Webs of affiliation were of particular importance for women of lower, or even middling, rank, offering one of the few ways whereby they could attempt to provide some kind of economic security for themselves and their children. If a woman's husband died or left her, or if normal sources of household income were otherwise disrupted, she might be forced to draw upon informal kinds of aid. To accumulate a pool of social credit, held in reserve in case of need, women could share food with others, loan goods or money, bestow gifts when their income was more than required for immediate consumption, tend a neighbor during illness, or take in a needy relative or an orphaned child. Women's social-credit networks flourished in communities characterized by several

9 Robert Jütte, *Poverty and Deviance in Early Modern Europe* (Cambridge, 1994), 84, citing the sociologist Donald Warren without specific reference, and 85, citing Martin Dinges, "Self-Help, Assistance, and the Poor in Early Modern France," paper presented at the conference, "International Perspectives on Self-Help," Lancaster, England, July 1991.

common features: the absence of an effective governmental system that provided social security to those in need, social patterns that did not require that the extended family take care of all its members, limited opportunities for individual advancement through reinvestment of excess income, and a breakdown of older patterns that emphasized family or communal values in favor of a more individually focused and profit-oriented system.

Such informal associations are inherently difficult for historians and sociologists to study. Unorganized interactions leave no records of their own and are normally mentioned only indirectly in other kinds of sources. Even modern studies, in which the volume of evidence from survey research is so much greater, reveal more about structured institutions with officers, membership lists, and regular meetings than about informal social gatherings. Only recently, for example, has earlier research on declining community involvement and its deleterious impact upon democratic institutions, based solely upon participation in formal organizations, been expanded and, in some cases, modified by consideration of such activities as card playing with friends or—in the British context—going to a pub. Since studying networks of social credit among lower-status women in the past is particularly challenging, given the dearth of explicit documentation, we must look for indirect signs of their existence in historical sources and literary texts.[10]

Later medieval and early modern England provides some information about how female networks of mutual assistance operated. In this setting, we can examine the qualities that caused women to be respected and valued and how social attitudes affected women's participation in social networks; we can also see what kinds of pressure tended to enforce or undermine informal female associations and how ideas about women's nature and roles

10   Newer analyses of social capital include Putnam's opening comments at the conference, "Patterns of Social Capital: "Stability and Change in Comparative Perspective," Harvard University, December 4, 1997, and Peter A. Hall, "Social Capital in Britain," paper presented at the Bertelsmann Stiftung workshop on social capital, Berlin, June, 1997. Some scholars, including many Africanists, feel that because history and literary criticism employ different types of evidence and have developed distinct methods of analysis, historians ought not use fiction or drama as a source of information about the past. I am persuaded, however, that we profit by trying to break down the separation between scholarly fields. In using literary evidence, I am not arguing that it accurately represents "reality" but rather that it can provide a valuable reflection of attitudes and tensions present within a given culture.

changed as new economic, demographic, political, and religious patterns emerged. This addition of a gendered component expands our understanding of social capital, showing how women's informal social networks functioned alongside men's more organized institutions. (Since female associations relied upon a certain degree of trust and shared norms among their members, they probably would not have thrived unless similar values were present, at least to some extent, among men as well; boys are rarely socialized on the basis of entirely contrary social attitudes than girls.)

A variety of sources from the later fourteenth and fifteenth centuries make clear both that English women routinely engaged in social interactions with each other and that male authors were uncomfortable about these contacts. Women gathered in their houses, at the market, or in alehouses to chat; they brought their domestic tasks to another person's house so they could talk while working together; they knew the personal histories of all their neighbors and used informal social pressure to ensure conformity to the values that they deemed important. When women gave birth, they were surrounded by other women—a midwife, a servant, and a few neighbors or relatives. Those of higher status had a larger attendance. Forty days after giving birth, women came to church with a group of female peers to be "churched" (a ceremony that, in Catholic terms, was intended to purify or cleanse new mothers and, after the Reformation, to give thanks for their safe deliveries). Before the Reformation, the churching ritual, described by Gibson as "women's theatre," was raised to the community level once a year when women participated in the traditions of Candlemas, which included a procession around the church with all of the parishioners—female as well as male—carrying lighted candles in celebration of the churching of the Virgin Mary after Jesus' birth.[11]

The fact that women commonly talked, worked, gave birth, took part in religious ceremonies, and even drank in the company of their female peers was troubling to many men. Moral and religious works, for example, portrayed women as excessively gregarious, devoted to gossip and hence vulnerable to sins asso-

---

11   See, for example, Alan Macfarlane, *The Family Life of Ralph Josselin* (London, 1970); David Cressy, *Birth, Marriage, and Death: Ritual, Religion and the Life-Cycle in Tudor and Stuart England* (Oxford, 1997), esp. 55–79, 197–229; Gail McMurray Gibson, "Blessing from Sun and Moon: Churching as Women's Theater," in Hanawalt and David Wallace (eds.), *Bodies and Disciplines* (Minneapolis, 1996), 139–154.

ciated with the tongue. Chaucer's wife of Bath in *The Canterbury Tales* (1386–1400) emphasizes her ties with female friends, despite the importance placed on her five consecutive husbands in her prologue. She regularly called on her women companions, going "fro hous to hous, to heere sondry talys." She bragged that she confided secrets to her "gossyb dame Alys" that she would not have told to her parish priest, and she passed along disparaging information about men to her niece and another close female friend. (A "gossip" was originally a co-godparent or a god-sibling, but the term came to be used for any close friend of the same sex.) Her insistence that women had a social world of their own, one in which they discussed and even laughed at men behind their backs, contributes to Chaucer's ambivalence about this un-contained character.[12]

The powerful tension between women's close social interactions and male concern about the independence that such contacts promoted is evident in the "Noah" play in the Chester mystery cycle. Whereas Noah's wife is commonly presented as argumentative and disobedient in the religious plays produced by English towns (she ridicules Noah for building the ark and is unwilling to get into it when the rains begin), she is represented in a more complex and potentially sympathetic manner in the Chester play. When Noah orders her to enter the ark, she refuses to do so unless she is joined by "my gossips everyechone. . . . They shall not drowne, by sayncte John, and [if] I may save there life." Then, in an emotionally charged scene, she joins her female companions outside the ark, singing a drinking song—"The Good Gossips' Song"—as the waters rise around them: "The fludd comes fleetinge in full faste, on everye syde that spredeth full farre. For fere of drowninge I am agaste; good gossippe, lett us drawe nere./ And lett us drinke [bef]or wee departe, for oftetymes wee have done soe." At the end, her sons carry her forcibly into the ark, leaving her friends to disappear beneath the flood.[13]

---

12   See, for example, Arthur Brandeis (ed.), *Jacob's Well: An English Treatise on the Cleansing of Man's Conscience* (London, 1900), I; D. M. Grisdale (ed.), *Three Middle English Sermons from the Worcester Chapter Manuscript F.10* (Leeds, 1939); McIntosh, "Finding Language for Misconduct: Jurors in Fifteenth-Century Local Courts," in Hanawalt and Wallace (eds.), *Bodies and Disciplines,* 87–122; Fred N. Robinson (ed.), *The Works of Geoffrey Chaucer* (Boston, 1957; 2d ed.), "The Wife of Bath's Prologue," ll. 525–550, p. 81.
13   Play III, "Noah's Flood," in Robert M. Lumiansky and David Mills (eds.), *The Chester Mystery Cycle* (London, 1974), ll. 200–246, pp. 50–53.

A representation of women's social ties that reveals the existence of informal networks of credit comes from works directed,
ostensibly, at a female audience. The most popular genre, as
measured by the number of surviving manuscripts and its continued reworking from the mid-fourteenth through the end of the
sixteenth century, was a poem of advice given by a mother (the
"Good Wife") to her daughter. Presented in simple rhyme and
meter, these works assume that women had regular contact with
one another, both in private homes and in public areas. The
daughter is warned not to go too often into town, moving from
one house to another looking for the company of her friends, and
not to spend too much money when at the market or in a tavern
(though, interestingly, those sites are not portrayed as inherently
harmful or evil). The poems also assume that women routinely
loaned goods to each other, advising the daughter not to borrow
"too gladly" lest she become greedy for more, nor to display her
borrowed clothing or other goods in an attempt to appear wealthier than she is: "For at the ending, Home will [go] the borrowed
thing." Moreover, women with excess income are told to welcome their neighbors with meat and drink. Although charity to
the poor was a moral virtue in itself, defense of this kind of
generosity came in far more pragmatic terms: "[L]ove well thy
neighbour thee beside" because of the need to prepare for an
uncertain future, for fear of the bad "thing that may thee betide."[14]

Other kinds of evidence about women's social credit relationships become available in the sixteenth and early seventeenth
centuries. Diaries and household account books document the
frequent visits of women to their neighbors, friends, and nearby
family/kin, whether for just a meal or for a few days' stay. Young
married women, who commonly returned to their mother's home
for the birth of their first child, often assisted their elderly parents
later in their lives. The custom of gift giving, especially at New
Year's, embedded women within a web of reciprocal relationships
in which an economic component was concealed beneath a ve-
neer of social goodwill. Wills reveal that women were more likely
than men to make personal bequests in their wills—such as

---

14   See, for example, "How the Good Wijf Taughte Hir Doughtir," in Frederick J. Furnivall
(ed.), *Early English Meals and Manners: The Babees Book* (London, 1868); Tauno F. Mustanoja
(ed.), *The Good Wife Taught Her Daughter, The Good Wyfe Wold a Pylgremage, The Thewis of
Gud Women* (Helsinki, 1948) (the quotations from the latter come from a 1597 version, the
language of which is more familiar to modern readers [210–216]).

clothing, household goods, or small amounts of cash—to their friends, neighbors, and extended kin, not just to members of their immediate families, suggesting not only that women were involved in extensive social networks but also that they might have been fulfilling obligations as yet unreciprocated. Women also made frequent bequests to named, individual poor people. Whereas men tended to distance themselves from the poor, leaving money to parish poor-relief officials or other charitable institutions, women's interactions with the poor often retained a direct, personal quality.[15]

Closely tied to female networks of social credit was the issue of what it meant to be a good or respectable woman. In later medieval England, and among poorer members of society in succeeding centuries, female virtue was described in terms of neighborliness, generosity, and accommodation to the needs of others. Participation in systems of reciprocal assistance was entirely in keeping with that ideal. Women involved in trade could join, too, so long as their profits remained modest and any excess was shared with others. Moreover, a given woman's reputation was determined largely by her female peers, through informal conversations about whether her actions conformed to what they saw as appropriate behavior.

During the later sixteenth and early seventeenth centuries, however, an alternative definition of female merit rose to prominence, challenging older patterns of social credit. Building upon a secondary strain within medieval thought but adding new intensity to it, the dominant early modern gender ideology focused on the dangers of female speech and sexuality. A good woman was expected to remain at home, where her father or husband could better control her words and behavior. Alehouses and markets were perceived as hotbeds of misrule and possible sin. In characteristic hegemonic fashion, this patriarchal discourse was accepted, at least nominally, by most women. For example, local women showed considerable concern with the sexual behavior and inappropriate speech of their neighbors in the informal judgments made at the community level. This new definition stemmed, in part, from such practical factors as demographic

15 See, Macfarlane, *The Family Life of Ralph Josselin;* M. St. Clare Byrne (ed.), *The Lisle Letters* (Chicago, 1981), 6v.; McIntosh, *Community Transformed,* 86; Sylvia Bugbee, "Women's Social Universe in Sixteenth-Century England: Evidence from Wills," paper delivered at the Western Conference on British Studies, Fort Worth, Tex., October 1997.

pressure and altered marriage patterns for women, increased urbanization, the early stages of capitalism, new forms of craft production and agriculture, and lack of employment for male household heads, but it was buttressed by the social messages of Protestantism and Puritanism and by the desire of more powerful people to maintain control at all levels—a situation that fed into the emergence of a national state.[16]

Powerful forms of enforcement backed the new standards of female propriety. One derived from the way in which the statutes of 1598 and 1601 defined and awarded poor relief. In the traditional, late medieval pattern, most charity was administered informally, with personal contact between donor and recipient; women were the primary providers of assistance to the poor, since food and clothing were common forms of aid. Indeed, because a major purpose of social-credit networks was to ensure help when needed, it was not ignominious for those in need to go to friends or neighbors for assistance if they were already involved in a reciprocal relationship with them. When institutionalized poor relief was established, however, wealthier members of villages or towns became less willing to provide informal assistance since they were required to pay taxes for the poor. Thus were needy people distanced socially from their more prosperous neighbors; informal networks of social credit became less likely to cross socioeconomic lines.

Women who hoped to qualify for locally supported poor relief had to pass the behavioral qualifications stipulated by the new ideological formation and enforced by the men who served as local overseers of the poor. Poor-relief officials might regard women who had been valued under the old system for their social engagement with female peers in unfavorable terms. According to the newer values, if women worked harder and saved their resources, rather than sharing them with others, they would not be forced to ask for public assistance. By the early seventeenth century, poor relief for women was restricted largely to respectable

16 See, for example, David Underdown, "The Taming of the Scold: The Enforcement of Patriarchal Authority in Early Modern England," in Anthony Fletcher and John Stevenson (eds.), *Order and Disorder in Early Modern England* (Cambridge, 1985), 116–136; Fletcher, *Gender, Sex and Subordination in England, 1500–1800* (New Haven, 1995); Laura Gowing, *Domestic Dangers: Women, Words, and Sex in Early Modern London* (Oxford, 1996); Laura K. Deal, "Whores and Witches: The Language of Female Misbehavior in Early Modern England, 1560–1650," Ph.D. diss. (Univ. of Colorado, 1996); McIntosh, *Controlling Misbehavior,* esp. 186–208; *idem,* "Response."

elderly widows who had fallen upon hardship through no fault of their own. Poorer women continued to participate in networks of mutual assistance, though no longer with approval from the dominant ideology.[17]

Accusations of witchcraft increased dramatically during the period that saw the new gender ideology articulated and imposed (c. 1560 to 1640). The majority of those charged were women. Witchcraft allegations could be used to damp down older forms of female social credit. As detailed local studies have shown, there is little evidence in England of a belief in formal contracts with the devil, covens of witches, or wild nighttime rides on broomsticks. Instead, people thought of witchcraft as a person's use of supernatural power for revenge. Hence, charges of witchcraft grew out of tensions between neighbors or families. Further, whereas early feminist scholars regarded the surge of witchcraft allegations in later sixteenth- and seventeenth-century England as a classic example of patriarchal abuse of women, more recent work shows that women were deeply involved in the history of ill will that culminated in formal accusations and prosecutions of witchcraft. Many charges of witchcraft grew out of altercations between women over such issues as acquiring and sharing food, bearing and raising children, and providing charitable assistance—issues that once lay at the heart of reciprocal social-credit systems but were now being set aside in favor of an ideology better adapted to the needs of the emerging capitalist system. Community values were less important than those that justified and reinforced individual advancement.[18]

A fictitious, but plausible, composite picture, derived from the narratives given in detailed community studies, illustrates how witchcraft might play into this new system. Widow Gedge, an elderly poor woman living alone in a village who finds herself without food at the end of a hard winter, calls at the kitchen door

---

17 *Idem*, "Local Responses to the Poor"; Felicity Heal, *Hospitality in Early Modern England* (Oxford, 1990); Tim Wales, "Poverty, Poor Relief and the Life-Cycle: Some Evidence from Seventeenth-Century Norfolk," in Richard M. Smith (ed.), *Land, Kinship and Life-Cycle* (Cambridge, 1984), 351–404.

18 Marianne Hester, "The Dynamics of Male Domination Using the Witch Craze in 16th- and 17th-Century England as a Case Study," *Women's Studies International Forum*, XIII (1990), 9–19; Keith Thomas, *Religion and the Decline of Magic* (New York, 1971); Macfarlane, *Witchcraft in Tudor and Stuart England* (London, 1970); Clive Holmes, "Women: Witnesses and Witches," *Past & Present*, 140 (1993), 45–78; James A. Sharpe, *Instruments of Darkness: Witchcraft in England, 1550–1750* (London, 1996).

of her more prosperous neighbor, yeoman Cotton's wife, and asks
for something to eat. According to the older pattern, Widow
Gedge would probably have established prior ties with Mistress
Cotton, but even if she had not, conventional morality taught
that a woman who had extra should share it willingly with the
needy. Recall that the "Good Wife" advised her daughter to give
freely of her goods, for "Treasure he hath that [the] poor feedeth."
In the new ethic, however, Mistress Cotton refuses to give any
assistance, perhaps even lecturing Widow Gedge about her lack
of prudence and initiative. The angry widow grumbles or curses
as she leaves. A few weeks later, a cow—or a child—belonging
to the Cotton household becomes ill. Mistress Cotton, who
believes in the existence of witchcraft, thinks back to her exchange
with Widow Gedge. Not only does she have reason to feel guilty
because she turned her neighbor away but also, perhaps, because
her husband bought land at a lowered price from Widow Gedge's
deceased husband at a time when Gedge was in serious debt,
thereby contributing to that family's poverty. Her response, however, is punitive rather than charitable: She accuses Widow Gedge
of witchcraft.[19]

Wealthy women, too, created networks of social interaction
to produce capital. Collections of correspondence are a valuable
source. McNabb has analyzed the letters sent to Lady Honor Lisle,
wife of Arthur Plantagenet, Lord Deputy of Calais, during the
1530s and those received by a widowed gentlewoman, Lady Joan
Barrington, during the 1620s. McNabb argues that because even
women of high rank "rarely had access to the political, economic,
and cultural capital through which men exercised power," they
had to rely on the creation and employment of social capital. By
performing an action for another as a practical investment, women
built up "social credit among friends and influential people that
could then be recalled if ever the original agent was in need of
assistance." McNabb places these letters into categories based upon
the particular kind of social credit involved: giving presents to
display affection or secure favors; aiding petitioners seeking religious patronage or lay employment; helping with the education or
placement of children and adolescents; and assisting with marriage
negotiations. Even women who had powerful husbands or other

---

19 Mustanoja (ed.), *The Good Wife Taught Her Daughter,* 159 (spelling modernized).

male relatives were careful to cultivate their own contacts with those who could help them if necessary.[20]

For aristocratic women, informal networks could bring political as well as social benefits. In a study of how the households of the nobility and the powerful gentry attempted to forge connections with the royal court during the earlier sixteenth century, Harris stresses the importance of women in building and maintaining alliances. She demonstrates how women worked to further their families' interests by creating dynastic and personal networks, established through such activities as placing their children in the homes of their kinfolk, friends, and patrons; paying regular visits to each other's houses; giving presents; and securing offices, annuities, and other favors for their peers and dependents. Harris notes that women pursued these social activities deliberately and consciously "to strengthen their own networks and to perpetuate them into the next generation."[21]

Among women of lower status, loosely structured systems of social assistance created social capital different from that generated by formal community institutions, though the returns were profound. Most important, and as intended, participants gained some degree of security, focused on downside risks (that is, the possibility that their circumstances could worsen). Their concern was to protect themselves against their husbands' death or other causes of lowered income, not to seek chances to move upward in wealth or status. The opportunity costs of creating and acting within such a system were low, since women had few, if any, other ways of investing their time or economic resources. They could expect neither to achieve substantial improvement in their standard of living through their own activities (an upside gain) nor to accumulate enough money of their own to protect themselves and their families against unexpected problems (an alternative form of downside insurance). Close contacts also produced secondary forms of social capital for women. These interactions, and a sense of reciprocal obligation among them, promoted trust and the development of cooperative skills, including how to resolve

20 Jennifer McNabb, "The Use of Social Capital by Women of the Upper Ranks of Early Modern England," paper presented at the Western Conference on British Studies, Fort Worth, Tex., October 1997; Byrne (ed.), *Lisle Letters,* I–II; Arthur Searle (ed.), *Barrington Family Letters, 1628–1632* (London, 1983).
21 Barbara Harris, "Women and Politics in Early Tudor England," *Historical Journal,* XXXIII (1990), 259–281.

conflict at an informal level. Conversations led to shared norms, and the exchange of information could be useful in economic or social terms.

From a political or economic standpoint, the externally beneficial social capital created by these women's networks was negligible. After all, the participation of women (and the poor) in formal community institutions was limited, and the transportable social capital created by their own unstructured associations modest. Moreover, for all but the wealthiest women (those with wider geographical ties), strong reciprocal bonds among those who saw each other regularly might have accentuated locally defined group identifications, perhaps even to the detriment of trust and cooperation with people at a greater distance. In economic terms, because women were the primary producers and sellers of ale, and sometimes bread, between 1300 and 1500 in England's smaller communities, their social skills, information, and access to credit provided by participation in a reciprocal network might have had the potential to facilitate market activity. In practice, however, their trade was almost entirely local, involving consumable goods made from supplies generated within the region; women do not seem to have competed in the market by lowering prices or increasing their volume of goods. (All items of a given type were supposed to be sold at a standard price, set by local authorities; relatively few small markets had outside buyers eager to purchase such items for subsequent resale in larger cities.) Hence, female networks might seem to have hindered, rather than to have promoted, the growth of a market economy.

But examination of female roles within the household leads to more subtle conclusions. The increased security, trust, and shared norms produced by women's associations probably had a positive impact upon the social attitudes of their husbands and male relatives, as well as on the children and adolescent servants in their households. They taught by example that cooperation was a realistic and productive strategy, that others shared their values, and that the world around them made sense. Likewise, the availability of information and experience in problem solving enhanced women's ability to raise children who were emotionally prepared to take advantage of opportunities. All of these benefits would have been magnified in periods of rapid change.

Social capital must be analyzed in terms that fit particular circumstances. Social capital does not necessarily promote "modernizing" goals like the emergence of a civil society, democratic processes, or economic growth. The forms of capital produced by unstructured female networks in England illustrate a contradictory pattern; the customary social values that sustained these groups conflicted with an emerging ideology that stressed individual responsibility and advancement, thereby impelling England's transition into a capitalist economy within which advanced political forms would develop. Accordingly, the particular definition of social capital that comes to us from sociology, political science, and economics is not ideally suited to the study of informal women's networks. Although works like Coleman's *Foundations of Social Theory* or Putnam's *Making Democracy Work* include examples of simple exchanges of equipment or labor between individual farmers and such weakly structured organizations as rotating credit associations, their emphasis is on how social capital contributes to wider social and political developments. For economists too, capital of any kind is an input factor, interesting for its direct, measurable effects, or outcomes. Since reciprocal assistance systems among women of lower rank generated relatively little obvious public good, the standard definition offers at best a blunt analytical tool.[22]

A more helpful approach derives from the work of Bourdieu, especially *Outline of a Theory of Practice*—based upon his anthropological fieldwork among the Kabyle people of Algeria—which presents his conception of symbolic capital. Already popular with both literary critics and historians, the idea can be extended readily to social capital. Most of Bourdieu's examples pertain to a non-industrialized society; he makes no teleologically driven assumptions that social interactions are important only insofar as they lead to certain economic/political developments. Because his understanding of symbolic capital stems from a culture that was not affected by industrialization and that had markedly different roles for men and women, it also applies to premodern societies and to settings in which women differ from men in their creation and use of social capital.[23]

Bourdieu stresses that the economic foundation of symbolic capital and its role in expressing power is normally kept hidden. Acts of gift giving or purchasing prized goods carry weight pre-

22 James S. Coleman, *Foundations of Social Theory* (Cambridge, Mass., 1990), esp. 300–321; Putnam, *Making Democracy Work*, esp. 163–185.
23 Pierre Bourdieu (trans. Richard Nice), *Outline of a Theory of Practice* (Cambridge, 1977).

cisely because they are described and accepted as virtues in their own right. No one speaks of the economic benefits or the elevation in status or authority that they may bring. That social capital, too, may be created for reasons other than those articulated is an important observation when considering informal credit networks. Even in our own society, if Susan helps to tend Mary's older children after Mary has a new baby, Susan will probably say that she was happy to do so ("that's what neighbors/friends are for"), rather than pointing out that she thereby has earned an equivalent favor from Mary, or someone else who might have heard about her kindness. Because not all social capital is alike, we need to have a diverse array of conceptual tools that allow us to analyze its nature and impact in specific cases.

FEMALE SOCIAL NETWORKS IN SOUTHERN NIGERIA, 1900 THROUGH 1960   Although women's networks similar to those of late medieval and early modern England have been observed in many different cultures and periods, the Yoruba and Igbo societies of southern Nigeria between 1900 and 1960 offer a particularly interesting comparison. Like England between 1300 and 1640, Nigeria was experiencing rapid economic development with increased emphasis on market production, the growth of more centralized political institutions, the introduction or expansion of new religious systems, and, by the later part of each period, pronounced demographic rise and increased urbanization. As in England, these transformations led to ideological conflict about women's proper social and economic roles. That tension is most clearly visible with respect to female market traders in Yoruba and Igbo communities.[24]

Yoruba and Igbo women have engaged in trading activity as far back as evidence extends. At a lower economic level, many

24   This discussion does not operate from the veiled imperialist assumption that England had already advanced to modern forms by 1640 whereas Africa retained simpler, or backward, patterns well into the twentieth century. Fruitful crosscultural comparisons do not entail reductionist notions of necessary institutional progression or rigid patterns of development. This account must be regarded as preliminary, based upon initial work on a new research project.

Another example of informal networks comes from the rural communities of early New England, where people entered into unstructured, but cumulatively extensive, reciprocal relations with each other, involving social as well as economic credit. See, for example, Daniel Vickers, "Competency and Competition: Economic Culture in Early America," *William and Mary Quarterly*, XLVII (1990), 3–20; Laurel Thatcher Ulrich, *A Midwife's Tale* (New York, 1990).

women during the nineteenth and twentieth centuries set up stalls in community markets, where they sold food or other agricultural goods, drink, and domestic items. Their trading was generally limited to their own town or village, and the prices and volume of the goods sold were low. Normally, women brought to the market their own household's extra agricultural goods, slightly processed food, or locally produced items like pots. Alternatively, they sometimes purchased a small quantity of manufactured goods, commonly textiles, to sell at somewhat higher prices in the market. The primary (and socially accepted) goal of these lesser traders was to make enough profit to buy food and other supplies for their own families that day. Although saving for larger purchases was a secondary aim, if present at all, after 1900, some women began to use trading profits to pay for their children's schooling.[25]

Competition within the local markets was active but restricted: For example, women in adjacent stalls might bargain with potential customers about the exact volume and price of a commodity that they all sold. Social pressure, and a low level of profit, kept the women from reducing or raising their prices beyond certain limits, and nobody bought large volumes of goods within

25 See, for example, Niara Sudarkasa, *Where Women Work: A Study of Yoruba Women in the Marketplace and in the Home* (Ann Arbor, 1973); Simi Afonja, "Changing Modes of Production and the Sexual Division of Labor among the Yoruba," *Signs,* VII (1981), 299–313; Toyin Falola, "Gender, Business, and Space Control: Yoruba Market Women and Power," in Bessie House-Midamba and Felix K. Ekechi (eds.), *African Market Women and Economic Power* (Westport, 1995), 23–40; Margaret M. Green, *Ibo Village Affairs* (New York, 1964; orig. pub. 1947); Susan M. Martin, *Palm Oil and Protest, An Economic History of the Ngwa Region, South-Eastern Nigeria, 1800–1980* (Cambridge, 1988); Ekechi, "Gender and Economic Power: The Case of Igbo Market Women of Eastern Nigeria," in House-Midamba and *idem* (eds.), *African Market Women,* 41–57; Judith Van Allen, "'Aba Riots' or Igbo 'Women's War'? Ideology, Stratification, and the Invisibility of Women," in Nancy J. Hafkin and Edna G. Bay (eds.), *Women in Africa* (Stanford, 1976), 59–85.

Although the description in this article applies broadly to both Yoruba and Igbo communities, women traders have generally been more prominent and independent in the former than in the latter. The high level of Yoruba urbanization contributed to larger and more specialized markets and to increased middle-distance trade. Further, Yoruba women were expected to contribute to the family's income and control their own resources. Women also continued to play important roles in traditional religion and culture, expressed in a range of rituals and linguistic genres. The custom or legacy of polygyny, which remained much stronger among the Yoruba than among the Igbo, facilitated the movement of older wives into the trading world. See, for example, Emmanuel D. Babatunde, "Ketu Myths and the Status of Women," *Journal of the Anthropological Society of Oxford,* XIV (1983), 301–306; Henry and Margaret Drewal, *Gelede: Art and Female Power among the Yoruba* (Bloomington, 1983); Sara Berry, *Fathers Work for Their Sons* (Berkeley, 1985); Karin Barber, *I Could Speak until Tomorrow: Oriki, Women and the Past in Yoruba Towns* (Washington, D.C., 1991); Andrew Apter, *Black Critics and Kings: The Hermeneutics of Power in Yoruba Society* (Chicago, 1992).

these small trading spheres. Transportation facilities were poor and transaction costs high. In economic terms, small-scale female traders functioned as a benignly run cartel that hindered the formation of a fully competitive market. Trading had strong social components as well. It gave women the opportunity to interact with each other on a regular basis, to share the latest news, and to engage in the pleasure of haggling—all of which occurred within the marketplace, a setting controlled, at least in part, by women and recognized as their space.

A few women, especially in the major commercial centers, entered into longer distance trade with a larger volume of goods. The almost legendary Madam Tinubu was the most important middleperson between Lagos and the interior during the 1850s and 1860s, using her private army to support trade in slaves, ammunition, palm oil, salt, and tobacco. By the opening decades of the twentieth century, more women were discovering the potential of entering into trade with Europeans, or at least with European-made goods. Omu Okwei, "the merchant queen of Ossomari," was perhaps the most powerful of the Igbo women who "controlled the vast system of wholesale marketing and distribution of the Onitsha market" between c. 1900 and 1929. Starting with trade in palm produce and foodstuffs and progressing to imported textiles, tobacco, hardware, and other provisions, she later served as an agent for chiefs and other influential men, acquired a fleet of trucks and canoes, loaned money at exorbitant rates, and traded in currency. In a fictitious representation, Emecheta shows how Ma Palagada, a wealthy trader in Onitsha during the 1920s, used the adoption of Christianity and Western-style education for the younger women of her household as a way to enhance her own social and economic status.[26]

Market activity could bring political power as well, both individually and institutionally. Madam Tinubu helped the Egba in their war against Dahomey and opposed the policies of the British consul in Lagos. In traditional societies, a female official within each town was responsible for women's aspects of the community, especially the marketplace (the *Iyadole/Iyaloja* among the Yoruba and the *Omu* in Igbo areas); some of these women

---

26 See, for example, Nina E. Mba, *Nigerian Women Mobilized* (Berkeley, 1982); Felicia Ekejuba, "Omu Okwei, the Merchant Queen of Ossamari," *Nigeria Magazine,* XC (1996), 213–220; Buchi Emecheta, *The Slave Girl* (New York, 1977).

acquired considerable influence not only in trade but also in political arenas. Igbo female traders were at the center of the 1929 uprisings against British taxation, known as the (Aba) Women's War. The market women of Lagos, who were highly organized as early as the 1920s, continued as a powerful force throughout the colonial period, controlling their own trade, influencing economic decisions at a higher level, and taking vigorous part in political matters.[27]

Although women continued to dominate local trade during the nineteenth and twentieth centuries, massive changes in the broader context worked to limit their economic and political influence, introducing tension between their traditional social functions and independent economic activity. The net impact of colonialism and its interaction with the indigenous patriarchal system led to a gradual, if uneven, curtailment of women's roles as traders and authority figures. From the 1920s onward, conflict was visible along gender lines, as women's economic potential threatened their customary position as wives and mothers. Ogunyemi perceived these developments as related: Because the marketplace was a public space for women, it therefore served as "a metonym for colonial space in which the colonized (for the purposes of this postulate, women) though at the center, ultimately have minimal control, since the colonizers (that is, the men) have already disempowered them with their insistent gaze directed to undermine women's potential economic power."[28]

The lesser market women of southern Nigeria created and used networks of social credit to provide essential insurance. The

27 See, for example, Oladipo Yemitan, *Madame Tinubu: Merchant and King-Maker* (Ibadan, 1987); Bolanle Awe, "The Iyalode in the Traditional Yoruba Political System," in Alice Schlegel (ed.), *Sexual Stratification: A Cross-Cultural View* (New York, 1977), 144–160; Bolanle Awe, "Iyalode Efunsetan Aniwura (Owner of Gold)," in *idem* (ed.), *Nigerian Women in Historical Perspective* (Ibadan, 1992), 55–71; Kamene Okonjo, "The Dual-Sex Political System in Operation: Igbo Women and Community Politics in Midwestern Nigeria," in Hafkin and Bay (eds.), *Women in Africa,* 45–58; Harry Gailey, *The Road to Aba* (New York, 1970); Van Allen, "'Aba Riots' or Igbo 'Women's War'?"; Chikwenye Okonjo Ogunyemi, *Africa Wo/man Palava: The Nigerian Novel by Women* (Chicago, 1996), 48–55; Cheryl Johnson, "Madam Alimota Pelewura and the Lagos Market Women," *Tarikh,* VII (1981), 1–10.

28 See, for example, Martin, "Slaves, Igbo Women and Palm Oil in the Nineteenth Century," in Robin Law (ed.), *From Slave Trade to 'Legitimate' Commerce* (Cambridge, 1995), 172–195; Kristin Mann, *Marrying Well: Marriage, Status, and Social Change among the Educated Elite in Colonial Lagos* (Cambridge, 1985); *idem,* "Women, Landed Property, and the Accumulation of Wealth in Early Colonial Lagos," *Signs,* XVI (1991), 682–706; Judith Byfield, "Innovation and Conflict: Cloth Dyers and the Interwar Depression in Abeokuta, Nigeria,"

extended family could not be counted upon to look after a woman in need, especially if she had left her home community: Neither Yoruba nor Igbo custom required that a man's brother take his widow as his own wife. Nor did British colonial officials or missionaries attempt to establish formal systems of social welfare. Although lesser market women might be able to save or borrow money through their own activity, they could seldom generate enough credit to provide security for themselves by such means. Involvement in an informal social network was potentially more valuable in terms of the amount and nature of the assistance that it could offer. As in England, market women living within traditional value systems could take active part in these social groupings, provided that their trading was done on a small scale and at a level roughly commensurate with that of other local women. Any substantial profits had to be distributed through gifts or loans to others, not kept for individual consumption or for reinvestment in a greater volume of trading goods. Since the avenues for personal self-advancement within customary patterns were scarce, offering no socially approved mechanisms whereby a woman could use her income in other ways, the opportunity costs of taking part in a social-credit system were low.[29]

Standards of appropriate female behavior in both Yoruba and Igbo cultures reinforced systems of group interaction and hence the production of social capital. Women were praised for sharing their wealth: Generosity was regarded as a good in itself, and accumulation as inacceptable selfishness. Helping people in need

---

Journal of African History, XXXVIII (1997), 77–99; Van Allen, "'Sitting on a Man': Colonialism and the Lost Political Institutions of Igbo Women," *Canadian Journal of African Studies,* VI (1972), 165–181; Ifi Amadiume, *Male Daughters, Female Husbands: Gender and Sex in an African Society* (London, 1987); Martin, *Palm Oil and Protest;* Ogunyemi, *Africa Wo/man Palava,* esp. 49.

29 Women could participate, for example, in a voluntary credit/savings association known as an *esusu,* in which each member made small but regular money payments and the full sum gathered was then given back to the participants on a rotational basis. (William Bascom, "The *Esusu:* A Credit Institution of the Yoruba," *Journal of the Royal Anthropological Institute,* LXXXII [1952], 63–69; Falola, "Money and Informal Credit Institutions in Colonial Western Nigeria," in Jane I. Guyer [ed.], *Money Matters: Instability, Values and Social Payments in the Modern History of West African Communities* [Portsmouth, N.H., 1995], 162–187; Anthony J. Nwabughogu, "The *Esusu:* An Institution for Capital Formation among the Ngwa Igbo: Its Origin and Development to 1951," *Africa,* LIV [1984], 46–58.) My focus here upon women is not intended to suggest that Nigerian men did not have similar kinds of interactions or that social capital was generated only by women.

was particularly commendable. Indeed, men and women alike fostered close ties with others, including advice and assistance as needed, on economic as well as social grounds. (There is little Bourdieuian emphasis on concealing the economic underpinnings of this symbolic capital.) Emecheta's novel, *The Joys of Motherhood,* for example, describes how a poor Igbo father—now in Lagos— chastised his son when he complained about the arrival of new relatives in the household, "calling him a selfish boy and saying that if he was not careful he would grow into a selfish man who no one would help when he was in difficulty." To emphasize the point, the father "put the fear of the Devil" into his son by telling him about a white man who had suffered a solitary death—a terrible fate for an Igbo—"because he was minding his own business."[30]

As women began to move away from traditional settings, the relationship between participation in the market economy and involvement in customary patterns of community-focused social relationships often became strained, especially during the 1920s through the 1940s, when Nigeria's colonial rule and integration within the international economy, based on exports, were both being strengthened. Women who immigrated from villages or small towns into the larger cities were likely to encounter more competitive forms of trade, as well as Western-style values and education that offered them new opportunities to use their income for greater material comfort or to advance their children. Thus they were encouraged to focus on the upside potential of their marketing activity. Yet, women who operated competitively as traders in one of the major cities had to extricate themselves from the traditional networks that generated social capital: It was difficult to maintain close personal ties and customary levels of generosity with friends, relatives, and neighbors if deeply engaged in market activity for individual profit. Hence, they could find themselves isolated and helpless if unexpected difficulties arose.

Most market women in the cities were involved in some kind of organization, usually informal, that combined economic and social functions. Women often needed a loan of capital with which to set up urban trading in the first place. In *The Joys of Motherhood,* when Nnu Ego, the young Igbo wife of the chastising

30 Emecheta, *The Joys of Motherhood* (New York, 1979), esp. 121.

father discussed earlier, found that she could not provide for her household in Lagos on what her poorly paid husband gave her, she was rescued from her despair by other women who had moved to Lagos from her home village, who gathered for sociable monthly meetings. They "taught her how to start her own business . . . , let her borrow five shillings from the women's fund, and advised her to buy tins of cigarettes and packets of matches," which she could sell at a profit. With her income from these sales, she was able to buy adequate food for her family and pay back her loan from the women's group. But involvement in trading by no means guaranteed economic security. Despite her ongoing participation in the market, Nnu Ego remained destitute whenever her husband provided no income. Her trading profits were not adequate to support her family alone; nor did her culture intend them to be so.[31]

Women who engaged in market activity at any level might find themselves seriously at risk if they abandoned participation in social networks. As an old and impoverished woman returning to her village, Nnu Ego reflected that "she would have been better off had she had time to cultivate those women who had offered her hands of friendship; but she had never had the time. What with worrying over this child, this pregnancy, and the lack of money, coupled with the fact that she never had adequate outfits to wear to visit her friends, she had shied away from friendship, telling herself she did not need any friends, she had enough in her family. But had she been right?" The answer given by the novel is "no." Because she had excluded friendship, Nnu Ego died alone at the side of a road after a night of confused wandering, thus paying the price for the kind of isolated behavior about which her husband had warned her son many years before. Conflict between the distributive norms reflected in traditional networks of social credit and a desire to accumulate wealth was common in societies experiencing rapid transition into global capitalism, but the pressure was probably most acute for women, since they were more deeply embedded in customary notions of social collectivity.[32]

Rejection of traditional gender roles compounded these difficulties. Women who engaged in market activity with their

31 *Ibid.*, 52.
32 *Ibid.*, 219.

husbands' approval to help support the household were fine, but women who used trade to support themselves and their children, independent of men, or who set aside their duties as wives and mothers to seek profit for themselves caused great consternation. These concerns interacted with female social networks. In *The Joys of Motherhood,* for example, a younger wife of Nnu Ego's brother-in-law came to Lagos with her daughters after her husband's death and began to make money, thereby obtaining a much more comfortable way of life, as well as the capacity to send her girls to a convent boarding school. Her relatives and old friends, bitter at being left behind, scorned her decision and saw her eventual withdrawal from the struggle to become a high-grade prostitute as another sign of her distorted values.

In southern Nigeria, as in early modern England, witchcraft accusations tended to keep women in line with expected female roles, but in this case, they were the older values of reciprocal social engagement and assistance rather than the newer, more individualistic or accumulative patterns. Community members used suspicion of witchcraft to prevent women engaged in trade from achieving too much prosperity, especially if they violated other gender expectations as well.

A particularly forceful account appears in Echewa's novel, *I Saw The Sky Catch Fire,* a remarkable representation of female identity, social interaction, and power during the 1920s, which is presented as a fictionalized historical background to the (Aba) Woman's War. After her husband's death, Ahunze, a childless Igbo woman of grandmotherly age, "a seasoned trader," declined to marry any of her suitors, choosing instead to live alone in the village. When her deceased husband's goods were stolen and her animals poisoned by angry neighbors, Ahunza began to save her market earnings, using them to buy larger stores of trading goods. As she prospered in the cloth trade "beyond what was imaginable for a woman, . . . she had the unwomanly boldness to travel to distant markets," bringing home European textiles; "men and women from far and near regularly mobbed her market stall to buy her latest acquisitions." With this wealth she invested in farms and palm trees and loaned money. The awe and fear felt by other local people at her success led to suggestions that she had made a pact with the spirits, perhaps Mami-Wota, the river goddess, to give up marriage and childbearing in return for success in trade. In the end, she was hacked to death by her husband's brother and her house set on fire. Echewa's narrative accentuates many of the themes presented a generation earlier in Nwapa's pathbreaking novel, *Efuru,* which stressed the inherent conflict between the traditional female roles of wife/mother and one woman's attempt to create some degree of independence for herself through trade.[33]

Apter suggested that the witch-finding movement known as the Atinga cult that swept the southern part of West Africa in the 1940s and 1950s was intimately associated with the social and economic power of female traders during a period when the price of cocoa boomed on the world market. In Atinga practice, (male) cult leaders entered a settlement to identify (female) witches and provide protective medicine against their activities. In Yoruba areas, they destroyed shrines and altars associated with the *orisa* cult, a religious movement in which women predominated. Apter argued that the expansion of large-scale cocoa production and economic prosperity produced social as well as economic tensions, with particular implications for gender relationships. These pressures affected "competition between co-wives and their children, inheritance disputes, lineage optation, segmentation and fission, and, most important, the tug of war between women's economic autonomy in the marketplace and subordination at home." He noted, in particular, that "trading capital, like the power of witchcraft itself, was now transmitted from mother to daughter." Atinga was a powerful—if short-lived—weapon that discouraged the development of women's fuller participation in the public economy at the expense of their customary social roles.[34]

The kinds of social capital created by the social and economic interactions of Nigerian market women resemble what we saw in the English context. Informal assistance networks generated unquestionable internal benefits. In addition to their insurance function, they provided information for their members through

---

33   T. Obinkaram Echewa, *I Saw the Sky Catch Fire* (New York, 1992), 123–160; Flora Nwapa, *Efuru* (London, 1966), which served as an acknowledged model for Emecheta's *The Joys of Motherhood.* See also B. Hallen and J. O. Sodipo, *Knowledge, Belief and Witchcraft* (London, 1986), which highlights the need to recognize the differences between witchcraft in early modern England and modern Africa.

34   Apter, "Atinga Revisited: Yoruba Witchcraft and the Cocoa Economy, 1950–51," in Jean and John Comaroff (eds.), *Modernity and its Malcontents: Ritual and Power in Postcolonial Africa* (Chicago, 1993), 111–128. The issue of how women transferred wealth and power to their daughters had different valences in matrilineal Igbo communities: Philip Nsugbe, *Ohaffia: A Matrilineal Ibo People* (Oxford, 1974).

contact with each other and any outsiders who came into the marketplace. The conversation of women traders about economic, social, and political matters was a form of education especially important for people moving from villages into cities. Some of this capital may have been transportable to other community settings, especially among Yoruba women who had well-defined roles in religious and cultural spheres. In the leading cities, where market women were highly organized, the economic and political benefits presumably were stronger. Sekoni emphasized the wider social importance of bargaining among Yoruba market women, based on an understanding of each party's current economic and social situation; he noted that this process reinforced "the notion that social life depends on exchange and negotiation." Within the household, the impact of female social capital generated in the market was mixed. Although the husbands of lesser traders may have profited from the economic and social advantages derived from their wives' market activity, many of them were probably keenly aware of the disruptive potential of the women's heightened independence. Children, too, benefited from the social capital that their mothers produced, but they could also hardly fail to learn what happened if traditional social roles were abandoned too overtly or fully.[35]

In external terms, female networks did not necessarily lead to enhanced trust outside their own ranks. Nor did their operation among women traders promote economic development; their members did not push prices down, encourage long-distance trade, or lower transaction costs. Laterally focused systems of social capital are probably most attractive during periods when a previously stable society and economy are becoming more dynamic. As that transition continues, however, such systems will almost certainly impede the growth of the newer forms, perhaps even becoming a hindrance to the ability of individual members to take advantage of the changed system.

This article offers several arguments about the ways in which historians define and employ the concept of social capital. The material presented here forces us to extend the chronological

35 Ropo Sekoni, "Yoruba Market Dynamics and the Aesthetics of Negotiation in Female Precolonial Narrative Tradition," *Research in African Literature*, XXV (1994), 33–46.

confines of existing research by demonstrating that English communities during the transition from later medieval to early modern patterns contained many organizations that produced social capital of value not only to their own members but also to the wider community. We must avoid any temptation to assume that externally beneficial social capital originated in the eighteenth, or even the sixteenth, century, or that it is necessarily linked to such relatively modern forms as a civil society, free market economy, or democratic political institutions.

The English evidence likewise demands that we question the current emphasis on voluntary organizations when examining social capital. Public institutions in which certain members of the community are required to participate can produce useful social returns just as effectively as can groups that people join entirely by choice. We need to include the fullest possible array of organizations in our assessment of how social capital is created and employed.

Finally, we must insist that historical study of social capital move beyond formal organizations, ones dominated normally by men (or occasionally women) of high local status. Structured institutions are indeed likely to have left good records, facilitating historical research, but we must be sensitive to evidence of the informal networks that flourished especially among men of lower rank and women. To ignore these social interactions and the benefits that they generated would be to slip back inadvertently into a narrower and more elitist view of what is historically important. Because the nature and effect of the social capital generated by informal networks were different from those produced by formal organizations, we must be prepared to adjust our theoretical framework to fit the particular case. A thoughtful analysis of the roles of gender and social status in the production of social capital that borrows conceptual tools from anthropology, as well as from sociology, political science, and economics, has much to contribute.

Jack P. Greene

Social and Cultural Capital in Colonial British America: A Case Study

Social capital is a relatively new concept that political scientists and sociologists have developed to distinguish certain social resources from others, namely, financial or investment capital, physical capital in the form of fixed or movable material resources, and human capital in the form of individual knowledge and technical skills. As employed by modern social scientists, such as Putnam, social capital consists of the organizations and connections that foster cooperation, trust, participation, the exchange of information, civil interaction, and coordinated activity in pursuit of social goals. An expression of the traditional social science concern with outcomes, the concept has proven useful to explain or predict the emergence of civil society, the development and growth of market economics, and the achievement of political democracy.[1]

Whether the concept can be equally useful to historians remains to be seen. Far less concerned with how to attain the specific goals that modern society deems desirable, historians are principally interested in understanding and characterizing the myriad processes and dynamics that have made societies of all different shapes and sizes work in particular places at specific times. For their purposes, the present social science definition is too narrow, too instrumental, too whiggish, and too Western. To become a useful tool of analysis for historians, the concept must be rendered applicable to a wide variety of contexts over time and space. More specifically, this article suggests that it must be redefined and expanded to include not just traditions of civil interaction but the entire range of institutions, practices, devices, and learned behaviors that enable collectivities and individuals to render physical spaces productive and social and cultural spaces agreeable. In this

Jack P. Greene is Andrew W. Mellon Professor in the Humanities, Johns Hopkins University. He is the author of *The Intellectual Construction of America: Exceptionalism and Identity from 1492 to 1800* (Chapel Hill, 1993); *Negotiated Authorities: Essays in Colonial Political and Constitutional History* (Charlottesville, 1994).

1   See Robert D. Putnam, with Roberto Leonardi and Raffaella Y. Nanetti, *Making Democracy Work: Civic Traditions in Modern Italy* (Princeton, 1993).

expanded usage, *social capital,* or, perhaps better, *social and cultural capital,* refers to all of those elements of the larger inheritance that cultures pass along to succeeding generations for later members to perpetuate, modify, discard, or reconstitute in new places.

Using the English or, after 1707, British experience as a case study, this article examines the role of social and cultural capital in the construction of new overseas societies during the early modern era, and the transformation of many of those societies into states beginning in the last quarter of the eighteenth century. More specifically, it focuses upon three aspects of this subject. First is the extent to which New World settlers relied upon their Old World inheritance in constructing European-style societies in the Americas. Second is the way in which the selective use of inherited forms of social capital and their subsequent refinement and elaboration provided the foundations for the emergence of recognizably civil societies in the New World well before some of those societies undertook to make themselves independent states. Third is the continuing importance of these colonial social creations in determining the character of the new federal nation formed by parts of British North America between 1776 and 1800.

The global dimensions of the Seven Years' War focused the attention of European analysts as never before upon the scope, significance, and transformative character of European involvement overseas. Published in 1757 in two volumes, William and Edmund Burke's *An Account of the European Settlements in America* provided the first comparative history of European activities in the Americas. In 1770, the Abbé Raynal, issued his much more ambitious multi-volume *Philosophical and Political History of the Settlements and Trade of Europeans in the East and West Indies,* which, as the title announced, covered not just the Americas but also Africa and Asia. Although both the Burkes and Raynal were deeply critical of European treatment of Amerindians and the enslavement of millions of Africans for labor throughout the New World, they also displayed a profound appreciation of the achievements of Europeans overseas: their success in expanding their trade over much of the globe and in bringing much of the Americas and portions of Africa and Asia under their hegemony. As Raynal announced in the first sentence of his first volume, the "discovery of the new world, and the passage to the East Indies by the Cape of Good Hope," had obviously turned out to be "one of the most important events in the history of the human species."[2]

What particularly impressed these and other contemporary analysts was what Smith referred to as the extraordinary "progress of all the European colonies in wealth, population, and improvement." Smith's lengthy discussion "Of Colonies" in *An Inquiry into the Nature and Causes of the Wealth of Nations,* issued in 1776, provided the most systematic and penetrating analysis of early modern European colonization in the Americas published up to that time. In Smith's view, the English, many of whose colonies had demonstrated phenomenal growth and development over the previous half century, had been most impressive in this regard. But the Portuguese in Brazil had built "a great and powerful colony" that contained a larger "number of people of European extraction" than any other "colony in America"; the Spanish, presiding over by far the widest extent of country, had built a populous and thriving empire with several cities that were larger than any to be found in the colonies of other nations; and the French colonies, following a series of slow starts, had exhibited "more rapid" development during the eighteenth century. Of the major colonizing powers, only the Dutch, according to Smith, had "been languid and slow" in their colonizing "progress."[3]

Among the measures that Smith used to chart this comparative "progress"—occupied territory, "wealth, population, and improvement"—improvement was the most fundamental. Following scores of earlier observers dating back to the earliest encounter between Europeans and Amerindians, Smith emphasized the primitive social state of the Americas at the time of the encounter and the backwardness of the Amerindians who occupied them. Christopher Columbus, he said, encountered "a country quite covered with wood, uncultivated, and inhabited only by some tribes of naked and miserable savages." The whole of America contained only "two civilized kingdoms," Mexico and Peru, and even they had "no cattle fit for draught," the llama, an animal whose "strength" was "a good deal inferior to that of a common

2 William and Edmund Burke, *An Account of the European Settlements in America* (London, 1808; orig. pub. 1757), 2v.; Guillaume Thomas François (Abbé) Raynal (trans. J. Justamond), *Philosophical and Political History of the Settlements and Trade of Europeans in the East and West Indies* (London, 1798), I, 1.
3 Adam Smith (ed. R. H. Campbell and A. S. Skinner) *An Inquiry into the Nature and Causes of the Wealth of Nations* (Oxford, 1976; orig. pub. 1776), II, 567–571.

ass," being the "only beast of burden." With the plow being wholly "unknown among them," Amerindians "were ignorant of the use of iron. They had no coined money, nor any established instrument of commerce of any kind. Their commerce was carried on by barter. A sort of wooden spade was their principal instrument of agriculture. Sharp stones served them for knives and hatchets to cut with; fish bones and the hard sinews of certain animals served them for needles to sew with; and these seem to have been their principal instruments of trade."[4]

What contemporary European and European-American observers found so remarkable was that in a little less than three centuries, Europeans and their descendants had transformed the "unwholesome," thinly inhabited, largely uncleared, and almost wholly uncultivated "desert[s]" that they had found in America into cultivated, cleared, populous, and improved spaces, many of which were experiencing rates of economic and demographic growth, and degrees of social and cultural development, without parallel in the known history of the West. Most observers—the Burkes and Raynal, for instance—were content simply to record these phenomena, occasionally pausing to condemn or to praise selected aspects of them. For Smith, however, these phenomena cried out for explanation, and no early modern writer thought more deeply or wrote more penetratingly about them than he.[5]

The explicit question that Smith posed about Europe's early modern overseas experience was why so many "new colonies" seemed to prosper: Why, as he put it, did the "colony of a civilized nation which takes possession, either of a waste country, or one so thinly inhabited, that the natives easily give place to the new settlers, [advance] more rapidly to wealth and greatness than any other human society." As his phrasing of the question suggests, the destruction or retreat of Amerindian cultures provided part of the explanation. So also, he emphasized, did the generous resource endowment that settlers often found in America and their situation far from the metropolitan states to which they were attached. While "plenty of good land" operated both as an invitation to settlement and as an incentive to industry, their location placed "them less in the view and less in the power of their mother country," thereby providing settlers with a maximum amount of

---

4 *Ibid.*, II, 559, 567–569; Burke and Burke, *Account of the European Settlements,* I, 21.
5 Smith, *Inquiry,* II, 597–598.

"liberty to manage their own affairs their own way" and to construct economies, societies, and polities that would enable them to make all that they could "of their own produce" and to employ "their stock and industry in the way that they judge[d] most advantageous to themselves."[6]

But, to Smith, the principal reason why Europeans turned out to have had such a tremendous competitive advantage over the Amerindians in the development of the Americas was the rich social and cultural baggage that they brought to that project. When they emigrated to the Americas, Europeans carried with them the accumulated cultural inheritance of an old and, in Smith's view, much more advanced civil society. The principal elements of that inheritance that Smith singled out for special emphasis were "a knowledge of agriculture and of other useful arts," a "habit of subordination," and "some notion of the regular government" that took "place in their own country, of the system of laws" that supported that government, and "of a regular administration of justice." Smith might have extended this list to include a wide range of social and economic skills, technological know-how, established systems of land tenure and law, and traditions of self-discipline and time management, as well as a variety of economic, legal, social, and civic institutions, tools and technologies, widespread literacy and numeracy, and a knowledge of animal husbandry.[7]

In effect, Smith called attention to the important extent to which the cultural inheritance of European colonizers provided them with a vast "storehouse of resources" that, in selective combinations, was far "superior to what" could have grown "up of its own accord in the course of many centuries among savage and barbarous nations." Coming from societies that were already highly commercialized, Europeans entered the contest for America with a decided advantage over the less advanced societies of the Amerindians. Reinforced by continuing access to metropolitan markets, knowledge, and inventions, settlers had the social and technical capacity to construct new "European-style" societies outside of Europe, thus ensuring that they would be the ones to determine the shape of the social landscapes that developed through interactions with the aboriginal inhabitants, and enabling

6 *Ibid.*, 564, 567, 572–573, 582.
7 *Ibid.*, 564–565.

them to function effectively within the broader early modern Atlantic economy. In the words of Hume, Smith's fellow Scot, America was a "noble" and well-endowed country that had been "kept desolate by the wild manners of the antient inhabitants."[8]

With this analysis, Smith highlighted the crucial importance of social and cultural capital in European overseas successes during the early modern era. To employ the concept, *social and cultural capital,* in this context is to liberate it from the usage of modern social science. Building on Smith's insight, this article examines the new societies of British America to make some preliminary suggestions about the role of social and cultural capital in the early modern colonizing and overseas state-building process.

Several attributes of social and cultural capital, as it functioned in the colonizing process, deserve remark. One was the transferability that Smith emphasized. Settlers could carry social and cultural capital to new places, combine it with labor and investment capital, and transform—often, radically—Amerindian social and cultural landscapes into English-style spaces complete with English-style economies, social systems, and cultural arrangements.

Another attribute of social and cultural capital was its extraordinary adaptability. Settlers and other occupants could put the social and cultural capital that they carried with them to a wide variety of uses in many different sorts of socioeconomic contexts and ecological zones. In early modern English America, these zones extended from the lush tropical island of Barbados to the bleak shores of Newfoundland.

A third, and closely related, feature of social and cultural capital was its partibility. Out of the rich storehouse of available social tools and knowledge, settlers could select whatever was most useful to their specific efforts at social reconstruction in a particular space. In the process, they discarded much and, in the course of adjusting to the new situations in which they found themselves, simplified or modified everything from economic practices and social organization to law, and even language.[9]

---

8   *Ibid.,* 564; E. L. Jones, "The European Background," in Stanley L. Engerman and Robert E. Gallman (eds.), *The Cambridge Economic History of the United States. I. The Colonial Era* (Cambridge, 1996), 125; David Hume, *The History of England* (London, 1778), VI, 186.

9   The classic, and still most analytically impressive, study of the selectivity and simplification of European social capital in a New World setting is George M. Foster, *Culture and Conquest: America's Spanish Heritage* (Chicago, 1960). See also R. Cole Harris, "The Simplification of Europe Overseas," *Annals of the Association of American Geographers,* LXVII (1977), 469–483.

A fourth attribute of social and cultural capital in the colonizing process was its enhancibility, in two general ways. The first was by invention. By trial and error, settlers gained knowledge about such fundamental concerns as crop production, product shipment, or housing forms to meet the new conditions that they found or the specific objectives that they developed in their new situations. The second way was by imitation, learning from other peoples and cultures. To cite a few well-known examples, from Amerindians, they borrowed techniques of maize cultivation and processing; from the Portuguese, they imported the culture and technology of sugar production and the institutions of the plantation and chattel slavery; and from enslaved Africans, they learned to improve rice cultivation.

Such invention and borrowing produced new pools of social and cultural capital, combinations of transplanted and acquired knowledge, practices, and institutions that constituted important components in the new English-style societies. This new social and cultural capital was also transportable to other and newer settlements—that of Virginia being reproduced in neighboring Maryland and North Carolina, that of eastern New England in western New England, and that of Barbados in the Leeward Islands, Jamaica, and South Carolina. All of it went through a pattern of adaptation, selection, and enhancement similar to that which had characterized the construction of the earliest spaces of English colonial enterprise in the Americas.

In the thinly populated societies that characterized the early generations of English colonizing, the human capital of particular individuals with specialized skills effectively translated into social capital, even though during the initial stages of English occupation, transplanted social and cultural capital everywhere went through a winnowing or simplification process. The simple societies with which settlers began had no outlet, or need, for some of the specialized skills by which some immigrants had sustained themselves in old England. Finding no employment in their trades, weavers, fullers, and dyers from East Anglia, for instance, became farmers in New England, and their clothmaking skills died with them.

Similarly, many of the complexities of Old World societies had no function in simple New World societies. In the process of discarding the superfluous, settlers lost much knowledge and many Old World forms of social and cultural capital. Hence, as the earliest colonies—in the Chesapeake, New England, and the West Indies—slowly became more complex and in need of more refined forms of social and cultural capital, their inhabitants often lamented the earlier loss of such forms, fearing that they had lapsed into a state of creolean degeneracy that fell far short of metropolitan standards. In this situation, as Smith remarked, "there was not, perhaps, at that time either in Europe or America a single person who foresaw or even suspected the rapid progress" that the colonies would make during the next half century.[10]

Indeed, some of the very elements that stimulated such fears provided the means for the colonists' social and cultural delivery. Trade, continuing immigration, governmental interactions with metropolitan agencies of political supervision, and ongoing cultural exchanges in science, religion, and politics made them a part of an expanding transatlantic "information pool," reinforced their inherited cultural preferences for things British, and, by gaining them access to metropolitan social and cultural capital, held out the possibility for the replenishment, expansion, and updating of that social and cultural capital in New World places. Improved transportation and communication resulting from better navigation aids, more efficient and safer ships, more numerous sailings, the development of postal services, and closer economic integration had the same effect. Moreover, high rates of growth and development during the first three-quarters of the eighteenth century signalled the colonies' expanding capacities for acquiring metropolitan social and cultural capital and successfully incorporating their acquisitions into British-American cultures.[11]

The expansion of Britain's American colonies in North America was evident in virtually every sector of life, especially after about 1715. Still clustered in a series of noncontiguous nuclei close to the Atlantic seaboard in 1710, the population began to spill out in all possible directions. By the 1760s and 1770s, there was one long continuum of settlement stretching from Georgia to Maine, and new centers emerging in Nova Scotia and in East and West Florida. The white settler population soared during the

---

10 Smith, *Inquiry*, II, 597–598.
11 Jones, "European Background," 104. See Ian K. Steele, *The English Atlantic 1675–1740: An Exploration of Communication and Community* (New York, 1986).

same period, rising from about 318,600 in 1710 to c. 1,326,300 in 1760—an increase of more than 1,100 percent!

Demographic growth was particularly impressive among the continental colonies. The number of whites was doubling every twenty-five to thirty years, jumping from 286,785 in 1710 to 1,275,163 in 1760. The black population, the overwhelming majority of which was slave, grew from 181,511 to 646,305 in all the British colonies, and from 44,386 to 317,906 in the continental colonies. Stimulated by the continuing availability of land and the high levels of economic opportunity to meet the demands of both the growing population and an expanding overseas commerce, the increase in the number of whites on the continent was the result of both continuing immigration and a vigorous natural increase that seems to have been a function of a combination of declining mortality, younger marriages, higher fertility, and better nutrition. The growth of black population was testimony to the increasing capital and labor resources of slave purchasers and, in the continental colonies, to a sturdy natural increase.[12]

Economic growth was also impressive during these years. Every available indicator—number of slaves, personal wealth, volume of agricultural production, value of exports and imports (from Britain), and quantities shipped in the coastal trade—demonstrates steady growth before 1740 and extraordinary growth thereafter. During the six decades after 1700, the volume of agricultural production increased at least sixfold, the value of overseas exports about fourfold, and the value of imports from Britain nearly sevenfold. Recent estimates suggest that the gross national product (GNP) multiplied about twenty-five times between 1650 and 1770, increasing at an annual average rate of 2.7 percent for British America as a whole and 3.2 percent for British North America. This increase may have represented a real per capita annual growth rate of 0.6 percent, which was twice that of Britain. By the time of the American Revolution, this vigorous economic growth had produced a standard of living that might have been "the highest achieved for the great bulk of the [free] population in any country up to that time."[13]

12   Greene, *Pursuits of Happiness: The Social Development of Early Modern British Colonies and the Formation of American Culture* (Chapel Hill, 1988), 177–181.

13   John J. McCusker and Russell R. Menard, *The Economy of British America, 1607–1789* (Chapel Hill, 1985), 51–61; Alice Hanson Jones, "Wealth Estimates for the American Middle

Accompanying this impressive territorial, demographic, and economic performance was a rapid development and massive accumulation of human, social, and cultural capital. In the economic sphere, it was manifested in a greater specialization of production, leading to lower production costs; better transportation, resulting in lower distribution costs; more efficient markets; tighter organization; and rising technical capacity. Occupational structure became increasingly complex; the commercial sector more highly skilled and internally differentiated; the professions—including law, ministry, and medicine—more specialized; arts, trades, and women's work more expert; and agricultural output more efficient, as farmers and slaves learned to adapt old products and experiment with new ones.

The proliferation of social and human capital was also observable in the social realm. It was responsible for the emergence of an increasingly complex society with an ever-larger range, more dense distribution, and more deeply established agglomeration of social institutions, including families and kinship groups; neighborhoods and hamlets; port cities and administrative towns; stores and artisanal establishments; local judicial and administrative institutions; churches; and transportation facilities, including roads, bridges, ferries, and a few canals.[14]

In the cultural sphere, it was evident in the increasing availability of knowledge through a broad spectrum of educational, cultural, social, economic, and religious institutions and through a rising volume of books, magazines, and newspapers of colonial, British, and European origin accessible to the colonists. It gave rise to a general expansion of schooling, including more institutions of higher learning; rising levels of English literacy, which, running well above 70 percent of adult male settlers, was higher than in Britain; the establishment and expansion of both private and public libraries; an increasingly vigorous press with the capacity to publish books, pamphlets, newspapers, and other reading material; and a rash of voluntary associations, such as coffee-house groups, chambers of commerce, professional societies, fraternal

Colonies, 1774," *Economic Development and Cultural Change,* XVIII (1970), 130; *idem, The Wealth of a Nation to Be: The American Colonies on the Eve of the Revolution* (New York, 1980), 302–303; *idem,* "Wealth and Growth of the Thirteen Colonies: Some Implications," *Journal of Economic History,* XLIV (1984), 250–252.

14 Greene, *Pursuits of Happiness,* 184–187.

organizations, literary clubs, salons, tea tables, assemblies, and other imitations of the forms of polite society that characterized the metropolis.[15]

The massive increase in colonial social and human capital represented by these developments fostered the emergence of a European-style civil society throughout Britain's American colonies. According to Seligman, the concept of civil society as a voluntary union of people "existing independently of the state" had its origins in eighteenth-century England and Scotland and received "its fullest articulation in the Scottish Enlightenment," Smith being perhaps its principal analyst and exponent. Yet, as Seligman observes, contemporaries looked across the Atlantic for the primary "historical model of this theory." The new republican polity of the United States "provided for the philosophers of the eighteenth and nineteenth centuries (and for many thereafter) the model of civil society, with its voluntary associations, separation of Church and State, federalist (as opposed to Statist) concepts, and protection of individual liberties."[16]

Seligman's observations implicitly raise the question of how much this model of civil society was the product of the American Revolution and how much it was informed by earlier colonial British-American social experience. Some scholars have been so intent upon assimilating the American Revolution to the great European revolutions—emphasizing its revolutionary character and radical discontinuity with the American past—that they have largely neglected to explore the bearing of earlier American social experience upon the events and developments of the American Revolution.

The conception of the Revolution, and the creation of a national political system as *the founding* and of the people who presided over those events as *the founders,* has encouraged this

15 See Lawrence A. Cremin, *American Education: The Colonial Experience 1607–1783* (New York), 545, 551, 553: David Lundberg and Henry F. May, "The Enlightened Reader in America," *American Quarterly,* XXVIII (1976), 262–292; Richard D. Brown, *Knowledge Is Power: The Diffusion of Information in Early America, 1700–1785* (New York, 1989); Richard L. Bushman, *The Refinement of America: Persons, Houses, Cities* (New York, 1992); David S. Shields, *Civil Tongues & Polite Letters in Early America* (Chapel Hill, 1997).
16 Adam B. Seligman, *The Idea of Civil Society* (New York, 1992), 3, 5, 61–62. On the origins and early development of the idea of civil society, see also Marvin B. Becker, *The Emergence of Civil Society in the Eighteenth Century: A Privileged Moment in the History of England, Scotland, and France* (Bloomington, 1994).

neglect. When it intends nothing more than the founding of the American national state, such language elicits no objection. There was no American state and, hence, no political entity or political society that could be called America before the middle of 1776; the American state so much celebrated by contemporary European philosophers and American political analysts did not come into being until the late 1780s.

Yet, if we are thinking about the civil societies in those areas of America that became the United States, such a conception is fraught with serious problems. As Smith and his American contemporaries were well aware, those civil societies were not "founded" during the late eighteenth century; they had already constructed themselves through a long process lasting, in all but one case, between a century and a century and three-quarters. When these societies came together to form the American nation between 1775 and 1800, what they experienced was a second founding. This is not merely a semantic or an academic quibble, especially not for a social historian or for any analyst concerned with understanding eighteenth-century American conceptions of civil society. To conceive of the establishment of the colonies as the first founding is to call attention both to their long histories as political societies at the time of the Revolution and to open up the possibility of understanding the important relationship between those histories and the contemporary understanding of civil society in late eighteenth-century America.

From the beginnings of English colonization early in the seventeenth century, both the actual process of settlement—of social formation—and contemporary conceptions of that process facilitated the emergence of ideas about the nature of civil society and the priorities that they represented. Indeed, the idea of what a civil society ought to be might well have been the most important form of social and cultural capital that settlers brought with them from the Old World. Through every stage of the colonizing process, and from Barbados north to New England, this inherited standard operated as a framework for identification. Largely oblivious to its tragic effects upon the indigenous inhabitants, settlers and land developers conceived of it as a massive civilizing project. Deeply aware of its profound transformative effects, they thought of themselves as engaged in a laborious but noble effort to conquer a wilderness by felling forests; creating fields, orchards, and pastures; substituting domestic for wild animals; and otherwise bringing the land under their mastery. In the process, they deliberately changed landscapes that to them appeared rude and barren, turning them into civil spaces that represented extensions of the English or other European places to which they were politically, economically, culturally, and emotionally attached and on which they relied for their norms of a civil society.[17]

First founders of every new society in colonial English America secured possession of the land by treating with or defeating the Indians, clearing the wilderness, and introducing whatever forms of agriculture seemed most appropriate. To supply their wants during the earliest phases of this process, they frequently reverted to more primitive forms of economic and social activity—hunting, like the Indians, or, in many cases, grazing and raising livestock. But their larger project was always the establishment of settled agricultural, commercial, and civil societies of the kind that they had left behind in the Old World. As they reconfigured the physical landscape into farms, estates, and urban communities, and inscribed it with property lines, they began the slow process of implanting, refining, and accumulating the social and cultural capital that would form the foundations for the articulation of a civil society.

Whether they entered into explicit formal compacts (as, for instance, in Plymouth), or whether, far more commonly, they simply adapted the well-known practices and rules of English common law to their new situations, they quickly established civil polities, the principal purposes of which were little more than to protect their habitations against Amerindians or rival Europeans, to govern relations among themselves, and to secure the property that they were creating and accumulating through their own industry and activities. From these early beginnings, the "natural progress" of agriculture, and the development of the commercial networks that made it profitable, settled "the affairs of society on an easy and secure foundation" and provided settlers with the economic and social wherewithal to cultivate a civil life. The result, as Smith noted, was a "natural progress in the arts" that led ineluctably in the direction of a civility and refinement that stood

17 See Greene, *The Intellectual Construction of America: Exceptionalism and Identity from 1492 to 1800* (Chapel Hill, 1993).

in stark contrast to conditions among neighboring Amerindians, who, despite the example of the settlers, "still continue[d] in the most rude and uncultivated state of society."[18]

In the experience of colonial British-Americans, moreover, this process was not limited to the earliest, or first, foundings. Rather, as many late eighteenth-century observers pointed out— among them Crèvecouer and Williams, whose 1794 *Natural and Civil History of Vermont* is certainly the most extensive, systematic, and sophisticated contemporary analysis of the "state of society" in America—settlers who headed for the "interior parts of the country" continually repeated the experience of the earlier coastal settlers. At first, they hunted like the Indians, but slowly, in Crèvecouer's words, they began changing the "hideous barbarous country" of the "great woods" into "fine, well-regulated district[s]," increasingly characterized by "a general decency of manners" and sophisticated commercial and social infrastructures, including stores, taverns, courthouses, churches, and other institutions. After the first two or three generations of settlement, colonial British North America in its various zones—from the primitive frontier to what Crèvecouer called middle zones and to the polite and more heavily commercialized east—exhibited the full range of stages through which contemporary social theorists conjectured that societies passed in their advance to commercial civilization.[19]

Dating from the first foundings and deeply rooted in the colonial British-American experience, this understanding of social development as progress from rudeness to refinement, from less to more advanced forms of social organization, and from passion and self-indulgence to reason and self-control was, by the middle decades of the eighteenth century, thoroughly engraved in the collective consciousness of free colonial British-Americans. Long before the American Revolution, colonial British-American social development had functioned as a blueprint—an elaborate historical demonstration, evident in literally thousands of cases—of the process by which civil society took shape.

18 Smith, *Inquiry,* II, 565; James Wilson, "Lectures on Law," in Robert Green McCloskey (ed.), *The Works of James Wilson* (Cambridge, Mass., 1967), I, 231; William White and Wilson, "The Visitant," 5, *Pennsylvania Chronicle* (Philadelphia), 29 Feb. 1768.
19 Samuel Williams, *Natural and Civil History of Vermont* (Walpole, N.H., 1794), II, 352; J. Hector St. Jean de Crèvecouer, *Letters from an American Farmer* (New York, 1957), 42–43.

As settlers and other contemporary analysts conceived of it, the history of the colonies was only incidentally about war and politics or about religious matters (other than in New England, which was atypical of colonial British-American cultural development). Rather, it was the more significant story of the *social* transformation of significant portions of North America and the West Indies in little more than a century and a half, a grand story richly and endlessly illustrated in the successful rise of individuals to competence, substance, and fortune. Witness Crèvecouer's recounting of the career of Andrew, the Hebridean, "a poor man, advancing from oppression to freedom; from obscurity and contumely to some degree of consequence—not by virtue of any freaks of fortune, but by the gradual operation of sobriety, honesty, and emigration." Throughout the colonizing process, this transformation of the wilderness into improved, European-style, civil spaces comprised the principal story that informed, connected, and gave meaning to the lives of the millions of free people who took part in it.[20]

Moreover, the characteristics associated with the societies that had taken shape as a result of this transformation were, in many respects, almost a perfect example of contemporary Scottish Enlightenment theories of civil society. As products of both necessity and volition, the new societies of colonial British America were, preeminently, societies of independent freeholding families composed of "free and independent men" and "sensible" women deeply engaged in their pursuits of individual happiness. Notwithstanding the fact that many of those men and women found their happiness in the possession of black slaves, in economic exploitation of social dependents, and in sweeping and intensive cultural imperialism, the societies that they created, according to many observers, often exemplified the characteristics that Enlightenment thinkers associated with the idea of civil society: concentration on agriculture; economic prosperity; social equality among the free segments of society; well-regulated families; concentric circles of neighborhoods, associations, institutions, and markets that provided public arenas for social interaction and fostered hospitality, industry, activity, and a powerful impulse toward improvement; mild, if not always "perfect freedom and equality" of religion;

20 *Ibid.,* 64.

benign, cheap, and highly participatory government that was suspicious of the intrusions of foreign power as well as nonlocal authority; modest civil establishment and low taxes; deep hostility to privilege; and "warm and uniform attachment to liberty."[21]

Long before they formally became republican in 1776, the British colonies in America were republican in manner and government. In Smith's words, settlers enjoyed virtually complete "liberty . . . to manage their own affairs in their own way." They were governed by locally elected assemblies that were not only dedicated to that "equal and impartial administration of justice which renders the rights of the meanest British subjects respectable to the greatest, and which, by securing to every man the fruits of his own industry, gives the greatest and most effectual encouragement to every sort of industry" but also were far more representative, far less corrupt, and far more responsive to their constituents than was the British House of Commons. As Wilson later explained, such political arrangements engraved upon the character of colonial British-Americans two of the principal "virtues" associated with the idea of civil society, "the love of liberty and the love of law."[22]

According to Williams' explication of Smith's and Wilson's insights, "in the state of society which had taken place in America," the foundations of its "freedom were laid, long before the nations of Europe had any suspicion of what was taking place in the minds of men." Not some "artificially contrived" system "of political checks, balances, and arrangements," then, but the distinctive social conditions that colonial British-Americans had created during their earlier histories constituted the "extensive and permanent cause" of the "system of American Republicanism." Williams defined it as the belief that government should limit itself to three simple functions: "Do justice, protect property, and defend the country."[23]

The "natural, easy, independent situation, and spirit, in which the body of the [free] people were found when the American war

21 Wilson, "Lectures on Law," I, 81; White and Wilson, "The Visitant," 3, *Pennsylvania Chronicle,* 8 Feb. 1768; Greene, *Pursuits of Happiness;* Williams, *Natural and Civil History of Vermont,* II, 423; Wilson, "Oration Delivered on the Fourth of July 1788," in McCloskey (ed.), *Works of Wilson,* II, 777.
22 Smith, *Inquiry,* II, 585, 610; Wilson, "Lectures on Law," I, 72.
23 Williams, *Natural and Civil History of Vermont,* II, 358–359, 426.

came on" and the broad "civil freedom" that they enjoyed, Williams explained, were the "constant product and effect" of the societies that the founders—that is, the *first* founders—and their descendants and later immigrants had constructed. In such conditions, "the common farmer of America had a more comprehensive view of his rights and privileges than the speculative philosopher of Europe ever could have of the subject." Political writers during the Revolution, like Thomas Paine, met with such "amazing success," not "because they taught the people principles, which they did not before understand; but because they placed the principles which they had learned" from "the state of society in America . . . in a very clear and striking light, on a most critical and important occasion."[24]

In these essentially self-regulating communities, society, in Wilson's words, was not "the scaffolding of government" but government "the scaffolding of society." The end of government and law was to "protect and to improve social life" by making sure that the lands, goods, chattels, and rights "collected by the labour and industry of individuals" should remain, inviolably, "their property"; the measure of a good government was the extent to which it promoted "the peace, happiness, and prosperity, the increase, and the affections of the people." What better demonstration could there have been of that fundamental principle of civil society that "the happiness of society" ought to be "the *first* law of every government"?[25]

Long before they could have read the works of the Scottish Enlightenment, colonial British-Americans had subscribed to the ideas that society—what the Scots meant by the term *civil society*—was anterior to government; that the function of laws, governments, and constitutions was to promote the ends of civil society, especially to facilitate the pursuit of happiness by the individuals therein; and that for most people, such pursuit would be conducted far more satisfyingly within the family, neighborhood, or local civic institutions than in the small political arenas that characterized the colonies.

---

24 *Ibid.*, 429–431.
25 Wilson, "Lectures on Law," I, 86, 88, 233; Williams, *Natural and Civil History of Vermont*, II, 415; Wilson, "Considerations on the Nature and Extent of the Legislative Authority of the British Parliament (1774)," in McCloskey (ed.), *Works of Wilson*, II, 723.

In the colonial British–American case, civil societies, in the European sense, were not the product of but the precondition for the American Revolution. They were not so much the result of independent nationhood or newfound revolutionary resources or sensibilities as of an ongoing process of social and cultural capital transfer, refinement, and accumulation that had begun during the century and a half following the first founding of English colonies in the Chesapeake, New England, and the West Indies. From this perspective, what historians call the American Revolution needs to be understood as an effort to perpetuate and improve the benefits of the civil societies that were already in place by the last decades of the colonial era. Both the civic autonomy that colonial British-Americans sought through independence and the institutional structures that they created during the last quarter of the eighteenth century were expressions of the preexistent social and cultural capital that they were determined to preserve.

Neither settlers nor metropolitans during the colonial era fully understood the larger implications of the social accomplishments of American settlers. Settlers did not think of their societies as a "new model of the social order." On the contrary, like Smith, they continued to consider the Old World as the "great mother" who had supplied and replenished much of the social capital that the settlers and their descendants had been able to refine, expand, and accumulate in the process of building English societies in American places. Only gradually during the intense constitutional discussions about the structure of the British Empire, the necessary attributes of republican polities, and the proper "form of government for an extensive empire" that took place from the mid-1760s to the early 1790s did people on either side of the Atlantic come to an appreciation of the extent to which the "historical development" of colonial British America was "paradigmatic of a broader and more general change in sensibility, values, and world views."[26]

During the late eighteenth century, at the time of the *second* founding, colonial American social experience had a profound bearing upon American conceptions of civil society and its relationship to government. Experientially and conceptually, the first and second foundings were of a piece; any discontinuities between them were little more than an elaborate resolution of political and

26 Seligman, *Idea of a Civil Society,* 16, 91; Smith, *Inquiry,* II, 590, 623.

intellectual contingencies that arose within the radical civil societies that colonial British-Americans had constructed between 1607
and 1776. Precisely because of their radical character, these societies could both construct a profoundly conservative revolution
and serve as paradigmatic for the civil societies emerging in the
Old World.

Gerald Gamm and Robert D. Putnam

The Growth of Voluntary Associations in America, 1840–1940

Americans are a civic people. Next to the mass political party, probably no aspect of American democracy has been more celebrated than the long-standing proclivity of Americans to join voluntary associations. According to Schlesinger, we are "a nation of joiners." The joining began in the middle of the eighteenth century, it flourished in the revolutionary committees that undergirded the War of Independence, and it has continued ever since. "Considering the central importance of the voluntary organization in American history there is no doubt it has provided the people with their greatest school of self-government," Schlesinger writes. "Rubbing minds as well as elbows, they have been trained from youth to take common counsel, choose leaders, harmonize differences, and obey the expressed will of the majority. In mastering the associative way they have mastered the democratic way."[1]

Schlesinger understood that he was revisiting and updating Tocqueville's famous argument. More than a century earlier, Toc-

Gerald Gamm is James P. Wilmot Assistant Professor of Political Science and History, University of Rochester. He is the author of *The Making of New Deal Democrats: Voting Behavior and Realignment in Boston, 1920–1940* (Chicago, 1989); *Urban Exodus: Why the Jews Left Boston and the Catholics Stayed* (Cambridge, Mass., 1999).

Robert D. Putnam is Stanfield Professor of International Peace, Harvard University. He is the author of *Making Democracy Work: Civic Traditions in Modern Italy* (Princeton, 1993); *Bowling Alone: Civic Disengagement in America* (New York, 1999).

Earlier versions of this article were presented at the annual meeting of the Social Science History Association, New Orleans, 1996; the annual meeting of the Organization of American Historians, San Francisco, 1997; and the conference on "Civic Engagement in American Democracy," Portland, Maine, 1997. The research for this article was funded by a grant from the Pew Charitable Trusts and a fellowship, for Gamm, from the Woodrow Wilson International Center for Scholars. The authors received particularly helpful comments from Nancy Cott, Marshall Ganz, Peter Dobkin Hall, Tom Sander, Theda Skocpol, Margaret Weir, and Robert Westbrook. For much of the research and data collection, the authors are indebted to Melissa Buis, Brad Clarke, Jay Goodliffe, Isa Helfgott, Tom Keating, Lisa Laskin, Jonathan Leeman, Martin Schulke, and Aaron Wicks. The authors would also like to thank Cindy Adams, Louise Hayes, Brian Roraff, Mario Salguero, and Chris Warren for additional research assistance. Special thanks go to Louise Kennedy and Tom Sander for their help in managing this project.

1 Arthur M. Schlesinger, "Biography of a Nation of Joiners," *American Historical Review*, L (1944), 24.

queville had contended that the abundance of American civil associations contributed to the stability of American democracy. Civil associations, he insisted, were more crucial than political associations to a democratic society. "If the inhabitants of democratic countries had neither the right nor the taste for uniting for political objects, their independence would run great risks, but they could keep both their wealth and their knowledge for a long time," Tocqueville argued. "But if they did not learn some habits of acting together in the affairs of daily life, civilization itself would be in peril."[2]

Tocqueville did not intend his remarks to serve as a warning to Americans. Neither did he hesitate to acknowledge ways in which political activity nurtured civil activity. As Skocpol demonstrates, the nation's dense network of associations flourished alongside mass party organizations and depended in many ways on the activities of the state. "The early U.S. postal system both grew out of and furthered a congressional representative system that encompassed virtually all white men," Skocpol writes. "It furthered ever-intensifying communications among citizens, pulling more and more Americans into passionate involvements in regional and national moral crusades and electoral campaigns."[3]

Tocqueville was deeply impressed by the level of voluntary activity that he found in the United States, and he regarded the American case as an exemplar for the democratizing world. He observed a society where the commitment to voluntary associations was constant and unyielding. Generations later, Schlesinger argued that American civil society was at least as strong and vibrant as it had been in Tocqueville's day. In the years since Schlesinger wrote his essay, scholars have researched a vast array of associations and produced a substantial and impressive literature. One association and one community at a time, this scholarship has quietly undermined the textbook image of associations established by Tocqueville and Schlesinger. Modern research suggests that associational life is a variable, not a constant. Yet, Tocqueville's claim that "Americans of all ages, all stations in life, and all types of disposition are *forever* forming associations" remains definitive.[4]

---

2 Alexis de Tocqueville (ed., J. P. Mayer; trans., George Lawrence), *Democracy in America* (Garden City, 1969; orig. pub. 1835–1840), 514.
3 Theda Skocpol, "The Tocqueville Problem: Civic Engagement in American Democracy," *Social Science History,* XXI (1997), 463.
4 Tocqueville, *Democracy in America,* 513 (emphasis added).

Understanding both the historical accuracy of this textbook image and the circumstances in which associations flourish is an urgent task. During the last generation, according to Putnam, Americans have deserted the church pew, the union hall, the Parent–Teacher Association, the Elks lodge, and even the bowling league. By many measures—though not all—the level of civic engagement in the United States has declined since the 1960s. Americans are less connected with one another in voluntary associations (at least in the conventional forms to which their parents were accustomed), as well as in less formal settings. Levels of trust and political involvement have fallen sharply. Associations are, to be sure, not the only form of social capital, but as Tocqueville underscored, they have been a particularly significant form in the United States.[5]

If the textbook image is correct—if the American attachment to voluntary organizations has remained consistent throughout the nation's history—then the recent decline in civic engagement represents an unprecedented, and serious, event. If, however, the textbook image is not correct and periods of overall associational decline have alternated with periods of associational expansion, then the past not only gives context to the present but offers potential explanation for the current drift away from civic involvement. Reversing that drift requires understanding the regional, political, and institutional sources of associational vigor and the character of communities where association building has historically been most successful.

That analysis is a large task. In virtually every city and town, Americans have built dense, complex networks of voluntary associations: churches, clubs, lodges, choirs, mutual-aid societies, and sports teams. The institutional history of voluntary associations is the history of many hundreds of thousands of institutions that are obscure, scattered, and often small. A systematic analysis of association building throughout the United States means locating and analyzing many forms of associations, in many regions, in large cities and modest towns, over long periods of time.

To conduct that analysis, we have gathered data, generally at ten-year intervals, from a sample of twenty-six cities and towns for the period 1840 to 1940 (not yet including 1930). The prin-

---

5 Putnam, "Bowling Alone: America's Declining Social Capital," *Journal of Democracy,* VI (1995), 65–78; *idem, Bowling Alone: Civic Disengagement in America* (New York, 1999).

cipal body of data is drawn from city directories, which include comprehensive lists of a large variety of associations. We also gathered data from organizational directories compiled and published by associations themselves, to assess the validity of city directories as a source of data and to obtain membership statistics for local associations. Drawing on these various bodies of evidence, we analyze long-term trends in American associational development, regional patterns of associational strength, and the relationship of associational development to immigration, industrialization, and urbanization.

Though rates of growth differed from association to association, we find that most types of associations grew rapidly in number, relative to population, between 1850 and 1900, with slower growth through 1910. Between 1910 and 1940, the incidence of associations stagnated and even declined. This finding confirms many studies of individual types of associations—the late nineteenth century was a time of unusually vigorous associational growth.

But our evidence conflicts directly with the common contention that associational growth was directly related to urbanization, industrialization, and immigration. For we find that associational life was most vibrant—and its growth most sustained—in the small cities and towns of the hinterland, rather than the great cities of the Northeast or Midwest. Throughout this period, associations existed in greater numbers in the West than in the East. Although some level of urbanization appears to have been a prerequisite for regular associational activity—town residents can organize in more formal ways than isolated farmers— associational activity was consistently weakest in large, rapidly growing cities. The finding that small cities and towns, especially those with low levels of population growth, became the strongholds of American associational life from the mid-nineteenth century to the mid-twentieth century suggests the need for a reexamination of basic assumptions about the course of American political and social development.

CITY DIRECTORIES AND ORGANIZATIONAL REPORTS   To measure national patterns of association building, we located sequences of city directories from twenty-six cities and towns. They range in size from large places like St. Louis and Boston—two of the nation's five largest cities at the turn of the century—to small places like Rome, Georgia; Junction City, Kansas; Boise, Idaho; and Bath, Maine. These cities vary not only in size but in region, timing of urbanization, level of industrialization, level of immigration, growth rate, and ethnic distribution.[6]

For each city or town, we identified, at intervals of about ten years, every association listed in the annual city directory. In total, we gathered data from 224 directories, identifying 65,761 voluntary associations. With small exceptions, this group includes all non-government and non-business organizations and associations listed in the directories. The functional area of these associations spanned the full gamut of American civic life, from the Peoria Main-Street Presbyterian Church and the Galveston Austrian Slavonian Benevolent Association, to the Lathers, Wood, Wire, and Metal Union Local No. 68 (Denver) and the St. Lawrence O'Toole's No. 32 Lodge of the Catholic Knights and Ladies of America (St. Louis). About 28 percent of the associations in these cities were churches or other religious organizations, 30 percent were fraternal or sororal organizations, and the remainder had other sorts of economic, social, cultural, and political purposes.[7]

City directories are not available from all cities for the earliest years; indeed, many of these cities did not exist in the 1840s and 1850s. Thus, our earliest samples include only Boston, Charleston, Lowell, St. Louis, and Peoria. By 1870, our coverage expands to twenty towns and cities, and by 1890, all twenty-six sites. We

6 Although not strictly a random sample, we selected our research sites to be broadly representative. In the case of large and medium-sized cities, we selected the sample to maximize diversity along several dimensions and then searched for city directories for each city in the sample. In just two cases (Brooklyn and Minneapolis) were we unable to locate directories with associational listings covering at least the period 1870 to 1920. In the case of smaller cities and towns, we were more constrained. The choice of small cities was made only after a long search—in the Library of Congress, university research libraries, and state and local historical societies throughout the country—for small-city directory series that covered as long a time span as possible.

7 Because Sunday schools are not listed consistently in city directories, we have omitted them from our analysis in the rest of this article. (By contrast, churches and synagogues seem to have been listed comprehensively by directory compilers in virtually all our sites.)

Henceforth, we report not the total number of associations in any city but the number of associations per 1,000 people. When we illustrate multi-city data in figures, we compute averages across all sites that are available for a given decade, rounding off-year directories up or down to the nearest census year. We use the actual city-directory years, without any rounding, in the regression analyses.

give equal weight to each site; evidence from a small town like Boise counts as much in our data as evidence from a big city like Boston. This approach permits generalizations about associational life in cities and towns of various size, eliminating any bias in favor of big-city data. After all, many more Americans at the turn of the century lived in Boises (1890 population, 2,311) than in Bostons (1890 population, 448,477).

Our sample suggests that city directories tended to appear when a population reached a few thousand inhabitants. Consequently, data drawn from city directories inevitably slight the large numbers of Americans who lived on farms or in smaller villages throughout this era. Even Boise, a minor, isolated town, was more urban than the places where most Americans lived in the late nineteenth century. Although most of the analysis in this article emphasizes trends and patterns of associational growth in cities and towns, we also gathered national and local membership numbers for Masonic lodges and Episcopal churches to assess differences in association formation between urban and rural America.

The city directories themselves appear to have been compiled with diligence and care. To check their accuracy, we gathered independent lists of associations published in various organizational registers. For example, we compared a list of Episcopal churches included in the 1930 *Living Church Annual* with the lists of Episcopal churches that appeared in eight city directories that year; the correspondence was exact, or nearly so, in every case. Synagogues, too—even the smallest, most poorly organized ones—appear to have been accurately listed in city directories. As Gamm discovered in researching Boston's churches and synagogues, the list of synagogues in the 1919 city directory was even more accurate than the corresponding list that appeared in that year's *American Jewish Year Book*. Official reports about local chapters of other organizations demonstrate that various types of associations—such as Rotary clubs, the Salvation Army, Masonic lodges, and the Daughters of the American Revolution—were accurately listed in city directories throughout this period.[8]

---

8   *The Living Church Annual: The Churchman's Year Book & American Church Almanac, 1930* (Milwaukee, 1930); Gamm, *Urban Exodus: Why the Jews Left Boston and the Catholics Stayed* (Cambridge, Mass., 1999). See also Appendix B.

But city directories did not list all organizations with such consistency. Some major forms of associations—local political party organizations and individual school chapters of the National Congress of Parents and Teachers—were generally not listed at all in city directories. Others, such as local affiliates of national labor federations and the General Federation of Women's Clubs, were listed incompletely. These are serious omissions. As we proceed to the next stage of this project, we intend to search for and analyze data for groups that were not listed consistently in city directories so as to develop a more comprehensive view of associational life than the directories themselves can afford.

Still, as a systematic source of data, the city directories are unparalleled. Their limitations do not suggest any consistent bias, except, perhaps, against ephemeral and newly organized associations. Middle-class women's clubs and PTAs were not listed consistently, but immigrant, low-status synagogues and fraternal organizations were listed with exquisite thoroughness. Omissions do not appear to be related to city size, to the size of immigrant populations, or to the social status of organizations. The directories represent an excellent source for understanding trends and patterns of associational strength. We are unaware of any comparably broad sample of civic life in American towns and cities of the nineteenth and early twentieth centuries.[9]

Since city directories generally list associations but not the number of members in each association, we have supplemented the directory data with data collected from various organizational reports. To determine the membership numbers of local associations, we examined hundreds of publications and unpublished reports in the Library of Congress, in Widener Library, and in other Harvard libraries, and we contacted the offices of many national and local organizations. This article presents evidence from the most comprehensive reports available, including data from many, or all, of our twenty-six sites, for the following organizations: Masonic lodges, Episcopal churches, affiliates of the General Federation of Women's Clubs (GFWC), and Rotary clubs. By examining these membership data in tandem with the group

9 Peter R. Knights, *The Plain People of Boston, 1830–1860: A Study in City Growth* (New York, 1971), 134–135; Stephan Thernstrom, *The Other Bostonians: Poverty and Progress in the American Metropolis, 1880–1970* (Cambridge, Mass., 1973), 285–288.

lists that appear in the city directories, we can analyze the relationship between numbers of separate organizations and numbers of members.[10]

TIMING   Scholars generally assert that the late nineteenth and early twentieth centuries comprised an age of great associational activity. Beginning in the 1870s and extending into the 1910s, new types of associations proliferated, as did chapters of new and pre-existing types of associations, and associations increasingly federated into state and national organizations. The diverse literature about many different types of associations suggests strongly that this was the era when the voluntary structures of American civil society assumed modern form.

Still, this same scholarship demonstrates that patterns of growth and decline varied sharply from group to group. Existing studies of associations do not identify any particular time within the period 1870 to 1920 when most associations experienced growth or decline simultaneously. The literature attests to the remarkable diversity of associational experiences during this era rather than to any overarching commonality of experience. Additional literature, especially studies of specific cities and towns, complicates the overall image further, suggesting that even this broad period might not encompass the most important periods of growth.

Trends in Association Building: Existing Scholarship   Religion and politics appear to have been the most important organizing forces from the late eighteenth to the early nineteenth century. The American Revolution itself was the product of a network that united political leaders throughout the colonies. The Committees of Correspondence, the Stamp Act Congress, the Continental Congress, the Sons of Liberty, and groups that gathered regularly in taverns contributed to the movement for national independence. Indeed, as Fischer shows, Paul Revere's ride succeeded only because of the prior existence of well-organized militias in each town that he alerted. After independence, the creation of a national government led to the organization of competing political parties. By the 1830s, local party organizations,

10   This search was conducted by Jonathan Leeman, who led the effort to compile a massive body of reports to supplement the city-directory data. This article analyzes evidence from the reports that include the fullest sets of membership numbers.

linked together in national federations, helped structure the nation's politics.[11]

The Second Great Awakening invigorated and extended religious organizations in the first decades of the nineteenth century. Methodist and Baptist churches flourished in this era—though, according to Finke and Stark, this general expansion masked declines in Episcopalian, Congregational, and Presbyterian churches. In communities across the country, Americans established Bible and tract societies, missionary societies, temperance groups, and benevolent associations. Sunday schools, too, were organized in these years.[12]

By the 1830s, temperance societies, reform and benevolent societies, and lyceums existed throughout most of the country, and abolitionist groups, linked together through the American Anti-Slavery Society, had been organized in much of the North. "The associational fervor began to subside around the mid-1840s," Ryan states, in her study of Utica and surrounding villages. "Until then, however, much of community life seemed organized around these associations." The Masons, transplanted from England in the late eighteenth century, had declined in popularity after the middle 1820s. But other groups, like literary clubs and college fraternities, had slowly begun to emerge. This was the America that Tocqueville found.[13]

Although studies of specific types of association often neglect the 1840s and 1850s, Blumin regards the era as a great age of

11   David Hackett Fischer, *Paul Revere's Ride* (New York, 1994); Schlesinger, "Biography."
12   Roger Finke and Rodney Stark, *The Churching of America, 1776–1990* (New Brunswick, 1992); Donald G. Mathews, "The Second Great Awakening as an Organizing Process, 1780–1830: An Hypothesis," *American Quarterly*, XXI (1969), 23–43; Nathan O. Hatch, *The Democratization of American Christianity* (New Haven, 1989); Charles C. Cole, Jr., *The Social Ideas of the Northern Evangelists, 1820–1860* (New York, 1954); Anne M. Boylan, *Sunday School: The Formation of an American Institution, 1790–1880* (New Haven, 1988).
13   Mary P. Ryan, *Cradle of the Middle Class: The Family in Oneida County, New York, 1790–1865* (Cambridge, 1981), 105. See also *idem, Civic Wars: Democracy and Public Life in the American City during the Nineteenth Century* (Berkeley, 1997); Schlesinger, "Biography"; Carl Bode, *The American Lyceum: Town Meeting of the Mind* (New York, 1956); David Rothman, *The Discovery of the Asylum: Social Order and Disorder in the New Republic* (Boston, 1971); Rowland Berthoff, *An Unsettled People: Social Order and Disorder in American History* (New York, 1971); Nancy Cott, *The Bonds of Womanhood: Woman's Sphere in New England, 1790–1835* (New Haven, 1975); James Brewer Stewart, *Holy Warriors: The Abolitionists and American Slavery* (New York, 1976); Paul Boyer, *Urban Masses and Moral Order in America, 1820–1920* (Cambridge, Mass., 1978); Paul Aaron and David Musto, "Temperance and Prohibition in America: A Historical Overview," in Mark H. Moore and Dean Gernstein

association building. "Voluntary organizations had existed before," Blumin argues, "but it was in the three decades preceding the Civil War that formal associations became so numerous, so elaborately organized, so appealing to so many people, so various in purpose, and in many instances so powerful, that this may fairly be called an era of voluntary institutional innovation without parallel in American history." Religious revivals in these years contributed to the steady growth of religious and moral-reform associations. Bible societies, temperance groups, cultural groups, militias, fire companies, and sports clubs abounded in this period. The American YMCA movement began in the 1850s; between 1851 and 1854, residents in twenty-five cities organized local YMCAS.[14]

Although many associations emerged in the first half of the nineteenth century, scholars generally argue that associations enjoyed their greatest flowering between 1870 and 1920. But the specific timing of this expansion—as well as any decline in this era—appears to have differed from group to group. The Grand Army of the Republic (GAR), a veterans' organization organized in the late 1860s, grew enormously in the 1880s, and the American Legion was founded at the end of World War I. Settlement houses were established across the country in the 1890s, 1900s, and 1910s. Nativist groups, including the American Protective Association and the Immigration Restriction League, flourished in the 1890s. College fraternities, sororities, and athletic clubs expanded rapidly in the 1880s and 1890s, and fraternities and sororities on various campuses began to organize national structures. The Boy Scouts,

(eds.), *Alcohol and Public Policy: Beyond the Shadow of Prohibition* (Washington, D.C., 1981); Jed Dannenbaum, *Drink and Disorder: Temperance Reform in Cincinnati from the Washington Revival to the WCTU* (Urbana, 1984); Kathleen Smith Kutolowski, "Freemasonry and Community in the Early Republic: The Case for Antimasonic Anxieties," *American Quarterly,* XXXIV (1982), 543–561; Charles F. Ferguson, *Fifty Million Brothers: A Panorama of American Lodges and Clubs* (New York, 1937); Helen Lefkowitz Horowitz, *Campus Life: Undergraduate Cultures from the End of the Eighteenth Century to the Present* (New York, 1987).
14 Stuart M. Blumin, *The Emergence of the Middle Class: Social Experience in the American City, 1760–1900* (Cambridge, 1989), 192. See also *idem, The Urban Threshold: Growth and Change in a Nineteenth-Century American Community* (Chicago, 1976); Ryan, *Civic Wars;* Timothy L. Smith, *Revivalism and Social Reform: American Protestantism on the Eve of the Civil War* (Baltimore, 1957); L. L. Doggett, *History of the Young Men's Christian Association* (New York, 1909); Charles Howard Hopkins, *History of the Y.M.C.A. in North America* (New York, 1951).

Girl Scouts, and Camp Fire Girls were organized in the 1910s. In rural America, farmers organized the Grange in the late 1860s and 1870s and the Farmers' Alliances in the 1880s. Working-class men and women began establishing large labor organizations, and social, cultural, and athletic clubs grew steadily in number. YMCAs, for example, grew continuously from the 1860s through the 1910s.[15]

Men's fraternal groups increased rapidly between the late 1860s and late 1890s. "Every fifth, or possibly every eighth, man you meet is identified with some fraternal organization," wrote Harwood in 1897. The nation's largest fraternal organizations that year—Masons, Odd Fellows, Knights of Pythias, Ancient Order of United Workmen, and Modern Woodmen of America—each reported hundreds of thousands of members. In the 1910s, as the popularity of traditional fraternal associations reached its peak, men began founding and joining service clubs like Rotary, Kiwanis, and Lions.[16]

15 Wallace Evan Davies, *Patriotism on Parade: The Story of Veterans' and Hereditary Organizations in America, 1783–1900* (Cambridge, Mass., 1955); Rodney G. Minott, *Peerless Patriots: Organized Veterans and the Spirit of Americanism* (Washington, D.C., 1962); David Bennett, *The Party of Fear: From Nativist Movements to the New Right in American History* (Chapel Hill, 1988); John Higham, *Strangers in the Land: Patterns of American Nativism, 1860–1925* (New Brunswick, 1988); Barbara Miller Solomon, *Ancestors and Immigrants: A Changing New England Tradition* (Cambridge, Mass., 1956); Ferguson, *Fifty Million Brothers;* John Robson (ed.), *Baird's Manual of American College Fraternities* (Menasha, Wisc., 1968; 18th ed.); David I. Macleod, *Building Character in the American Boy: The Boy Scouts, YMCA, and Their Forerunners, 1870–1920* (Madison, 1983); D. Sven Nordin, *Rich Harvest: A History of the Grange, 1867–1900* (Jackson, 1974); Lawrence Goodwyn, *Democratic Promise: The Populist Moment in America* (New York, 1976); Robert C. McMath, Jr., *American Populism: A Social History, 1877–1898* (New York, 1993); Alan Dawley and Paul Faler, "Working-Class Culture and Politics in the Industrial Revolution: Sources of Loyalism and Rebellion," *Journal of Social History,* IX (1976), 466–480; Stephen Hardy, *How Boston Played: Sport, Recreation, and Community, 1865–1915* (Boston, 1982); Melvin Adelman, *A Sporting Time: New York City and the Rise of Modern Athletics, 1820–1870* (Urbana, 1986); John S. Gilkeson, Jr., *Middle-Class Providence, 1820–1940* (Princeton, 1986); Steven Riess, *City Games: The Evolution of American Urban Society and the Rise of Sports* (Urbana, 1989); Karen Blair, *The Torchbearers: Women and Their Amateur Arts Associations in America, 1890–1930* (Bloomington, 1994); Hopkins, *History of the Y.M.C.A.*

16 W. S. Harwood, "Secret Societies in America," *North American Review,* CLXIV (1897), 617, also 620. See also Schlesinger, "Biography"; Lynn Dumenil, *Freemasonry and American Culture, 1880–1939* (Princeton, 1984); Mary Ann Clawson, *Constructing Brotherhood: Class, Gender and Fraternalism* (Princeton, 1989); Jeffrey A. Charles, *Service Clubs in American Society: Rotary, Kiwanis, and Lions* (Urbana, 1993); Clifford Putney, "Service Over Secrecy: How Lodge-Style Fraternalism Yielded Popularity to Men's Service Clubs," *Journal of Popular Culture,* XXVII (1993), 179–190.

Women's associations also grew during these years. The Crusade of 1873/74, led by women, reinvigorated the temperance movement and resulted in the formation of the Women's Christian Temperance Union (WCTU), which quickly expanded to include a variety of social issues on its agenda. In the 1890s, as the WCTU begin to decline, new groups had begun to emerge—for instance, the GFWC, established in 1890 by leaders of local clubs, and new single-issue associations, like the Anti-Saloon League and the National American Woman Suffrage Association, which competed for women's loyalties in the 1900s and 1910s.[17]

Immigrants and African-Americans created an array of associations. Germans, who immigrated in large numbers in the middle nineteenth century, supported an especially dense network of associations through the 1910s. After Emancipation, blacks organized mutual-aid societies and social clubs, often drawing on existing church organizations. In the late nineteenth and early twentieth centuries, Italians, Jews, Poles, and other immigrants from eastern and southern Europe organized mutual-aid societies, free-loan societies, social and recreational clubs, churches and synagogues, and newspapers. National fraternal organizations, like B'nai Brith and the Knights of Columbus, attracted large numbers of members at the turn of the century. The National Urban League, established to advance racial equality, was organized in 1910.[18]

17 Ruth Bordin, *Woman and Temperance: The Quest for Power and Liberty, 1873–1900* (Philadelphia, 1981); Aaron and Musto, "Temperance and Prohibition," 146–147; Anne Firor Scott, *Natural Allies: Women's Associations in American History* (Urbana, 1992); Skocpol, *Protecting Soldiers and Mothers: The Political Origins of Social Policy in the United States* (Cambridge, Mass., 1992); Jack S. Blocker, Jr., *Retreat from Reform: The Prohibition Movement in the United States, 1890–1913* (Westport, 1976); K. Austin Kerr, *Organized for Prohibition: A New History of the Anti-Saloon League* (New Haven, 1985); Richard F. Hamm, *Shaping the Eighteenth Amendment: Temperance Reform, Legal Culture, and the Polity, 1880–1920* (Chapel Hill, 1995).

18 Kathleen Neils Conzen, "Immigrants, Immigrant Neighborhoods, and Ethnic Identity: Historical Issues," *Journal of American History*, LXVI (1979), 603–615; James M. Berquist, "German Communities in American Cities: An Interpretation of the Nineteenth Century Experience," *Journal of American Ethnic History*, IV (1984), 9–30; Scott, "Most Invisible of All: Black Women's Voluntary Associations," *Journal of Southern History*, LVI (1990), 3–22; Susan D. Greenbaum, "A Comparison of African American and Euro-American Mutual Aid Societies in 19th Century America," *Journal of Ethnic Studies*, XIX (1991), 95–119; Samuel L. Baily, "The Adjustment of Italian Immigrants in Buenos Aires and New York, 1870–1914," *American Historical Review*, LXXXVIII (1983), 281–305; John Bodnar, *The Transplanted: A History of Immigrants in Urban America* (Bloomington, 1985); Shelly Tenenbaum, "Immigrants and Capital: Jewish Loan Societies in the United States, 1880–1945," *American Jewish History*, LXXVI (1986), 67–77; Daniel Soyer, *Jewish Immigrant Associations and American Identity in New York, 1880–1939* (Cambridge, Mass., 1997).

Finke and Starke argue that church membership grew steadily from the colonial era onward, whereas Holifield contends that membership levels changed little through the nineteenth and twentieth centuries. Still, scholars generally agree that the late nineteenth and early twentieth centuries witnessed American churches dramatically expanding their institutional roles. Older, mainline Protestant congregations, as well as newer congregations—black and white, Catholic, Jewish, and Protestant—set up Sunday schools, women's and men's clubs, study groups, literary societies, charitable associations, and various social clubs. The Salvation Army, an evangelical Protestant vehicle for ministering to the urban poor, first established in Britain, was organized in the United States in 1880.[19]

Trends in Association Building: City-Directory Data   Associational data from the city directories confirm the broad patterns of growth suggested by the scholarly literature. Figure 1 offers an overview of the basic trend, showing steady growth in associational life throughout the second half of the nineteenth century, accelerating between 1880 and 1900, slowing after 1900, and actually reversing after 1910. The average city directory reported 2.1 associations per 1,000 population in 1840, a figure that by 1910 had more than doubled to 5.4 associations per 1,000 population—when the populations of nearly all of those cities were many times larger than they had been a few decades earlier. The per capita number of associations in 1920 remained stable over the succeeding two decades.[20]

Examining the trends for various types of associations, we find variation in the degree to which different groups conformed

19   Finke and Stark, *Churching of America;* E. Brooks Holifield, "Toward a History of American Congregations," in James P. Wind and James W. Lewis (eds.), *American Congregations* (Chicago, 1994), II; Boylan, *Sunday School;* Aaron I. Abell, *The Urban Impact on American Protestantism, 1865–1900* (Cambridge, Mass., 1943); Jay P. Dolan, *The American Catholic Experience: A History from Colonial Times to the Present* (Garden City, 1985); Gilkeson, *Middle-Class Providence;* Evelyn Brooks Higginbotham, *Righteous Discontent: The Women's Movement in the Black Baptist Church, 1880–1920* (Cambridge, Mass., 1993); Hopkins, *Rise of the Social Gospel in American Protestantism, 1865–1919* (New Haven, 1940); Jenna Weissman Joselit, "The Special Sphere of the Middle-Class American Jewish Woman: The Synagogue Sisterhood, 1890–1940," in Jack Wertheimer (ed.), *The American Synagogue: A Sanctuary Transformed* (Cambridge, 1987); Diane Winston, "Boozers, Brass Bands, and Hallelujah Lassies: The Salvation Army and Commercial Culture in New York City, 1880–1918," unpub. Ph.D. diss. (Princeton Univ., 1996).

20   This pattern is similar to that recently reported in a wholly independent study by Peter Dobkin Hall (personal communication) about associational life in New Haven, Connecticut, between 1850 and 1950, also based on city-directory listings.

Fig. 1 Associational Density, 1840–1940

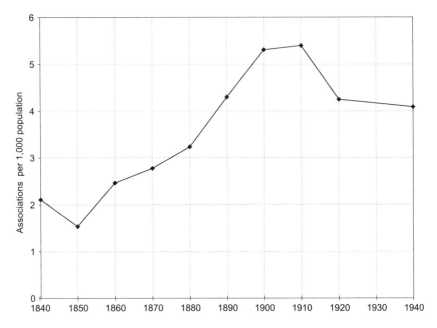

to the basic pattern of late nineteenth-century growth and early twentieth-century decline. As Figure 2 shows, churches and other religious groups, which together constituted roughly one-third of all associations in the directories, conformed to the basic trend. Fraternal groups, too, followed this trend, rising nearly tenfold (relative, as always, to population) through the second half of the nineteenth century, then declining sharply after 1910. The Masons represented the most important exception to this rule: The oldest and largest of the fraternal orders, the Masons experienced little growth in the nineteenth century and only minor decline in the first decades of the twentieth century. Social, cultural, and be-nevolent groups, like churches and fraternal organizations, also grew in number through the late nineteenth century and then declined in the 1910s.

Other organizations diverged from this general pattern. As Figure 2 shows, various types of economic groups experienced little growth through the 1870s. But, between 1880 and 1900, as industrialization transformed American society, business groups, professional groups, and labor unions multiplied; only agricultural groups remained relatively stagnant. The growth in numbers of labor unions at the end of the nineteenth century was particularly dramatic. Labor unions, business groups, and agricultural groups all experienced additional growth between 1920 and 1940, due, probably, to the impact of the New Deal. Women's groups and youth groups followed similar patterns of growth until 1880. Between 1880 and 1900, while youth groups grew 30 percent, women's groups more than tripled in number. After 1900, the relative density of both groups declined at the same rate. The steep rise in the number of women's groups in the late nineteenth century is consistent with the findings of a rich literature about women's organizations. Among ethnic associations, most of the growth came surprisingly early, between 1850 and 1860. After decades of stagnation, their number declined after 1910. Since a large proportion of ethnic associations were German, the twentieth-century decline largely reflected the demise of a public German-American culture. The incidence of explicitly African-American associations followed the more typical pattern, more than doubling between 1890 and 1910, before beginning the familiar post-1910 slump.

The last third of the nineteenth century was a time of dramatic proliferation of voluntary associations. The population of America's towns and cities was multiplying rapidly, and the number of organizations was growing even faster. This period of associational ferment came to an abrupt halt in the first years of the twentieth century. Although existing literature amply documents the rise of associations in the late nineteenth century, it speaks less to this period of decline. The same basic pattern of growth, followed by stagnation, was found in cities and towns throughout the country, though not all groups contributed in the same degree to this dynamic.

Trends in Association Building: Membership Data   Numbers of groups, however, tell only part of the story of association building. In assessing the role of associations in civil society, the numbers of people participating in groups matters at least as much as the sheer number of associations. Association building involves at least two basic stages. In the first stage, an entrepreneur, or group of entrepreneurs, initiates an organization. In the second stage, new members join. An analysis of the membership figures

Fig. 2 Associational Densities of Various Groups, 1840–1940

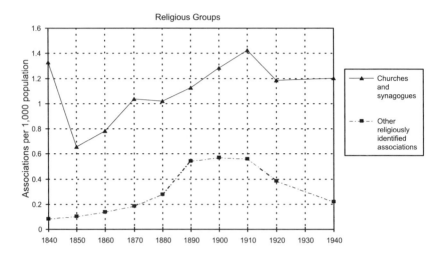

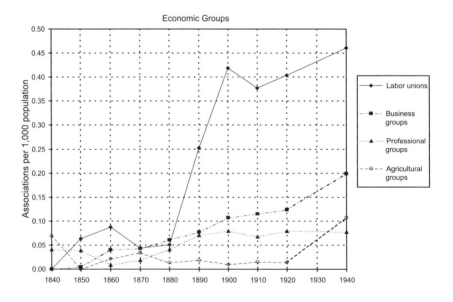

Fig. 2 Continued.

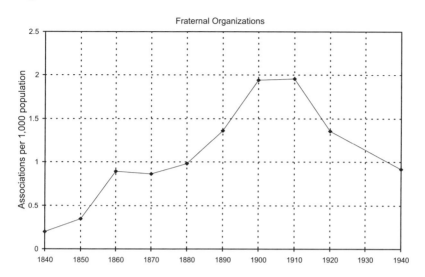

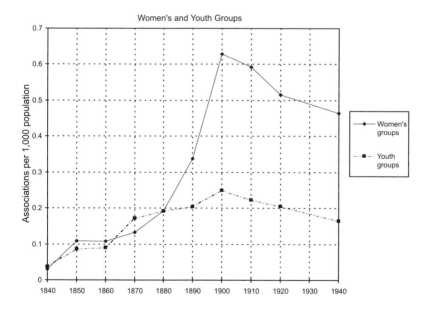

available for roughly 750 of the individual groups represented in the city directories suggests that the average group size might have grown by 20 percent a decade between 1860 and 1900, the very period when the number of groups was exploding. These data are too sparse to support a detailed quantitative analysis, but they suggest that the growth in group numbers charted so far understates the overall growth in membership during the associational boom of the late nineteenth century.[21]

Although city directories report membership numbers only sporadically, systematic data on membership are available in reports compiled by the groups themselves. For membership data, we located four sets of directories of local chapters compiled by national organizations. In each case, we compared lists of groups in these reports to lists gleaned from the city directories, coding and analyzing membership data for every local group. We report data for the Masons (1860, 1880, 1900, 1920, and 1940), Episcopal churches (1883, 1891, 1901, 1910, 1920, 1930, and 1940), the GFWC (1901 and 1911), and Rotary clubs (1930 and 1940). We collected Masonic data for thirteen of the twenty-six cities in the directory sample; data for the three other types of associations reflect all twenty-six cities.

The number of Masonic lodges and Episcopal churches grew little in relation to population through the second half of the nineteenth century. Unlike newer fraternal organizations and most other churches, relatively small numbers of new Masonic lodges and Episcopal churches were organized during the heyday of association building. But, as Figure 3 shows, the average memberships of Episcopal churches and Masonic lodges rose steadily through the nineteenth and early twentieth century. Perhaps relatively stagnant and well-established groups like Masons and Episcopalians grew by attracting new members to existing chapters, whereas newer groups, like the GFWC and the Rotary, grew by establishing new clubs. Clearly, though, the development of associational life in the second half of the nineteenth century was due not only to a proliferation of groups but to growing

---

21 The average size of the groups for which membership figures are reported in the city directories is about 200 members; ancillary evidence suggests that this estimate may be biased upward, since smaller groups were less likely to report membership figures. City directories after 1900 include virtually no evidence on membership, so we cannot continue this directory-based analysis of membership into the twentieth century.

Fig. 3 Trends in Chapter Size in Four Organizations, 1860–1940

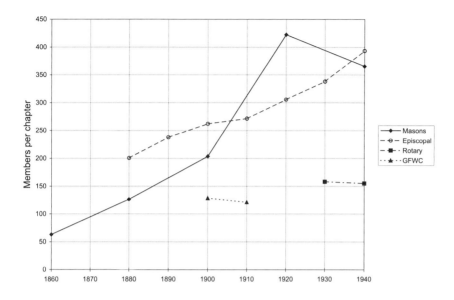

SOURCE   Membership directories of respective organizations, based on city directory sites (see Appendix B).

memberships in many of those groups. To understand these various patterns—and to explain why some cities and some groups experienced greater growth than others—we must examine explanations for why Americans increased their civic engagement so vigorously in the last third of the nineteenth century.

LOCAL CONTEXT: REGIONS, CITIES, AND IMMIGRANTS   Virtually all scholars agree that the growth of associations in the period 1870 to 1920 was due to the impact of industrialization, urbanization, and immigration on traditional communal attachments. Wiebe maintains that the railroad and the telegraph brought the nation's separated "island communities" into an integrated national sphere. According to Bender, the communal small-town orientation of the United States changed decisively in the 1870s. He rejects Wirth's contention that "the city is characterized by secondary rather than primary contacts," insisting instead that communal, face-to-face interactions continued to exist in urban places.

But Bender asserts that segmented organizations became increasingly prominent in the last decades of the nineteenth century.[22]

Economic and demographic changes disrupted patterns of work, leisure, churchgoing, and family roles. Women and men began to seek gender-defined associational attachments outside the home, adults began consciously to structure the social and educational worlds of children, native-born Americans sought to reform their own lives and the lives of immigrants, and African-Americans and immigrants created organizations to respond to the erosion of traditional community interactions. Association building, in short, according to this argument, was a product of the same forces that created the great cities of the Northeast and the Midwest.

Regions, Cities, and Immigrants: Existing Scholarship   To explain the growth of associations, some scholars have argued that middle-class reformers organized voluntary associations to exert social control over working-class men and women. Industrialization, accompanied in most cases by rapid urban growth and an influx of immigrants, upset long-standing economic and social relationships. In response, middle-class leaders established temperance societies, churches, YMCAs, playgrounds, kindergartens, and other associations. While acknowledging that leadership in many associations came from the middle class, other scholars emphasize the benevolent aspect of these organizations, suggesting that they were created to assist and strengthen immigrant and working-class communities rather than to control poor people's behavior.[23]

22   Louis Wirth, "Urbanism as a Way of Life," *American Journal of Sociology*, XLIV (1938), 12. See also Robert H. Wiebe, *The Search for Order, 1877–1920* (New York, 1967); Thomas Bender, *Community and Social Change in America* (Baltimore, 1978), 108–110.
23   Hopkins, *History of the Y.M.C.A.*; Cole, *Social Ideas*; Clifford S. Griffin, "Religious Benevolence as Social Control, 1815–1860," *Mississippi Valley Historical Review*, XLIV (1957), 423–444; Joseph Gusfield, *Symbolic Crusade: Status, Politics and the American Temperance Movement* (Urbana, 1966); Berthoff, *Unsettled People*; Blocker, *Retreat from Reform*; Boyer, *Urban Masses*; Elizabeth Dale Ross, *The Kindergarten Crusade: The Establishment of Preschool Education in the United States* (Athens, 1976); Paul E. Johnson, *A Shopkeeper's Millennium: Society and Revivals in Rochester, New York, 1815–1837* (New York, 1978); Dominick Cavallo, *Muscles and Morals: Organized Playgrounds and Urban Reform, 1880–1920* (Philadelphia, 1981); Rivka Shpak Lissak, *Pluralism and the Progressives: Hull House and the New Immigrants, 1890–1919* (Chicago, 1989); Hopkins, *Rise of the Social Gospel*; Abell, *Urban Impact*; Joseph Timberlake, *Prohibition and the Progressive Movement, 1900–1920* (Cambridge, Mass., 1963); Allen F. Davis, *Spearheads for Reform: The Social Settlements and the Progressive Movement, 1890–1914* (New York, 1967); Lois W. Banner, "Religious Benevolence as Social Control: A Critique of an Interpretation," *Journal of American History*, LX (1973), 23–41; Boylan, *Sunday School*.

In many cases, however, immigrants and other working-class people themselves organized associations. Labor unions, mutual-aid societies, and immigrant churches and synagogues were established and led by their members. According to Berthoff, "The immigrants, who had been accustomed to a more tightly knit communal life than almost any American could now recall, were quick to adopt the fraternal form of the American voluntary association in order to bind together their local ethnic communities against the unpredictable looseness of life in America." Hardy argues that immigrants and working-class people competed with reformers in the design of playgrounds and community centers.[24]

Many associations explicitly excluded working-class people as well as all blacks, Jews, and Catholics from membership. Exclusion assumed many forms, some relatively innocuous and others blatantly nativist. Most scholars suggest that elite clubs, immigration-restriction groups, the second Ku Klux Klan, and colonial and Revolutionary hereditary societies represented reactions to the influx of immigrants into American cities. Even professional associations—from the American Historical Association to the American Bar Association and organized baseball—established their professional status by erecting high and occasionally racist barriers to entry.[25]

In addition to disrupting class and ethnic relationships, industrialization and urbanization disrupted gender relationships. Challenges to traditional gender roles, according to various scholars, help explain the proliferation of women's clubs, women's temperance groups, and men's secret fraternal associations in the late nineteenth century. The Boy Scouts and men's athletic clubs represented efforts to strengthen boys and men whose masculinity was threatened by the sedentary nature of urban life. In social clubs, reform associations, YWCAs, and churches, women could enter the public sphere while continuing to promote domestic

24 Berthoff, *Unsettled People,* 273. See also Hardy, *How Boston Played;* Dawley and Faler, "Working-Class Culture and Politics"; Randall M. Miller, "Introduction," in *idem* and Thomas D. Marzik (eds.), *Immigrants and Religion in Urban America* (Philadelphia, 1977); Timothy L. Smith, "Religion and Ethnicity in America," *American Historical Review,* LXXXIII (1978), 1155–1185; Dolan, *American Catholic Experience;* Bodnar, *Transplanted.*

25 Davies, *Patriotism on Parade;* Solomon, *Ancestors and Immigrants;* Kenneth Jackson, *The Ku Klux Klan in the City, 1915–1930* (New York, 1967); Bennett, *Party of Fear;* Higham, *Strangers in the Land.*

values. Black women and Jewish women, like middle-class white Protestant women, organized an array of church and synagogue societies.[26]

Finally, other scholars argue that associations helped working-class and middle-class men cope with the new uncertainties of an industrialized age. "Fraternal lodges proliferated most exuberantly in the towns and cities of the industrial age," Berthoff argues. "The city dwellers now swarmed into the refuge which the secret society offered from its uncertainties." Membership in a fraternal organization or a veterans' organization gave men a stable identity that travelled with them as they moved from city to city. Membership, whether in the Masons or in the Grand Army of the Republic, also gave men entrance into a world where brotherhood, cemented by sacred ritual, still mattered more than relations between workers and employers. More tangibly, these organizations often offered selective benefits to members, like life insurance and cemetery plots, at a time when families could no longer rely on tight communal and kinship networks.[27]

What these disparate theories share is the assumption that the growth of associations in the late nineteenth and early twentieth century was closely related to industrialization, immigration, and urbanization. "Voluntary associations, always significant American institutions, took on increasing importance in the late nineteenth century," Keller argues. "The American propensity to join," according to Keller, was strengthened by "the social and economic needs of immigrants, workers, city-dwellers," as well as by "the generally unsettled character of life in a time of industrialization." Emphasizing middle-class occupational and professional groups, Wiebe, too, concludes that these voluntary associations were "not only concentrated in the cities but generally appeared first in the

26 Bordin, *Woman and Temperance;* Paula Baker, "The Domestication of Politics: Women and American Political Society, 1780–1920," *American Historical Review,* LXXXIX (1984), 620–647; Mark Carnes, *Secret Ritual and Manhood in Victorian America* (New Haven, 1989); Clawson, *Constructing Brotherhood;* Skocpol, *Protecting Soldiers and Mothers;* Charles, *Service Clubs;* Putney, "Service Over Secrecy"; Macleod, *Building Character;* Riess, *City Games;* Jodi Vandenberg-Daves, "The Manly Pursuit of a Partnership Between the Sexes: The Debate Over YMCA Programs for Women and Girls, 1914–1933," *Journal of American History,* LXXVIII (1992), 1324–1346; Winston, "Boozers, Brass Bands, and Hallelujah Lassies"; Joselit, "Special Sphere"; Higginbotham, *Righteous Discontent.*

27 Berthoff, *Unsettled People,* 272, also 274. See also Davies, *Patriotism on Parade;* Dumenil, *Freemasonry;* Clawson, *Constructing Brotherhood,* 146–149; Charles, *Service Clubs;* Putney, "Service Over Secrecy."

older, larger, and more industrially developed ones, mostly in the Northeast."[28]

Regions, Cities, and Immigrants: City-Directory Data Data from the city directories conflict sharply with this conventional account. For this analysis, we divided the sample of twenty-six cities by region as well as by city size, immigrant population, and growth rate; the resulting categories are displayed in Table 1. Multivariate analysis reported below confirms the basic findings of this categorization and distinguishes among these factors. Our expectation, given the existing historical literature, was that the late nineteenth-century boom in civic associationism would be earliest, strongest, and most enduring in the large, rapidly growing, immigrant-teeming cities of the Northeast, where social and economic change was most dramatic.

That expectation proved to be wrong. In fact, large cities supported fewer associations, relative to their population, than small cities. Fast-growing cities and cities with large immigrant populations supported fewer associations than slow-growing, predominantly native-born cities, and cities in the Northeast supported fewer associations than cities in the West, Midwest, or South. The spurt in associationism at the end of the nineteenth century was greatest not in the burgeoning metropolises (though it was visible there), but precisely in the smaller cities and towns of the heartland.

Although the general trend of nineteenth-century growth and early twentieth-century decline characterized groups throughout the country, significant regional differences existed. Throughout the entire period—from 1860 until 1940—cities in the Northeast reported fewer groups, relative to their population, than cities in other parts of the country. As Figure 4 shows, those differences became especially strong after 1890 and remained substantial through 1940. Association building, which had begun more or less simultaneously across the country, remained vigorous longer in the Midwest and West than in the East. Between 1920

---

28 Morton Keller, *Affairs of State: Public Life in Late Nineteenth Century America* (Cambridge, Mass., 1977), 517; Wiebe, *Search for Order,* 127. Keller also attributes the growth of voluntary associations to "agrarian loneliness," but it is not clear that farmers were growing more isolated in the late nineteenth century than they had been in previous times.

Table 1 Research Sites by City Size, Immigration, and Growth Rate

	CITY SIZE			IMMIGRATION			GROWTH RATE		
	SITE	DATA BEGIN[a]	POPULATION (000s) IN 1890	SITE	DATA BEGIN	FOREIGN-BORN RESIDENTS (MEAN, 1870–1920)	SITE	DATA BEGIN	POPULATION GROWTH (TOTAL, 1880–1920)
High	St. Louis	1821	452	Lowell	1832	39%	Portland	1863	1369%
	Boston	1830	448	San Francisco	1850	39%	Boise	1891	1194%
	San Francisco	1850	299	Milwaukee	1847	35%	San Antonio	1878	685%
	Milwaukee	1847	204	Boston	1830	34%	Denver	1866	620%
	Denver	1866	107	Scranton	1861	32%	Des Moines	1867	464%
				Brookline	1871	32%	Little Rock	1871	396%
							Brookline	1871	369%
							Milwaukee	1847	296%
Mean			302			35%			674%
Analysis begins[b]		1850			1850			1870	
Medium	Lowell	1832	78	Portland	1863	29%	Rome	1881	249%
	Scranton	1861	75	Marysville	1853	28%	Scranton	1861	201%
	Troy	1850	61	Leadville	1880	28%	Junction City	1887	181%
	Charleston	1841	55	Troy	1850	25%	Peoria	1844	160%
	Des Moines	1867	50	St. Louis	1821	24%	St. Louis	1821	121%
	Portland	1863	46	San Antonio	1878	24%	San Francisco	1850	117%
	Peoria	1844	41	Burlington	1865	24%	Boston	1830	106%
	San Antonio	1878	38	Denver	1866	21%	Pekin	1861	102%
	Galveston	1856	29	Pekin	1861	20%	Burlington	1865	100%
	Little Rock	1871	26	Galveston	1856	20%	Galveston	1856	99%
				Peoria	1844	19%			
Mean			50			24%			144%
Analysis begins		1850			1860			1860	

Low								
Burlington	1865	15	Des Moines	1867	15%	Lowell	1832	90%
Brookline	1871	12	Bath	1867	14%	Bowling Green	1877	88%
Leadville	1880	10	Adrian	1870	13%	Bath	1867	87%
Adrian	1870	9	Boise	1891	12%	Adrian	1870	51%
Bath	1867	9	Junction City	1887	11%	Charleston	1841	36%
Bowling Green	1877	8	Little Rock	1871	7%	Troy	1850	27%
Rome	1881	7	Charleston	1841	6%	Marysville	1853	26%
Pekin	1861	6	Bowling Green	1877	4%	Leadville	1880	-67%
Junction City	1887	5	Rome	1881	2%			
Marysville	1853	4						
Boise	1891	2						
Mean		8			9%			42%
Analysis begins	1870			1870			1850	

[a] "Data begin" refers to year in which city directory data first became available.
[b] "Analysis begins" refers to decade in which reliable cross-site averages became available.
SOURCE United States Census reports.

Fig. 4   Associational Densities, by Region, Percentage of Foreign-Born
Residents, City Growth Rate, and City Size

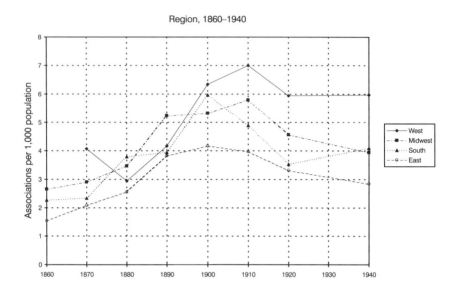

Region, 1860–1940

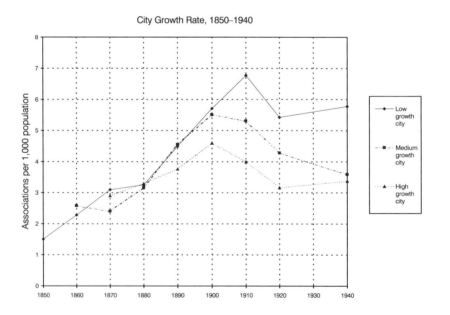

City Growth Rate, 1850–1940

Fig. 4 Continued.

Percentage of Foreign-Born Residents, 1850–1940

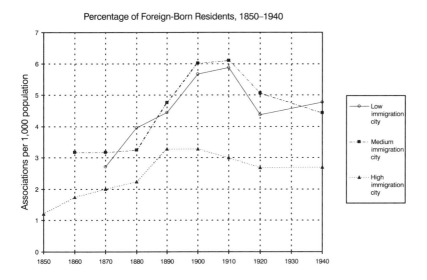

City Size, 1850–1940

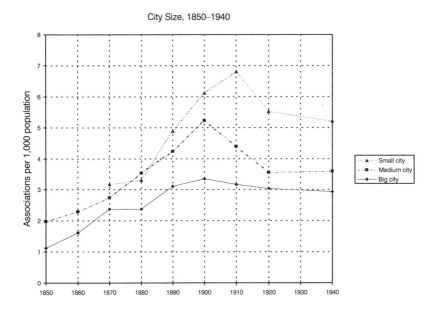

and 1940, the average western city supported nearly twice as many associations per capita as the average eastern city.[29]

Writing in the first half of the nineteenth century, Tocqueville and Olmsted discovered an especially high level of associational activity in the Northeast. However, this regional distinction appears to have dissipated by 1860. If Tocqueville's and Olmsted's accounts are accurate, the level of associational activity in the Northeast was especially high in the first half of the century. In the second half of the nineteenth century, according to the city-directory data, regional differences in associational activity were muted, and associational levels in the Northeast became relatively low in the early twentieth century. Unlike that in the West and Midwest, associational activity in the Northeast dampened, rather than flowered, during the era of intense industrialization, urbanization, and mass immigration.[30]

Immigration itself does not appear to have stimulated the nineteenth-century increase in associationism. Rates of immigration at the height of the associational boom at the end of the nineteenth century were not much higher than comparable rates at mid-century, before the boom. Moreover, as already noted, ethnic-based associations (the organizational form most directly a response to immigration) did not increase throughout the second half of the nineteenth century. Nor can the concentration of immigrants in specific places explain the growth of associations. According to the city-directory data, the wave of association building that swept across the country in the second half of the nineteenth century was concentrated precisely in cities with low numbers of foreign-born residents. As Figure 4 shows, both the number of associations and the rate of increase in associational activity was consistently lowest in the cities with the largest populations of immigrants.

To be sure, not all migration in nineteenth-century America was international. Much of it reflected movement from the American countryside to the burgeoning American city. Might

29 In aggregate terms, associational density in the South was greater than that in the Northeast, though less than that in the West and Midwest. Associationalism in the South, however, was heavily concentrated in churches; secular associational density in the South was no greater than in the Northeast.
30 Tocqueville, *Democracy in America;* Adam Gopnik, "Olmsted's Trip," *The New Yorker,* 31 March 1997, 96–104.

urban growth itself (and the social and economic upheaval that it signified) have been the primary cause of the associational boom? The evidence suggests not. A comparison of three sets of cities, grouped according to their rate of population expansion between 1880 and 1920, indicates that slow-growing cities, as Figure 4 shows, supported relatively larger numbers of associations than fast-growing ones. Through 1880, the trend lines of associational growth were virtually identical for these three different kinds of cities. Thereafter, however, a gap opened up between fast- and slow-growing cities; by 1910, the density of associations in slow-growth cities was two-thirds greater. Rapid urbanization was not the engine of associational development.[31]

Our most fundamental test of the conventional theory of associational growth explores differences in the experience of large cities with that of smaller cities and towns. The last graph in Figure 4 displays patterns of associational development for three sets of cities—the five largest cities in our sample, with an average population of 302,000 in 1890; ten medium-sized cities, with an average population of 50,000; and eleven small cities and towns, with an average population of 8,000. Strikingly, not only were the levels of associationism significantly higher in the smaller localities, but the upward trend was significantly longer and stronger there than in the metropolitan centers. The periods of greatest associational growth end in the largest cities in 1890, in the medium-sized cities in 1900, and in the smallest cities and towns in 1910. In 1870 the smallest cities in our sample had barely one-third more groups per capita than the largest cities (3.2 per 1,000 residents, compared to 2.4). By 1910, the gap had so widened that the smallest cities had more than twice as many groups (6.8 per 1,000 residents, compared to 3.2).

This basic pattern—faster, longer-lasting associational growth in smaller towns and cities—characterized a wide range of groups: women's groups, fraternal organizations, churches and synagogues, and social and recreational clubs. Although in some cases, the density of groups, such as business groups and labor unions, was not related to city size, no groups seem to have flourished more in big cities than in small cities and towns. The late nineteenth-

---

31 Slow-growing cities in this era were expanding about 1 percent per annum, as compared with roughly 7 percent per annum for fast-growing cities.

century civic mobilization was concentrated in smaller cities and towns, not in the major metropolitan areas.

Regions, Cities, and Immigrants: Multivariate Analysis   As our attention shifts from the *when* of the nineteenth-century upturn in civic engagement in America to the *where,* our evidence is sharply at odds with conventional theory. But grouping cities into categories—whether by size, region, immigrant population, or growth rate—does not permit us to analyze how these characteristics interact nor to assess their relative significance for associational development. Only multivariate statistical analysis can allow us to distinguish the most important factors associated with associational vitality. Moreover, this sort of analysis enables us to be more precise in our tests of alternative hypotheses. So far, for example, we have looked only at whether cities that grew rapidly during the 1880 to 1920 span differed from those that did not, but not at whether associationism in a particular year was related to growth during the previous decade. Similarly, big cities tended to have more foreign-born residents, but the preceding analysis could not tell whether it was their size or their immigrant mix that inhibited group formation.

This section reports results of the multiple regression analysis designed to test the leading hypotheses for associational density. In broad outline, it seeks to predict aggregate associational density in a given city in a given year, using such independent variables as population size, population growth rates, percentage foreign-born, region, and year. The analysis assesses the effect of any given variable, holding all other variables constant—implicitly comparing, for example, eastern and western cities of the *same* size, ethnic composition, and growth rate. The basic pattern in our results, summarized in Table 2, is clear, strong, and highly significant, both statistically and substantively.[32]

32   The statistical analysis presented here applies to the aggregate number of community organizations, not to every single type of organization taken separately. We have undertaken comparable analyses of the density of specific associational forms. Our basic findings—emphasizing population size, growth, region, and time—also apply specifically to the density of all secular groups, fraternal groups, women's groups, and several other categories of group. But the prevalence of church organizations is correlated only with population size and region, not with population growth or time, perhaps because the main denominational organizations were mostly in place before our story opens. The incidence of business, professional, and labor groups is unrelated to any of the factors considered here and perhaps reflects, instead, differences in community economic structure not captured by our current data.

Given the multiple sources of random "noise" inevitably present in data collected in twenty-six separate communities for ten decades by hundreds of different individuals, our

Table 2 Predicting Total Associations per 1,000 Population

	UNSTANDARDIZED COEFFICIENTS		STANDARDIZED COEFFICIENTS		
	B	STD. ERROR	BETA	t	SIG.
(Constant)	3.726	1.435		2.597	0.01008
Years since 1800	0.136	0.026	1.656	5.313	0.00000
(Years since 1800)^2	−0.0006	0.0001	−1.324	−4.314	0.00002
LN(population)	−0.727	0.078	−0.464	−9.299	0.00000
Change in LN(pop.) in previous decade	−1.049	0.269	−0.222	−3.897	0.00013
Western site	1.925	0.327	0.342	5.881	0.00000
Midwestern site	1.082	0.283	0.221	3.817	0.00018
Southern site	0.378	0.302	0.071	1.254	0.21119

NOTES $R^2 = 0.515$; adjusted $R^2 = 0.499$; standard error of estimate = 1.573.

Population size and growth. The most powerful predictor of associational density is (logged) population size. Across our nationwide, century-long sample of 224 site years, the average associational density is 3.9 groups per 1,000 inhabitants. Against that backdrop, an increase of one order of magnitude in population size (from 1,000 to 10,000 residents, for example, or from 10,000 to 100,000 residents) was associated with a relative decline of 0.7 groups (per 1,000 inhabitants). Thus, ceteris paribus, a city of 500,000 would be expected to have 1.4 fewer groups (per 1,000 residents) than a city of 5,000. In fact, there is some suggestion in the data that the negative effects of size on associationism tended to rise over time, as urban agglomeration increasingly dampened associational life.[33]

Population growth over the preceding decade seems also to have been a powerful independent depressant of associationism. The regression results imply, roughly speaking, that compared with an identical city that experienced no growth, a city that tripled in size during the previous decade would suffer a relative

rather parsimonious model accounts for a surprisingly high proportion of the measured variance in associational density (adjusted R^2 = .51). Each of the regression coefficients that we discuss below is statistically significant at the .00002 level or better.

33 Because of the skewed distribution of the population size and growth data, we have logged these variables in our equations. This strategy amounts to saying that the difference between 1,000 and 10,000 residents is comparable to the difference between 10,000 and 100,000, rather than to the difference between 100,000 and 109,000.

204 | GERALD GAMM AND ROBERT D. PUTNAM

decline of about 1.05 groups per 1,000 residents. Since the rate
of population change during the preceding decade varied dramatically—from −38 percent (Bath, Maine, in 1931) to roughly +4,000
percent (San Francisco in 1852)—this result implies that a significant fraction of the variation in associationism may be attrib-
utable to differences in growth rates.[34]

Taken together, these two findings imply that—contrary to
the interpretation of associationism as the product of rapid demographic change—both immediate growth pains and the cumulative results of growth independently inhibited the development
of civic associations. With hindsight, it might seem plausible to
attribute this unexpected result to the unsettling effects of geographical mobility and transiency on civic associations. The late
nineteenth century was a time of astonishingly high rates of
residential mobility for urban dwellers. Much contemporary sociological work on the correlates of associational membership has
found that mobility undermines community connectedness,
though Thernstrom, reviewing the historical evidence, reports no
"consistent relation between population stability and either city
size or population growth rates." Seen against the backdrop of
massive population movements, the associational boom of the late
nineteenth century becomes all the more impressive.[35]

Sectional differences. As foreshadowed earlier, a third, and
even less anticipated, correlate of associational density is region.
To be sure, our detailed results confirm some predictable regional
distinctions: GAR chapters were rarer in the South; groups identified as "Negro" or "colored" were more common there; eastern
cities reported more party organizations and western cities more
nonpartisan reform groups; and so on. Such particularities were
overlaid, however, on more fundamental regional disparities.
Considering all groups combined, and with other factors controlled, midwestern cities had 1.1 more groups per 1,000 residents
than northeastern cities, and western cities had 1.9 more groups
per 1,000 residents than comparable northeastern communities.

34 Population change is measured here as the difference between the log of population in
the year of the directory and the log of that city's population ten years earlier.
35 Thernstrom, *Other Bostonians*, 224. See also Knights, *Plain People of Boston;* Clyde Griffen,
"Workers Divided: The Effect of Craft and Ethnic Differences in Poughkeepsie, New York,
1850–1880," in Thernstrom and Richard Sennett (eds.), *Nineteenth-Century Cities* (New
Haven, 1969); Edward Kopf, "Untarnishing the Dream: Mobility, Opportunity, and Order
in Modern America," *Journal of Social History,* XI (1977), 206–227.

Some aspects of the regression analysis hint that these sectional differences became stronger over time.

Why this regional disparity? The statistical evidence tends to exclude some obvious possibilities. The timing of urbanization—whether a given city, regardless of its current size, had reached a population of 30,000 by 1830 or 1880, for example—is uncorrelated with associational density. Controlling for other factors, immigration, too, appears to have little or no impact on associationism. Since immigration itself neither boosted nor dampened general associational life, the bivariate relationship shown in Figure 4 reflects the fact that immigrants tended to congregate in bigger cities, where, as already seen, associations were relatively scarcer. In any event, immigration cannot explain the sectional differences.

A final hypothesis that we considered for the relative weakness of associations in the East was the concentration of Catholics there. Catholic associations, most of which were tightly bound up in the life of a single parish, might have been less likely to be listed in city directories than Protestant associations. Schools, community centers, and mutual-aid societies, which for Protestants and Jews often appeared in city directories as discrete organizations, were, in the case of Catholics, sometimes not listed apart from the church itself. It is possible, too, that the vertical, hierarchical structure of Catholicism, in contrast with the congregational structure of Protestantism and Judaism, might have made it relatively difficult for Catholics to acquire the skills and habits necessary to form other associations. But, at least so far, we find little support for either hypothesis in our data. There is no relationship, positive or negative, between the density of Catholic churches in a city and the density of its associational life generally.[36]

In short, neither the age of northeastern cities, nor their ethnic complexion, nor their religious composition can explain their lower organizational vitality. We have not yet been able to explore empirically another possible reason for the regional disparities in associationism—the relative strength of party machines. "The party organizations constructed in the cities and states of the

36   Putnam, with Roberto Leonardi and Raffaella Y. Nanetti, *Making Democracy Work: Civic Traditions in Modern Italy* (Princeton, 1993); Sidney Verba, Kay Lehman Schlozman, and Henry E. Brady, *Voice and Equality: Civic Voluntarism in American Politics* (Cambridge, Mass., 1995).

West were," Shefter argues, "weaker and more narrowly based than their counterparts in the Northeast." We too find more party organizations in the East, and we suspect that machine-related associational activities were underrepresented in city directories. Moreover, deeply entrenched party organizations, dispensing patronage and organizing regular activities, might have frustrated the emergence of competing types of associations. Of course, the relationship might have been exactly the opposite: Strong party organizations might have stimulated the growth of voluntary associations. Whether regional differences in civic vitality turn out to be explained by political organization or by something else entirely, resolving this mystery may well provide important clues for our broader puzzle—the remarkable efflorescence of civic organizations in the late nineteenth century, followed by an era of organizational withering.[37]

Time. The empirical significance of that broader puzzle is reinforced by the fact that, even after controlling for population size, growth rates, immigration, and several other factors, time itself remains an important predictor of the density of community associations. Statistically speaking, this effect appears in a quadratic form in our equations, corresponding to the curvilinear pattern portrayed in Figure 1. Each successive decade of the nineteenth century was associated, statistically speaking, with an increase of roughly 1.4 associations per 1,000 inhabitants. This gross estimate of change across the century is higher than the observed change for two reasons. First, the rapid and sustained urbanization of these decades tended to depress associational vitality by itself. Second, as the decades passed, the decennial gains in associational density gradually diminished and eventually reversed. In our analyses, both the positive first-order effect and the negative second-order effect of time appear highly significant.

To be sure, "time" itself is hardly a substantive cause of change. Rather, it represents the operation of some still poorly understood process of change. In essence, our statistical analysis underscores the central fact that some other factor or combination of factors—not yet identified, but neither immigration nor urbanization—first animated and then dissipated civic energies in

37   Martin Shefter, "Regional Receptivity to Reform: The Legacy of the Progressive Era," *Political Science Quarterly*, XCVIII (1983), 459–460.

American communities during the last half of the nineteenth century and the first half of the twentieth.

Regions, Cities, and Immigrants: Membership Data   Official membership directories confirm the basic, unexpected finding of the city-directory data: Associationalism was strongest in smaller cities and towns. The evidence illustrated in Figure 5 comes directly from reports issued by the associations themselves, covering the same sites as our city directories. All four types of associations—Rotary clubs, General Federation of Women's Clubs, Episcopal churches, and Masons—conformed to the same pattern throughout the nineteenth and early twentieth century. Relative to population, the largest numbers of local chapters existed in the smallest cities; the fewest chapters existed in the largest cities. The numbers of local chapters in medium-sized cities fell midway between the two extremes. Thus, chapter density was inversely related to city size.

An obvious objection to this finding is that the number of groups bears little, if any, relation to the numbers of men, women, and children participating in these associations. To conclude that Bath supported more Episcopal churches per capita than Boston is to say nothing about the relative numbers of churchgoers in Bath and Boston. Intuition suggests that the average Episcopal church in Boston was larger than the average church in Bath. Trinity Church, for example—the magnificent edifice in Boston's Copley Square—could not have had a counterpart in any small or even medium-sized city—though, even in Boston, Trinity Church was an anomaly, by far the largest of the city's many Episcopal churches. It is possible that differences in the sizes of average congregations more than compensated for the fewer number of churches in big cities. Economies of scale—relatively fewer but larger organizations in bigger cities—might make our "finding" about the effects of city size a mere methodological artifact of counting groups, not members.

But that is not the case. As the second graph in Figure 5 shows, the average memberships of these four types of associations was not directly related to city size. In three of the four cases—women's clubs, Episcopal churches, and Masonic lodges—the average chapter in a medium-sized city boasted more members than the average big-city chapter. To be sure, big-city associations were larger in size than small-city associations, but in none of

Fig. 5   City Size and Organizational Memberships

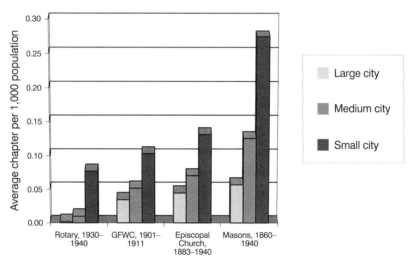

City Size and Chapter Density
in Four Organizations

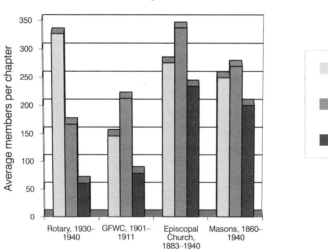

City Size and Chapter Size
in Four Organizations

Fig. 5 Continued.

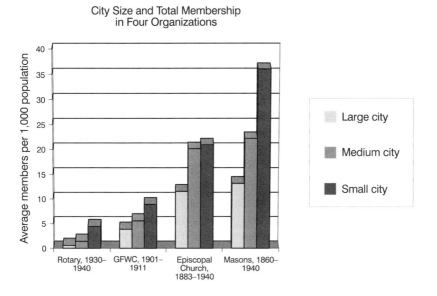

City Size and Total Membership
in Four Organizations

these three cases was the difference great. For example, big-city Masonic lodges averaged about 250 members each, as compared with 200 members per small-city lodge. Yet, lodges themselves were five times more common in small cities. The one exception to this pattern, the Rotary club, had a peculiar organizational structure. In 1930 and 1940, nearly every city, whatever its size, supported one Rotary club; hence, data on the membership of the "average" club are identical with data on the number of members in the entire city.

The implication of these data on membership size is obvious. If small cities supported many more associations than big cities, and if average chapter sizes were not strongly related to city size, then many more people in small cities than in big cities participated in associational life. The last graph in Figure 5 illustrates this pattern. In all four organizations, total membership levels per capita were much higher in small cities than in big cities; as was true with the numbers of chapters, medium-sized cities constituted a middle case. The differences between the three sizes of cities were persistent over time. For every type of organization and in every year for which we examined data, small cities consistently reported substantially larger numbers of members, as a proportion of the city population, than large cities. In short, the basic finding of this part of our study—that the associational boom in the last years of the nineteenth century and the first years of the twentieth was concentrated in the smaller cities and towns of the periphery, not the major metropolitan centers—is no mere methodological quirk, but a serious historical puzzle to be solved.

In the last decades of the nineteenth century, Americans created and joined an unprecedented number of voluntary associations. In Peoria and St. Louis, in Boston and Boise and Bath and Bowling Green, Americans organized clubs and churches and lodges and veterans' groups. Everywhere, in small towns and in great metropolises, the number of voluntary associations grew. The number of associations rose sharply through the second half of the nineteenth century, and then, soon after the turn of the century, it began to decline and stagnate. Looking back, at the verge of another new century, we discover that civil society in the United States has not grown steadily stronger over time, but by fits and reverses. The foundation stone of twentieth-century civil society was set in place by the generation of 1870 to 1900.

This was the age of great migrations, urbanization, and industrialization, and, since that time, scholars have emphasized the growth of voluntary associations in the nation's great cities. They have argued that the expansion of civil society in the late nineteenth century was a direct response to the turbulence that women and men were experiencing. Associations, in this account, were buffers softening the impact of economic and social change. They were institutions created to rebuild the human attachments that had been ruptured as cities grew, as families left farms and ancient villages, and as the Industrial Revolution pulverized community. Once established in the great metropolitan centers, these institutions, according to this account, began to emerge in smaller cities and in towns.

But the systematic evidence we have gathered is not consistent with such an interpretation. Cities, even great industrial cities teeming with immigrants, were not the initiators and propellants of American civil society. Voluntary associations were more apt to flourish in small cities and towns than in large metropolises. The relationship between city size and number of groups—and the relationship between city size and total number of members in these groups—is powerful and negative. Between the mid-nineteenth century and the mid-twentieth century, voluntary associations grew most quickly and proliferated most heavily in the smallest cities and towns. The civic core was in the periphery, away from the big cities and outside the Northeast.

Still, this periphery was urban. Rural Americans, living in farms and in small villages, appear not to have organized the types of associations found in cities. Figure 6 compares the numbers of Episcopal church members and Masons in the entire United States population with the numbers in our basic city sample. In every year illustrated in this figure, levels of participation were substantially higher in our twenty-six cities than in the country as a whole. The inference is straightforward: Urban Americans joined churches and lodges in larger numbers than rural Americans. Tocqueville "discovered democracy not just in association," Ryan observes, but "in relatively dense human settlements, towns, villages, or cities."[38]

Urbanization was a prerequisite for association building. Yet, among cities, it was in the smallest and slowest-growing of the cities—the cities that stood, literally, on the urban periphery—where associational development was most vigorous. Not only does this generalization about associational development account for differences between big cities and small cities; it also accounts for the great surge in associational activity during the second half of the nineteenth century and for its relative stagnation in the twentieth century. Perhaps, too, it was the shifting of the urban periphery from the Northeast to other parts of the country that explains Tocqueville and Olmsted's observations about the many associations in the Northeast during the 1830s and 1850s, and explains the relatively small numbers of associations in the Northeast during the late nineteenth and early twentieth century. In the second half of the nineteenth century, the Northeast—relative to the Midwest and, especially, the West—had already experienced its period of initial urban growth.

The hypothesis that the changing geography of the urban frontier contributed to regional differences in associational density is a hypothesis that we cannot test with the evidence at our

38 Ryan, *Civic Wars,* 9.

Fig. 6 Episcopal Church and Masonic Memberships in United States and City Samples

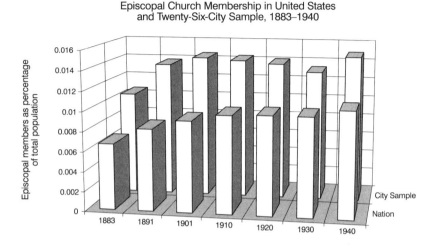

Episcopal Church Membership in United States
and Twenty-Six-City Sample, 1883–1940

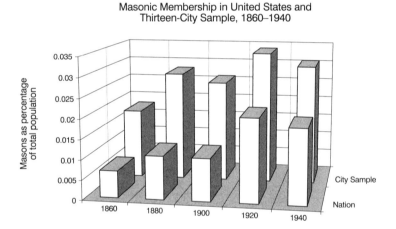

Masonic Membership in United States and
Thirteen-City Sample, 1860–1940

disposal. A related hypothesis, which we considered, was that city directory compilers were simply more assiduous in ferreting out associations in the "booster" communities of the West and Midwest. But the evidence does not support this hypothesis at all. The types of groups that appeared in relatively larger numbers in the directories of the West and Midwest included groups like the

Masons and Episcopal churches; careful comparisons of the city directories with independent membership listings demonstrate that the city directories accurately reflected the real number of groups in the various cities. The bounty of groups outside the Northeast does not appear to have been an artifact of how directories were compiled.

One possible explanation for this puzzle about the awakening of American civil society is that associations are created and sustained most easily in communities that are relatively small and homogeneous. In these places, where residents are more likely to know one another, the cost of not participating regularly in voluntary activities is probably higher than in a bigger city: Free riders are more subject to social or economic sanctions. Consequently, fearing sanction, small-town residents would be more likely to organize and join associations than big-city residents. If this theory is accurate, small, homogeneous cities would produce a larger number of associations than bigger cities. One difficulty with this theory, however, is that it is not dynamic. Although it predicts higher levels of associations in smaller communities, it does not explain what caused the sharper growth in voluntary associations during the late nineteenth century. The argument that this growth occurred as a defensive reaction to the disruptive forces of industrialization, immigration, and urbanization cannot explain why the defensive reaction occurred simultaneously in small and big places; the railroad and telegraph could not have carried the city's problems to the country in so instantaneous a fashion.

An alternate approach might be to emphasize a specific facet of the industrial age—the newly structured division between work and leisure time—and to posit competition among various entrepreneurs to provide for leisure activities. Some entrepreneurs might have built amusement parks, ballparks, boxing arenas, symphony halls, vaudeville houses, nickelodeons, theaters, and, in the twentieth century, movie palaces. Other entrepreneurs might have opted to promote voluntary associations, building Masonic temples, clubhouses, handsome stone churches, or perhaps organizing societies and clubs that met in livingrooms and schoolrooms. Like industrial-era jobs, associations conformed to regularly scheduled meeting times and depended on organization. Big cities at the turn of the century boasted professional ballparks, amusement parks, and vaudeville houses; small cities did not. If this theory of competing entrepreneurs is correct, voluntary associations would indeed have sprouted more rapidly in small cities than in big cities, since the professional-entertainment industry was less competitive in smaller cities, although this comparative advantage of voluntary associations in smaller places would have eroded as movie theaters and amusement parks proliferated later in the twentieth century.[39]

A third hypothesis might emphasize the role played by national and translocal entrepreneurs in organizing voluntary associations. As Skocpol shows, associations frequently expanded by spawning offshoots in different cities and states. Initiative for a new local group could come as much from above as from below—and the structures and goals of national associations often suggested a close relationship to the political sphere. "Networks of national, state, and local units allow associations to mediate between local people and political parties and legislators," Skocpol argues. "For much of American history, in fact, extralocal 'levels' of voluntary federations were founded prior to most local groups. Foundings of local units fanned out 'sideways,' with encouragement and support from state and national leaders, until the 'normal' template of a complete U.S. voluntary association was fully filled in." Presumably, this structure encouraged national associational organizers to emphasize the numbers of cities and towns in which their associations were organized, rather than the percentage of a given city's population that belonged to the association. Such a strategy would yield a pattern in which, in per capita terms, associational density was negatively related to city size—except in rural areas and very small towns, which national organizers would have neglected altogether. The data are consistent with this pattern. However, this hypothesis cannot explain why associational formation stagnated in the early twentieth century, even as political interest groups thrived.[40]

---

39 John Kasson, *Amusing the Million: Coney Island at the Turn of the Century* (New York, 1978); Gunther Barth, *City People: The Rise of Modern City Culture in Nineteenth-Century America* (New York, 1980); Francis Couvares, "The Triumph of Commerce: Class Culture and Mass Culture in Pittsburgh," in Michael Frisch and Daniel Walkowitz (eds.), *Working-Class America: Essays on Labor, Community, and American Society* (Urbana, 1983); Riess, *City Games;* Roy Rosenzweig, *Eight Hours for What We Will: Workers and Leisure in an Industrial City, 1870–1920* (Cambridge, 1983); David Nasaw, *Going Out: The Rise and Fall of Public Amusements* (New York, 1993).
40 Skocpol, "Tocqueville Problem," 470, 471.

The great growth in voluntary associations was rooted in smaller cities and towns, and it was stimulated by local as well as by national organizers. This growth coincided with the nationalizing forces of industry and government, which emanated from metropolitan centers. As we continue our research, we are examining how associational growth in the late nineteenth century coincided with the decline of local party organizations and the first stirrings of interest groups and Progressive-era political-reform movements. Once we achieve a better understanding of why American civil society in that era grew most strongly in the smaller cities of the Midwest and West, we will be in a better position to see the dynamic connections between civil society and civic engagement. We may also be better positioned to assess the condition and prospects of American civil society at the end of the twentieth century.[41]

APPENDIX A: CITY DIRECTORIES

Adrian, Mich.—1870, 1882, 1890, 1900, 1911, 1921, 1940
Bath, Maine—1867, 1871, 1880, 1887, 1888, 1896, 1900, 1902, 1912, 1919, 1931, 1937, 1947
Boise, Idaho—1891, 1903, 1911, 1919, 1943
Boston, Mass.—1830, 1841, 1850, 1860, 1870, 1880, 1890, 1900, 1910, 1920, 1940
Bowling Green, Ky.—1877, 1886, 1905, 1914, 1923, 1940
Brookline, Mass.—1871, 1881, 1891, 1901, 1911, 1920, 1943
Burlington, Vt.—1865, 1870, 1883, 1891, 1901, 1910, 1920, 1940
Charleston, S.C.—1849, 1852, 1859, 1860, 1868, 1870, 1879, 1881, 1890, 1900, 1910, 1920
Denver, Colo.—1866, 1871, 1873, 1881, 1891, 1901, 1911, 1920, 1940
Des Moines, Iowa—1867, 1871, 1882, 1890, 1900, 1910, 1920, 1940
Galveston, Tex.—1856, 1859, 1870, 1874, 1881, 1890, 1901, 1911, 1921, 1941
Junction City, Kans.—1887, 1905, 1909, 1911, 1921, 1927, 1948
Leadville, Colo.—1880, 1890, 1902, 1909, 1918
Little Rock, Ark.—1871, 1882, 1890, 1901, 1910, 1920, 1940
Lowell, Mass.—1832, 1841, 1851, 1861, 1870, 1881, 1891, 1901, 1911, 1921, 1940

41 Baker, "Domestication of Politics"; Richard L. McCormick, "Public Life in Industrial America, 1877–1917," in Eric Foner (ed.), *The New American History* (Philadelphia, 1990); Skocpol, *Protecting Soldiers and Mothers;* Elisabeth S. Clemens, *The People's Lobby: Organizational Innovation and the Rise of Interest Group Politics in the United States, 1890–1925* (Chicago, 1997).

Marysville, Calif.—1853, 1861, 1870, 1895, 1904, 1922, 1940
Milwaukee, Wisc.—1847, 1852, 1858, 1861, 1871, 1881, 1891, 1901,
  1910, 1920, 1940
Pekin, Ill.—1861, 1870, 1877, 1893, 1902, 1904, 1909, 1910, 1921, 1941
Peoria, Ill.—1844, 1851, 1861, 1871, 1881, 1891, 1901, 1911, 1920, 1940
Portland, Ore.—1863, 1870, 1880, 1890, 1900, 1910, 1920, 1940
Rome, Ga.—1881, 1888, 1899, 1904, 1913, 1922, 1940
San Antonio, Tex.—1878, 1882, 1891, 1902, 1911, 1922, 1940
San Francisco, Calif.—1850, 1852, 1860, 1869, 1880, 1890, 1900, 1910,
  1921, 1940
Scranton, Penn.—1861, 1870, 1881, 1891, 1901, 1910, 1920, 1940
St. Louis, Mo.—1821, 1836, 1838, 1863, 1871, 1881, 1891, 1901, 1910,
  1920, 1941
Troy, N.Y.—1852, 1860, 1870, 1880, 1890, 1900, 1910, 1920, 1940

APPENDIX B: MEMBERSHIP DIRECTORIES
(BY ASSOCIATION AND YEAR)

DAUGHTERS OF THE AMERICAN REVOLUTION
Montgomery, Susan J. *Deeds Not Dreams: One Hundred Year's Service by
  California Daughters.* Glendora, Calif., 1991.

EPISCOPAL CHURCHES
*The Living Church Annual: An Almanac and Calendar for the Year of Our
  Lord 1883.* Cooper Union, N.Y., 1883.
The Living Church Quarterly, 1891. Milwaukee, Wisc., 1890.
The Living Church Quarterly, 1901. Milwaukee, Wisc., 1900.
*The Living Church Annual and Whittaker's Churchman's Almanac: A Church
  Cyclopedia and Almanac, 1910.* Milwaukee, Wisc., 1910.
*The Living Church Annual and Churchman's Almanac: A Church Cyclopedia
  and Almanac, 1920.* Milwaukee, Wisc., 1920.
*The Living Church Annual: The Churchman's Year Book & American Church
  Almanac, 1930.* Milwaukee, Wisc., 1930.
The Living Church Annual: The Year Book of the Episcopal Church, 1940.
  Milwaukee, Wisc., 1940.

GENERAL FEDERATION OF WOMEN'S CLUBS
General Federation of Women's Clubs. *List of Officers and Directors,
  Federation Secretaries and Committees, State Federations, and List of Fed-
  erated Clubs.* Philadelphia, Penn., 1901.
General Federation of Women's Clubs. *Directory.* No city, 1911.
Colorado Federation of Women's Clubs. *Yearbook.* Denver, Colo., 1928.
Helen M. Winslow (ed.), *Annual Register of Women's Clubs and National
  Organizations in America, 1930–1931.* Shirley, Mass., 1931.

JEWISH SYNAGOGUES
American Jewish Year Book, 5680. Philadelphia, Penn., 1919.

MASONIC LODGES
Proceedings of the Grand Lodge of Iowa of Ancient Free and Accepted Masons Held at Burlington, June 5, 1860. Muscatine, Iowa.

Proceedings of the Grand Lodge of Kentucky at a Grand Annual Communication Held in the City of Louisville, 1860. Frankfort, Ky., 1860.

Proceedings of the Grand Lodge of Maine at Its Annual Communication. Portland, Maine, 1860.

Proceedings of the Grand Lodge of the Most Worshipful & Honorable Fraternity of Free and Accepted Masons of the State of Missouri, 5860. St. Louis, Mo., 1860.

Proceedings of the Most Worshipful Grand Lodge of A.F. of South Carolina at the Annual Communication, 1860. Charleston, S.C., 1861.

Proceedings of the Most Worshipful Grand Lodge of Georgia at the Annual Communication for the Year 5860. Macon, Ga., 1860.

Transactions of the Grand Lodge of F&AM of the State of Michigan, 1860. Detroit, Mich., 1860.

Transactions of the Grand Lodge of the Most Worshipful and Honorable Fraternity of F&AM of the State of New York, 1860. New York, N.Y., 1860.

Proceedings of the Most Worshipful Grand Lodge of Ancient Free and Accepted Masons of the Commonwealth of Massachusetts, 1856 to 1864 Inclusive. Boston, Mass., no date.

Official Proceedings of the Most Worshipful Grand Lodge F&AM, 1880. Macon, Ga., 1880.

Official Proceedings of the Sixtieth Annual Communication of the Most Worshipful Grand Lodge AF&AM of the State of Missouri, 5880. St. Louis, Mo., 1880.

Proceedings of the Grand Lodge of Iowa of Ancient Free and Accepted Masons. Davenport, Iowa, 1880.

Proceedings of the Grand Lodge of Kentucky F&AM 81st Annual Communication, 1880. Louisville, Ky., 1880.

Proceedings of the Grand Lodge of the Most Ancient and Honorable Fraternity of Free and Accepted Masons of the Commonwealth of Massachusetts, 1880. Boston, Mass., 1880.

Proceedings of the Most Worshipful Grand Lodge of AF&AM of the Territory of Idaho at Its Thirteenth Annual Communication, 1880. Washington, D.C., 1880.

Proceedings of the 104th Annual Communication of the Most Worshipful Grand Lodge of A.F. of South Carolina, 1880. Charleston, S.C., 1881.

Transactions of the Grand Lodge of F&AM of the State of New York, 1880. New York, N.Y., 1880.

Transactions of the Grand Lodge of Michigan, 1880. Grand Rapids, Mich., 1880.

Proceedings of the Most Worshipful Grand Lodge of AF&AM of the State of Maine, 1879–1881. Portland, Maine, 1881.

Annals of the Grand Lodge of Iowa AF&AM, 1900. Davenport, Iowa, 1900.

Annual Communication of the Grand Lodge of Georgia F&AM, 1900. Rome, Ga., 1900.

Centennial of the Grand Lodge of Kentucky F&AM, 1900. Louisville, Ky., 1900.

Official Proceedings of the Eightieth Annual Communication of the Most Worshipful Grand Lodge AF&AM of the State of Missouri, 5900. St. Louis, Mo., 1900.

Official Proceedings of the 33rd Annual Communication of the Most Worshipful Grand Lodge of AF&AM of the State of Idaho, 1900. Boise, Idaho, 1900.

Proceedings of the Grand Lodge of F&AM of the State of New York—119th Annual Communication. New York, N.Y., 1900.

Proceedings of the Most Worshipful Grand Lodge of AF&AM of the Commonwealth of Massachusetts for the Year 1900. Boston, Mass., 1901.

Proceedings of the Most Worshipful Grand Lodge of Ancient Free & Accepted Masons of Oregon—15th Annual Communication. Portland, Ore., 1900.

Proceedings of the Special Communication of May 15 and August 4, 5900, of the 124th Annual Communication of the Most Worshipful Grand Lodge of A.F. of South Carolina. Abbeville, S.C, 1901.

Transactions of the Grand Lodge of Michigan, 1900. Port Huron, Mich., 1900.

Official Proceedings of the 99th Annual Communication of the Grand Lodge AF&AM of the State of Missouri. No city, 1919.

Annals of the Grand Lodge of Iowa AF&AM, 1920. Davenport, Iowa, 1920.

Annual Proceedings of the Grand Lodge of Kentucky F&AM, 1920. Louisville, Ky., 1920.

Official Proceedings of the 53rd Annual Communication of the Most Worshipful Grand Lodge of the State of Idaho, 1920. Boise, Idaho, 1920.

101st Annual Communication—Grand Lodge of Maine, 1920. Portland, Maine, 1920.

Proceedings of the Grand Lodge of F&AM of the State of New York—139th Annual Communication. New York, N.Y., 1920.

Proceedings of the Most Worshipful Grand Lodge of AF&AM of the Commonwealth of Massachusetts for the Year 1920. Cambridge, Mass., 1920.

Proceedings of the 134th Annual Communication of the Grand Lodge of Georgia F&AM. Alton, Ga., 1920.

Transactions of the Grand Lodge of Michigan, 1920. Saginaw, Mich., 1920.

Proceedings of the 185th Annual Communication of the Most Worshipful Grand Lodge of AFM of South Carolina, 5922. Columbia, S.C., 1922.

Proceedings of the Grand Lodge of F&AM of the State of Michigan, 1939. Detroit, Mich., 1939.

Annals of the Grand Lodge of Iowa AF&AM, 1940. Mason City, Iowa.

121st Annual Communication—Grand Lodge of Maine, 1940. Portland, Maine, 1940.

Proceedings of the Grand Lodge of F&AM of the State of New York—159th Annual Communication. New York, N.Y., 1940.

Proceedings of the Most Worshipful Grand Lodge of AF&AM of the Commonwealth of Massachusetts for the Year 1940. Cambridge, Mass., 1941.

Proceedings of the 154th Annual Communication of the Grand Lodge of Georgia F&AM, 1940. Macon, Ga., 1940.

Proceedings of the 203rd A.C. of the Most Worshipful Grand Lodge of AFM of South Carolina, 5940. Columbia, S.C., 1940.

Seventy-Fourth Annual Communication of the Most Worshipful Grand Lodge of Ancient Free & Accepted Masons of Idaho, September 1940. Boise, Idaho, 1940.

Official Proceedings of the Grand Lodge AF&AM of the State of Missouri at Its 121st Annual Communication. No city, 1941.

Proceedings of the Grand Lodge of Kentucky F&AM—141st Communication. Louisville, Ky., 1941.

NATIONAL CONGRESS OF PARENTS AND TEACHERS

National Congress of Parents and Teachers. *Proceedings of the Thirty-Second Annual Meeting.* Washington, D.C., 1928.

ROTARY CLUBS

1930–31 Official Directory of Rotary International. Chicago, Ill., 1930.

1940–41 Official Directory of Rotary International. Chicago, Ill., 1940.

SALVATION ARMY

Salvation Army Yearbook, 1930. No city, 1930.

Mary P. Ryan

Civil Society as Democratic Practice: North American Cities during the Nineteenth Century

On the threshold of the twenty-first century, many scholars and citizens are grasping for some sense of societal purpose more substantial and satisfying than the aggregated narcissism that triumphed in the last. Yet, the various formulations of the object of this quest, "Social capital," "civic engagement," "the public sphere," or "civil society," strike contradictory chords of meaning. "Social capital" might ring pleasantly in the ears of social scientists, but to some humanists, it emits a discordant economistic sound. "Civic engagement" might recall the pieties of a citizenship class convened a half century ago, which alternately comfort and repel. Gold-plated philosophical terms like "civil society" and "the public sphere" come enmeshed in a thicket of theoretical writing, much of it bound to parochial Western political theory. While the range and variety of issues that this special issue of the journal calls forth is to be applauded, such heterogeneous expectations can also lead to confusion and miscommunication. Thus, at the outset, let me state my own particular interpretation of what is at stake in the contemporary discussions of social capital.

The concept of social capital is a strategic vantage point from which to mount a discussion of a number of critical and interrelated concerns that have made their way into dispersed personal libraries and private offices for at least the last decade: first, the discovery of an extensive network of women's organizations that undergirded American political history (especially the development of the welfare state); second, a theoretical search for the "public" that is invigorated by an extensive list of authors, ranging from Alexis de Tocqueville to Jürgen Habermas; and finally, that noisy, sometimes surly face-off between multiculturalism and its critics.

Mary P. Ryan is Margaret Byrne Professor of American History, University of California, Berkeley. She is the author of *Women in Public: Between Banners and Ballots, 1825–1880* (Baltimore, 1990); *Civic Wars: Democracy and Public Life in American Cities during the Nineteenth Century* (Berkeley, 1997).

Between my empirical research about public life in American cities during the nineteenth century and these broader issues, I have forged the following rough formulation of the critical importance of social life to political history: Sustained, associated action is an essential condition for, and component of, democratic politics. (At times I have sounded like a civic cheerleader for the organizational panache, that, at least since Tocqueville's visit in the 1830s, has been regarded as a character trait of Americans). Indeed I value this social acumen in itself, but not only for itself. I look beyond simple quantitative measurement of social capital or civic organizations toward some substantive civic goals, namely, the furtherance of democratic participation and the pursuit of social justice.

According to these standards and purposes, the concept of "civil society," especially as formulated by Cohen and Arato, is the most useful conceptual foundation on which to mount a research project. Cohen and Arato "locate the genesis of democratic legitimacy and the chances for direct participation . . . within a highly differentiated model of civil society itself." It follows from this premise that civil society can be found far and wide, in any place where "free and unconstrained association and discussion" reign. But civil society, so broadly construed, will not always represent, or even foster, genuine public democracy. My own search for effective democratic practice has taken me to a variety of social spaces—from exclusive clubs to scrappy social movements. What I found was a melange of political practices that will not fit neatly into a single classification—neither Putnam's social capital nor Tocqueville's voluntary association, nor even Habermas' public sphere. In the United States during the antebellum period, citizens and outsiders filled urban public spaces with a whole panoply of institutions and practices that activated, exercised, and expanded what has always been an imperfect democracy.[1]

---

1   Jean L. Cohen and Andrew Arato, *Civil Society and Political Theory* (New York, 1992), 19. See Robert D. Putnam, with Roberto Leonardi and Raffaella Y. Nanetti, *Making Democracy Work: Civic Traditions in Modern Italy* (Princeton, 1993); Tocqueville (trans. Henry Reeve), *Democracy in America* (London, 1835–1840), 2v.; Habermas (trans. Thomas Burger and Frederick Lawrence), *The Structural Transformation of the Public Sphere* (Cambridge, Mass., 1989).

This essay treats three very select places during approximately the second quarter of the nineteenth century: New York, New Orleans, and San Francisco—sites of investigation chosen for several purposes. First, this research strategy centers the analysis squarely within the chronology of the American democratic revolution, focusing on the period after the War of Independence, when republican ideology and mixed constitutions (at the state and federal levels) had set the stage for an explicitly democratic practice. By 1825, democratic expectations were firmly installed in a relatively widespread male suffrage that delegated public decisions to popularly elected officials who met in deliberative legislative bodies and were held accountable to their constituents. The operation of these basic democratic institutions is most visible at the local level, and it is particularly vivid in nineteenth-century American cities.

Basing my analysis in three rapidly growing and particularly diverse ports serves a second purpose: It puts severe pressure on the process of association, which Tocqueville among others regarded as the special cultural capital of homogeneous Anglo-Saxon populations (often personified by the New England town meeting). During the pivotal years of this study, roughly 1825 to 1860, these cities doubled in size nearly every decade (New York reaching more than 750,000 in population). At the same time, the foreign born came to constitute nearly half the total residents, and often the majority of the voters. Although hardly typical American settlements, New York, New Orleans, and San Francisco spanned a whole continent of urban experience, displaying a wide range of cultural and demographic patterns. Not far removed from Spanish and French, as well as English, colonial institutions and harboring everything from financial capitals to slums, slave quarters, and Chinatowns, these cities put the possibilities for democratic civic life to a rigorous test.

The simplest body of evidence about antebellum civil society is found in the city directories that were published in most American towns of significant size late in the eighteenth century. Even though these listings underrepresented levels of association, they turn up an extraordinarily large and diverse accounting of what were called "societies." A contrast between these maps of organized social life and their contemporary analog, telephone directories, is instructive. The latter read like a monotonous compilation of names and addresses, prefixed with a list of government offices and supplemented with a huge consumers' guide to shops and businesses. The names of voluntary associations that occasionally appear within these lists are neither labelled nor aggregated to delineate any distinctive social space within the dense landscape of homes, businesses, and government services. (The task of charting social space from the World Wide Web is too dizzying to contemplate.) The early city directories projected a different morphology of urban social life.

The New York Directory for 1786 (when the city's population was 23,614) set the pattern. The table of contents identified the basic cell structure of the community: first, the politically elected officials (from the Congress to the state assembly, the city, and the county of New York); next, the local lawyers and notary publics, followed by the learned professions (ministers, physicians, bank directors, professors at Columbia); and finally, a miscellaneous compendium of organizations grouped under the category of "Members of Abolition Society and other Societies." The other "societies," though only six in number, articulated the general principles of association in the eighteenth century. The purpose of the first one listed—the "Society for promoting the Manumission of Slaves, and protecting such of them as have been, or may be liberated"—is self-explanatory; the second, the Society of Cincinnati, was a seed of the first party system, an association of incipient Federalists. Both had a clear political intent, suggesting an American variant on Habermas' bourgeois public sphere—a place of free discussion organized outside the state apparatus where public opinion took form. Like analogs in London and Paris, the Abolitionist Society met "in the Coffee-house" and the Society of Cincinnati was divided into two districts "for the sake of frequent communications." Following these societies, in order, were social clubs—the Saint Andrews' Society and the Masons—occupational associations—the Gold and Silver Smiths, the General Society of Mechanics and Tradesmen, and the "Society of Peruke Makers and Hair Dressers, etc."[2]

Before the eighteenth century had closed, the habits of sustained association had been established in the City of New York:

2 David Franks, *The New York Directory* (New York, 1786), 94–103.

Some associations (like the antislavery society) challenged established institutions and enunciated the principles of political opposition; others (like the guilds of silversmiths and lawyers) took shape around social and economic distinctions. All of them opened up a place of civic discussion between state and individual. The subsequent decades would expand and elaborate this space, in New York and elsewhere.

The testimony of city directories indicates that the 1830s and the 1840s were an era of especially hearty growth in the number and variety of associations. Leafing forward through the New York directories to 1840 indicates a geometrical increase in the number of associations. By then, the table of contents was differentiating societies into several categories, favoring the term *institution* as the generic title for the separate building blocks of civil society. "Medical Institutions, Institutions of Fine Arts, and Literary and Scientific Associations" linked men of the elite professions according to specific civic interests or avocations, from the study of history and sacred music to political affiliation. Many clubs met weekly, sometimes in their own handsome buildings with substantial libraries and an air of conviviality. The United States Naval Lyceum, for example, aimed to "promote the diffusion of knowledge, to foster harmony, and a community of interest in the service." Other clubs were devoted to mutual improvement, especially among the young and those employed at the level of clerk.[3]

The Directory of 1840 added yet another category of association—"Religious, Benevolent and Moral Institutions." Clearly a by-product of the Second Great Awakening, this category added no less than fifty-six associations to the civic roster. Under the familiar names of Bible society, relief society, tract society, and Sunday school, women joined men at the penumbra to civil society. Eight of these societies were open to women, married and single, honoring them with titles like president, treasurer, and manager.[4]

Religion and morality were not monolithic values in antebellum America. Alongside the denominational variety of Protestantism (seen in the hundreds of different churches enumerated

3 *New York as It Is: Containing a General Description of the City of New York* (New York, 1840), 67–113.
4 *Ibid.*, 75–108.

in New York's directory), co-existed a number of Catholic and Jewish societies that gave identifiable civic status to recent immigrants and different language groups. Associations with such names as the Society for the Education of Orphan Children of the Jewish Persuasion, Roman Catholic Benevolent Society, French Benevolent Society, the German Society, and St. Patrick's Society revealed the cosmopolitan character of urban volunteerism.[5]

The spirit of joining had taken sufficient root by the early nineteenth century to sustain growth beyond the Northeast. The first New Orleans directory was issued in 1805, a few months after the Louisiana Purchase; it was a mere unadorned list of names. By 1822, however, the spirit of association was flourishing under southern skies and bursting with ethnic and religious diversity. Nineteen lodges, many schools, several orders of masons (with names like "Le Conseil de Royal Secret" or "L'Etoile Polaire"), "a number of benevolent and charitable societies," and a female asylum endowed by a "rich bachelor" (Julien Pydras) testified to the proliferation of associations in what was then a bicultural city. A decade later, civil society in New Orleans had become multicultural, hosting organizations from far-flung corners of the world—"The Hibernian Society of New Orleans for the Relief of Unfortunate Irishmen," for one.[6]

If a French, Catholic, southern city could be so enamored of associational life, it is no wonder that the western pioneer outposts did not turn out to be civic slackers. San Francisco Bay had hardly been settled in 1854 when the encampment of miners en route to and from the gold fields published a directory with a full contingent of fraternal lodges. No less than eight Masonic chapters and six chapters of odd fellows announced their weekly meetings, built public halls, and welcomed such ethnic variants as "the Harmony Lodge (German)" of the IOOF. Four weekly chapter meetings of the Sons of Temperance, as well as two "Temperance Taverns," offered refuge from the temptations of "Baghdad by the Bay." Other benevolent contingents formed as French, German, Hebrew, and New England Associations; the old bases of Protestant benevolence were covered by Bible, orphan, tract, and Sunday-school societies, and supplemented with newer members of the Christian coalition like the YMCA and the Ladies Protection

---

5 Ibid., 102, 106.
6 New Orleans Directories (1805), 33; (1811), 34.

and Relief Society. If the only objective were to locate a point in the American past when habits of vigorous voluntary association were well established, the investigation could conclude well before the Civil War in the North, South, and West.[7]

Yet, for all their variety and energy, these voluntary institutions fell far short of the democratic ideal in themselves, and in relation to the civic whole. Religious benevolent associations often featured an exclusive, top-heavy membership. The earliest associations, in particular, boasted patrician founders, restricted membership, hefty fees, and condescending attitudes toward the beneficiaries of their largesse. Sometimes benevolent associations took profit from their deployment of social "capital," their purpose hidden behind such benign descriptions as industrial schools or employment agencies, or such titles as "Society for the Encouragement of Faithful Domestic Servants." The last-named was a New York society that started in 1825, announcing its purpose as "the promotion of good feelings between employers and servants and to induce the latter to remain as long as possible in their places." Other associations were even more blatant in their advertising, including such membership perks as access to employees who worked far below the market wage rates.[8]

These early blemishes on civic noblesse oblige were only faint omens of the class connotations that voluntarism would assume in the Gilded Age. The depressed economy of the 1870s would bring this unseemly side of civil society into the limelight, especially during the cold of winter. Witness the *New York Tribune*'s Dickensian account of a "holiday scene" on Thanksgiving Day in 1875. The story began with the image of a "great number of ladies and gentlemen of the highest social standing and greatest wealth, merchants and business men whose names are well known in the community" making a pilgrimage to the slum of Five Points, carrying holiday dinner to "the crowd of hungry little people . . . of the squalid neighborhood—old men hobbling on crutches, young men and boys dressed in rags, and women carrying little children in their arms. They waited hour after hour, their numbers constantly increasing, for the opening of the doors." Meanwhile, the regular beneficiaries of this elite society were inside the Five Points House of Industry, proving their worthiness by pious

---

7 *Lecount and Strong's San Francisco City Directory for 1854* (canvassed and compiled by Frank Rivers) (San Francisco, 1854).
8 *Longworth's American Almanac, New York Register, and City Directory* (New York, 1830).

recitations and song. This holiday ritual made even the *Tribune* reporter queasy: He noted that some of the poor "in spite of their hunger seemed to shrink from having their eating made a spectacle for curious eyes." Such a condescending display of social capital exposes a dimension of association that, though not often noted in Tocquevillian celebrations of democracy in America, was built into the very foundation of nineteenth-century civic life.[9]

Most associations were more democratic and egalitarian. Humbler lodges and mutual-benefit associations soon outnumbered elite religious and benevolent societies. The fraternal encampments of odd fellows, journeymen, or reformed drunkards dissolved class differences in common rituals and abundant good spirits. Their purpose, like that proclaimed by the St. Nicholas Society of New York, was little more than "Good fellowship and social intercourse . . . and charity toward those of them who may have fallen into decay." By mid-century, such associations of mutual care and support had woven a finely meshed safety net around much of the urban population.[10]

At the western outpost of fraternalism, in the extraordinarily diverse congregation of San Francisco, mutual-benefit organizations served as prefabricated social shelters for thousands of lonesome pioneers. These associations, which fell somewhat arbitrarily under the categories of both benevolence and protective societies, were initiated according to two major principles—either occupational or ethnic. Those with the former orientation included everyone from cigar makers and stevedores to surgeons and the chamber of commerce; those with the latter often included such generic sources of mutual capital as the "Savings and Loan Society," which, in its own words, came into being so "that by means of it the members may be enabled to find a secure and profitable investment for small savings," as small, in fact, as $2.50.[11]

Other protective societies served ethnic clienteles. The Eureka Benevolent Society, established in 1850, for example, aimed "to assist poor and needy Hebrews in want or sickness." Its monthly fee of $1 per member soon mounted to $10,000 in capital. The German General Benevolent Society, by collecting the same fee from 700 members, accumulated sufficient funds to

9 *New York Tribune*, 26 Nov. 1875.
10 *New York as It Is*, 105.
11 *San Francisco Directory for the Year Commencing June 1, 1859* (San Francisco, 1859), 391.

erect its own building, a hospital fitted with steam baths, a garden, and fountains, all valued at $20,000. Five San Francisco associations identified themselves as "Hebrew" societies, among them the Ladies Society of Israelites and the Ladies United Hebrew Benevolent Society ("for the assistance of Hebrew women who may require it"). Separate but friendly benevolent associations shot up in San Francisco—Irish (3) British, French, Swiss, Scandinavian, and Slavonic. The Societa Italiana di Mutua Beneficenza, for example, reported that it had secured "by arrangement with the French Benevolent society, ample accommodations" at the hospital of the latter "excellent institution." The variety of social organizations that took such quick root in these diverse cities indicates that American associationism was not simply an offshoot of an Anglo-Protestant cultural predisposition.[12]

The proliferation of mutual-benefit associations, fast on the heels of evangelical religious associations—especially among the foreign born—also serves as a caveat to those who would read the record of American voluntary association nostalgically backward to a small-town mentality forever lost. The wealth of associations testifies just as well to urban social diversity, or to competition between many parochial, close-minded groups. The propagation of societies says as much about tribalism as about concern for common civic good. Although most species of association educated its members to those organizational skills and habits of cooperation needed to make democracy work, some exhibited antisocial impulses as well, excluding those who were different, condescending to those deemed inferior, converting those judged to be less enlightened, and retreating from the rigors of the urban melting pot into villages of their own kind.

The gender boundary was the deepest of all trenches between associations. Not a single entry in the city directories indicated that men and women joined the same associations. The one known case of gender integration—the anti-slavery movement of the 1830s—did not issue a public invitation to women and presented the usual all-male list of officers. Women's associations exhibited a separate set of values, as illustrated by the Ladies Protection and Relief Society: "The object of the society is to render aid and protection to women in need and distress, residents

12 *San Francisco Directory for the Year Commencing July, 1860* (San Francisco, 1860), 440–445.

or strangers. All persons acquainted with any cases of distress or want are requested to give information at this office. All respectable women in want of protection, employment in families, or as needle-women, by applying at the office, will receive immediate attention." No word about the mutual accumulation of social or economic capital is spoken herein, nor is there a hint of the robust conviviality of lodgemen.[13]

The male side of the divide gave play to a greater variety of needs and talents—the meeting in saloons by mutual-benefit associations, the spirited debating societies for ambitious clerks and lawyers, and the soldering of lucrative business connections at the chamber of commerce. All of these associations were aggressively masculine. The raison d'être of some, however, was not just masculine; it was distinctly puerile. The secret rites of societies of "knights," "redmen," and other "odd fellows" enacted fantasies of escape from female kin through male bonding. One San Francisco chapter of the Odd Fellows went by the name of "The Patriarchal Branch," its chief called "D. D. Grand Sire."[14]

The metaphor of social capital describes the operations of these early American associations aptly. They did accumulate material and cultural resources within select groups—based on class, ethnic, religious, and gender affiliations. Associations were not, however, intrinsically linked to the more public, disinterested civic world; nor did they necessarily conform to even the stripped-down liberal definition of the public realm, which guaranteed certain inalienable rights. The constitutional guarantee of free assembly did not extend to these private associations, even though a number of the most exclusive benevolent associations received state subsidies. Only by extension, and only under particular historical circumstances, was association a nutrient of democracy.

The high political stakes and the shifting context of the contemporary debate about civil society make this obvious point worth emphasizing. The institutionalization of civil society and expansion of social capital occurred at a time when America's political culture explicitly adhered to high standards of democracy. America's achievement of popular sovereignty and representative government, however, did not automatically bring inclusive and

13 *Lecount and Strong's San Francisco City Directory,* 250.
14 *Ibid.,* 254.

egalitarian ideals to the voluntary associations: The political sphere was at least open to all adult white men on an equal basis, regardless of birthplace, wealth, or religion. The fact that women had access to their own associations but not the franchise only underscores the point. The overwhelming majority of "ladies" who joined societies would not even imagine, much less demand or secure, title to the vote and the rights of full citizenship. Membership in a society was no guarantee of a share in public decision making nor of any input in the creation of a political democracy. For that we must look to other places in civil society.

Social capital is too blunt a measure to guage the vitality and extent of democratic politics. At least three additional factors are necessary to encompass the democratic practices of antebellum Americans: social inclusion, genuine participation, and power to affect the public realm. Simple social organizations, no matter how extensive, do not satisfy these criteria. The records of the city directories sometimes indicated that associations were often exclusive rather than inclusive, that they disdained, or even prohibited, partisan political discussions on their turf, and that they delegated what some consider public responsibilities—like care of the poor, the orphaned, and the sick—to self-serving coteries.

By focusing only on group formation, we might overlook other conditions that are key to making democracy work. The city directories are a paltry record of civic engagement compared with another obvious way of documenting public life, the press. By the 1830s, urban newspapers reached almost the entire adult population. The New Orleans' directory listed no less than fifteen local newspapers and periodicals—in German, French, and English. In New York, censuses numbered local periodical publications in the hundreds. Examination of just a few shows a society teeming with civic engagement, of a passionate, contentious, and not always civil sort.[15]

The first daily newspapers—like the *New York Evening Post,* which commenced publishing in the 1820s—provide a dynamic picture of how the units of civil society were activated and how they performed. On a typical day in New York City, the chamber

15   Michael Schudson, *Discovering the News: A Social History of American Newspapers* (New York, 1978); Donald Schiller, *Objectivity and the News: The Public and the Rise of Commercial Journalism* (Philadelphia, 1981); Richard R. John, *Spreading the News: The American Postal System from Franklin to Morse* (Cambridge, 1995).

of commerce met to discuss tariff policies, the volunteer firemen paraded in front of city hall to celebrate their thirty-fifth anniversary, and "all who [were] desirous of becoming members [were] respectfully invited to attend" a meeting of the Dry Goods Clerks Association. An equally crowded calendar of association came into focus in the South, at least in the winter months when the weather was tolerable and the risk of contacting cholera or yellow fever had abated. Papers like the *New Orleans Picayune* were replete with articles about parades, festivals, balls, and meetings sponsored by various associations. The press charted the movements of diverse congregations into the city streets: for example, unskilled dock workers or proud screwmen from the cotton mills, different ethnic groups, or even an occasional contingent of free men of color.

Associations were especially welcome in San Francisco of the 1850s, a boomtown desperate for civilizing institutions. In what would become an all-too-familiar California practice, when the state legislature decided to cut costs by closing a public hospital, civil society came to the succor of the needy, winning accolades in the press: "Considering the varied and conflicting interests of individuals composing the community of San Francisco and in view of our peculiar and incongruous social elements it may be deemed wonderful that so much has been accomplished for the benefit of many by our benevolent institutions. Many of these institutions were organized during a period of our local history when all other objects seemed lost to view in the pursuit of wealth." After singling out the Protestant Orphan Asylum, Ladies Protective Relief Society, the Riggers and Stevedores, as well as the Hebrew, Eureka, and German mutual-benefit associations for special commendation, the *Daily Alta Californian* sighed with relief that "many of our charitable societies have become established beyond the need of pecuniary assistance from the Public." The picture that emerges from the press confirms and expands the meaning of voluntary societies. In an emergency, separate associations would come together to create a patchwork of civic responsibility. However segmented, civil society could assume the social breadth and vitality to meet public needs.[16]

The press accounts also indicated that the voluntary civic realm was more than a sum of these organized parts. Civic action

16 *Daily Alta Californian*, 22 Apr. 1955.

did not depend on pre-existing organization. It was so pervasive and entrenched an urban habit that the *New York Press* reserved a full column for notices of "Public Meetings"—events that mixed "regular meetings" of associations with ad hoc assemblies for anything from public relief to honoring a deceased hero. In 1827, for example, this eclectic column noted a funeral procession for Thomas Emmett, the Irish hero, a gathering of neighbors to install a pump, and a meeting called "by the desire of a number of respectable individuals . . . who are desirous of relieving the Greeks in their present most distressing need."[17]

Public assemblies hidden in minor presses augment this already high quotient of civic engagement. *The Workingmen's Advocate* called its readers to a "Great Public Meeting" with "express resolution posted at [a previous] meeting of 3000 mechanics and the working men." The New York papers testified that the practice of the public meeting was more than a local custom. A report on a Philadelphia meeting, called in opposition to the movement to abolish slavery, carefully detailed the convening process: "[I]n pursuance of publick notice, an immense assemblage of the young men of the City convened yesterday afternoon in the spacious hall of Musical Study Society." Moreover, papers in New York, Philadelphia, and other cities served as organizers and moderators, as well as recorders of public meetings. The *New York Evening Press* had already established its role as a monitor in 1827 when it reported that the Federalists were plotting a secessionist convention in Harrisburg: "A plan is underway or quite matured by certain gentlemen in Albany to agitate the city to its center, by convening a public meeting of the inhabitants at an early date, for the purpose of choosing delegates."[18]

Participants in public meetings were not just joiners but alert citizens capable of creative and effective public action. They deployed well-honed political knowledge about how to call meetings, court the press, locate meeting space, summon support, make alliances, create publicity, and scrutinize the activities of others. Furthermore, no membership fees, pedigree, or elite sponsors were required for these ubiquitous *public* events, which were more democratic, more active in their mode of civic engagement, and

17 *New York Evening Press*, 2 Jan. 1827.
18 *Ibid.*, 7 July 1827, 27 Aug. 1835.

more eclectic in their civic possibilities than typical voluntary associations were. Antebellum city people developed a repertoire of procedures—notifying the press, convening in open-air, central locations, drafting and ratifying resolutions, and publicizing actions—and adapted them to multiple public goals.

Public meetings routinely reported in the city newspapers also document another, emphatically political, species of "human capital" that was much in evidence during debates about both national and local issues. The most lavish display of this civic resource took place at partisan events. Daily headlines announced papers' favorite causes, such as the *New York Evening Press*' headline, "Great Triumphant Meeting of the People," about a gathering of Democrats. Such hyperbole did not rebound to Gotham's glory alone. The "Great Democratic Meeting in Boston," "Great Public Festivals in St. Louis," and "Public Meetings in the South versus the Abolitionists" received ebullient reviews in New York City. Public assemblies called in San Francisco in the 1850s employed a new term, the "Mass Meeting." The "very large meeting of the democracy in the plaza" in May 1850, for example, followed on an "issuance of a call for a mass meeting" six weeks earlier. Its purpose was to "[effect] an organization of the Democratic Party."[19]

The Jacksonian Democrats in New York City during the 1820s and 1830s were the impressarios of the public meeting. Andrew Jackson's election was heralded with "[s]uch a meeting [as] we believe, was never before held in New York. Tammany Hall, from the place where the chairman sat to the door, was crowded to breathless suffocation; there was scarce room for another man to budge himself in. The stair case, the passages, the public rooms below, were equally thronged with persons pressing vainly for admittance. The street in front of the hall, and the sidewalks for a considerable distance each way were covered with a multitude." Although the *Evening Press*—a fervently Jacksonian organ—duly reported that the faction allied to John Quincy Adams held its meetings in Tammany Hall, it hailed its own party as the champion of the Irish and of workers and smeared members of its rival as affluent monopolists. These public meetings were

19 See Ryan, *Civic Wars: Democracy and Public Life in American Cities during the Nineteenth Century* (Berkeley, 1997), 94–131.

the crucibles of the two-party system; they contain the richest vein of civic engagement, the very bedrock on which democratic opposition was effectuated.[20]

Election campaigns were the stormy centers of democratic and participatory civil society. The bombastic headlines of the Jacksonian Press were the overture to democracy in America—for example, "A Great Meeting of Adopted Citizens," and "Another Triumphant Expression of the Voice of Democracy." During the spring election of 1834, New Yorkers mounted ward meetings throughout the city to nominate and ratify candidates for every office on the ballot. At the moment of electoral climax, civil society staged a classic democratic ritual: "When the doors of the great room were thrown open, the whole vast space was instantly and completely filled with a dense mass of citizens, all eager to raise their voices in behalf of the object." A few days later, the editor of the *Evening Press* put democracy on the line:

> The crisis is come. Tomorrow commences the struggle and three days will decide whether the Bank of the United States or the constituted authority chosen by the free voices of the people shall govern this great country. . . . The struggle between the two great parties has now resolved itself into a war of the rich against the poor—of private interest against public liberty, of MONEY against MEN. . . . Come forth then stern, proud, unchangeable and independent Democrats . . . and teach these mean, yet proud aristocrats who sell their souls for discounts, the memorable lesson that they can neither cheat you under the masks of friendship, nor bully you as apes and enemies. Come to the polls without noise, confusion, arrogance or fear. Give your votes like Freemen who know the value of their own rights, while they respect the rights of others.[21]

Meanwhile, the Whig opposition staged a "Tremendous" meeting at the Exchange, where "every avenue leading to the big room was one solid mass of human flesh." Still the battle had hardly begun. Election morning found Whigs and Democrats confronting one another in Masonic Hall near Wall Street, as well as in the rougher neighborhoods of the sixth ward: "Armed, ferocious and half mad bands of desperadoes throng in the streets

20 *New York Evening Press,* 3 Nov. 1827.
21 *Ibid.,* 5–12 Apr. 1834.

killing peaceable men." Epithets of "low Irish" and "damned Irish" were mixed with swipes at hypocritical merchants and their officious clerks. Literal mud and a few bricks flew through the partisan air until the ballots were counted, the victorious Whigs celebrated, and the losing Democrats conceded, restoring civic quiet.[22]

We have come to take this particular kind of civic engagement for granted—its demagogery, inflated rhetoric, venal motivation, vote tampering, and simple silliness. In the 1830s, such electoral antics were defiantly democratic acts. By a combination of organization and competition, challenge to established authority, and legitimation of opposition, political parties installed democratic representatives in positions of state power. These partisan battles—a kind of routine civic warfare—also defended and gradually expanded the rights of citizens.

In the 1840s and 1850s, for example, the Democratic Party of New York successfully repelled attempts to limit the voting rights of recent immigrants, some of whom carried their newly won franchise to San Francisco, where they posted a Tammany Hall placard on a tent in Portsmouth Plaza. These fledgling California Democrats were able to install a full network of ward organizations and public meetings; the Whigs were too weak to put up much of an opposition. The second party that formed in 1854 was something of an aberration: The Know-Nothing Party, a nativist association, was organized in secrecy, drawing its political capital from principles of social exclusion and mistrust. The Democrat's electoral victory over the Know-Nothings that year generated such opposition that within a few months of the election, thousands of San Franciscans organized themselves into a lynch mob that drove the Democratic Party underground.

Such vigilantism and nativism represent a kind of social and political resource that we might not want to reclaim as our civic heritage. They are reminders of the volatility and risks of popular and participatory democracy. As the *San Francisco Daily Alta* put it on the eve of the Vigilante insurrection: "What a curious thing is government. Who can explain, who comprehend it? It has taken a great many generations to work out the problem of democracy

22   *Ibid.*

as it has been developed in the United States and it sometimes goes astray."[23]

In 1854, American democracy was a partial and fragile institution. Although the nativist attempt to exclude immigrants from democracy would go down to electoral defeat, millions of other Americans were political exiles in the land of their birth. Before 1850, no government—local or national, North or South—seriously considered female suffrage, and only a few states permitted non-whites to vote. Before the Civil War, the principles of exclusion were clear and the boundaries firm all across the country. The delegates to the California State Constitutional Convention of 1849 stretched logic to the breaking point to deny citizenship to Indian tribesmen, native residents of Mexican origin, and African-Americans and grant it to "white men only." The racial lines of democracy were also being tested and redesigned in New York, where a sequence of referenda denied suffrage to the vast majority of African-Americans, save a few men of sufficient property. By statute and pervasive prejudice, the majority of Americans were kept out of electoral procedures and representative government, the most important areas of civic engagement.

Yet, not all of the possible routes to a workable democratic civic center have been exhausted. Although non-whites and women were not found at the voting booth or at party caucuses, small prescient numbers of them mobilized in another critical arena of civil society, the sphere of social movements. Several points of civic contention early in the last century manifested the rudiments of social movements—for example, the issue of slavery, the grievances of working men, and the role of women in society. Because all of the groups involved mounted civic actions from a position outside the legal framework of political society, explicitly challenging dominant public opinion and expectation, they were compelled to devise distinctive ways to capitalize on the civic resources available.

Like other flanks of civil society, social movements were built on the foundation of voluntary associations and public meetings and caught up in the momentum of partisan politics. When, in 1844, George Evans announced the formation of a "New and

23   *San Francisco Daily Alta,* 7–31 May 1855.

Important Movement of the Working Men," he was registering the maturation of a political practice that he had been nurturing since the 1820s but had roots in the eighteenth century. Ever since property-less artisans had mobilized in behalf of American independence and championed the federal constitution, unenfranchised manual workers had served as templates of political innovation. By the 1840s, the *Workingman's Advocate* could report the existence of a strong network of trade unions. A typical cell, like the New York Society of Journeymen House Carpenters, pursued such familiar objectives as providing for "the decent internment of deceased members," but it also demanded "equitable prices and just and reasonable wage." Trade associations were common in American cities by mid-century. The Riggers and Stevedores Union Association of San Francisco, for example, was organized in 1853 "for the regulation of wages and protection of each other." These mobilizations of manual workers gave a faint, but recognizable, shape to the independent labor movement—a loose aggregation of associations that had specific economic goals and regularly flexed their muscles with "turnouts" to raise wages.[24]

Organized manual workers also formed an explicitly political front. By the 1820s, the Working Man's Party presented its own slate of candidates for public office and advocated specific public policies. The Democratic Working Men's General Committee to Protect Equal Rights lobbied political parties to curtail prison labor during the election of 1835. The young labor movement was a major force in the democratic revolution of the Jacksonian period. Leaders like Evans pushed Tammany Hall toward opposing property restrictions on the franchise, adopting decentralized ward-level organizations, attacking the Second Bank of the United States, and championing the "producing classes." As Hugins put it, the Working Men's Party "democratized the Democracy." It also converted the political margins into the political avant garde, presenting an early textbook exhibition of how social movements operate. It was launched "at a numerous meeting of Mechanics and other Working Men of the City of New York, held pursuant to public notice, at Wooster Street Military Hall," which resolved to exert pressure on major political parties through coalitions with

24 Walter Hugins, *Jacksonian Democracy and the Working Class* (Stanford, 1960), 57; *San Francisco Directory for the Year Commencing June 1, 1859*, 391.

other associations—notably, the Society for the Protection of Industry and Promotion of National Education.[25]

By 1844, Evans could translate these ad hoc programs into a concise formulation of how to effect political mobilization: "By providing information, By printing and circulating tracts calculated to give information to the people on these important subjects, By corresponding, reporting with similar societies in other towns and cities, By promoting the gradual extension of the associations through the states of the Union." This movement expired in the depression of 1837, but labor rose again in the 1850s when scores of worker associations convened in the city-wide Congress of Trades. Soon after mid-century, when industrial production had spread outside the northeast, similar networks emerged in the workingmen's clubs of San Francisco and the trade associations of New Orleans.[26]

Working men were not the only citizens who took advantage of the open civic spaces of antebellum cities to promote unpopular causes. The reform efforts of the American Anti-Slavery Society—listed in the New York City Directory under the category of Moral Institutions—were fuelled by a unique blend of social capital and moral–political passion. Its distinctive manner of civic engagement was stated in its preamble:

> The object of this Society is the entire abolition of slavery in the United States. While it admits that each state, in which slavery exits has, by the Constitution of the United States, the exclusive right to legislate in regard to its abolition in said state, it shall aim to convince all our fellow-citizens, by arguments addressed to their understandings and consciences, that slave-holding is a heinous crime in the sight of God, and that the duty, safety and best interests of all concerned, require its immediate abandonment, with expatriation. The Society will also endeavor, in a constitutional way, to influence Congress to put an end to the domestic slave trade.

Welding the moral intensity of Protestant grace to the political framework of the federal constitution, the Antislavery Society created the civic space from which to influence public opinion and stir up agitation. By 1840, the Society's headquarters in New

25 Hugins, *Jacksonian Democracy,* 220; *Working Man's Advocate,* 31 Oct. 1829.
26 *Ibid.,* 29 and 30 Oct. 1829, 16 Mar. 1844.

York had spawned almost 1,000 auxiliaries in nine states, distributing journals nationwide on a weekly, monthly, and quarterly basis.[27]

The anti-slavery movement mobilized ingenious forms of political capital at the grassroots level, where it tapped the moral concerns and organizational skills of women, who used boycotts, fairs, petition campaigns, and poetry to enlist support. After the Civil War, female abolitionists formed a movement for women's suffrage. The major claimant for that civic status before that was the Female Moral Reform society, which captured a few headlines in New York during the 1830s and in 1848. It managed to enact its own view of women's best interest into state law—the Seduction Act of 1848, an anemic statute of dubious efficacy that punished violators of a young woman's virtue with a $25 fine. Nonetheless, this law demonstrated that with enough ingenuity and obstinance, even the most marginalized citizens could find the political leverage to change public policy.[28]

Like women, African-Americans in nineteenth-century cities found ways to assert their rights and opinions and to exercise citizenship without official portfolio. They aired their grievances—slavery in the South and discrimination in the North—through a number of civic venues—mixed gender, mixed race associations, like the American Anti-slavery Society; national conventions; several state referenda campaigns; and such grassroot organizations as militia companies, newspapers, and fraternal orders. Neither the social death of slavery nor the political death of disenfranchisement left African-Americans bereft of political capital. The power that these associations accumulated cannot be exaggerated. They provided the original yeast from which followed the realignment of a major party, a sectional division, and eventually the end of slavery, after the most devastating war in United States history. Yet, this early movement of African-Americans was seldom even noted in the official roster of voluntary associations.[29]

27 *New York as It Is,* 99–100.
28 See Carroll Smith Rosenberg, *Disorderly Conduct: Visions of Gender in Victorian America* (New York, 1985); Ryan, *Women in Public: Between Banners and Ballots, 1825–1880* (Baltimore, 1990).
29 See James Horton and Phyllis Field, *The Politics of Race in New York: The Struggle for Black Suffrage in the Civil War Era* (Ithaca, 1982); Jean Fagin Yellin and John Van Horne (eds.), *The Abolitionist Sisterhood Women's Political Culture in Ante-Bellum America* (Ithaca, 1994).

Although it would take another generation for local associations of labor, women, and civil-rights advocates to congeal into well-oiled national organizations capable of effecting federal policy, the defining characteristics of powerful social movements were apparent by 1850. The exertion of organized political pressure in behalf of minority opinions added a critical dimension to public democracy. The evidence from antebellum cities indicates that at least three levels of civic organization are essential for a viable democracy, and only one of them corresponds with the kind of social capital generated in the garden variety of voluntary association, or all-American club. Membership in the societies listed in an antebellum city directory could inculcate social skills and organizational talents essential to democracy—the ability of citizens to work together, to create social meaning, and to voice concerns in the public sphere. The importance of simple social capital made associating a habitual, almost reflexive, quality of American cultural citizenship. Even though the network of lodges and ethnic brotherhoods represented a narrow range and a particularistic assertion of civic interests, often serving parochial interests and consolidating an inequitable distribution of power and resources, they established a first line of defense against the concentration of monolithic state power.

Open and public discussions about the needs of the whole polity, however, were not the stock-in-trade of the voluntary organizations, either locally or nationally. Debates about issues that went beyond private concern and tackled social differences were the province of the public meetings and were orchestrated most effectively by political parties. Partisan institutions were probably the most pervasive, most populous, and most vociferous organizations in antebellum civil society. They performed two critical services: First, they used the electoral process to bring the concerns of citizens to the government's attention and, second, they initiated the spirit and practice of political opposition that was just as critical to democracy as the simple acts of joining and organizing. This strategic differentiation of civil society was achieved at the grassroots level, in the wards, public halls, and street corners of antebellum cities. Yet, however engaged in social dialogue and cognizant of political difference, parties were neither pure democracies nor boundless communities. As many of their critics bemoaned, professional politicians' sense of public responsibility stopped just outside the voting booth and far short of identifying the rights and needs of all. In fact, during the nineteenth century, it was confined within the narrow realm of white-male suffrage.

Working democracy required another mechanism to keep civil society open at its margins. Before 1850, America's disenfranchised, relatively powerless citizens began to build up this political capital by means of social movements. It is neither an accident nor a simple function of demography that much of the history of American social movements concentrates on those who were excluded from participation during the formative period of American democratic institutions: non-whites, women, and, at the very outset, workingmen without property. Denied the political capital of the vote, and the economic capital of the propertied classes, these groups devised distinctive means of civic engagement: petition campaigns, public demonstrations, extensive organizational networks, and strategic alliances. By the midpoint of the nineteenth century, something more complex than Putnam's social capital, Tocqueville's voluntary associations, or Habermas' public sphere had evolved in the new American republic. A combination of associations, public meetings, parties, and social movements had created a highly differentiated structure for empowering citizens and practicing democracy.

Some of the critical ingredients of this civil society resembled the makings of the bourgeois public sphere that Habermas located in eighteenth-century European capitals, especially those that connected opposition to the absolutist state with the expansion of market capitalism. The imprint of merchant capital is unmistakable, almost tautological, in the city directories of the early nineteenth century. The directories were originally business propositions, created to facilitate trade; it is hardly surprising that they gave pride of place to banks, insurance companies, and later railroads. One of the earliest, most ubiquitous associations—often prominently placed in the directories—was the chamber of commerce, an association of the leading tradesmen of the city. It is a relatively easy matter to adapt Habermas' concept of the structural foundation of the public sphere to American conditions; the advance of market capitalism faced little state interference in the American colonies. The English Board of Trade was a pushover compared with the European monarchies and the mercantilist ministers, and national independence won the new American republic a relatively clear slate on which to expand individual enterprises and form mutually beneficial trade associations.

This is not to say that political institutions were immaterial to the luxurious growth of the voluntary civic sector. The civic identity of even a business organ like the city directory was shaped around government. Most directories began with a proud listing of state, federal, and local officials, and some charted the passage of time according to a national political calendar. *Longworth's New York Directory* for 1820, for example, marked its date on the frontispiece as "the thirty-fifth Year of American Independence." San Francisco's first directories bore the title, "General Directory of Citizens and a Business Directory of Dealers," but they gave top billing to "The Organization of the Different Branches of Municipal Government and the Laws regulating the Same: together with a Description of the Different associations."

America's civil society, and the payoff of social capital, drew momentum from the economic transformations of the Atlantic world but took form around the centering institutions of constituted government. The basic political scaffolding was laid in place by the American Revolution and its immediate consequences. Routine political practice in an antebellum city testifies to the widespread comprehension of basic civic lessons, especially the outlines of the constitutional order and federal system of government. This political knowledge became second nature to countless citizens who organized themselves into societies with "presidents" and "vice presidents," "by-laws" and "constitutions." Anyone who frequented a ward meeting or party rally knew something about how to draft resolutions, and could quote from the Bill of Rights, particularly the guarantees of free speech and assembly.

Another item in the Bill of Rights, freedom of religion, activated a second major source of civic engagement. The flood of Protestant evangelical societies issued directly from the political separation of church and state. It did not flow from some innate character trait of Protestants or outpouring of revivalist zeal; it evolved as a political strategy designed to assert specific ideological influence in the free market of religious belief. Much of the bloated condition of association in the second quarter of the nineteenth century is due to the formation of evangelical institutions aimed at propagating Protantism once the state no longer funded an established ministry. The American Home Missionary

Society, for example—"a voluntary, unincorporated association, formed by persons of the Presbyterian, Congregational Associated Reformed and Reformed Dutch Churches"—came into being in 1826 for the express purpose of spreading the gospel among the poor. In ten years, it sent 755 missionaries into 27 states and territories and 1,000 congregations or missionary districts, at an expense of $92,108.[30]

The evangelical enthusiasm of the antebellum period, though not strong enough to penetrate to the unsavory climate of New Orleans, spread quickly to the West. The officers of the San Francisco Bible Society, whose listings in the city directory claimed the title "esquire" rather than cowboy, boasted that they had issued 8,594 Bibles, in English, Spanish, and other European languages. Benevolent associations stepped in where the liberal state refused to tread, propagating Anglo-Protestant culture to the far shores of America's voluntary network. The proliferation of religious and benevolent associations gained added incentive from competition with the Catholic churches and Jewish temples of new immigrants.[31]

Religious diversity was only one shade in the rich palette of differences that invigorated civil society in the United States. The cell-like structure of antebellum public life expanded through a process of social differentiation and along lines of civic competition. Disagreement about a wide array of political and social issues—religious belief, partisan loyalty, public policy, reformist causes, and economic needs, as well as race, ethnicity, and gender identities—operated as a major catalyst for the proliferation of associations in antebellum cities. The vitality of civil society, in other words, does not necessarily depend on social trust. On the contrary, in antebellum American cities, it sometimes thrived on the leaven of difference, debate, even open conflict. This civic contention arose in tandem with democratic participation.

No map of civil society's tributaries in antebellum America is complete without reference to geographical, as well as economic and political, factors. Like political parties, associations for the purpose of religious benevolence were nurtured by a federal system that recreated and augmented civic organization at every

30 New York as It Is, 79–81.
31 Lecount and Strong's San Francisco City Directory, 255.

geographical level of government from the ward to Washington. The importance of spatial considerations for associations is also evident in both architecture and the urban plan. City directories gave special listings not just to societies but to their meeting places, some of which were local landmarks that had their names engraved in stone above the street: Hibernia Hall, The Merchants Exchange, Odd Fellows Hall. The San Francisco business directory for 1854 listed six entries under "Public Halls." Tellingly, "City Hall," the seat of legitimate government, was just one architectural landmark in a diversified public landscape. In a highly differentiated civil society with heterogeneous and scattered associations, the government office building was no more than the first among equals. It might have had a central location, a halo of classic ornament, a high dome, and often a large room for public assembly, but so did many public halls, some of them available for hire.

One last geographical feature of civil society might be tautological, but it is significant nonetheless. By their very nature, the major port cities in this investigation were especially conducive to civic vitality and democratic practice. Cities of a certain size and diversity, like New York, New Orleans, and San Francisco, provided the critical mass, social diversity, and concentrated human interaction that nourished a profusion of civic organizations. The distinctive pattern of urbanization in nineteenth-century America compounded the significance of this geographical factor. In the United States, new and instant cities emerged at the same time as older ones grew larger in population, thereby multiplying the sites where vigorous civil societies might appear. Space was far more than a metaphor for civic organization. Antebellum urban places provided particularly fertile habitats in which civic associations could emerge, grow, and propagate.

In the last analysis, the discrete factors mentioned in this analysis find their meaning and power only in conjunction with one another and within a unique historical context. American civic society, like Habermas' public sphere, Tocqueville's voluntary associations, or even Putnam's Renaissance republics, evolved in tandem with small-scale, locally grounded sites of market capitalism. The three port cities described herein were bustling entrepôts of international commerce, at a time of nascent and fluid economic power. Small entrepreneurs, like civic-minded individuals, had ready access to social resources with which to consolidate and advance their interests. In fact, business enterprises and civic associations drew on the same legal basis for accumulating capital through associated action—the general law of incorporation. City governments, local banks, turnpikes, and the ladies relief associations all applied to the state for corporate charters. At the municipal level, civil society and state power were analogous one to the other, and in this historical moment, relatively balanced in social power and political influence. Free enterprise and free association were not poles apart; nor was society divided by a gulf between private and public, individual and state, the realm of freedom and the domain of government. Such was the setting in which American democracy originated and matured.

A century later, the global scale of economic organization has destroyed the equilibrium between business corporations and civic associations, and democracy may hang in the balance. Although no transhistorical formula is available to determine what valences of state, capital, and civil society are necessary to make democracy work, this case study at least introduces some nuance into our understanding of these critical relationships. Social capital, one of the most elemental forms of civil society, is not a sufficient political force to challenge the concentration of power in the late twentieth century. Even simpler times required more to create effective democracy. The political resources assembled in the past by mass democratic parties and radical social movements are also essential to a democratic polity, first to create it, then to expand it, and now to keep it alive.

Elisabeth S. Clemens

Securing Political Returns to Social Capital: Women's Associations in the United States,

1880s–1920s   *Social capital* has proven exceptionally fruitful as a metaphor. By invoking financial imagery, this phrase points to the generative power of social ties, their capacity to produce social goods such as economic growth or effective governance. But metaphors are also dangerous, not least because they assert multiple dimensions of similarity, some of which may be inappropriate or positively misleading. Prominent among these potential false parallels is the presumption that social capital is marked by the same portability or fungibility that makes financial capital such a powerful motor of economic growth and transformation. In its purest form, economic capital is not tied to particular persons, places, or objects, but "presents itself as an independent substance, endowed with a motion of its own, passing through a life-process of its own, in which money and commodities are mere forms which it assumes and casts off in turn." Social capital, by comparison, is fundamentally embedded, rooted in "norms of reciprocity and networks of civic engagement." The very term "social capital" embodies a seeming paradox—a deeply embedded capacity for social action that is transposable from one setting to another, from one domain to other diverse projects.[1]

Elisabeth S. Clemens is Associate Professor of Sociology, University of Arizona. She is the author of *The People's Lobby: Organizational Innovation and the Rise of Interest Group Politics in the United States, 1890–1925* (Chicago, 1997); "Organizational Repertoires and Institutional Change: Women's Groups and the Transformation of U.S. Politics, 1890–1920," *American Journal of Sociology*, XCVII (1993), 755–798; co-editor, with Walter W. Powell, of *Private Action and the Public Good* (New Haven, 1998).

The author would like to thank the Social and Behavioral Sciences Research Institute at the University of Arizona and the Young Faculty Fellows Program of the Program on Nonprofit Governance, Center on Philanthropy, University of Indiana, Indianapolis, for financial support. She is also grateful to Patrick Ledger and Kris McIlwaine for help in collecting the biographical data.

1   Karl Marx, "The General Formula for Capital," in Robert C. Tucker (ed.), *The Marx–Engels Reader* (New York, 1978; 2d ed.), 335. James S. Coleman, *Foundations of Social Theory* (Cambridge, 1990), 300–321, is explicit about the limited fungibility of social capital. Robert D. Putnam, with Roberto Leonardi and Raffaella Y. Nanetti, *Making Democracy Work: Civic Traditions in Modern Italy* (Princeton, 1993), 167.

In its operation, social capital involves a certain alchemy, transforming personal ties, trust in specific persons, and localized capacities for collective action into such macrosocial outcomes as economic performance and political efficacy. This transmutation, however, is fraught with tension. A closer analysis of the ways that social capital is tied to individuals and organizations reveals dynamic processes and strategic opportunities rather than a steady conversion of interpersonal trust into social goods. This structure of social capital constitutes a terrain for politics and a landscape that is reconfigured through politics.

In the course of political contests, social capital is generated and destroyed, enrolled in or disengaged from collective action. Indeed, the hallmark of successful organizers is their ability to harness informal networks and noninstitutional capacities to collective action in the pursuit of social change. Consequently, an analysis of how social capital is enrolled in politics must begin by exploring its distribution at different levels of analysis and mapping those levels onto one another. Individuals with ties to one another do not always belong to the same associations; nor do these associations necessarily take compatible positions across a range of issues or invoke similar positions within public debates. Hence, the relative location of the multiple forms of social capital—personal skills, interpersonal ties and trust, formal organizations, and the cultural norms that legitimate collective action—presents distinctive obstacles to, and opportunities for, their deployment.

In United States political history, few efforts to enroll informal networks and voluntary associations in political projects match the accomplishments of the "woman movement" of the late nineteenth and early twentieth centuries. Without benefit of the vote, women both gained the vote and helped to lay the foundations of a distinctively maternalist welfare state. To invoke the language of nineteenth-century philanthropy, the consolidation and ultimate fragmentation of the woman movement presents an "object lesson" in the political uses of social capital.

LOCATING SOCIAL CAPITAL   Social capital can be located in at least three ways or, more precisely, at three levels of civic society. First, trusting relationships, or social ties, may exist between individuals; such ties may or may not be constituted within formal organizations or associations. At this level, social capital refers either to the skills and capacities of individuals for social action or to the web of ties among individuals. Two dimensions of variation should be noted: Skills acquired in one set of interactions may be more or less easily transposed to another; informal networks of trust and friendship may or may not coincide with memberships in formal organizations. The genius of nineteenth-century voluntary associations lay in both their cultivation of transposable routines for acting collectively (for example, Roberts Rules of Order) and their elaboration of national federations grounded in the sociability of communities and friendship networks.[2]

The formation of these associations created social capital at a second level, changing "the relations among persons . . . in ways that facilitate action." Formal organization transforms a network of interpersonal ties into a system of roles and routines. New members are more easily integrated and expansive campaigns more easily coordinated. In addition, the establishment of formal organizations creates a new kind of social network—ties between organizations, constituted through either formal alliances or the joint memberships of individuals. When interorganizational and interpersonal networks diverge, recruitment and rupture are possible.[3]

Finally, these interpersonal networks and formal associations were both embedded in cultural categories that structured discourse about civic life. Although the care of the infirm and the moral education of children might be the objects of either a woman's club or a local Women's Christian Temperance Union, the public identities of these organizations gave distinctive meanings to their efforts. Organizations anchor meaning; they "provide a visible interpretive frame upon which the otherwise slippery and ineffable character of institutional life can be firmed up." Particularly before survey research promised direct access to individual opinions, organizations served as critical signals of positions within public debate.[4]

2 Sidney Verba, Kay Lehman Schlozman, and Henry E. Brady, *Voice and Equality: Civic Voluntarism in American Politics* (Cambridge, 1995).
3 Coleman, *Foundations,* 304.
4 John W. Mohr and Francesca Guerra-Pearson, "The Differentiation of Institutional Space: Organizational Forms in the New York Social Welfare Sector, 1888–1917," in Walter W. Powell and D.L. Jones (eds.), *Bending the Bars of the Iron Cage: Institutional Dynamics and Processes* (Chicago, forthcoming).

Given its multiple locations, or forms—individual, organizational, and cultural—social capital may not aggregate neatly from interpersonal ties into broader networks of collective action, nor be easily transposed to one new project as to another. Tensions are generated when levels do not map cleanly onto one another. An association identified with one goal might also be committed to another one that a member might find deeply offensive. The resulting conflicts underscore a more general theoretical point: The ability to transpose social capital cultivated at the individual level to larger projects of collective action is limited by the available organizations, as well as the location of those organizations within the cultural categories of public discourse.

Exploring the intersection of individual participation, formal organization, and political culture sheds light on the dynamics of recruitment and training, on the mobilization of political coalitions, and on the sources of rupture in the web of group affiliations. Consider the following puzzle: Drawing on membership records, recent research has documented that membership in the Moose, Elks, Masons, and other fraternal organizations in the United States increased significantly during the second half of the nineteenth century and into the early decades of the twentieth. What does this surge imply about the creation and distribution of social capital? The answer depends on how individual memberships mapped onto formal organizations. Imagine a town in which both the Masons and the Knights of Pythias boasted 100 members in one decade and 200 during the next. Among the possible scenarios are that 100 previously unaffiliated individuals joined the Masons, and another 100 became Knights; *or* all of the Masons joined the Knights of Pythias, and vice versa.[5]

From the viewpoint of maximizing participation, recruitment of the unaffiliated would be the more promising development for a democratic polity. In the context of late nineteenth-century American politics, however, a third possibility was most promising: Political influence increased with both broader participation and greater ties among associations. Few cases illustrate this process

5 Gerald Gamm and Putnam, "Association Building in America, 1840–1940," paper presented at the conference, "Civic Engagement in American Politics," Portland, Maine, 1997. A later version was presented at the conference, "Patterns of Social Capital: Stability and Change in Comparative Perspective," Harvard University, December 4–6, 1997. A revised version appears herein as "The Growth of Voluntary Associations in America, 1840–1940," 511–557. Theda Skocpol, "The Tocqueville Problem: Civic Engagement in American Democracy," *Social Science History,* XXI (1997), 455–479.

more clearly than the "woman movement," an associational effort of the (largely) disenfranchised to shape political and civic life in localities, states, and nation. But the eventual decline of the woman movement also provides important lessons for understanding how networks of voluntary associations can create the conditions for faction, schism, and demobilization.

THE WOMAN MOVEMENT   "Women's clubs are the big sticks of society," proclaimed a commercial postcard of the time. This sentiment reflected the extraordinary growth of women's associations and celebrated their political accomplishments. Recent studies amply document how these mass-membership women's organizations shaped political culture and social policy prior to World War I, despite women's disenfranchisement. This conjuncture of associational activity and the absence of formal political standing provides an exceptional case for the analysis of social capital and the consequences of its effective deployment.[6]

For all this associational energy, many women still desired the right to vote. Their agitation for woman suffrage was part of a broader field of political activity in which shifting segments of the woman movement were caught up in changing alliances with the many reform and political movements that mobilized Americans across the divisions of gender. Indeed, much of the strength of the official suffrage organizations came not from the length of their own membership rolls but from their ability to form working relationships with male-dominated associations and, perhaps more important, to draw on the support of other large, often federated, women's associations. Of these, two were of particular importance—the Women's Christian Temperance Union (WCTU) and the General Federation of Women's Clubs (GFWC). In terms of membership, the National American Woman Suffrage Association

6   The copyright of the postcard is 1910. Paula Baker, "The Domestication of Politics: Women and American Political Society, 1780–1920," *American Historical Review*, LXXXIX (1984), 620–647; Clemens, "Organizational Repertoires and Institutional Change: Women's Groups and the Transformation of U.S. Politics, 1890–1920," *American Journal of Sociology*, XCVIII (1993), 755–798; idem, *The People's Lobby: Organizational Innovation and the Rise of Interest Group Politics in the United States, 1890–1925* (Chicago, 1997); Robyn Muncy, *Creating a Female Dominion in American Reform, 1890–1935* (New York, 1991); Anne Firor Scott, *Natural Allies: Women's Associations in American History* (Urbana, 1991); Kathryn Kish Sklar, *Florence Kelley and the Nation's Work: The Rise of Women's Political Culture, 1830–1900* (New Haven, 1995); Skocpol, *Protecting Soldiers and Mothers: The Political Origins of Social Policy in the United States* (Cambridge, 1992).

(NAWSA) was dwarfed by both. The WCTU had long endorsed woman suffrage, but the GFWC did not pass an endorsement until 1914. Women committed to civic engagement could choose to join any or all of these organizations, each of which made distinctive, if sometimes overlapping, demands on the polity.[7]

Although it was the smallest of the three over much of this period, NAWSA provides a valuable lens for detecting the structure of association and activism within the woman movement. This structure was not equivalent to the formal hierarchy of any single organization but was constituted by the combined trajectories of individual affiliation and activism that can be illuminated by collective biography. Rather than focusing on the leadership of particular organizations, activist women were identified through the official NAWSA history. Due to the hybrid nature of the organization—an 1890 merger of the American Woman Suffrage Association, with its state-level strategy, and the National Woman Suffrage Association, which was committed to winning an amendment to the federal constitution—its history was written in two ways. Although much of the narrative centered on national campaigns for women's rights, two volumes included state-by-state reports of suffrage activity. To a far greater extent than the standard organizational history, these sources offer a window onto broader patterns of associational activity.[8]

These state-level reports were used to construct a concordance of approximately 500 names from which those women who were mentioned as active in reports from at least four states were selected (lecturing in South Dakota counted; writing a letter to the South Dakota suffrage organization did not). Women who restricted their activity to a single state or to national politics, or who were not residents of the United States were excluded, producing a final list of ninety women. Biographical information was located for seventy-nine women and birthdates for seventy-one (the basis for all tables and percentages). Unlike many collective biographies that select on the basis of organizational prominence, thereby focusing on those individuals who con-

7 Karen J. Blair, *The Clubwoman as Feminist: True Womanhood Redefined, 1868–1914* (New York, 1980), 119.
8 Susan B. Anthony and Ida Husted Harper, *The History of Woman Suffrage, 1883–1900* (Indianapolis, 1902), IV; *idem, The History of Woman Suffrage, 1900–1920* (New York, 1922), VI.

structed careers primarily within a single voluntary association, this strategy of selection captures the interpersonal and interorganizational networks central to the analysis of social capital.[9]

When aggregated, individual careers of participation produce an overview of the changing field of associational activity that constituted the woman movement (or at least the portion of it related to woman suffrage). "Ties" among associations are captured by individual affiliations with formal organizations. Assuming that joint membership goes hand in hand with the formation of individual-level ties, it is meaningful to speak of the intersection of activist networks or individual social capital with voluntary associations, particularly for officeholding in organizations with activist cores of no more than a few hundred at a given time, and rarely even that. Ninety-five out of 241 possible delegates attended the 1894 NAWSA convention in Washington D.C.; 544 out of a possible 725 came to Atlantic City in 1916. Archival research confirms the density of ties among activists; those who did not know someone directly often knew which of their acquaintances to ask for information about her.[10]

The civic lives of these women reveal the dynamic relationship of voluntary association and political participation during the decades surrounding the turn of the century. Formal organizations, and the relationships among them, constituted a complex terrain upon which women sought to build expansive and effective coalitions. The following sections consider this interorganizational field from the perspective of the generation of social capital through recruitment and training; the consolidation of interorganizational alliances through activist careers; and the multiple sources of rupture within the woman movement. Although recognized as a pioneering exemplar of constitutional-amendment politics and of the "new lobby" of the 1920s, the woman movement failed to generate the much-anticipated, and much-feared, "woman's bloc" in the wake of the constitutional amendment

9 For collective biographies, see Linda Gordon, "Black and White Visions of Welfare: Women's Welfare Activism, 1890–1945," *Journal of American History*, LXXVIII (1991), 559–590; Catherine Harris and Inzer Byers, "Social Backgrounds and Ideologies of Women Active in Woman Suffrage and Social Reform, 1870–1930," *Quarterly Journal of Ideology*, XII (1988), 61–84; Carole Nichols, *Votes and More for Women: Suffrage and After in Connecticut* (New York, 1983); Susan Ware, *Beyond Suffrage: Women in the New Deal* (Cambridge, 1981).
10 NAWSA, *Proceedings* (1894), 89–91; (1916), 112–113. By 1916, delegates were no longer listed by name in the "Report of the Committee on Credentials."

guaranteeing the right to vote regardless of sex. Carefully knit together during the decades of struggle for suffrage, the web of affiliation linking women's associations proved fragile when confronted with world events and competing organizational identities.[11]

TRAINING AND RECRUITMENT: THE CREATION OF NEW SOCIAL CAPITAL   The significance of these women's associations did not lie in their size alone, but in their routine practices and relationships among organizations. During the late nineteenth century, the widespread development of a distinctive women's organizational culture, exemplified by the women's club movement, facilitated multiple affiliations of organizations and causes. Adopting an organizational model from the male fraternal societies, the early clubwomen created social spaces that were intended to transform the system of separate spheres, at least insofar as women expanded their awareness beyond the boundaries of domestic life. In the most intimate associations, the parlor and literary clubs, women would prepare book reports and make oral presentations to a circle of friends. Such gatherings laid the foundations for a gradual transformation in women's politics by developing and diffusing organizational skills. At club meetings, women spoke in public and voiced their own opinions. As one California clubwoman concluded, "club life and club work has been the necessary school for citizenship."[12]

Lessons learned in one setting could be put into action elsewhere. Women's organizations provided recruiting grounds for one another. This recruitment might be explicit, as when prominent suffragists were invited to speak to women's congresses, parliaments, and clubs. As activists from Oregon concluded, "The woman's club is the cradle in which to develop suffragists"; however, "[w]e must not let the women's clubs be satisfied with doll politics, but make them feel that we need the real thing." But suffragists also recognized the strategic advantages of slowly coaxing women to the suffrage cause by involving them first in less

11 Clemens, *People's Lobby*, 294–308; Nancy F. Cott, *The Grounding of Modern Feminism* (New Haven, 1987), 85–114.
12 Mary I. Wood, *The History of the General Federation of Women's Clubs: For the First Twenty-two Years of Its Organization* (New York, 1912), 99–103; Mary S. Gibson, *A Record of Twenty-Five Years of the California Federation of Women's Clubs* (1927), 67.

radical efforts, as members of nonpolitical organizations. In the words of Catharine Waugh McCulloch, a prominent Illinois lawyer and judge,

> I think every State should make mothers joint guardians and you will doubtless find less objection to this than suffrage. You can unify your women on a mild measure like this and get them trained to work with suffragists. The federated clubs and women's church organizations and fraternal societies will pass resolutions for this.
>
> If you fail to pass your bill and your associated women are indignant + complain that they really need the ballot to accomplish anything important for women, well you have taught the women by a splendid object lesson. If you succeed, you have one law to your credit which will encourage you to press on.[13]

Organizational skills were generalized through parliamentary drills, lecture courses, formal suffrage schools, and legislative institutes, rather than being acquired solely as individuals passed through a pre-ordained sequence of organizational offices. Emphasis was placed on the rotation of participation, from the selection of a new person to chair each meeting of a local club to the limited, two-year term for presidents of the GFWC. Formal officers were encouraged to develop the parliamentary skills needed to run an orderly and inclusive meeting. Women without formal office served as skilled field organizers and activists.

Just as skills were not tightly tied to formal offices, leadership also depended on an individual's position within a wide and complex network of personal ties. Individual women might be invited to assume a leadership position in a new locale, based on their personal ties within the national movement. Such ties extended beyond the local networks usually stressed in community studies of the suffrage movement. Emma Smith DeVoe, for example, was active in suffrage campaigns (either as an organizer or as a speaker) in Washington, Wisconsin, South Dakota, and Illinois. But for all her far-flung and highly praised role in the fight for suffrage, DeVoe's only staff position with NAWSA was as one of a number of "National Lecturers." Despite serving on powerful

13 G. Thomas Edwards, *Sowing Good Seeds: The Northwest Suffrage Campaigns of Susan B. Anthony* (Portland, 1990), 159, 190, 232; Gibson, *Record,* 5; McCulloch to Alice Locke Park, November 5, 1908, Box 1, PK 227, Alice Locke Park Correspondence (henceforth ALPC), Huntington Library, San Marino, Calif.

committees, including legislation, petition, and work, she was not part of the central organizational hierarchy. DeVoe's career suggests that NAWSA—and perhaps other women's organizations— relied on at least some women for whom high levels of sustained activism did not lead to formal leadership positions but nonetheless established ties across state-level associations.[14]

Organizational skills were a critical resource for the movement which activists sought to conserve even when patterns of affiliation were disrupted. Writing to a San Francisco suffragist in 1902, Carrie Chapman Catt praised Alice Park:

> The woman in Montana that I always considered the very best worker there, and most intelligent, although I never saw her, moved from that state to California some years ago. She lived up in a mining town. She has just moved to San Francisco. . . .
>
> I have written her to ask her to join the club in San Francisco. I wish you would see that she has a special invitation to attend the very next meeting there is, and ask her to come and introduce herself to you. As I have said, I do not know her personally, but I have corresponded with her for a number of years and I think she is a splendid woman. I believe you could make good use of her when she is made familiar with the work.

Within three years, Park was acting secretary of the California Equal Suffrage Association.[15]

This nonhierarchical, lateral mobility was a critical source of "connectedness" within the woman movement. Interorganizational ties constituted by joint memberships were encouraged by the widespread cultivation of organizational skills, the recruitment strategies of NAWSA, and the general disinclination to maintain clear organizational hierarchies. All of these conditions facilitated the development of social capital—understood here as either organizing skills or interpersonal ties—by individual women, as well as the movement of individual organizers across locales and campaigns. These individual careers combined to produce a formidable network of associations.

14 Naomi Rosenthal et al., "Social Movements and Network Analysis: A Case Study of Nineteenth-Century Women's Reform in New York State," *American Journal of Sociology*, XC (1985), 1022–1054.
15 Catt to [Clara M.] Schlingheyde, November 22, 1902, PK 158, ALPC; "Minutes of the Executive Board," August 5, 28, 1905, PK 155, ALPC.

ACTIVIST CAREERS AND THE WEB OF GROUP AFFILIATION   One key to understanding how social capital is transposed from one local project to others lies in the concept of "bridging social capital," or the distinction between "strong" and "weak" social ties. Both bridging social capital and weak ties link relatively dense local networks, constituting a critical medium for the flow of new information and the coordination of large-scale collective action. Within the woman movement, the accumulation of bridging social capital is evident in patterns of multiple membership and joint officeholding.[16]

Although the women in Table 1 were selected for their suffrage activity, almost 37 percent held office in the WCTU at some point in their activist careers; some members of earlier cohorts were also associated with antebellum temperance societies not included in this tabulation. A number of women—Clara Hoffman, Frances Willard, and Judith Ellen Foster—held no formal office in NAWSA, establishing their prominence as suffragists using the WCTU as their primary vehicle. The relationship between suffrage and temperance organizations was not a constant. A comparison of birth cohorts reveals few links based on joint officeholding between NAWSA and the WCTU in later generations, and none at all in the cohort of the 1880s. For cohorts born in the 1860s and 1870s, connections to the GFWC were much

Table 1   Associational Officeholding by Birth Cohort

	NAWSA[a]	WCTU	GFWC
TOTAL (*N* = 71)	84.5%	36.6%	32.4%
b. 1810s (*n* = 4)	75.0%	25.0%	25.0%
b. 1820s (*n* = 2)	50.0%	50.0%	0.0%
b. 1830s (*n* = 8)	62.5%	37.5%	50.0%
b. 1840s (*n* = 12)	91.6%	83.3%	16.6%
b. 1850s (*n* = 15)	100%	40.0%	20.0%
b. 1860s (*n* = 14)	85.7%	21.4%	71.4%
b. 1870s (*n* = 9)	77.8%	11.1%	33.3%
b. 1880–90 (*n* = 7)	85.7%	0.0%	0.0%

[a] Does not include officeholding in the National Woman Suffrage Association or the American Woman Suffrage Association.

16 Mark Granovetter, "The Strength of Weak Ties," *American Journal of Sociology*, LXXVIII (1973), 1360–1380.

stronger. But, again, none of the 1880s cohort of suffragists held office even in the more secular of the two pillars of the woman movement.[17]

These pulses in affiliation represent something analogous to a "founding effect," in which "organizations formed at one time typically have a different social structure from those formed at another time." Networks also bear the imprint of history. For the earliest generation of suffragists, the struggle for women's rights was interwoven with abolitionism; for the cohorts in their twenties and thirties during the 1870s—the era of the "Woman's Crusade" against saloons—the WCTU was an important focus for organized activity. Twenty years later, women of the same age were drawn to membership in the GFWC, established in 1890.[18]

Both these spikes in affiliation underscore the significance of the broader organizational context for the development of movement organizations and interorganizational networks. Within NAWSA, the shift in orientation from moral reform to domestic politics produced tensions within the leadership, particularly between Elizabeth Cady Stanton and Susan B. Anthony. Twenty years later, the club-oriented organizers recruited by Anthony were themselves rejected by younger activists who had strong ties to the British suffragettes, an orientation to direct action, and very little connection to the central organizations of the American woman movement. The capacity of any given association to recruit new members depended, in part, on the changing configuration of informal social networks, the range of organizational vehicles, and the relationship of these associational alternatives to the categories of political discourse.

The decline of multiple officeholding in the NAWSA, GFWC, and WCTU among the youngest birth cohorts contrasts with the

---

17 Although it has often been claimed that the WCTU was a critical training ground for suffrage activists, some scholars have argued that this reputation was based primarily on the programmatic commitment to suffrage championed by WCTU leader Frances Willard but that it was not reflected in actual ties between the WCTU and suffrage organizations. The organizational affiliations of the seventy-one suffrage activists in this study, however, tell a more complex story. Apparently, women were more apt to move from the WCTU to suffrage organizations than vice versa, and the links between the WCTU and suffrage were stronger in the Midwest and South than in the Northeast. For contrasting interpretations, see Ruth Bordin, *Woman and Temperance: The Quest for Power and Liberty, 1873–1900* (Philadelphia, 1981), 118–123; Rosenthal et al., "Social Movements," 1046.

18 Arthur L. Stinchcombe, "Social Structure and Organizations," in James G. March (ed.), *Handbook of Organizations* (Chicago, 1965), 154.

high level of interorganizational connectedness that characterized the nineteenth-century woman movement. This decline was not simply the result of the deaths of a few key leaders who served as boundary-spanners. Breaking down the sample by position within NAWSA (national hierarchy, state organizer, no office) reveals no consistent pattern, apart from the unsurprising one that those without any position in NAWSA were more likely to hold office in one of the other major women's associations. Read against debates among women activists, the declining interconnectedness of the woman movement reflects the decay of the normative frameworks of municipal housekeeping and maternalist social politics advocated by large, relatively cross-class federations such as the GFWC and the WCTU. To the extent that younger women continued to be active in associations after the suffrage victory, they were more likely to belong to civic and peace organizations. This development foreshadowed the retreat of elite women from their role as bridging social ties within a broader field of women's associations.[19]

In the decades surrounding the turn of the century, however, significant levels of interorganizational connectedness were not restricted to associations dedicated to women's issues. Shifting from the more stringent requirement of joint officeholding to joint membership, Table 2 illustrates the embeddedness of the woman movement within a wider associational field. These estimates of associational involvement are necessarily conservative because of the limited availability of obituaries and entries in biographical dictionaries; the threshold of activity required for mention in such sources; and the exclusion of two common associational activities, simple party affiliation and church membership. These limitations notwithstanding, the overall level of activity is impressive. Of the total possible combinations of individuals and types of association ($71 \times 12 = 852$), 37 percent are documented in these sources. Clearly, the suffrage movement was firmly embedded in a broader field of associational activity.

19 Women were coded as members of the NAWSA hierarchy if they ever held national office, including the position of field secretary but excluding membership on national committees. NAWSA organizers include all other women holding office or committee positions in the national organization or state affiliates. Skocpol, "Unravelling From Above," *The American Prospect*, XXV (1996), 20–25.

Table 2 Affiliations with Types of Association, by Birth Cohort

	WOMAN SUFFRAGE	CIVIC	CLUBS	TEMPERANCE	PEACE	SOCIAL WELFARE	PARTY	LABOR	PROFESSIONAL	RELIGIOUS	PHILANTHROPICAL	FRATERNAL	AVERAGE
1810s (n = 4)	100%	25%	25%	50%	25%	25%	—	—	—	—	—	—	2.5
1820s (n = 2)	100%	100%	—	100%	—	50%	—	100%	—	50%	50%	—	5.5
1830s (n = 8)	87%	37%	62%	50%	62%	37%	12%	12%	37%	25%	—	—	4.3
1840s (n = 12)	92%	25%	25%	83%	33%	17%	33%	25%	25%	42%	8%	—	4.1
1850s (n = 15)	100%	53%	73%	47%	47%	33%	40%	47%	20%	13%	27%	13%	5.1
1860s (n = 14)	93%	71%	79%	21%	29%	50%	50%	21%	50%	14%	14%	—	4.9
1870s (n = 9)	89%	100%	44%	11%	44%	67%	44%	67%	22%	22%	33%	—	5.4
1880s (n = 7)	100%	43%	14%	—	57%	14%	29%	—	29%	—	—	—	2.9
Total (n = 71)	94%	55%	51%	41%	41%	37%	34%	31%	28%	16%	16%	3%	

To view Table 2 as a cross-section, or snapshot, of the web of association, however, would overestimate the density of interorganizational ties. These patterns of membership were constructed over lifetimes—often impressively long—in which women formed and broke ties to particular associations. A sense of this dynamic can be captured by comparison across birth cohorts. Temperance activity declined markedly for suffragists born after the 1850s, as did club ties for those born after the 1860s. Peace activities, particularly those evoked by World War I, mobilized suffragists of all ages. Civic activities, understood as efforts to promote a better and more just society, were a consistent complement to suffrage work, although the specific organizations changed over the decades, from the Society for Prevention of Cruelty to Animals to the American Civil Liberties Union and the National Association for the Advancement of Colored People. Rarely, however, were suffrage efforts connected with fraternal groups and philanthropic activities (for example, serving as trustee of a college or arts organization). Nevertheless, the basic conclusion is that beyond the connections generated among women's associations, suffragists were also affiliated with associations active in other civic causes, creating an interorganizational web that facilitated the movement of skilled organizers and resources from one cause to another and provided personal foundations for associational alliances. Out of this matrix of individual skills, interpersonal ties, and interorganizational coalitions, activists sought to secure political returns to social capital.

The growing literature on women's political culture during the nineteenth and early twentieth centuries provides ample documentation of the extent to which activists were able to generate political leverage from informal social networks and voluntary associations (see note 6). Whether in pursuit of social legislation, or in promotion of the arts and public institutions, women's associations made major contributions to the infrastructure of state intervention and civic life. Yet, to stop with a celebration of the accomplishments of these women's organizations would leave a distorted picture of the relationship between social capital and political mobilization. By enrolling informal networks into associations and associations into coalitions, organizers also incorporated sources of potential schism within the web of group affiliations.

RUPTURE: THE FRAGMENTATION OF SOCIAL CAPITAL   With respect to any single goal, the multiplicity of organizations in the woman movement offered strategic opportunities, allowing activists to choose among collective identities as they mobilized coalitions. Under these conditions, however, any event that highlighted the latent conflicts between affiliations and identities threatened the viability of these wide-ranging alliances. As the coalition in support of woman suffrage grew, the number of potential sources of schism also increased.

Associations served not only as recruiting grounds for one another, and as anchors in the web of affiliations woven by the careers of activists, but also as public signals of distinctive positions within political debates. These signals were not univocal, although suffrage organizations struggled to maintain a single-issue campaign. As the College Equal Suffrage League of Northern California warned, "[L]et equal suffrage and equal suffrage alone be the issue of your organization. If your association allows itself to become identified with Socialism, Women's Christian Temperance work, reforms for working women, or any other measure, it will be at the expense of alienating the interest of some of the friends of your own cause." Although a single issue such as suffrage could be advocated by multiple associations, suffrage pursued by a temperance organization meant something different than suffrage pursued by clubwomen who had a public presence concerning issues of social welfare and "cities beautiful." California temperance advocates were amused, for example, when "[l]etters were received by women prominent in the cause of Suffrage, warning them to keep clear of 'White Ribboners,' and not to be compromised by the Temperance element, but the ladies to whom these appeals were sent were found to be nearly all official members of the W.C.T.U." Insofar as individual activists were members of multiple organizations, they could pursue the cause of suffrage—or be recruited to it—wearing a number of different hats.[20]

Because organizations were linked to multiple causes, and causes could be promoted by multiple associations, the opposition to any group might seek to undermine its activities by linking it to more controversial groups. The uproar about "free love" in the

20   College Equal Suffrage League of Northern California, *Winning Equal Suffrage in California* (1913), 13; Mrs. Dorcas James Spencer, *A History of the Women's Christian Temperance Union of Northern and Central California* (Oakland, n.d.), 66–67.

nineteenth century and the Red Scare of the 1920s both document the vulnerability of the woman movement to such tactics. But given the character of the interassociational field, rifts might easily open even in the absence of any intentional effort to disrupt the network. Partisan politics, class conflict, and a war-induced choice between pacifism and preparedness all strained—and sometimes broke—the interpersonal ties that had knit together an impressive alliance of voluntary associations.

Party Politics   The partisan fragmentation of the woman movement was the unintended consequence of intentional action. As the connection of suffrage activists to major women's organizations weakened by the first decades of the twentieth century, their ties to party politics increased. Along with many other reformers of the late nineteenth century, suffrage activists joined in the condemnation of party politics. Yet, the criticism of then-current partisan practices did not necessarily imply a complete aversion to partisanship. A surprising number, including even the earlier cohorts, expressed partisan identification at some point—42 percent of those born prior to 1850, compared with 56 percent of those born between 1850 and 1890.[21]

The organizational commitment to nonpartisanship espoused by many women's associations should be understood not as a direct reflection of individual preferences but as a strategy to suppress divisions within the suffrage associations. Suffrage organizations worked to increase the distance between official organizational non-partisanship and the personal commitment of activists; formal organization was an important signal to other political actors. Accusations of undue partisanship were not infrequent and, in some cases, led to a permanent break with the suffrage movement. For example, Laura Johns, an experienced organizer from Kansas and president of the state's Women's Republican Club, gave up her affiliation with NAWSA in the wake of accusations that she had spent suffrage funds to support the Republican cause. For this sin, she has been largely expunged from the historiography of the woman-suffrage movement.[22]

But even short of erasure from organizational memory, individual activists risked sabotaging the suffrage effort through the

21   Clemens, *People's Lobby,* 17–40, 206–224.
22   Wilda M. Smith, "A Half Century of Struggle: Gaining Woman Suffrage in Kansas," *Kansas History,* IV (1981), 88.

expression of partisan sympathies. Organizers were well aware of this possibility, and consciously suppressed political loyalties for the suffrage cause. Laura Gregg (Cannon) was explicit about the strategic rationale for this decision yet felt it at odds with her strong sense of partisan (and class) loyalty:

> You ask if I am a Socialist, and if I would be willing to keep my personal opinion in abeyance, etc. Of course I recognize that the Suffrage movement must try to win the votes of all classes, and that Socialism is a bugbear to Democrats and Republicans, and I therefore think it better that work among what we call the middle class people should be done by women of less radical opinions, as they honestly see the suffrage movement from the middle class viewpoint, while if a Socialist is speaking to the same people, she must continually curb herself, or else speak more radically than the middle class people will stand.[23]

But for all her discomfort with the middle-class nonpartisan-ship of the suffrage movement, Gregg was one of the most active (albeit largely forgotten) organizers in the movement, working in fifteen states over a period of twenty-nine years. Neither the official nonpartisan stance of suffrage organizations nor the aver-sion of some activists to parties should be taken as indicative of an absence of partisan loyalties among suffragists. Indeed, these loyalties help to explain both the fragmentation and incorporation of women activists after their enfranchisement.

These patterns of partisanship are surprising in two respects. First, the absolute level of partisanship is higher than expected, given the association of the woman suffrage movement with either nonpartisanship or the "party in power" strategy imported from British parliamentary politics by the Congressional Union. After all, prominent figures in the suffrage movement often expressed their lack of attachment to the party system. Throughout the woman movement of the late nineteenth century, the condem-nation of partisanship had been a constant theme. A "pox on both your houses" was the official attitude of woman-suffrage organi-zations: "The Republicans, in the person of Mr. Hitchcock, formally offered us money yesterday, but we refused it because it

---

23 Cannon to Anne Martin, February 19, 1914, Box II, Anne Martin Papers (henceforth AMP), Bancroft Library, University of California, Berkeley.

came from the committee. The truth is that they are unwilling to give us money unless we will give up our independence and become an annex of the G.O.P. When I am with the G.O.P.'s I'd rather die than be one. But I feel the same way when I am with Democrats, so I think I'll go into a convent."[24]

Of the thirty-eight women found to have expressed some degree of partisanship, nine identified themselves as Republicans, fifteen as Democrats, and fourteen as members of third parties, including the People's Party, Prohibition, and various socialist parties. This Republican minority is surprising, given that party's support for both abolition and prohibition, but there are two reasons for the unexpected Democratic affinities of suffrage activists: One was the widespread support for Woodrow Wilson's effort to keep the United States out of World War I and, after the war, to constitute the League of Nations as a means for avoiding future conflicts. This connection between feminism and pacifism was of long standing. The second reason, however, stems from a tendency to misread the partisan affiliations of elite eastern suffragists (who did tend toward the Republican party) for the national situation. Brought out from New York City to campaign in small towns throughout Nevada in 1914, Gregg was surprised by the partisan basis of support for woman suffrage. Writing to Anne Martin, the leading suffragist in the state, she explained,

> Well, I could not get a single thing clinched until a leading Democrat who wanted to give Squires a drubbing persuaded a couple of women to try to get a hearing for me in the church, and the fact that the minister's wife heard me speak in the conference in Reno, helped to land that opportunity.
>
> And as soon as that was secured, Democrats, Bull Moosers and Socialists all began boosting for the meeting, all unbeknown to me, and Sunday morning I nearly collapsed with amazement when I was told over the phone that a leading Democratic woman said she would serve on the committee. I knew the Rubicon was crossed there. . . .

24 In an oral history, Mabel Vernon, an organizer for the National Woman's Party, acknowledged, "I didn't vote very many times. The time that I distinctly remember voting was for Adlai Stevenson. I went to Delaware to vote for Adlai." This reluctance to vote partly reflected her residence in Washington D.C., but her remarks also suggest a deeper distaste for partisanship ("Speaker for Suffrage and Petitioner for Peace," Bancroft Library, University of California, Berkeley, 1976, 78). Abby Scott Baker to Martin, September 21, 1916, Box I, AMP.

Of course I do not know the politics of all who signed, but in going over the list this morning I do not find the name of a single Republican with whom I had talked, while I do recognize Democrats, Socialists and Progressives, and there is no doubt but that the men of these parties got behind the women and pushed them.[25]

This organizer's surprise foreshadowed the fragmentation of the woman movement. Building a national suffrage coalition across a highly regionalized party system, the suffragists built potentially destructive partisan differences into the network of associational alliances. Antoinette Funk, a prominent congressional lobbyist for NAWSA and one of the first women lawyers in Illinois, feared "the avowed policy of the [Congressional Union] to strike at the Democratic Party as a whole, . . . and to make war on Democratic members regardless of their friendliness or unfriendliness or their willingness to vote for or against suffrage legislation." These differences became clearer when some women chose to become active in party organizations after they either gained, or anticipated gaining, the right to vote within their own states.[26]

Reflecting on the two party conventions of 1920, Mrs. George Bass, chair of the Women's Bureau of the Democratic National Committee, praised both the greater number of her party's women delegates and their active role in the convention. Emphasizing the importance of practical political experience rather than words of support, Mrs. Bass concluded "Which party has given a greater honor to women by giving them the greater opportunity for party responsibility and party service?" At the same convention, Susan FitzGerald of Massachusetts became the first woman to nominate a candidate at a national Democratic convention, approaching the podium to the strains of "Oh, You Beautiful Doll."[27]

Although western women voters made the most dramatic electoral contribution to Wilson's 1916 victory, even in the eastern states, women offered strategic advantages to the Democratic party

---

25 Cannon to Martin, 1914?, Box II, AMP.
26 "Mrs. Funk, Suffragist, for Wilson," *New York Times,* 7 Sept. 1916, 6; "Suffragists Lose in Rules Committee," *New York Times,* 18 Jan. 1914, sec. II, 2.
27 William H. Crawford, "Mrs. Bass Presents Democracy's Claims," *New York Times,* 21 Sept. 1920, 10; *New York Times,* 1 July 1920, 1.

insofar as women's organizations cross-cut patterns of partisan dominance and institutional strength. Following their enfranchisement in 1917, women in the state of New York were in the vanguard of the Democratic party in regions where no (male) Democrat had dared to go. The party, with its resources and institutional standing, was available to be commandeered by newly enfranchised women as an organizational vehicle. Ironically, in gaining the vote, women lost the insulation from partisanship that had facilitated the construction of an encompassing national alliance for woman suffrage.[28]

Class Conflict   If the tension generated by political partisanship increased with suffrage victories in the various states, the strains resulting from the effort to construct a movement of women—crossing boundaries of class and, less frequently, of race—were a persistent source of rupture within the woman movement. The secondary literature offers plentiful examples of conflicts between privileged and working women in such organizations as the Women's Trade Union League. Unlike associations explicitly dedicated to cross-class alliances, the woman-suffrage movement has often been portrayed as overwhelmingly middle and upper-middle class. Although this study confirms the general point, there were some suffragists with roots in the working class, but they have been all but invisible in the historical record.

As with partisanship, Gregg provides particularly keen insights into the tensions incorporated within the associational field. She made a living at organizing, but her career was not structured along either bureaucratic or professional lines. She had strong ties to the Western Federation of Miners, counted labor activist Mother Jones as "a very dear personal friend," and repeatedly crossed class lines in her efforts for woman suffrage. Her allegiances, however, were with labor rather than the middle class. Writing Martin in Nevada about her work in Pennsylvania, she complained,

> it bores me to pieces to keep up the clothes to go among that class of people. With my mind concentrated on the campaign I don't like to give any more thought to clothes than to keep my waist and skirt from getting divorced, and a sufficient number (but not all) of the hooks and eyes in place.

28   "Hearst Fight Spurs Woman Democrats," *New York Times,* 10 July 1922, 15.

But to stop in the middle of strenuous work to dress for teas and luncheons takes more out of me than half a dozen speeches, and I am sure that I can accomplish very much more if I can cut that kind of work out altogether.[29]

The social capital generated in these women's clubs was embedded in a distinctive class culture potentially hostile to the maintenance of certain "bridging" ties. Despite her discomfort with the conventions of "club life," however, Gregg followed the standard suffrage circuit through the middle- and upper-middle-class organizations central to the woman movement of the time. The last trace of her is as a speaker at a New York City peace rally in 1917. A worker in the Washington headquarters of the National Woman's Party noted,

You may be interested to know that Mrs. Kerlin recently received a letter from Mrs. [Laura Gregg] Cannon expressing regret for her conduct in N.J. in 1915 and the trouble she made. Mrs. K. thinks she must want to come back into the state for some reason, and is trying to overcome the feeling against her which resulted from her doings. I believe she did Miss Martin incalculable harm, tho I never have been able to find out what she said about her. *It seems that the fact that such a woman was sent by Miss Martin, in itself, prejudiced the women against Miss M.*[30]

As to what happened in New Jersey, only further research will tell.

On a theoretical level, Gregg's career offers important insights. First, even in organizations with formal bureaucratic structures, sustained high-level activism may not correlate with prominence in the organizational hierarchy. Although Gregg was regularly employed by NAWSA, her links to labor and the left made it unlikely that she would officially represent it. Second, the presence of individuals whose careers link together diverse associations has important consequences for the strength and strategy of a movement, allowing varying orientations to multiple constituencies and audiences. Although Gregg, as an individual, strug-

29   Cannon to Martin, June 3, 1914, February 18, 1915, Box II, AMP.
30   "Pacifists Condemn and Praise Wilson," *New York Times,* 11 Feb. 1917, sec. I, 6; Katharine Fisher to Vernon, November 8, 1918, Box 1, Mabel Vernon Correspondence, Bancroft Library, University of California, Berkeley (emphasis added).

gled to reconcile her radical politics with the middle-class sensibilities of NAWSA, her ties to other groups broadened the constituency of the organized suffrage movement. Third, bridging social ties can break. Where political networks link distinctive class cultures or groups committed to multiple causes, the resulting coalitions will be fragile.[31]

War   In addition to the durable differences of party and class, women's associations were confronted by the unanticipated fallout of historical events. Divisions over the equal-rights amendment in the 1920s have been used to explain the fragmentation of the core group of suffrage activists, but the woman movement was also savaged by ideological divisions generated by World War I. Days after the beginning of the conflict in Europe, women in New York City began planning a "peace parade," modelled on the suffrage parades that were a standard component of their repertoire. Many suffragists were on the planning committee, including five members of this sample: Harriot Stanton Blatch, Mary Garrett Hay, Harriet Laidlaw, Catt, and Charlotte Perkins Gilman. Yet, pacifism was not a seamless extension of suffrage activism. The war exacerbated the intersection of multiple networks, ultimately straining interorganizational ties and feeding internal faction.

Women's pacifism was not simply a response to the outbreak of war, but the joint product of the war and prior ties to pacifist groups, including various socialist organizations. Of the earlier cohorts, Julia Ward Howe belonged to the Women's Peace Congress of the 1870s; Belva Lockwood and Frances Willard to the Universal Peace Union; and Ada Bowles, May Sewall, and Alice Blackwell to the American Peace Society. These women and others in the sample also attended international peace conferences in the decades before World War I. Still others—Anna Shaw and Mabel Vernon among them—had strong ties to Quaker colleges.

With the outbreak of World War I, the mobilization of women for peace turned, in part, on the prior existence of "peace-minded feminists." These women, however, belonged to organizations typically led by men who were uncomfortable allying with the suffrage network. In addition, the female member-

---

31   In 1904, Gregg was defeated by five votes for election as second auditor (NAWSA, *Proceedings* [1904], 53). Such contested elections were relatively rare.

ship of the old-line peace societies was not uniformly in favor of woman suffrage. Thus, whereas joint membership in peace societies and suffrage organizations had been relatively unproblematic prior to the war, the increased salience of those ties created a debate about the proper form of women's organization in support of peace. As the war continued, the "pacifist movement" was increasingly divided into peace and "women's peace" movements.[32]

A parallel rift in suffrage networks developed when some—but far from all—women were drawn to the peace movement as the war began. When suffrage activists espoused a commitment to pacifism and non-intervention, they strained their relationship with the more moderate women's groups, including the clubs, the membership of which was also more conservative and likely to support preparedness, and later defense, activities. The once gradual continuum of organizations in the woman movement—so crucial to the recruitment strategies of suffragists—was disrupted. Suffragists who made a primary commitment to peace advocated a strategic (albeit temporary) abandonment of suffrage; activists whose primary commitment was to suffrage were reluctant to embrace public pacifism for fear of alienating a large part of their constituency. Some of the leaders of the NAWSA, notably Anna Howard Shaw, decided to embrace defense work. Other NAWSA board members, however, "continued their suffrage activities along with their war work and directed all suffragists to do the same. They had not forgotten that their predecessors had abandoned suffrage work during the Civil War and had remained disenfranchised." Although the onset of the war was a "political opportunity" for some of the leadership, the opportunity could be exploited only at the cost of activating latent divisions in the activist network.[33]

The war changed the meaning of the intersection between the suffrage and pacifist networks. The shift toward pacifism and away from the NAWSA's single-minded focus on women's rights exposed women activists to new institutional constraints and sanctions. Although Jane Addams would go on to win the Nobel Peace Prize, "Saint Jane" never regained her mainstream reputa-

---

32 Barbara J. Steinson, *American Women's Activism in World War I* (New York, 1982), 26.
33 *Ibid.*, 310.

tion of the prewar era. The revolutions in Europe and the widespread strike activity in the United States after the war precipitated a full-fledged Red Scare. Among women's organizations, the conservative charge was led by the Daughters of the American Revolution, once part of the broad women's reform coalition. From the National Consumer's League to the International Sunshine Society, women's groups were accused of Bolshevism. The political accomplishments of women's associations, along with the politicization of such traditionally feminine concerns as pacifism and social welfare, stripped the woman movement of much of its protective cultural cover.

POLITICS AND THE TRANSFORMATION OF SOCIAL CAPITAL   Mobilized from the mid-nineteenth century through World War I, the woman movement exemplifies the capacity of individuals to construct vehicles for civic engagement, even when their rights as political citizens are explicitly denied. The web of affiliations woven by these activists during the course of their careers, however, existed both as a network of interpersonal ties and as a field of formal organizations linked to one another by *both* the joint membership of individuals and their positions relative to the categories that structured political and social discourse. This double existence of the woman movement—its presences as both a network of individuals and of organizations—offered opportunities as well as dangers for the construction of a broad alliance in favor of woman suffrage. The existence of multiple organizations committed to a particular cause created a strategic space in which activists could choose "which kind of woman" would be perceived as supporting a particular cause. But almost every individual activist confronted competing loyalties; the commitments of one organization might strain activists' ties to another, disrupting the broader network of affiliation.

The tensions between individual networks and the associational field suggest more general questions for the study of the formation, deployment, and fragmentation of social capital. In particular, the case of the woman movement underscores the importance of moving beyond quantitative questions—How many people participate? How often?—in order to map the distribution of social capital across multiple formal organizations and domains of civic activity. Such a cartographical exercise can reveal the social distribution of opportunities for forming encompassing civic alliances as well as locate potential sources of disruption and schism in the web woven by affiliation and participation.

Read in terms of the consolidation and fragmentation of social capital, the nineteenth-century woman movement raises questions about the historical trajectory of the capacity for collective action. Putnam's study of Italy suggests that regional differences in social capital endure for centuries, and the debate about social capital in the United States has been organized around an image of gradual decline during the second half of the twentieth century. Associational life in the nineteenth-century United States, by contrast, suggests a more rapid sequence of network construction and destruction on a scale of decades rather than centuries. In addition to the analysis of durable political institutions and cultures, analyses of social capital must attend to the more rapid tempo of political organization, strategy, and conflict. When individual networks, formal organizations, and cultural categories coincide, social arrangements are durable and present few opportunities for activists to harness social capital to struggles for social change. But where networks, organizations, and categories crosscut one another, social capital generates transformation more easily.

Second-Generation Civic America: Education, Citizenship, and the Children of Immigrants   The

onset of recurrent mass immigration forced the United States to deal with a new problem—"the preservation of the ability of people of dissimilar origins to act together under dissimilar conditions." Public institutions and ethnic groups faced the challenge of creating forms of social capital that would facilitate the crossing of boundaries for social and civic participation. Putnam has described the complex of networking, norms, and mutual social trust bringing together different groups in pursuit of common social and civic objectives as "bridging" social capital.[1]

Both the public schools and settlement houses of the Progressive era directed creative forces for organizing social and civic networks to overcome group divisions. These institutions were, in part, a reaction to the putative weakness of "bridging" social capital in immigrant communities in an attempt to advance public spiritedness and commitment to the public interest. Progressive-era educators and settlement workers, responding to the perception that the nation had become a society of myriad sub-communities isolated and alienated from each other, identified a "second-generation problem": Deprived of both upbringing in their ancestral homeland and assimilation into their host society, the children of immigrants existed in a transnational vacuum. To fill this civic void, schools and settlement houses exposed members of this second generation to an ideology of

Reed Ueda is Professor of History, Tufts University. He is the author of *Postwar Immigrant America: A Social History* (New York, 1994); *Avenues to Adulthood: Origins of the High School and Social Mobility in an American Suburb* (Cambridge, 1987); *West End House, 1906–1981* (Boston, 1981).

1   Oscar and Mary Handlin, *The Dimensions of Liberty* (Cambridge, Mass., 1961), 4. Putnam's analytical conception of bridging social capital concerns how "dilemmas of collective action" are overcome by "facilitating coordinated action" and "civic engagement" with communal life. The fact that bridging social capital in immigrant communities derived from premigration communal structures suggests that immigrants had a pre-existing facility for coordinating group activity. As Putnam notes, "Voluntary cooperation is easier in a community that has inherited a substantial stock of social capital." See Robert D. Putnam, with Roberto Leonardi and Raffaella Y. Nanetto, *Making Democracy Work: Civic Traditions in Modern Italy* (Princeton, 1993), 167, 168–171; *idem*, "The Strange Disappearance of Civic America," *The American Prospect*, XXIV (1996), 34–48.

Americanization and a program of citizenship training. These structures of civic acculturation had the potential to be converted into instruments for increasing their inclusion in politics and other spheres of public life.[2]

Two institutions—McKinley High School in Honolulu and the West End House in Boston—illustrated the creation of "bridging" social capital at the intersection of Progressive-era education and immigration. These institutions had core memberships—Japanese at McKinley and Russian Jews at the West End House—that derived from highly solidaristic immigrant communities with dense networks of cooperative and coordinated roles anchored in families and communal subgroups. Such factors of social capital intrinsic to organized ethnic life have been frequently associated with the pooling of resources and the mutual assistance necessary for popular investment in educational opportunity.

In the early twentieth century, the rate of investment in advanced schooling rose in many areas where a substantial degree of ethnic and religious homogeneity and communal stability existed. Japanese and Jewish immigrants tended to sponsor prolonged schooling and to seek high returns on the education of their children. A mobility ethic operationalized by intergenerational partnership propelled a voluntary quest for educational opportunity. Attendance at McKinley High School (in an era when most youngsters never moved beyond the eighth grade) and active membership in the West End House reflected a high degree of voluntary initiative.[3]

Other by-products of immigration—social marginality and the effort to overcome its barriers to opportunity—played a role in fostering the creation of "bridging" social capital. Japanese-Americans evinced a profound discrepancy between the first-generation (Issei) experience of exclusion from naturalized American citizenship and the second-generation (Nisei) experience of birthright American citizenship. The civic inequality of immigrant

2 Lawrence A. Cremin, *The Transformation of the School: Progressivism in American Education, 1876–1957* (New York, 1961), 115–126.

3 See Claudia Goldin and Lawrence F. Katz, "Human Capital and Social Capital: The Rise of Secondary Schooling in America, 1910 to 1940," paper originally presented at the conference, "Patterns of Social Capital: Stability and Change in Comparative Perspective," Harvard University, December 4–6, 1997, updated in this volume, 683–723.

parents stimulated the Nisei to organize and mobilize collectively for full participation in American public life and to represent their community in the public realm, in short to achieve civically and politically what had been denied to their parents. Likewise, the social marginalization of "new immigrants" from Europe in an era of restrictionist politics and discriminatory institutional policies stimulated in second-generation American Jews an organized quest for social justice and social opportunity.

MCKINLEY HIGH SCHOOL: DEMOCRATIC CITIZENSHIP AND CIVIC EN-
GAGEMENT   The educational history of the Nisei in early twen-tieth-century Honolulu is an empirically rich area for investigating the effects of schooling on the shaping of ethnic civic community. In Hawaii, during the 1920s and 1930s, Nisei students were the primary subjects of a progressive education program aimed at cultivating modern democratic citizenship, largely because Japa-nese-Americans were the islands' largest immigrant population from an alien culture. The mid-Pacific location of Hawaii, at the crux of American and Japanese geopolitical rivalry, added strategic urgency to the public school's task of securing Nisei loyalties. To progressive educators in Hawaii, the Japanese-American second generation represented the dangerous possibility of a sub-commu-nity isolated and alienated by an ineradicable racial nationalism.[4]

The post–World War I "Americanization" movement that shaped the development of progressive curricula in the public schools of Hawaii was not unlike the mainland cultural crusade

---

4 Stanford M. Lyman, "Generation and Character: The Case of the Japanese Americans," in *idem* (ed.), *The Asian in North America* (Santa Barbara, 1977), 151–176; Allison Davis, "The Public Schools in America's Most Successful Racial Democracy: Hawaii," unpub. ms. (Chi-cago, 1947); M. Kent Jennings and Richard G. Niemi, *The Political Character of Adolescence: The Influence of Families and Schools* (Princeton, 1974), 181–206; Territory of Hawaii, Depart-ment of Public Instruction, *Biennial Reports, 1919–1920, 1923–1924, 1925–1926, 1929–1930*; Ethel J. Spaulding (ed.), *We Americans in Hawaii: A Study of Citizenship Problems, Particularly as They Pertain to the People of Hawaii* (Honolulu, 1941); F. E. Stafford, "Character Education in the Schools of Hawaii," *Hawaii Educational Review*, XV (January 1927), 111ff; Miles E. Cary, "Summary High School Course of Study Work in Hawaii for the Year 1927–28," *Hawaii Educational Review*, XVII (September 1928), 4ff; Oren E. Long, "Then and Now in Character Education," *ibid.* (December 1928), 85ff; Charles Edgar Finch, "Citizenship Train-ing in Our Schools," *ibid.* (February 1929), 148ff; Akiyoshi Hayashida, "Japanese Moral Instruction as a Factor in the Americanization of Citizens of Japanese Ancestry," unpub. master's thesis (Univ. of Hawaii, 1933).

that sought to assimilate the children of immigrants from southern and eastern Europe. William McKinley High School, nicknamed "Tokyo High" because of the predominance of Japanese-American students, provided extensive exposure to the ideals of liberal democracy in its history, civics, and English courses. The teaching of American citizenship at McKinley composed the building blocks of national consciousness in the second-generation Nisei.[5]

The development of second-generation civic identity at McKinley can be gauged through an exploration of two sources—the *Pinion,* the weekly student newspaper, and a set of autobiographical essays written by Nisei students in 1926. The *Pinion* throws light upon how Nisei students came to see the public experience of participating in an educational program for Americanization. Issues published from 1925 to 1932 played a primary role in interpreting the institutional culture for civic acculturation at McKinley. The students on the newspaper's staff formed a representative ethnic cross-section of second-generation society in Hawaii, a large proportion each year consisting of Japanese-Americans. As campus journalists, they covered school activities, discussed courses, and offered opinion and editorial pieces, much as in papers at other American high schools. The students' autobiographical essays reveal how the educated members of the second-generation were building a new civic identity. An analysis of both records allows historians to reconstruct the engagement of the micro-worlds of ethnic subcultural identity and adolescent personality with the public world of official, nationalist identity. As will be shown, this triple interaction produced the bridging social capital possessed by a second-generation civic community.[6]

5 The Citizenship Education Committee, *Americanization Institute Papers* (Honolulu, 1919); Valentine Stuart McClatchy, *Assimilation of Japanese: Can They be Moulded into American Citizens* (Honolulu, 1921); E. Guy Talbot, "Making Americans in Hawaii," *American Monthly Review of Reviews,* LXXIII (1926), 280–285; Jisoo Sanjume, "An Analysis of the New Americans Conference from 1927 to 1938," unpub. master's thesis (Univ. of Hawaii, 1939); Eileen H. Tamura, *Americanization, Acculturation, and Ethnic Identity: The Nisei Generation in Hawaii* (Urbana, 1993), 56, 57. For a quantitative analysis of the ethnic composition of McKinley High School, see Cary, "A Vitalized Curriculum for McKinley High School," unpub. masters thesis (Univ. of Hawaii, 1930), tables IX and X, 27–28. Lawrence H. Fuchs, *Hawaii Pono: A Social History* (New York, 1961), 283–289; Oscar Handlin, *John Dewey's Challenge to Education: Historical Perspectives on the Cultural Context* (New York, 1959), 23–27.
6 William Carlson Smith, a sociologist trained at the University of Chicago, collected the student essays in 1926 with the cooperation of the Territorial Department of Public Instruction. See the William Carlson Smith Collection, "Life Histories of Students," Hamilton

The *Pinion*'s editorial policy focused on the vigorous and abundant school activities that promoted the greatness and privilege of American democracy. The *Pinion* articles described an institutional public culture shaped by civic knowledge and patriotic attitudes and explained to the institutional public how the Nisei students were absorbing American ways. The public high school created a powerful cultural medium to impress the ideas and practices of official Americanism on the children of immigrants. Essay and elocution contests, lectures, student government, and service programs were vehicles for teaching patriotism, citizenship, and democratic values.

The *Pinion* expressed the official public view of the institutional community on the experience of civic acculturation. By producing and consuming campus journalism, students made the new political language learned in the progressive classroom relevant to their wider institutional life. The editors of the *Pinion* wove the themes of official Americanism, taught to them in their English, social studies, and history classes, into their editorials and stories. Student writers clarified the civic meaning of school elections, activity programs, and athletics for their student readers.[7]

To the extent that student journalism expressed the high school's core values, it was the result of student writers and editors working within a stylistic and "values" paradigm set by administrators and teachers. The latter, however, did not manage or orchestrate *Pinion* journalism in a direct or heavy-handed fashion. The *Pinion* came to reflect an institutional paradigm; student editors consulted with faculty advisors and were "cued" indirectly by other teachers and administrators. From their classes, for example, *Pinion* writers learned their teachers' "worldview" and life perspectives, generally with respectful attention. This scholastic experience doubtlessly affected their public tone and judgment as student journalists. Still, a close and cumulative reading of *Pinion*

Library, University of Hawaii, Manoa (henceforth abbreviated as WCS) The autobiographies of sixty-six McKinley High School students were examined—thirty-five males and thirty-one females, average age of eighteen. The students in the sample were born in Hawaii, and their parents were born in Japan. John Bodnar, *Remaking America: Public Memory, Commemoration, and Patriotism in the Twentieth Century* (Princeton, 1992), 246.

7 *Pinion*, 21 Feb. 1927, 1; 8 March 1927, 1; 23 Jan. 1929, 3; 15 Nov. 1927, 1, 3; 12 Feb. 1926, 2; 19 Feb. 1926, 1–2; 26 Feb. 1926, 1–2; 19 March 1926, 1–2; 8 Feb. 1927, 1; 21 Feb. 1927, 1; 3 May 1927, 2.

text shows that authors were also free to express the tastes, humor, and life concerns of a generational peer culture.

The *Pinion* editors regularly ran articles on the country's public icons, especially on their birthdays. Presidents George Washington and Abraham Lincoln stood out as the foremost figures in the *Pinion's* gallery of heroic leaders, but other statesmen were also accorded tribute, most notably Benjamin Franklin, who was saluted as a leading contributor to American independence, and Theodore Roosevelt, who was hailed as a "statesman, nature lover, explorer [and] soldier." Editors of the *Pinion* also called attention to other important figures (not necessarily Americans) who had enriched American culture: John Keats, John Philip Sousa (composer of "The Stars and Stripes Forever"), George Eliot, Mark Twain, President William McKinley (the school's namesake under whose administration Hawaii was annexed to the United States), Robert Burns, President Grover Cleveland, Joseph Pulitzer, Thomas Edison, and Louisa May Alcott. By paying tribute to these luminaries, the *Pinion* editors hoped that they could inspire students to emulate their values and achievements.[8]

The *Pinion* strenuously advocated linguistic assimilation as a necessary step toward becoming good American citizens, particularly admonishing students who used "pidgin" English—a mixture of English, Hawaiian, and local idioms borrowed from "immigrant" languages. In 1926, with the strong backing of the *Pinion,* the high school held its first "Better English Week," which began with a campus parade. Instruction in public speaking, informal debate, and the art of conversation was introduced. To heighten the seriousness of the week's agenda, students served as monitors for speech behavior: "Policeman and sleuths will snoop around then, to 'nab' all who abuse any rules of grammar." A student-body grand jury indicted student offenders, and a pair of civics teachers subjected them to a mock trial. Students were urged to use proper English throughout the entire school year but especially during "Better English Week."[9]

Many Nisei described their participation in the institutional civic culture in histrionic terms, citing how such pride-inducing

---

8   These inspirational tributes to great cultural figures appeared with regularity in the *Pinion* issues of 1930 and 1931.

9   John E. Reinecke, "'Pidgin English' in Hawaii: A Local Study in the Sociology of Language," *American Journal of Sociology,* XLIII (1938), 778–789; *Pinion,* 12 March 1926, 1.

patriotic activities as Flag Drills, the Fourth of July celebration, and singing the national anthem. The symbols of democracy provided a sense of protection and security. The boys were eager to join the Reserve Officers' Training Corps to help defend their country. One Nisei declared his love for America in a pledge to "old glory." It was natural, many students perceived, for those who were born and educated in America, taught American ideals, and spoke the English language, to feel strong loyalty to America. Moreover, by being patriotic, they felt that they followed in the Japanese tradition of loyalty to one's country.

For Nisei students in prewar Hawaii, education was inseparable from the support system of their families. Nisei students appreciated their parents' willingness to participate in their education. Some parents were determined that their children advance as far in school as they could and actively advised them about "what subjects to take and what course to follow." The extent of parental support for education was described in the recollections of two McKinley High School students:

> After graduating from the elementary school, I was sent to the city. My father realized that the country school was not well equipped and he thought that his son should learn a little of his native language. I was fortunate to be the son to have this opportunity. This change had done a great deal to me. The change gave me an opportunity to read better books and gave me a chance to hear and to see better things.

> My parents were very much interested in our schools. They always consented if it was a school matter. My father is planning to make all of us go to the University. My eldest brother is now in the senior class of the University of Hawaii and my second brother is in the sophomore class of the same school. I am also planning to enter the University of Hawaii.[10]

In general, Nisei students saw their parents as going to extraordinary lengths to provide educational opportunity. Since their parents made great economic sacrifices to send them to high school and beyond, they were motivated to work as hard as possible on their studies.

10   McKinley essay (hereinafter MK)-75, MK-112, MK-213, WCS.

For Nisei at McKinley High School, American national consciousness and identity coexisted with formal institutions of Japanese culture. Many students in their autobiographies referred to the Japanese-language schools that they attended concurrently with their American public schools, many even into their secondary school years. A majority of students—including those who had dropped out of the Japanese-language schools in the elementary grades—thought that learning Japanese was indispensable for the development of communication and understanding between parents and children. In fact, one student believed that conflicts with parents took place because of the language gap. Another held that by improving communication between the generations, the Japanese-language schools helped to turn the Nisei into good citizens.[11]

Students also cited practical incentives for knowing the "mother" tongue. As one student argued,

> I believe we Japanese should go to the Japanese schools because when the big concerns want men to work for them they would rather have a "haole" [Caucasian] who speaks English, rather than a Japanese who isn't sure of himself. But if this person understands and speaks Japanese well, as well as English, this would help him because the "haole" wouldn't be able to understand the Japanese customers while the Japanese can understand both the English and Japanese customers and any employer would rather have a man who can do more work for him.

Another student expected that "in the future trade will be carried on with Orientals exclusively and in order to be friendly we must know this [Japanese] language." Some students felt, however, that knowledge of Japanese would be less valuable in the future when its usage declined in Hawaii.[12]

Students also described the Japanese-language school as a place to learn the history and values of their ancestral country, veneration for the aged, respect for teachers, love for education, obedience to law, and high standards of moral conduct. Through their texts and courses, they discovered a progressive, beautiful,

11 Misako Yamamoto, "Cultural Conflicts and Accommodations of the First and Second Generation Japanese," *Sociology and Social Research,* XXXIII (1949), 40–48.
12 MK-19, MK-1, WCS.

industrious, and culturally rich Japan. They were inspired by heroic sagas about loyal and courageous samurais and relived Japan's victory in the Russo-Japanese War. The education at the language school cultivated the Nisei's pride in their ethnic heritage.

Although they were not above criticizing particular groups, the Nisei students decried racial discrimination. The multiracial society of Hawaii helped to broaden their outlook about such matters. As one student discerned, the customs and values of all groups were growing more familiar to everyone. They were proud of racial harmony in Hawaii.

Students found sustenance for their cosmopolitan ideals in the democratic creed of equality and the Christian idea of universal spiritual brotherhood. The *Pinion* regularly advised students to preserve these traditional American values. During its coverage of Education Week in 1925, the editorial column instructed, "The strength, character, reputation and influence of a nation depend upon the education of the citizens. Education goes hand in hand with religion and piety . . . everything that is done or said in favor of better and still better education is a step toward God, country and humanity." In 1927, the keynote themes of Education Week were American freedom and the Christian spirit of service. The symbolism of the Fourth of July affirmed "the achievement of our national freedom" and of Christmas, "the life of the world's greatest religious teacher."[13]

The *Pinion* reported many other campus events that advocated the need for moral and religious instruction, often identified as Christian. At the first general student-body assembly of 1928, speakers discussed how to "strive for a better Christian character." Citing the Christian piety of Washington and President Calvin Coolidge, a student argued that religious character was indispensable to the making of good American citizens. Another speaker addressed the role of morality in American citizenship, reciting Roosevelt's words, "A man educated in mind, but not in morality, is a menace to society." A bishop invited to campus to lecture on the spirit of service praised American democracy as the creation of a people who comprehended "a right total view of the universe." He characterized Lincoln as a man imbued with the cosmic

13 *Pinion,* 23 Oct. 1925, 2; 15 Nov. 1927, 1–2.

spirit, pledged to God to abolish slavery for the sake of democracy. Democracy and Christianity were at the center of McKinley's civic life; they were universalizing creeds with the power to bring people together, a key concern of young people growing up in a multiracial society.[14]

Many students felt that they had to become actively involved in improving race relations. One girl admonished Niseis to be more outgoing and diplomatic:

> The Hawaiian-born Japanese should try to be friends with the haoles instead of criticizing each other. If they act friendly, the haoles would have no reason to go against them and the friendship would grow. Every race has some whose pride is above everything and who don't care to associate with those of different races and these are the ones who cause the unfriendliness between the races.

Many Nisei students supported programs and social activities to ease racial antipathy and to facilitate racial mingling, endorsing such organizations as the YMCA, Boy Scouts, and Girls Reserves.[15]

The *Pinion* guided its readers to link American democracy with Hawaii's unique role as a pluralistic society. The editors potrayed campus life at McKinley as building a multiracial egalitarianism that would serve as the foundation of democratic life. They used graphic and text devices to weave together the themes of partiotism and the civic unity of the world's races. The annual George Washington's Birthday issue of 1926 coupled an illustration of Washington drawn by a Nisei senior classman with an article entitled "All are Equal at McKinley; Spirit not Color, Counts." The point was that the harmonious interracialism at McKinley was based on American citizenship.[16]

The *Pinion* regularly referred to the racial diversity of the student body in its articles and editorials, adducing that more than ten races were represented among the students enrolled at McKinley High School. Articles encouraged students to feel that they were part of a historic project to realize American democracy as Hawaiian racial democracy. A feature entitled "All Races Meet and Play Together Here without Prejudice" declared, "McKinley

14 *Ibid.* 17 Jan. 1928, 3; 8 March 1927, 1.
15 MK-19, WCS.
16 *Pinion,* 19 Feb. 1926, 1.

High School is unique in that it is perhaps the only high school in the whole world where so many students of different races meet on equal ground . . . . Is there any place on earth that has so many different nationalities so Americanized?" Another article, "All Are Equal at McKinley," boasted, "With approximately two thousand three hundred students in McKinley high school, ninety percent are of races other that Caucasian, and yet there is no racial problem in the school. . . . [The reason] would be that they are mostly American citizens." In an opinion column, one editor cited students' responsibility to spread racial harmony not just in school or in America, but throughout the world.[17]

Despite the *Pinion*'s, strong emphasis on Americanism, various articles mentioned that the high school provided its students numerous opportunities to acquire knowledge and understanding of Japan and Japanese culture. The *Pinion* often highlighted campus events that dealt with inter-Pacific relations between the Territory of Hawaii and the United States, on one hand, and Japan, on the other.[18]

McKinley High School afforded opportunities for the Nisei students to deal publicly with issues of ethnic interest. The columns and reports in the *Pinion* suggested that even though the institutional culture was clearly American, it also permitted public explorations of Japanese-American identity. The features of Japanese culture were introduced to students often in a positive form. McKinley supported Japanese language instruction, a Nisei student organization, lectures on subjects related to Japan, and exchange programs with Japanese students. The ideological teaching of Americanism had the power to incorporate the second generation as American citizens, but this civic acculturation rested on an accommodation to ethnic pluralism. By recognizing the Niseis' interest in Japanese culture and international relations, McKinley allowed American citizenship to be compatible with the ethnic identity of Japanese-Americans.

This dual set of institutional opportunities probably helped to strengthen the identification of Japanese-Americans with an integrative American civic culture. According to an op-ed writer for the *Pinion,*

17 *Ibid.,* 2; 16 Jan. 1930, 2; 15 Dec. 1926, 16.
18 *Ibid.,* 1 Feb. 1927, 1; 16 Nov. 1928, 1; 15 Dec. 1926, 15; 2 Oct. 1925, 1.

All citizens have equal rights. The phrase is upheld by every student in high school. . . . With the students of different races, the class works and studies just as well as any class in any high school on the mainland. . . . No teacher has the impression that because of a student's color or race he should get a certain amount of attention. The teacher too thinks that every student has equal rights to learn. . . . [The students] are as friendly as if they were of the same race. . . . Not a thing about racial friendship prevails among the students and there is no antagonistic feeling there will be no racial problem to solve in McKinley high school.[19]

In their autobiographies, the Nisei tended to counter prejudice by accentuating their identity as American citizens. In the wider society as well as in the classroom, Nisei students endeavored to lay claim to their equal rights: "I am an American citizen so I think I should have equal rights as others." As loyal citizens, they were determined to make every effort to serve the United States: "We are true Americans and we must prove that we are true Americans." Their patriotism was an assertion that they belonged to America. The students deeply felt the need to show their citizenship because they worried that "white people do not consider American-born Japanese as Americans . . . they confuse largely . . . their native tongue [and] nationality." A student described the challenge of "doing away with racial clashes" to make Hawaii "one of the most successful laboratories of racial associations."[20]

The Nisei felt that their background as Japanese-Americans equipped them to overcome racial divisions and contribute to the democratic melting pot. One student expressed a fervor for promoting the common good of both their adopted and ancestral country, "to create a harmonious relationship." Another made a pledge for all Nisei, who had "the responsibility and duty to distinguish ourselves as ideal American citizens, and at the same time, to pay obedience and respect due to our Japanese parents," to establish "the foundation of the realization of World Wide Brotherhood." Yet another saw the desire to harmonize the relations of Japan and the United States as not only a personal cause but an international mission for which Hawaii was uniquely

19   *Ibid.,* 16 Jan. 1930, 2.
20   MK-173, MK-101, MK-204, MK-43, WCS.

positioned to serve. This task would be of the highest interest to the entire world. As Japanese-Americans with knowledge about both America and Japan, these students were in a good position to help improve relationships between the two countries.[21]

The emerging second-generation of Japanese-Americans fashioned an ideal of consensual democratic pluralism and undertook to install it in their public relations with the wider society. Despite a coercive campaign of Americanization in the 1920s that intended to homogenize the Japanese into Anglo-conformity, the second generation, with the aid of first-generation leaders, established a public image that combined American citizenship with Japanese-American ethnicity. The achievements of the Japanese of Hawaii disproved the idea that Asians were culturally unassimilable. Most important, the Nisei students at McKinley believed that their successful adoption of American democratic ideals was compatible with Japanese heritage. Students whose parents came from Asia were eminently prepared for full citizenship in a modern democracy.[22]

The Nisei of McKinley participated in a collective reenactment of the American founding. They re-invented their public persona to achieve what Sollors described as "the universal regeneration position," the renewal of the spiritual experience of democracy by every group. As Dewey expressed it in 1916,

> No matter how loudly anyone proclaims his Americanism if he assumes that any one social strain, any one component culture, no matter how early settled it was in our territory, or how effective it has proven in its own land, is to furnish a pattern to which all other strains and cultures are to conform, he is a traitor to American nationalism.[23]

WEST END HOUSE: THE MUTUALISM AND VOLUNTARISM OF CIVIC PATRIOTISM   In 1906, a boys' club was founded in one of Boston's immigrant districts of the West End. The West End House was endowed by James J. Storrow, Jr., a patrician who was active in municipal affairs and politics, but its staff and membership

21   MK-44, MK-45, MK-23, WCS.
22   Fuchs, *Hawaii Pono,* 283–284, 288, 291; Tamura, *Americanization* 48–49, 65.
23   Werner Sollors, *Beyond Ethnicity: Consent and Descent in American Culture* (New York, 1986), 87–88.

came from the neighborhood—newcomers from Russia, Italy, Poland, Ireland, and Greece. Second-generation American Jews constituted a large share of the membership, as well as the staff. Through sports and cultural programs, House members learned how to work as part of an organized group and to set their sights on self-improvement.[24]

Mitchell Freiman, the first director of the West End House, established its institutional ethos—namely, to prepare members for useful and productive citizenship. The coupling of self-help and teamwork was a reflection of the social ethic in a neighborhood of striving immigrant families. The competitive atmosphere of such structured group activities as athletics and debating created peer pressure to achieve personal and collective excellence. These shaping experiences had residual effects: An extremely active alumni association persevered to live up to the vision and expectation of the House founders.[25]

The West End House created an institutional matrix of mutual assistance. For example, from its inception it functioned as an informal employment agency. Newsboys—the first members of the club—helped each other to find employment by swapping routes and sharing knowledge. Alumni, who returned to visit the club, hired members as apprentices, office boys, and clerks. House members gained a network of personal contacts for obtaining jobs and occupational counselling. They also benefitted from interaction with older successful members and alumni who were willing to help with homework and give advice about colleges or professional schools.[26]

A 1980 survey of club alumni born before World War II showed high levels of education and occupational mobility. Of those sons born before 1920 whose fathers held blue-collar occupations, 98 percent went to high school, 31 percent entered college, and 24 percent attended professional or postgraduate schools. The sons from working-class families who were born between 1921 and 1940 attained comparable levels of education. Approximately 90 percent of the sons from working-class families

---

24 Robert A. Woods, *Americans in Process: A Settlement Study* (Boston, 1903), 36–38, 42–46, 107–127; Herbert J. Gans, *The Urban Villagers: Group and Class in the Life of Italian Americans* (Glencoe, Ill., 1962), 11–12.

25 Jacob M. Burnes, *West End House: Story of a Boys' Club* (Boston, 1934), 31–41; Ueda, *West End House, 1906–1981* (Boston, 1981), 137.

26 *Ibid.,* 125–126.

in both birth cohorts attained employment in white-collar jobs. A sizable cluster of House alumni had careers in the professions of law, medicine, and dentistry; others found their calling in business, journalism, academics, sports, and the entertainment field.[27]

The West End House encouraged a life-long dedication to neighborhood citizenship. Founded for the "mental" and "moral" advancement of its members, it provided forums, debates, speeches, and essay contests that taught the arts of civic advocacy. Discussions centered on municipal reform, immigration policy, pacifism, and socialism. Jacob Kahn, an immigrant son, published an essay in the House *Bulletin* called "My Heroes," which exposed the false heroism of the powerful and wealthy and described the true heroism of working people in the spirit of socialist struggle and the American dream of upward mobility through self-reliance and education. Kahn "worshipped people who honestly desire that children, instead of being sent to factories, be sent to schools and playgrounds, while their fathers will be given a good wage, in order that they may bring up healthy members of society." His "heroes were parents, who offer the best there is in them in order that their children may grow up to be useful, and honest citizens," and he expressed thanks to "people who do their utmost to end racial prejudice, and teach us that we are children of one common Father."[28]

The staff worked hard to foster the spirit of equality in the neighborhood and in the words of the founder, James J. Storrow, to keep the West End House "a club for all boys." The membership showed great ethnic diversity, and it kept changing as the West End changed. Team sports provided a context for interethnic understanding. Boys learned to rely upon teammates of different nationalities, to benefit from their unselfish play, and to sacrifice willingly for others. Competing together created ties of interdependence and mutual trust.[29]

27 Some of the House alumni who entered the legal profession became important figures in public service: Joel Cohen, the chief counsel for the Social Security Administration; Harold Kowal, counsel of the National Labor Relations Board; Irving Roginson, a federal judge; Charles Atwater, a United States diplomat in Thailand; John Higgins and Frank Tomasello, judges in the Massachusetts Superior Courts; and Samuel Peitchell, Joseph Schneider, and Benjamin Trustman, outstanding leaders in the legal profession. See Ueda, *West End House,* 126–136.
28 Burnes, *West End House,* 84–86.
29 Ueda, *West End House, 1906–1981,* 65–93.

The urban renewal of the West End in the late 1950s brought the end of the old neighborhood and the West End House. Instead of closing their doors forever, the Alumni Association began to explore new sites for the clubhouse in 1961. Throughout the 1960s, its leaders negotiated with officials and launched a massive drive to raise funds for the new House. They decided to locate in Allston, because the majority of Alumni Association members lived there or nearby. As the House Survey and Planning Committee explained, "The Alumni are an integral and vital part of the West End House and if this group becomes disinterested and stagnates, the organization will no longer be able to function as it has for the past sixty years."[30]

According to State Representative Norman Weinberg, the new location in Allston had a "melting pot atmosphere," more than half of its population being immigrants and their children. Because of its social diversity and its accessibility, the area received a flow of upwardly mobile people from the city. It seemed fitting for the West End House, by then led by second- and third-generation immigrants, to follow their natural constituency.

The civic bonds forged early in life became a valuable resource during the project of relocation. The majority of the Alumni Association felt that reestablishing the facility was the responsibility of those who had benefitted from the generosity of Storrow. An article in the *Boston Globe* described the alumni's commitment to the project as based on the sense of history and civic obligation that they had learned in their youth. In the words of George Kane, the director, "Don't we have an obligation to [our founders], and to their memories?" The colorful brochures sent out to alumni to solicit donations appealed to this attitude. One brochure, entitled "Rededicated to Service," displayed an artist's conception of the "New West End House" and announced that "the spirit will never die."[31]

Since this capital fund program was a unique event, rather than an annual campaign for operating costs, it required generous

30 "Minutes of the Board of Directors of the Alumni Association," May 1, 1961, June 5, 1961; "Report of Survey and Planning Committee—West End House Alumni Association," May 10, 1966; "Feasibility Study for a Proposed West End House Boys' Club in the Allston-Brighton Area," October 16, 1967; "The Most Needed Building in Town: A New West End House Boys' Club for Allston and Brighton," (n.d.); Letter from Benjamin Gargill to Norman S. Weinberg, July 19, 1967.
31 "West End House to Build 'Finest Boys Club in U.S.,'" 20 Aug. 1968, 1; Kane, "Dedication Speech for the New West End House," October 3, 1971.

gifts and numerous contributors. When the new clubhouse was dedicated in 1971, 1,283 contributors, large and small, had pledged $650,000 to the Building Fund.[32]

The grassroots mobilization of alumni donors to build a new West End House fulfilled Storrow's philanthropic agenda—his desire to help boys attain successful positions from which they could help others, in turn. The alumni who were aided by Storrow's philanthropy saw themselves as paying a debt. They returned the yield of their life achievements to the West End House so that a new generation could restart the cycle of civic patriotism.

DEMOCRATIC CIVIC COMMUNITIES OF THE SECOND GENERATION

Social capital accumulated early in the generational cycle at McKinley High School and the West End House, building into a resource for organizing collective endeavors in adulthood. The creation of this fund of social capital also facilitated the movement from particularistic ethnic identity to broader forms of collective identity.[33]

In Honolulu, the Nisei elite emerged from McKinley with a vision of universal citizenship, equal opportunity, religious ecumenicalism, intergroup tolerance, and ethnic pride. As second-generation Japanese who were ethnic outsiders, they were acutely aware of the obstacles and challenges. Nevertheless, through civic acculturation, they endeavored to transform their lives and change American society in Hawaii to establish a democratic pluralism that rose above the bounds of race.

The institutional culture portrayed in the *Pinion* shaped the bonds of civic community in the second generation. McKinley created a peer network in which students helped each other see citizenship as a transracial status that would bring them into the American mainstream. It also introduced ideological motifs with the potential to be appropriated for political mobilization.[34]

McKinley High School shaped the political worldview of many future leaders in the Japanese-American community. It

32 Ueda, *West End House, 1906–1981*, 147–153.
33 Marcus Lee Hansen, "The Problem of the Third Generation Immigrant," in Dag Blank and Peter Kivisto (eds.), *American Immigrants and Their Generations: Studies and Commentaries on the Hansen Thesis After Fifty Years* (Urbana, 1990), 192–193.
34 Cf. Gary Gerstle, *Working-Class Americanism: The Politics of Labor in a Textile City, 1914–1960* (Cambridge, 1989), 10, 177–187; idem, "The Politics of Patriotism: Americanization and the Formation of the CIO," *Dissent*, XXXIII (1986), 84–92.

taught the Nisei a new language of political democracy as applied and cultivated in student government, student journalism, and social studies. The vocabulary of equal rights would later shape the political language of racial democracy that former students there would use to express their quest for power in Hawaii. The McKinley experience created civic connections among new Americans of Japanese ancestry. During their rise in the Democratic party and their push to win statehood for Hawaii, the Nisei leaders mobilized politically through the networks established in the civic community of the public high school.[35]

The commemorative volume assembled by graduates, "A Hundred Years: McKinley High School, 1865–1965," pointed out the conjunction between the civic lessons learned at McKinley and the attainment of statehood for Hawaii. Excerpts from the "centennial day" speech of John A. Burns, Hawaii's Democratic governor, described McKinley's key role in teaching Hawaii's postwar generation that they were part of a democratic civic community and recognized "the many courageous superintendents and principals and teachers" who "steadfastly fought" for the right of Hawaii's children to learn about the meaning of the Declaration of Independence and the Constitution. For example, Miles E. Cary, McKinley's principal before World War II, constructed the high school's curriculum to motivate students "to change [their] environment," and after the war, Burns recalled, many did just that, as proved by Hawaii's achievement of statehood in 1959.

Burns further pointed out that "the distinguished McKinley alumni" had a central role in the changes that made Hawaii an "integral and essential part" of the United States. They helped to bring about not "merely the realization of Statehood," but also "the full appreciation of . . . American rights" that they had learned in McKinley's classrooms.[36]

The McKinley High School experience occurred at the geographical and social margins of American life, but it probably had

35 George K. Yamamoto, "Political Participation among Orientals in Hawaii," *Sociology and Social Research*, XLIII (1959), 359–364. Cf. "Spark Matsunaga: The Path to Understanding," *Japanese American National Museum Newsletter* (Summer 1990), 5; Fuchs, *Hawaii Pono*, 129, 283–284, 286–290.

36 Henry Y. K. Tom, Linda Y. Furushima, Paula T. Yano, *A Hundred Years: McKinley High School, 1865–1965* (Honolulu, 1965), 7.

parallels with the experiences of the educated second generation in the Polish, Jewish, Italian, Greek, and Armenian enclaves of the United States. Peer-group institutions in immigrant communities were designed to produce a common experience of acculturation. Observing the education of Japanese-Americans in Hawaii, one commentator noted, "The theory that the Oriental mind is essentially different from the Occidental mind no one who teaches in Hawaii would consider for a moment."[37]

Boston's West End House harnessed the immigrant ethic of self-help and teamwork to serve the wider community and to strengthen its democratic pluralistic foundations. Many of its former members fondly remembered the egalitarian fraternalism of club life: Lee Romanow, a prominent attorney, praised "the example set by the Director, Jack Burnes, whose dignity, manner, and sensitivity" applied to all the boys. Alan Skivsky felt that the House helped him to "grow emotionally, physically, and intellectually in a multi-ethnic, racial environment." Alfred Ferrara expressed gratitude to the club "where he learned to respect and trust other people who were not of the same faith." David Knopping spoke for many alumni when he stated that "caring for the welfare of boys of all religions and color" was an enduring legacy of the House.[38]

Gerstle has pointed out that civic education often helped European immigrant youths gain political self-consciousness and to pursue the goal of inclusive society. For example, Vito Marcontonio was a citizenship teacher in an Italian-American community center in East Harlem before he became a Congressman. Another example is Walter Reuther, who, as a German-American high-school student in his early twenties, joined a 4C club (standing for cooperation, confidence, comradeship, and citizenship), sponsored by the chamber of commerce, where he learned the civic values that laid the foundation for his later role as a national labor leader.[39]

The educational experiences of second-generation immigrant Americans helped to enlarge the possibilities for communication and social coexistence. Both at McKinley High School and the

37   Henry B. Restarick, "Americanizing Hawaii," *The Mid-Pacific Magazine,* VII (1914), 217–223.
38   Ueda, *West End House, 1906–1981,* 122–123.
39   Gerstle, "Politics of Patriotism."

West End House, the intensification of democratic social and civic networks within ethnic subgroups led to the extension of civic engagement beyond original group boundaries. McKinley High School students and West End House members established networks that fostered the interethnic and cosmopolitan dimensions of social trust, public activism, and voluntarism. These experiences set an agenda for joint and collaborative activity in public life that weakened parochial divisions and made group relations more open and permeable.

The educated members of the second generation were able to convert such structures of "socialization" as citizenship and ethical training into new forms of social capital for including themselves in public life and the social mainstream. They participated in the creation of the "bridging" social capital that underlay the rise of a public philosophy of democratic pluralism in the United States.

Second-generation leaders, who came into their prime years after World War II, sought to strengthen a public agenda that brought different groups together on an egalitarian basis. For example, National Brotherhood Week, sponsored by the National Conference of Christians and Jews since 1933, gained new prominence when, immediately after the war, President Harry S. Truman became its honorary chair and former Governor Harold E. Stassen of Minnesota presided over its events. The President of the National Conference saw far-reaching popular support for "the movement of spiritual motivation" represented by Brotherhood Week, the theme of which was "In Peace As in War— Teamwork." A Jewish religious leader hoped that the spirit of this event would engender a higher consciousness of how "the problems of the postwar world can be solved only through united cooperation." The editorial page of the *New York Times* summed up the continuing need for such public efforts as Brotherhood Week to help overcome divisions.[40]

In postwar American education, teachers, parents, and students grew receptive to improving intergroup relations and mutual understanding. Ginn and Company, the publisher, inaugurated the Tiegs–Adams Social Studies Series, which included such titles as *Your People and Mine* and *Your Country and Mine: Our American*

---

40 "Nation to Observe Brotherhood Days," *New York Times,* 17 Feb. 1946, 13.

Neighbors. These textbooks demonstrated how different ethnic groups and different nations learned to work together for a more harmonious world.[41]

Organized public and institutional efforts to spread an American creed of unifying democratic pluralism were facilitated by the bridging social capital accumulated through the second generation's collective education in the values of cosmopolitan democracy. Confidence in the mutually beneficial qualities of American diversity drew on direct experiences in neighborhood educational institutions, where different nationalities learned to work together in new civic communities. In the postwar decades, this popular attitude supported public policies to break down ethnic and racial barriers to the mainstream, resulting in a more sensitive relationship between the national whole and the ethnic part.

41 For example, see Josephine McKenzie, with Ernest W. Tiegs and Fay Adams, *Your People and Mine* (Boston, 1949), 6–7.

Claudia Goldin and Lawrence F. Katz

Human Capital and Social Capital: The Rise of Secondary Schooling in America, 1910–1940

> *The landlord who lives in town has only a financial interest and must be reached from the financial side. He may well be reminded that when he offers his farm for sale it will be to his advantage to advertise, "free transportation to a good graded school."*
>
> *Those who have no children to attend school are often indifferent as to school privileges, but they more than others should be interested in securing to the children of the whole community the best educational advantages possible. They may be secure and independent at present, but if they live out their years with no children to depend upon in old age, they must of necessity rely upon someone, they know not whom, who is today in the public schools. Their only safeguard lies in giving the best advantages possible to all.*
>
> *Iowa Biennial Report, 1912/13,*
> on the campaign for consolidated school districts

The United States led all other nations in the development of universal and publicly funded secondary school education, and much of the growth occurred from 1910 to 1940. The focus of this article is on why the "high school movement" occurred in America generally and why it occurred so early and swiftly in America's heartland—a region we dub the "education belt." Since Iowa was at the center of this belt, we use information from the unique Census of Iowa for 1915 at both the county and individual

Claudia Goldin is Professor of Economics, Harvard University, and Director of the Development of the American Economy Program at the National Bureau of Economic Research, where she is also Research Associate. She is the author of *Understanding the Gender Gap: An Economic History of American Women* (New York, 1990); and co-editor, with Michael D. Bordo and Eugene N. White, of *The Defining Moment: The Great Depression and the American Economy in the Twentieth Century* (Chicago, 1998).

Lawrence F. Katz is Professor of Economics, Harvard University, and Research Associate of the National Bureau of Economic Research. He is editor of the *Quarterly Journal of Economics;* co-editor, with Robert B. Freeman, of *Differences and Changes in Wage Structures* (Chicago, 1995).

The authors thank the Spencer Foundation for funding the collection of the Iowa State Census of 1915, the Russell Sage Foundation for leave support in 1997/98, and the National Science Foundation for a research grant. They also thank the research assistants who helped

level to explore the factors that propelled states like Iowa to embrace so expensive a public good as secondary school education.

Our framework emphasizes both individual (private) and community (public) factors. Of the factors usually grouped under the heading of "individual," we find that income or wealth levels and the opportunity cost of education—such as the availability of manufacturing jobs for youths—were crucial to the high school expansion. But we also locate such factors as homogeneity of community, the distribution of wealth or income, and the fragmentation of social, ethnic, and religious groups that influenced how social capital aided the production of human capital. In our case study of Iowa, as well as in our evidence for the entire United States, small towns and villages experienced the highest levels, and the greatest expansion, of high school education from 1910 to 1920. Most important was that the pecuniary returns to secondary school education were high—on the order of 12 percent per year. Social capital appears to have been the handmaiden of human capital, and it was more easily and rapidly accessed in areas with greater homogeneity and tightly knit communities.[1]

We end with a set of findings on the state-level relationship between *current* measures of social capital and early twentieth-century measures of economic, educational, and social indicators. A stronger correlation exists, at the state level, between an index of social capital today (combining measures of associational activity, social trust, and political/civic participation) and per capita

to code the Iowa data, including Allegra Ivey, who collected most of the rural sample and much of the urban one, Brigit Chen, Serena Mayeri, Todd Braunstein, Misha Dewan, Michael Cress, and Arvind Krishnamurthy. The authors also thank Edward Glaesar and Caroline Minter Hoxby for illuminating discussions and the participants at the conference, "Patterns of Social Capital: Stability and Change in Comparative Perspective," Harvard University, December 4–6, 1997, for useful suggestions. They are especially grateful to Robert Putnam for his social capital and educational indices.

1 There are many notions of social capital. The one that we employ is similar to that in James S. Coleman, "Social Capital in the Creation of Human Capital," *American Journal of Sociology,* Supplement to XCIV (1988), S95–S120. Like physical capital and human capital, social capital is a stock of productive matter that can be called upon to facilitate an action. But unlike human capital, social capital does not belong to, or inhere in, or reside in any one individual. Rather, it is part of a community, a network, a neighborhood, a country, a clan, or a family. It is more public than private; it is more social than individual. At times, it is more intangible than tangible because it exists in the relations among individuals.

taxable wealth in 1912 or per capita income in 1900 than between the same index and per capita income in 1994. A strong correlation exists between the high school graduation rate in 1928 and the index of social capital today. An equally high correlation exists between the graduation rate in 1928 and a current educational performance index (combining measures of test scores at various ages and the high school dropout rate). Social capital was not merely the handmaiden of human capital in the past; it appears to have survived many changes in the economy and society, serving a similar function today.

THE HIGH SCHOOL MOVEMENT: 1910 TO 1940   The period from 1910 to 1940 is often referred to as that of the "high school movement" in the United States, and the emergence of the high school as the "second great transformation" of American education. The period has been singled out as a special one in the history of education for good reason. The rise of the public high school was rapid across the entire United States. In 1910, just 9 percent of American youths earned a high school diploma, but by 1935, 40 percent did. The transition was even swifter in certain states and regions—in the three states of the Pacific region, for example, where about 10 percent of youths graduated from high school in 1910, and 60 percent by 1935. No other country underwent the transformation to virtually universal public secondary education at so early a date. Moreover, secondary schooling was an expensive undertaking. Putting a youth through four years of high school cost the same as putting the same youth through the first eight years of common or grammar school.[2]

2   Martin Trow, "The Second Transformation of American Secondary Education," *International Journal of Comparative Sociology,* II (1961), 144–166, places the "high school movement" in historical perspective. For sources to the various data cited on secondary school education, see Goldin, Appendix to "How America Graduated From High School: An Exploratory Study, 1910 to 1960," National Bureau of Economic Research-Development of the American Economy working paper 57 (Cambridge, Mass., 1994); *idem,* "America's Graduation from High School: The Evolution and Spread of Secondary Schools in the Twentieth Century," *Journal of Economic History,* LVIII (1998), 345–374. For comparative data, see Goldin and Katz, "Why the United States Led in Education: Lessons from Secondary School Expansion, 1910 to 1940," National Bureau of Economic Research (NBER) working paper 6144 (Cambridge, Mass., 1997); Fritz K. Ringer, *Education and Society in Modern Europe* (Bloomington, 1979).
      On the relative cost of primary and secondary education, see, for example, U.S. Bureau of Education, *Biennial Survey of Education, 1920/22* (Washington, D.C., 1924), 5. "In 1918 the

Because educational decisions are made primarily at a local level in the United States, the production of human capital depends largely on social capital lodged in small communities. The first tabulation of local school districts by the U.S. Office of Education in 1932 set the number at c. 130,000. It was probably even higher earlier in the period. But even as late as 1932 there were about 9,000 in Kansas, 7,000 in Nebraska, and 5,000 in Iowa. In 1925, the states (plus the federal government) supplied just 16 percent of all educational expenditures for kindergarten through the twelfth grade (K–12). States, to be sure, had powers in the educational realm besides those concerning the purse. Yet, after careful consideration, we conclude that the high school movement occurred at a grassroots level, despite the coordinating function of state governments and nationally acclaimed educators.[3]

The importance of the rapid move from the grammar (or common) school to that at the secondary level cannot be overemphasized. About 70 percent of the increase in years of education of the adult population from 1900 to 1970 was due solely to the increase in secondary school attendance and graduation. Without the rapid rise of the high school, America could not have put the G.I. Bill of Rights into immediate action after 1944 because American youth would not yet have graduated high school. Nor would the 1950s to 1970s have witnessed the enormous expansion of college education. Although we are not prepared to claim that the rise of the United States to international economic supremacy during the period was a direct result of the greater amounts of human capital held by the average American worker, our inves-

---

average cost in the United States per elementary school pupil enrolled was $31.65; per high-school pupil enrolled, $84.48." The difference would have been less if weighted by states, not individuals, because states with the most support to education would have had more students in high school.

3 Not all of the 130,000 school "attendance" districts were fully independent "fiscal districts" with control over their property taxes and spending. Iowa school districts appear to have had fiscal independence. Although the counties collected school district taxes and arranged for the exchange of "tuition" payments among the state's school districts, the county appears to have been simply the fiscal agent for the districts. The districts seem to have set tax and tuition rates, within the bounds of the various state laws and regulations. On the number of school districts, see U.S. Office of Education, *Biennial Survey of Education, 1930/32* (Washington, D.C., 1935); U.S. Bureau of the Census, *Historical Statistics of the United States: Colonial Times to 1970* (Washington, D.C., 1975), series H 412. For data on the share of various levels of government in school finance, see U.S. Bureau of Education, *Biennial Survey of Education, 1924/26* (Washington, D.C., 1928), Table 18, 593.

tigation of how important secondary schooling was to the high-tech industries of the 1910 to 1940 period finds that these industries took good advantage of the influx of high-school-educated youths in the labor market.[4]

The increased education of America's youth during the high school movement reflected a substantial commitment of the nation's resources to education. Although it is difficult, if not often inadvisable, to quantify "social capital," the commitment of resources in support of education by small communities seems one reasonable measure. Therefore, our indicator of social capital is the amount of public resources committed to education as a fraction of the total resources of the community, given by income. Figure 1 shows the amount spent on K–12 education by states and localities as a fraction of income by region and at the national level from 1910 to 1930 and from 1950 to 1970. We omit the Great Depression and World War II years because the large income fluctuations during these periods make the series less informative.

Our indicator of educational commitment rises steeply during the 1910s and for most of the 1920s. For the United States as a whole it remains at its 1930 level until the early 1950s, when it rises again. In 1970, the national level was about 4.5 percent, whereas it was 0.9 percent in 1910. More than half of that increase took place from 1910 to 1925. Some regions (the Pacific and the West North Central) were already committing more than 3 percent of their income to K–12 public education by the early 1920s, and they also had large public higher-educational expenditures on a per capita basis. Since these regions were rich, the fraction of

4 On the role of secondary-school advances in increasing the stock of education, see Goldin, "America's Graduation from High School," Table 1, 346. The World War II G.I. Bill of Rights is the subject of Keith W. Olson, *The G.I. Bill, the Veterans, and the Colleges* (Lexington, Ky., 1974) which, on the basis of a simple extrapolation, concludes that the bill had a negligible net impact on the number of men who went to college. Marcus Stanley, "The Impact of the World War II G.I. Bill on the College Graduation of Men," unpub. paper, Harvard University (Cambridge, Mass., 1997), using more sophisticated tools and cohort-specific data, finds that the bill increased the numbers of men graduating from college in the affected cohorts (born 1921 to 1927). Other possible effects of the G.I. Bill, for example the distribution of college students across universities, have not yet been examined thoroughly.

On the use of high school graduates by industry, see Goldin and Katz, "The Origins of Technology-Skill Complementarity," *Quarterly Journal of Economics,* CXIII (1998), 693–732.

Fig. 1   State and Local Elementary and Secondary Educational Expenditures as a Fraction of Regional Income or U.S. Personal Income

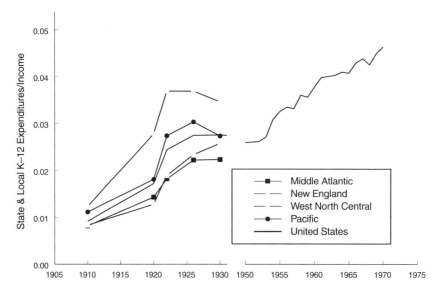

NOTES   The periods of the Depression and World War II are omitted because of large changes in the denominator—income. Although the income measures for 1910, 1920, and 1929 differ from that for the post-1950 period, the national number for 1929, derived from the state figures, is close to that in the national series used for the post-1950s. State income and population figures for 1922 and 1926 were interpolated from the data for 1920 and 1930 (1929 for the income data). Population figures were necessitated because the 1920 and 1929 income data are per capita. The K–12 expenditure data include current expenses and "outlays, new buildings, sites and new equipment" for public day schools. The data used to construct the regional data for 1910 to 1930, by separate states, contain virtually the same U.S. totals as in U.S. Bureau of the Census, *Historical Statistics,* series H 492, used for the post-1950s national series.

SOURCES   For K–12 expenditures, 1920, 1922, 1926, and 1930, see U.S. Bureau (or Office) of Education, *Biennial Survey of Education* [for year] (Washington, D.C., [year]). For post-1950, see U.S. Bureau of the Census, *Historical Statistics of the United States* (Washington, D.C., 1975), series H 492. For income in 1920, see Simon Kuznets, Ann Ratner Miller, and Richard A. Easterlin, *Population Redistribution and Economic Growth: United States, 1870–1950. II. Analyses of Economic Change* (Philadelphia, 1960); for 1929, U.S. Department of Commerce, Bureau of Economic Analysis, *State Personal Income by State Estimates for 1929–1982* (Washington, D.C., 1984); for post-1950 population, U.S. Bureau of the Census, *Historical Statistics,* series F 8, personal income. For 1910 and 1920, see U.S. Bureau of the Census, *Historical Statistics,* series A 195.

their income devoted to education represented an impressive absolute amount.[5]

The U.S. Bureau of Education explained the substantial increase in educational expenditures just after World War I by several factors: The war both unified and intensified the increase in educational expenditures throughout the country, plainly demonstrating to communities that they harbored poorly educated, illiterate, and physically unfit Americans. But in many sections of America, the single most important change that affected how much money went to education was the increase in high school attendance; each student year of upper grades cost about twice that of the lower grades. Furthermore, the length of the school year generally increased, as did the real cost of teacher's salaries in many parts of the country. The upshot of all of these factors was a cost of education that was escalating at a rate faster than that of income.[6]

What is most important about the history of the American high school in this context is that the modern version—one that we would easily recognize today—emerged c. 1910. Prior to 1900, secondary schools in much of America often trained youths to gain entry to particular colleges and universities in their vicinity. During the period of the high school movement, however, secondary education was transformed into training "for life," rather than "for college." In 1910, 49 percent of high school graduates continued to some form of higher education; by 1933, only 25 percent did. Secondary schools were granting more terminal degrees, not because college entry had declined but because high school entry had so greatly increased.[7]

5 For an analysis of public expenditures on higher education per capita, see Goldin and Katz, "The Origins of State-Level Differences in the Provision of Higher Education: 1890 to 1940," *American Economic Review,* LXXXVIII (1998), 303–308. See also Fred J. Kelly and John H. McNeely, *The State and Higher Education: Phases of Their Relationship* (New York, 1933), 257. Of the top fourteen states in 1930 by "receipts from state, county, or city of publicly supported higher education per [non-black] inhabitant 21 years of age and over," all but six are in the Pacific or West North Central regions and four of the six are in the Mountain region. One of the remaining two is South Carolina, because Kelly and McNeely exclude blacks from the denominator. The other is Oklahoma.
6 See the lengthy discussion in U.S. Bureau of Education, *Biennial Survey, 1920/22,* 1–9, on the increase in educational expenditures directly following World War I.
7 Our contributions to the literature on high schools include Goldin, "America's Graduation from High School"; *idem* and Katz, "Why the United States Led." Among the most-cited volumes are Edward A. Krug, *The Shaping of the American High School: 1880–1920* (Madison, 1964); *idem, The Shaping of the American High School: 1920–1941* (Madison, 1972), II; William

What were the reasons for the large influx of students into American high schools, and why did local government respond by building schools and staffing classes? Education at the secondary level is distinctive for being almost always publicly funded and supplied, both in the United States and elsewhere. Yet, it has almost none of the features of a public good and many of the characteristics of a private good. The relevant issue is one of timing rather than degree, since all communities in the United States, and most countries in the world, have undertaken public funding of secondary-school education at some point. Hence, the question is, Why did secondary schools diffuse so rapidly during this particular period?[8]

In nineteenth-century America, the high school had been attacked as an "elitist" institution. Local taxpayers were often united against its funding on the grounds that it would serve only a small and wealthy clientele who could afford to send their sons and daughters to college. Such debates continued across America as the high school movement spread. The funding of many early high schools, particularly outside major cities, was justified as a strengthening of the common-school system; high schools, after all, trained teachers for the lower grades. This argument, however, saw little use during the high school movement. Also rare was the argument that schools produced the literate populace necessary to maintain a great democracy; it was offered in behalf of the common-school revival, not the high school movement. The reasons given for championing secondary education were more mundane.[9]

J. Reese, *The Origins of the American High School* (New Haven, 1995). In the current article, we pay less attention to the special subject of secondary schooling in America's big cities than we have done in previous work. These issues have been the focus of many fine works, among them David Tyack, *The One Best System* (Cambridge, Mass., 1974); David F. Labaree, *The Making of an American High School: The Credentials Market and the Central High School of Philadelphia, 1838–1939* (New Haven, 1988); Joel Perlmann, *Ethnic Differences: Schooling and Social Structure among the Irish, Italians, Jews, and Blacks in an American City, 1880–1935* (New York, 1988). For data on the numbers of secondary-school graduates continuing to higher education, see Goldin, "America's Graduation from High School," Table 2, 351.

8   In this manner, the question we ask is similar to that in work on the diffusion of technological processes. See, for example, Zvi Griliches, "Hybrid Corn: An Exploration in the Economics of Technological Change," *Econometrica*, XXVI (1958), 501–522.

9   Michael B. Katz, *The Irony of Early School Reform: Educational Innovation in Mid-Nineteenth Century Massachusetts* (Cambridge, Mass., 1968), and Maris A. Vinovskis, *The Origins of Public High Schools: A Reexamination of the Beverly High School Controversy* (Madison, 1985), have

The first and foremost among them was the expected financial return to high school students c. 1910, even in the absence of a college education. But because the 1940 U.S. population census was the first to ask questions about education and earnings, concrete evidence in support of this claim has not been easy to locate. Elsewhere we have shown that, from 1890 to 1920, occupations common to high school graduates (for example, such ordinary white-collar workers as secretaries, bookkeepers, and typists) paid twice the monetary amount as did occupations that tended to employ individuals without high school training. In this study, we are able to estimate, more directly, the returns to years of schooling by using the manuscripts of the Iowa State Census of 1915—a unique document both for its time and for many years to come because of its information on education and earnings, among other variables. These data reveal that the financial return on high school in 1915 was substantial, on the order of 12 percent for each year completed. State school superintendents used such arguments to recommend new high schools and teachers. As the epigraph suggests, they also maintained that schools were good investments for property owners: If high schools were good for youths, they were also good for property owners in school districts that had them.[10]

Community cohesion was also a prominent rationale for the building and funding of high schools and for the consolidation of

---

different interpretations of the opposition of one community to the building of a high school. Katz sees the opposition based on class, whereas Vinovskis interprets it more pragmatically as a matter of which individuals lived closer to the proposed school. Early controversy about state and local financing of high schools is also taken up in Reese, *Origins*. See also Isaac Leon Kandel, *History of Secondary Education: A Study in the Development of Liberal Education* (Boston, 1930), particularly on the important Kalamazoo case of 1874, after which states no longer questioned whether localities had the authority to tax citizens to establish a high school. Kalamazoo thereby served to legalize the spread of the public high school in America by attaching its importance to that of the common school. For a discussion of the establishment of early high schools in Iowa to produce teachers for the common school system, see Clarence Ray Aurner, *History of Education in Iowa* (Iowa City, 1915), I, III. Although the early high schools charged tuition, through the "rate bill," individuals who promised to teach received a tuition waiver. As early as 1858, Iowa offered scholarships and stipends to students in the top half of their high school class, provided that they became teachers and served for the length of time that they had received the scholarship (I, 52–53).

10   For data on the wage structure by occupation, see Goldin and Katz, "The Decline of Noncompeting Groups: Changes in the Premium to Education, 1890 to 1940," NBER working paper 5202 (Cambridge, Mass., 1995).

small districts. Proponents warned about the possibility of migration from communities that did not provide adequate schooling. So important was the provision of secondary schooling to the children of rural America that youths often went to live with relatives in towns and cities when their local district did not provide such education, and sometimes entire families moved to the closest town when their oldest child graduated from the local common school. Hence, one good reason for building schools in rural America was "to stop the drift of the population to the cities."[11]

The second appeal in the epigraph concerns a pivotal factor in the expansion of public high schools. If the creation of a literate citizenry was not a good enough reason for publicly funded secondary schooling, the justification had to come from another market failure or externality—the inability of the capital market alone to effect the optimal transfer of resources both within and between generations. Communities composed of different generations, however, could solve this problem. First, the established members of the community could lend to young parents during the most stressful portion of their economic life cycle, when they are not yet at their peak earning capacity. Then, this generation could pay back the loan when it, in turn, became the next older generation. Selling that logic to a current older generation also meant selling the idea that an educated community conferred positive externalities as a place where the aged could depend on their neighbors. With this reasoning, the older generation would be convinced to buy into the plan, and the younger generation would not defect as it aged.[12]

Two points are important to make at this juncture. One is that a vibrant and self-replicating community was a blessing to older residents, especially in areas with long harsh winters. Another is that just because good schools induced some young people and families to stay put does not mean that extensive out-migrations did not flow from these areas. In many of the states of the

11   State of Iowa, *Iowa School Report, 1911/12* (Des Moines, 1912), 12. In Willa Cather's novel, *My Antonia* (Boston, 1918), which takes place in south-central Nebraska in the 1890s, Jim Burden's grandparents retire from farming and move to town so that he can attend the local high school.

12   For a similar argument see Gary S. Becker and Kevin M. Murphy, "The Family and the State," *Journal of Law and Economics,* XXXI (1988), 1–18.

Great Plains, for example, education was not just good for the existing community; it was also good for those who wanted to leave the region and give up farming.

A FRAMEWORK OF HIGH SCHOOL EXPANSION: PUBLIC AND PRIVATE CONCERNS   Attendance at, and graduation from, high school was considered beneficial to individuals and families because of its potential private returns. But communities were crucial; they, and only they, could provide the means by which all children could attend secondary school. Our implicit model of the expansion of high schools concerns both decision-making bodies.

At the family or individual level, consider the private decision of investing in education in a two-period framework. In period 1, the individual earns a wage of w_1 and does not attend school; in period 2, the same individual earns a wage of w_2. Alternatively, the individual can attend school in period 1, pay C in direct costs (for example, tuition, transportation, and books), and earn nothing. In period 2, however, the individual with schooling earns $E_2 > w_2$. Given a one-period discount rate of r, the decision to attend school in period 1 depends on whether

$$\frac{\frac{E_2}{w_2} - 1}{1 + r} > \frac{C + w_1}{w_2},$$

which simply means that the individual will go to school if the discounted returns to education (left side) exceed the first-period costs (right side).[13]

The simple framework leads us to consider the high school wage premium (E_2/w_2), the costs of education (direct, C/w_2, and indirect, w_1/w_2), and the discount rate (r), which is a measure of capital-market constraints facing individuals and families, as they affect the private demand for education. High school enrollment decisions are positively affected by the high school wage premium and negatively affected by the costs of education and the discount rate. The private demand for high school is also likely to depend positively on family wealth (or income) through an income effect on the consumption demand for education and by the easing of

13   On the human capital model, see Becker, *Human Capital* (New York, 1964).

capital-market constraints (that is, increased wealth effectively lowers r).

But this simple human-capital framework says nothing about one of the most obvious facts of education—its almost-ubiquitous public provision. Why do communities at the local, state, and national levels tax their citizens to provide education for other people's children? Public funding was part of an intergenerational loan. According to this view, homogeneous communities, in which people tend to remain and take an active interest in each other, would be more likely to provide intergenerational loans. In a manner similar to Coleman's notion of "closure," the degree to which community members saw themselves as part of a generational succession would determine their support for the high school, especially during its formative years.[14]

On the other hand, communities in which wealth or income was unequally distributed would encounter substantial opposition to the high school movement. Because schooling is a private good and because, before the 1930s, few legal constraints were in place to compel youths to attend high school, those at the bottom of the distribution could opt out entirely. Those at the top of the distribution might have opted out by attending private schools. Thus, the wider the distribution of income, the greater was the chance of encountering a political equilibrium in which the poor and the rich joined to defeat the public provision of a high school; such an equilibrium is aptly termed "the ends against the middle."[15]

14 By "closure" Coleman means the results of any mechanism that links social relationships to facilitate the drawing on social capital. For example, assume that school children do better when their parents take an interest in them and that parents are "shamed" when others see that they do not do homework with their children. Closure may be facilitated when parents get together and discuss how to help their children with homework. The parental meeting is a "social structure that facilitates social capital" (Coleman, "Social Capital in the Creation of Human Capital," S105). See also Coleman, *Foundations of Social Theory* (Cambridge, Mass., 1990), chap. 12, 300–321.

15 In 1917, for example, although thirty states had a maximum age of sixteen years for compulsory schooling, all but four granted labor permits at, or before, age fourteen, and the remaining four granted them at age fifteen. The education required for a labor permit was nowhere more than eight years and exactly eight years in just five states. In 1928, the maximum age of compulsory schooling had increased to eighteen in five states and to seventeen in another five states. But labor permits were still issued to those under sixteen in all but two states, and the education required for a labor permit was nowhere greater than eight years. The laws do not appear to have constrained youths to remain in high school, let alone to have graduated from high school. See Ward W. Keesecker, *Laws Relating to*

The "social capital" needed to produce human capital is a function of factors that create "closure," binding generations to each other and creating a belief that educated youth will later benefit older community members. Recent work has shown that communities fragmented by ethnicity or language or comprised of persons who migrated to the community in their older age tend to be less supportive of educational expenditures. In our empirical work, we use proxies for these variables: the fraction foreign born, the fraction Catholic, the fraction older than sixty-five years, and the distribution of wealth, itself proxied by another variable.[16]

Our exploration of the factors influencing high school expansion takes place at four levels of aggregation. First, at the national level, we look at variation in high school graduation rates for a cross section of states, and in attendance rates across different-sized cities and towns. We then focus on Iowa—a leading state in the high school movement—first at the county level and then at the family and individual level, using the Iowa State Census of 1915.

FACTORS INFLUENCING HIGH SCHOOL EXPANSION AT THE STATE LEVEL   Figure 2 graphs the percentage of youths in various regions of the United States who graduated from high school in the year given. The contemporaneous graduation rate is a "cleaner" variable than enrollment or attendance, in the sense that it permits less ambiguity in its meaning. Because we summarize our previous work in this section, we do not give data on all

Compulsory Education (Washington, D.C., 1929). See Dennis Epple and Richard E. Romano, "Ends Against the Middle: Determining Public Service Provision When There Are Private Alternatives," Journal of Public Economics, LXII (1996), 297–326, and Raquel Fernandez and Richard Rogerson, "On the Political Economy of Education Subsidies," Review of Economic Studies, LXII (1995), 249–262, for the role of income distribution in public-choice models of education.

16   James Poterba, "Demographic Structure and the Political Economy of Public Education," Journal of Policy Analysis and Management, XVI (1997), 48–66, finds that the greater the growth in the proportion of older people in U.S. states from 1961 to 1991, the lower was the growth in funding for K–12 education. Alberto Alesina, Reza Baqir, and William Easterly, "Public Goods and Ethnic Divisions," NBER working paper 6007 (Cambridge, Mass., 1997), finds a negative relationship between ethnic fractionalization and spending on "productive" public goods, including education, in a cross section of U.S. localities c. 1990.

Fig. 2 Public and Private High School Graduation Rates for Four Regions, 1910 to 1958

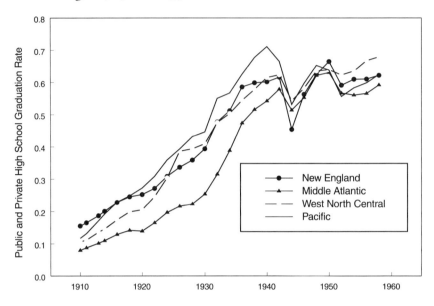

NOTES   The public and private high school graduation rate is the number of individuals graduating from high school in a state (summed to the regional level) divided by the number of seventeen-year-olds in a particular year. Graduation from high school includes those in public, private nonsectarian, and private-denominational schools, as well as individuals in the preparatory departments of colleges and universities.

SOURCES   See Goldin, Appendix to "How America Graduated from High School: An Exploratory Study, 1910 to 1960," National Bureau of Economic Research-Development of the American Economy working paper 57 (Cambridge, Mass., 1994) for details concerning the construction of the series.

regions in Figure 2. Rather, the figure shows the regions that included many of the leading states (New England, West North Central, and Pacific) and one region containing some of the nonsouthern laggards (Middle Atlantic). Although New England led the country in the proportion of its youth passing through secondary schools in 1910, it was soon eclipsed by many of the states in the West. By the mid-1920s, more than 40 percent of youths in the Pacific states were graduating from high school. Other leading states in the high school movement were those in the nation's heartland—prominent among them being Iowa, Kansas, and Nebraska. The states of the Middle Atlantic closed much of their gap with the leading states in the 1930s, when the Depression shut down the employment route for many youths.[17]

The maps of Figure 3 tell much the same story but highlight various areas of the country that figure prominently in our later discussion. In 1910, the darkest areas of the map, those with the highest rates of high school graduation, were in New England, although some were scattered in the mid-section of the nation. But by 1928, the highest graduation rates occurred clear across the mid-section of the United States, in "the education belt," stretching from the Pacific states through Utah, Colorado, Nebraska, Kansas, Iowa, Indiana, and then jumping to New England. The southern states, it is no surprise, lagged. Although we do not show this information in the graph, the South was behind in all periods of the high school movement, not simply because blacks were less educated; high school graduation rates for southern white youths were also below the nation's.

In a previous study, we analyzed the factors that encouraged high school graduation, attempting to explain why certain parts of the country led in the high school movement whereas others did not. We employed both state-level data at various points in time from 1910 to 1938, and city-level data in 1910, 1920, and 1930. In the state-level analysis, we looked at a series of cross sections, as well as at changes from 1910 to 1928 and 1928 to 1938. Some of the analysis is reproduced in Table 1.[18]

In keeping with the framework just discussed, our explanatory variables can be divided into two main types, the variables

17 Graduation rates are "cleaner" in the sense that most states accredited high schools and set standards for graduation, whereas enrollment rates could have been overstated for many reasons, including the state's method of funding local education. Some ambiguity remains, however, with regard to the quality of education and how it changed over time. The graduation rate is equal to the number of high school graduates (including those from private schools and the preparatory departments of colleges and universities) divided by the number of seventeen-year-olds in a given state during a particular year. It should be noted that the data in figures 1 and 2 are described in detail in Goldin, "Appendix," and were assembled from state-level data on public high schools, private high schools, and the preparatory departments of universities and colleges. Although they did not originate in the national graduation data given, for example, in U.S. Bureau of the Census, *Historical Statistics,* they track those national totals well. In all cases, they are contemporaneous data reflecting graduation from high school at a point in time and as a fraction of the youths in a state.

18 We have also estimated longitudinal models with state fixed-effects pooling data from 1910, 1920, and 1930. The results for the key variables are similar to those in the levels regressions presented in Table 1. But the effects of some variables (for example, percentage Catholic and manufacturing employment share) cannot be estimated precisely when state

Fig. 3 Public and Private High School Graduation Rates by State, 1910
and 1928

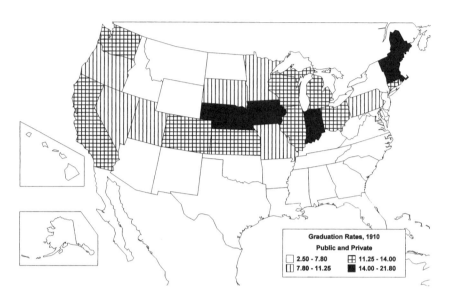

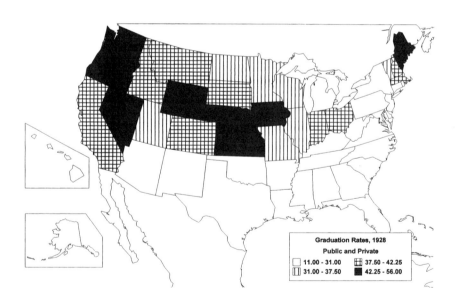

NOTES   See Figure 2. The shadings of the two maps allow an equal number of states to fall into each of the three shaded categories for the two years.

that influence the individual, or private, choice of education and the variables that affect the public, or social, choice of group action. Put another way, certain variables alter whether individuals invest in human capital, and certain others indicate whether social capital is available for the same investments. Some of the variables can be located in both arenas, though many are more clearly in one and not the other.

Table 1 presents cross-section regressions for 1910 and 1928, as well as a regression to explain the change in high school graduation rates from 1910 to 1928 as a function of initial conditions of states at the start of the high school movement in 1910. Because the regressions are cross-state, there are only forty-eight observations, and many of the variables of potential interest are collinear. The fraction Catholic, for example, is highly correlated both with the fractions foreign-born and urban; per capita income is similarly collinear with wealth per capita and agricultural income per farm worker. We have, therefore, chosen a set of variables that can stand in for many others.

In both 1910 and 1928, the high school graduation rate was positively related to various measures of wealth (or income) and negatively related to the opportunity cost of education (as proxied by the percentage of the labor force in manufacturing and the wage of manufacturing workers). Because educated labor was highly mobile, the wage relevant for those deciding whether to attend high school exhibited little cross-state variation. Hence, we do not include a measure of white-collar wages in the regressions. Yet, we find that states where a larger fraction of youth attended public colleges and universities in 1910 experienced faster growth in high school graduation rates from 1910 to 1928. Greater access to public universities is likely to have increased the private returns to high school, and it may also have been a reflection of the commitment of state residents to public education in general. Greater wealth in 1910 also hastened the growth of high schools from 1910 to 1928, whereas a larger share of manufacturing employment in 1910 modestly retarded it.

---

fixed effects are included, and coefficients are constrained to be constant over time, because of the strong persistence of state differences in these variables. For details, see Goldin and Katz, "Why the United States Led."

Table 1   Explaining Total (Public and Private) Secondary-School Graduation Rates by States, 1910 and 1928

	(1)	(2)	(3)
	1910	1928	1928–1910
Log per capita wealth, 1912 or 1922, $\times$ 10^{-1}	0.236	0.852	0.857
	(0.0901)	(0.368)	(0.260)
Fraction $\geq$ 65 years, 1910 or 1930	2.13	1.423	−1.749
	(0.260)	(0.788)	(0.737)
Fraction of labor force in manufacturing, 1910 or 1930	−0.0673	−0.144	−0.0495
	(0.0335)	(0.0972)	(0.0947)
Fraction Catholic, 1910 or 1926	−0.0913	−0.377	−0.265
	(0.0305)	(0.0867)	(0.0900)
South	−0.0449	−0.0935	−0.0735
	(0.00932)	(0.0272)	(0.0267)
New England	0.0444	0.100	0.0811
	(0.0121)	(0.0310)	(0.0333)
Males in public colleges/17-year-olds, 1910			1.09
			(0.384)
Auto registrations per capita, 1930, $\times$ 10		0.0568	
		(0.0230)	
Constant	−0.136	−0.468	−0.324
	(0.0709)	(0.273)	(0.199)
R^2	0.895	0.874	0.758
Root mean-squared error	0.0172	0.0451	0.0474
Mean (unweighted) of dependent variable	0.0882	0.291	0.212

NOTES   Standard errors are in parentheses; ordinary least-squares regressions, unweighted. Weighting by state population does not substantially affect the results. Number of observations is forty-eight for all regressions; the District of Columbia is not included. Arizona and New Mexico were territories until 1912 but are included in the data for 1910 states. The dependent variable in column (3) is the change in the total (public and private) high school graduation rate from 1910 to 1928; the independent variables in column (3) are measured in 1910 or the closest year possible.

SOURCES   For dependent variable, total (public and private) graduation rate by state, see Goldin, Appendix to "How America Graduated from High School: An Exploratory Study, 1910–1960," National Bureau of Economic Research-Development of the American Economy working paper 57 (Cambridge, Mass., 1994). Graduation rate divides by seventeen-year-olds in the state. Unweighted means of the independent variables are given in parentheses. For per capita wealth, 1912 ($1,934) or 1922 ($2,966), taxable wealth/population data come from U.S. Department of Commerce, *Statistical Abstract of the United States* (Washington, D.C., 1925). For fraction $\geq$ 65 years, 1910 (.0414), or 1930 (.055), see U.S. Bureau of the Census, *Historical Statistics* (Washington, D.C., 1975), 195–209. For fraction in labor force manufacturing, 1910 (.248), or 1930 (.254), see U.S. Bureau of the Census, *Thirteenth Census of the United States: 1910, Population* (Washington, D.C., 1912); U.S. Bureau of the Census, *Fifteenth Census of the United States: 1930, Population* (Washington, D.C., 1932), III. For fraction Catholic, 1910 (.150), or 1926 (.151), see U.S. Department of Commerce, *Religious Bodies: 1926* (Washington, D.C., 1930), I, Table 29. The 1910 numbers are derived from those of 1906 and 1916. All are expressed per state resident. South (0.354) includes the census divisions South Atlantic, East South Central, and West South Central. New England (0.125) is the census division of New England. For males in public colleges/17-year-olds, 1910 (.0316), see U.S. Department of the Interior, *Report of the Commissioner of Education* (Washington, D.C., 1910), Table 31, 850. Military academies receiving public support are excluded. Since the denominator includes both males and females, it is about equal to half the eighteen-to-twenty-one-year-old group of males. For auto registrations per capita, 1930 (0.224), see U.S. Bureau of Commerce, *Statistical Abstract of the United States* (Washington, D.C., 1940), Table 467.

Of most importance for the issues raised in this study, high school graduation is positively related to the proportion of the state's population over sixty-four-years old and negatively related to the proportion Catholic in both 1910 and 1928. In the 1928 regression, we also include a variable that captures important aspects of both the level and distribution of wealth. Since automobile registrations per capita in 1930 provide a count of those rich enough to afford a car, automobile registrations per capita summarizes mean wealth and its distribution in a form particularly relevant for decisions about the provision of a public good. It proxies the share of voters likely to favor financing so expensive a public good as high schools. At a high enough level of mean wealth, high automobile registrations per capita are likely to indicate a more equal distribution of wealth. No other variable has as large an effect on the high school graduation rate in the late 1920s and early 1930s as does automobile registrations per capita. The states with the highest in 1930—California, Nevada, Kansas, Nebraska, and Iowa—were also leaders in the expansion of high schools, as shown in the bottom panel of Figure 3. The strong positive effect of automobile registrations per capita on high school graduation rates in 1928, as shown in column (2) of Table 1, is apparent, even when state mean per capita wealth is also included as a regressor.

The distribution of wealth is an important input to the political and social decisions to fund high schools. Stability and homogeneity of community, as well as many of the more familiar and better-understood variables thought to affect human capital decisions, were important in the diffusion of the high school across America during the period of the high school movement. The state-level analysis points to many of the public and private factors that propelled the high school movement and reveals the types of states that led in secondary education. Because many of the leading states were rich agricultural areas, they were also thickly dotted with small towns and villages that served the agricultural hinterland. The high school movement appears to have found its greatest support in these small towns and villages.

Table 2 gives the full-time school attendance of sixteen- and seventeen-year-olds by size and type of place for 1910 and 1920 in all nonsouthern states. The attendance rates in the smallest towns were more than double those in the largest cities in 1910,

Table 2   "Full Time" School Attendance Rates for Sixteen- and Seventeen-Year-Olds: U.S. Non-South, by Size and Type of Place, 1910 and 1920

SIZE AND TYPE OF PLACE	1910 (%)	1920 (%)
Rural (unincorporated or < 1,000 population)	37.7	38.7
unincorporated	36.3	—[a]
incorporated and < 1,000 population	48.1	—[a]
Town (1,000 < 10,000 population)	40.5	43.9
1,000 < 2,500 population	45.7	47.3
2,500 < 10,000 population	37.7	42.0
Small city (10,000 < 25,000 population)	36.9	35.1
City (> 25,000 population)	26.1	31.7
25,000 < 100,000 population	31.5	35.9
100,000 < 500,000 population	28.8	33.8
≥500,000 population	21.3	28.2
Number of observations	9,607	11,955

[a] The 1920 data do not separate the unincorporated areas from the small incorporated villages.
NOTES   "Full time" school attendance means that the youth attended school at some point after September 1 of the previous year and was not currently working during the census year (that is, no occupation was given in the census). The pattern of results displayed in this table for both 1910 and 1920 are similar (but modestly attenuated) in logit models or linear regressions of full-time school attendance on a full set of indicator variables for size of place, as well as in detailed controls for race, foreign-born status, parents' foreign-born status, household head's occupation, and region.
SOURCES   1910 Public Use Micro-data Sample (PUMS) of the U.S. federal population census of 1910; 1920 Integrated Public Use Micro-data Sample (IPUMS) of the U.S. federal population census of 1920.

and, in both years, attendance rates declined monotonically as the size of place increased for incorporated areas. Even the unincorporated rural places of the United States, which were mainly farming areas of the open country, had higher attendance rates than did the larger cities. The site of the early high school movement appears to be those small communities in which social capital may have been the greatest. That many of the leading states in the high school movement through the early 1930s—such as Nebraska, Kansas, South Dakota, and Iowa—were also those that had large numbers of school districts relative to population (few people per school district) further indicates that the decisions made by small, wealthy, homogeneous communities facilitated expensive collective investments in high schools. We will return to the role of the small town in our analysis of the Iowa data.[19]

19   "Full time" attendance means that the youth attended school for at least one day since September 1 in the previous year and did not list an occupation. We include only nonsouthern states to avoid conflating rural and small town with the South in the simple cross tabulations. The attendance data in Table 2 probably overstate the proportion of youths in secondary

SECONDARY SCHOOLING IN THE HEARTLAND: CASE STUDY OF IOWA, 1915   Iowa was both an early leader in the high school movement and part of the education belt that formed in the 1920s. It was also among the richest states in the union on a per capita basis in both 1912 and 1922. In 1912, it ranked second, behind Nevada, and in 1922, fourth, behind Nevada, Wyoming, and South Dakota in per capita taxable wealth. It pioneered in the standardized testing of its youth, had a widespread system of private colleges and universities, established leading research centers in its public universities, and was the birthplace of agricultural extension in America. In the early twentieth century, Iowans wanted to make the superiority of their educational system known to the rest of the country and prove that their state was just as respectable as those of the northeast, from which many of their ancestors had come.[20]

With its 1915 population census, Iowa became the first state to request information from its citizens about their educational attainment and current school attendance. The responses, not surprisingly, allowed the state proudly to note that "for the first time there has been secured information showing the extent of education of the entire population and the results confirm the

---

schools, because the U.S. federal population censuses of 1910 and 1920 inquired whether an individual had attended school at least one day during the preceding year. Attendance could have been at a night, correspondence, industrial, music, commercial, private, parochial, or regular-day school, among others. Furthermore, many young people, especially in the open country, could have been attending common schools at age 16 and 17, not state-accredited high schools. Margaret E. Greene and Jerry A. Jacobs, "Urban Enrollments and the Growth of Schooling: Evidence from the U.S. 1910 Census Public Use Sample," *American Journal of Education,* CI (1992), 29–59, report similar results for 1910, regarding the role of small towns.

The cross-state correlation of school districts per capita in 1932 and the high school graduation rate in 1928 is 0.49. This significant positive relationship between the density of school districts and high graduation rates remains in high school graduation regressions that control for population density or the urban share of the population. It is apparent even when examining only states outside the South. But the number of school districts per capita is closely related to wealth, automobile registrations per capita, and agricultural income per farm worker; it is not statistically significant in such regressions that include proxies for wealth.

20 On per capita wealth data, see the sources in Table 1; Goldin and Katz, "Why the United States Led."

The city of Des Moines used its local commercial magazine, *Des Moines Wealth,* to broadcast the superiority of its school system in comparison with all others in the United States. "Des Moines therefore equals all and excels most cities in . . . school attendance in proportion to population, high school enrollment, number of teachers in proportion to the size of the school system, and salaries paid to the teachers. . . . Des Moines is recognized the country over as a grand school city" (*Des Moines Wealth,* II [June 1910], 15).

general belief that Iowa people rank very high in educational matters."[21]

The Iowa state census of 1915, like most other censuses, was a 100 percent sample of the citizens of the state. The volume, *Census of Iowa, 1915,* contains detailed tables that highlight aspects of the population by county. Its manuscript census, which consists of one three-by-five index card per person, has been filed by county, arranged alphabetically by last name. In 1986, the Church of Jesus Christ of Latter-day Saints microfilmed all the cards. Several researchers have collected samples from this unique census, but because of the idiosyncratic nature of these data sets, we have collected our own. Ours is a cluster sample of three large cities (Davenport, Des Moines, and Dubuque) and eight "rural" counties. Several medium-sized cities are also in our "rural" sample, as are a large number of smaller towns and villages. We have also assembled a county-level data set from the Iowa state census of 1915 and various federal censuses.[22]

Even though schooling rates were high in Iowa, the percentage of teenagers who currently attend high school and who ever attended high school show considerable variation across the state. Across Iowa's ninety-nine counties in 1914, the proportion of ten-to-twenty-year-olds with any high school ranged from 0.11 to 0.31, and the proportion of ten-to-eighteen-year-olds currently attending high school varied from 0.086 to 0.32. In 1914, high school enrollment rates (measured by the ratio of students in high schools to the population aged fourteen to seventeen years) by region ranged from a low of 0.143 in the South Atlantic to a high of 0.351 in New England. Thus, Iowa's counties spanned a range similar to that of all regions at the same time. To understand the reasons why communities did, or did not, invest in high schools during the early period of the high school movement, we first

21   State of Iowa, *Iowa State Census, 1915* (Des Moines, 1916), xxxvi. Only one other state (South Dakota in 1915) asked about educational attainment before the federal population census did in 1940. Iowa repeated the question in its 1925 state census.
22   Richard Jensen and Mark Friedberger, "Education and Social Structure: An Historical Study of Iowa, 1870–1930," unpub. paper, Newberry Library (Chicago, Il. 1976), collected a sample from the original cards stored in Des Moines and linked it to both the 1925 Iowa State Census and the federal population manuscripts. Daniel Scott Smith, "'The Number and Quality of Children': Education and Marital Fertility in Early Twentieth-Century Iowa," *Journal of Social History,* XXX (1996), 367–393, collected another sample designed for a fertility project.

explore, in Table 3, county-wide variation in high school education.

THE HIGH SCHOOL MOVEMENT IN IOWA: COUNTY-LEVEL ANALYSIS
The county-level data that we have at our disposal contain a rich set of variables. Many wealth and income variables are available, including per capita (or per farm) values for land and crops, and the assessment of property for taxes. Detailed information exists about church going, the number of congregations, the demographic and ethnic composition of the population, and the occupational distribution of the population in Iowa's counties c. 1915. The regressions presented in Table 3 are illustrative of a broader set of results using alternative wealth and income measures. Measures of county wealth and agricultural income have strong positive effects on high school and college attendance. None of the ethnic-composition variables matter once the proportion of the population with native parentage is included. The share of Catholics in the county population is negatively correlated with high school attendance, but the variable is highly collinear with the share of the population with foreign-born parents. The dependency ratio (fraction of those younger than five years) matters negatively for high school attainment and attendance rates, and indicators of the presence of a college in the county are positively related to high school attendance.

Of most interest regarding the issues raised in this study is that the proportion attending, or ever attending, high school reached a peak in those counties with the largest share of their population in the smallest of Iowa's towns—incorporated areas with fewer than 1,700 persons. The case of those who ever attended high school shows a 10 percentage point difference between the effects of county population share in the largest cities and those in the smallest towns. In the case of those currently attending, the difference is more than 4 percentage points, even in the reported regression models in Table 3 with controls for the income, wealth, and demographic composition of the population. The finding is similar to that derived from the somewhat less reliable school-attendance data in the 1910 and 1920 Public Use Micro-data Sample of the U.S. population census, and it appears to be robust even with the inclusion of wealth or income measures as controls. There appears to be compelling evidence that the early

Table 3 Determinants of High School and College Attendance at the County Level, Iowa, 1915

	(1) EVER ATTENDED HIGH SCHOOL		(2) CURRENTLY ATTENDING HIGH SCHOOL		
	β	STANDARD ERROR	β	STANDARD ERROR	MEAN
Proportion of 10-to-20-year-olds with some high school, col. (1)					0.196
Proportion of 10-to-18-year-olds currently attending high school, col. (2)					0.163
Value of cereals per farm $\times$ 10^{-3}, 1910	0.0524	0.0113	0.0212	0.00481	1.063
Per capita tax assessment $\times$ 10^{-2}					4.36
Proportion of population native born, with native parentage	0.103	0.0201	0.118	0.0251	0.613
Proportion of population < 5 years old	-1.092	0.360	-1.069	0.459	0.104
Whether college or university is in county (dummy variable)[a]	0.0256	0.00861			0.111
College students as a proportion of the population			0.650	0.169	0.00597
Whether county is on the Missouri or Mississippi (dummy variable)[b]	-0.0222	0.00678	-0.0113	0.00902	0.192
Proportion of population in incorporated towns with[b]					
population > 10,000 persons in 1915	0.130	0.0327	0.148	0.0361	0.104
population 2,500 ≤ 10,000 persons	0.169	0.0404	0.155	0.0491	0.126
population 1,700 ≤ 2,500 persons	0.222	0.0679	0.178	0.0859	0.030
population ≤ 1,700 persons[c]	0.237	0.0508	0.191	0.0642	0.208
Constant	0.0438	0.0922	0.0270	0.0678	
R^2	0.661		0.516		
Root mean-squared error	0.0236		0.0313		
Number of observations	99		99		

[a] College or university with a 1915 student population > 200.

[b] Omitted group is rural, unincorporated.

[c] Individuals living in incorporated towns and villages with less than 1,700 people.

NOTES   Dependent variable for col. (1) is the number of persons less than twenty-one years of age who ever attended high school (or college), divided by the number of persons ten to twenty years old in the county. Because colleges and universities often had preparatory departments, some people would have claimed to have attended college but not high school. Dependent variable for col. (2) is the number of persons ten to twenty years old currently attending high school, divided by the number of persons ten to eighteen years old in the county. Also included in the col. (1) regression is the fraction of ten-to-twenty-year-olds who were eighteen to twenty years old, to account for the age composition of the group. Value of cereals per farm is the total value of cereal crops produced in the county divided by the total number of farms in the county.

SOURCES   U.S. Bureau of the Census, *Thirteenth Census of the United States, Agriculture* (Washington, D.C., 1913), VI, for farm data; all other information is from State of Iowa, *Census of Iowa for the Year 1915* (Des Moines, 1915).

high school movement was most strongly felt in the small towns and villages of the West and Midwest.[23]

Why these small places had the highest rates of high school attendance is not entirely clear at this point. One possibility is that small-town America offered young people virtually nothing else to do during much of the year. In the open country, they could work on the farms, and they had limited access to secondary schools in any event. In the larger cities, they could find employment in a number of jobs. But those in the smaller towns may have had neither option.

Another potentially complementary reason is that small-town America was a locus of associations (religious, fraternal/sororal, business, and political organizations) that could have played an important role in galvanizing support for the provision of local publicly provided goods, including high schools. By all accounts, the towns and villages across America were teeming with such associations. Although they may not have provided the direct impetus for the high school movement, they certainly provide another indicator of community cohesion.[24]

We have attempted to assess the extent to which the differences in educational attainment by size of place reflect the density of such associations by adding a variable that measures the number of church congregations per capita to the regression specifications shown in Table 3. Church congregations per capita for Iowa counties c. 1915 were positively related to the share of the population in small towns and negatively related to the share in larger cities. The variable has a positive but insignificant relationship to the fraction of youth who ever attended high school, and its inclusion only slightly reduces the substantial gap in high school

23   These findings are also corroborated in an analysis, not presented here, using the individual-level data from our "rural" sample. We have matched the post-office addresses or town given in the Iowa census to information about the size of the town. Among fifteen-to-twenty-year-olds, those residing in towns of between 1,000 and 3,500 population attained the greatest number of years of high school and college. We also include controls for county, Iowa City, sex, church affiliation, nativity of parents, whether the household head was a farmer, and an indicator variable for whether the individual could be matched to a household head.
24   Gerald Gamm and Robert D. Putnam, "The Growth of Voluntary Associations in America, 1840–1940," published in this issue, find that the smallest towns in their sample had the largest number of associations per capita and that the largest cities had the smallest number. The towns in their study, however, are somewhat larger than those we are able to identify in the Iowa data.

attainment between the smallest towns and the largest cities found in column (1) of Table 3. In contrast, church congregations per capita has a strong positive and statistically significant relation to the fraction of youth currently attending high school. It attenuates the weaker differences by size of place when it is added to the specification in column (2) of Table 3. The greater high school attendance rates in small towns seems to be partially mediated by a thicker density of community and religious associations.

Even if associations were not the glue that bound the residents of small-town America closer together, other aspects of the small town might have been. Small towns simply had greater ethnic, religious, cultural, and economic homogeneity. Whatever the underlying reasons, we have uncovered convincing evidence that the smaller towns of Iowa had the highest rates of secondary-school attendance.

WHO GAINED FROM THE HIGH SCHOOL MOVEMENT IN IOWA, C.1915? Thus far, we have explored differences in high school (and college) attendance by county, showing the importance of county-specific factors that could reflect differences in social capital. The smallest towns and villages, literally at the edge of the prairie, had higher levels of school attendance than did the larger towns and cities. We now move to an analysis of the impact of individual factors, those generally reflecting family background. Social and group factors, however, remain integral to the analysis.

The data are a sample of the individual records from the Iowa State Census of 1915, the published version of which formed the basis of the county analysis, for three major cities (Davenport, Des Moines, and Dubuque) and eight counties, each without a city containing more than 25,000 people. The two parts of the sample are termed "three large cities" and "counties without large cities." These counties were not simply farming areas; they contained many of the towns and villages that featured in the previous discussion. The samples together contain more than 53,000 observations, almost equally divided between the cities and "rural" counties. Although the records were not arranged in family units, we have, with much success, used last names, birthplaces, addresses, and "card numbers" to reconstitute families. We describe the sample and our family reconstitution procedure in the Appendix.

The variable of interest is the school attendance of fifteen to eighteen-year-olds, who would have been most affected by the high school movement. We consider two variants: whether the youth attended *any* school in 1914 and whether the youth attended high school or college in 1914. Although in the larger cities and towns, schooling between the ages of fifteen and eighteen would generally have taken place in a secondary school, those at the younger end of the age range could still have been in grammar school, and assessors might not have differentiated between high school and regular school. In the more rural areas, however, youths often remained in common schools into their mid-teens, especially if their districts did not contain a secondary school. But by 1914, youths in rural Iowa no longer had to attend common schools to receive education beyond the usual eight years.

By an act of the thirty-fourth Iowa General Assembly, passed in 1913 after numerous attempts, all youths in Iowa had the right to attend a high school free of charge, even if their district did not have one, the tuition to be paid by their home district. This "free tuition" law, as it was termed, was one of many that states with large populations in the "open country" passed in the 1910s and 1920s. The response to the "free tuition" law in Iowa was an increase in high schools throughout the state; if taxpayers had to pay tuition, they might as well build their own schools. By 1914, according to the Iowa State Census of 1915, secondary-school attendance equalled 31 percent of all fourteen-to-seventeen-year-olds.[25]

25 The "free tuition" laws are not well known, and we have been unable to find a source documenting when each was passed. State education reports reveal that Nebraska's, first passed in 1895 but declared unconstitutional, was the earliest. A bill that met the constitutional objection was enacted in 1907 after two more unsuccessful tries. Some states (for example, California, Kansas, Oregon, and Washington) passed free tuition laws at the county level. By the mid-1920s, virtually every state with a large rural population had a free tuition law on its books. See William R. Hood, *Legal Provisions for Rural High Schools* (Washington, D.C., 1925).

The high school enrollment rate computed from the Iowa State Census of 1915, using the ratio of the number of individuals of all ages who indicated that they attended high school in 1914 to the total number of fourteen-to-seventeen-year-olds, is almost identical to an analogous one computed from a set of contemporaneous records from high schools. The former estimate is 31.1 percent, whereas the latter estimate is 31.5 percent. We compute the former estimate by weighting the figures derived from the two parts of our sample (large cities and counties without large cities)—the weights being chosen to produce estimates representative of the overall state population in large cities and in counties without large cities

Why did some youths attend high school and others not? Table 4 reveals the effects of family background and individual characteristics on school attendance within counties and cities. In the fifteen-to-eighteen-year-old group, and among those whom we could match to household heads, 31 percent attended high school (or college) in the large cities and 24 percent in the eight rural counties. Almost 57 percent attended any school in the large cities and 55 percent in the rural counties.[26]

Among the determinants of attendance in high school (or college)—columns (3) and (6) of Table 4—are such characteristics as sex, church affiliation, and own and parental birthplace. Features of the household head, such as occupation, years of schooling, and home or farm ownership, are also included. Not surprisingly, youths from privileged families had a far higher probability of attending high school than others. The son or daughter of a household head who was a white-collar worker and had graduated from secondary school was 30 percentage points more likely to attend high school in the large cities than was the child of a blue-collar worker with eight years of school. A similarly large gap in the rural counties is apparent between youths living with a head of household who was a white-collar worker and those living with one who was a farmer. Foreign birth, for the child or the parents, was far less important, once education and occupation of the household head are included. Girls were more likely to attend school in the counties without large cities but not in the three large cities. Many have reported sex differences in secondary-school education, particularly in industrial settings, but the Iowa data reveal smaller differences.[27]

---

in 1915. The procedure for latter estimate, derived from a completely different set of data, is in Goldin, "Appendix."

26 The rural attendance rates are lower than those in the three large cities because the rural data include those in the "open country." The data from the Iowa State Census of 1915 enable a more accurate calculation of the percentage of youths attending school than do the federal population censuses of 1910 and 1920. School attendance in the Iowa State Census is given in months. A few students attended school for fewer than six months; most attended for nine and some for eight.

All the regressions in Table 4 have also been estimated using logits and probits with no important change in the underlying conclusions. We report the easier-to-interpret linear-probability models with appropriately adjusted robust standard errors.

27 Head of the family status was inferred using a simple algorithm that bestows head status to a married male in the household who meets various age criteria with respect to the children, or to a widowed or divorced male in the household in the absence of a married woman. In

The coefficients on church affiliation have enormous significance. The 1915 Iowa State Census is the earliest known United States document to give information about education and religion, as well as various economic variables for a large representative sample. Affiliation with any of the New England Protestant churches, including Congregational, or with a Jewish synagogue, increased the probability of attending high school by 20 to almost 30 percentage points above that of a person with no church affiliation in the city sample. The effect in the rural counties was highest for Congregationalists but remained substantial for the other New England Protestants. Those with no church affiliation in the city sample had the lowest school attendance. Certain religious denominations, such as Congregational and Quaker, founded liberal arts colleges and universities and had a long-standing involvement in education. But the difference between the group with no church affiliation and the others might have been due to the association of church affiliation in 1915, like today, with sociability in other dimensions and thus with parental pressure to keep children in school.[28]

Family characteristics were undoubtedly important in determining high school attendance. The more privileged may have taken greater advantage of the public school system, but the vast majority of the children in Iowa's high schools had more humble backgrounds. In the city sample, 64 percent of the fifteen to eighteen-year-olds in households headed by high school graduates were attending high school (or college) in 1914, compared with 27 percent of those in households headed by non–high school

the rural sample, 86.3 percent of the household heads were male and 9.4 percent were widowed (or divorced) women. In both samples, only 5 percent of household heads were married women who either did not correctly state their marital status or whose husbands were not found in the census. The inclusion of head's income and country of origin dummies does not alter the main results.

On sex differences in high school enrollment and graduation, see Goldin, "America's Graduation from High School," and on co-education in general, see Tyack and Elisabeth Hansot, *Learning Together: A History of Coeducation in American Schools* (New Haven, 1990).

28 See Edward Glaeser and Spencer Glendon, "The Demand for Religion," Harvard University working paper (Cambridge, Mass., 1997) for the relationship between economic success and religion using modern data. They find that individuals claiming no religious belief have similar amounts of education than those with religious beliefs, but have far lower incomes. Note that the Iowa State Census asked "church affiliation," whereas Glaeser and Glendon use a question on religious belief. The variable in the 1915 Iowa State Census is an associational measure rather than one concerning beliefs.

Table 4 Determinants of School Attendance of Fifteen-to-Eighteen-Year-Olds, Youths Matched to an Adult Household Head, Iowa State Census, 1915

	COUNTIES WITHOUT LARGE CITIES[a]			THREE LARGE CITIES[b]		
	(1) MEANS	(2) ANY SCHOOL	(3) HIGH SCHOOL OR COLLEGE	(4) MEANS	(5) ANY SCHOOL	(6) HIGH SCHOOL OR COLLEGE
Female	.476	.021 (.022)	.037 (.019)	.502	.001 (.024)	.009 (.024)
Foreign-born	.020	-.209 (.086)	-.129 (.052)	.040	-.247 (.068)	-.112 (.064)
Native-born, with foreign-born father	.290	-.089 (.034)	-.097 (.029)	.274	.050 (.033)	.045 (.034)
Native-born, with foreign-born mother	.232	-.051 (.035)	.017 (.029)	.218	-.134 (.036)	-.101 (.036)
Church affiliation of youth						
Catholic	.195	-.054 (.033)	-.059 (.029)	.241	.080 (.037)	.065 (.036)
Lutheran	.095	-.030 (.047)	-.008 (.035)	.082	.067 (.050)	.072 (.045)
Congregationalist	.031	.255 (.064)	.283 (.072)	.022	.107 (.084)	.237 (.086)
New England Protestant[c]	.049	.108 (.054)	.124 (.053)	.056	.213 (.054)	.280 (.061)
Methodist	.088	.058 (.043)	.100 (.043)	.101	.137 (.045)	.139 (.047)
Baptist	.024	.006 (.077)	-.055 (.067)	.027	.270 (.070)	.021 (.081)
Other Christian religion	.102	-.003 (.041)	.063 (.035)	.127	.070 (.044)	.119 (.043)
Jewish	.000	—	—	.029	.124 (.082)	.210 (.089)

Family head's occupation, white collar	.123	.043 (.037)	.095 (.041)	.271	.153 (.031)	.185 (.033)
Family head's occupation, farmer	.544	-.118 (.026)	-.183 (.023)	.011	-.053 (.130)	.012 (.149)
Family head's years of schooling	8.15	.009 (.004)	.017 (.004)	8.32	.019 (.005)	.028 (.005)
Family owns farm or home	.662	.104 (.025)	.085 (.021)	.469	.046 (.026)	.048 (.025)
R^2		.200	.160		.234	.157
Sample size		1,806	1,806		1,413	1,413
Mean of dependent variable		.545	.243		.566	.306

[a] A large city is one with more than 25,000 people.

[b] The three cities are Davenport, Des Moines, and Dubuque.

[c] New England Protestant, other than Congregational, includes Presbyterian, Quaker, and Unitarian.

NOTES   The dependent variable in cols. (2) and (5) equals 1 if the youth reported attending any school (common, grammar, high school, or college) during 1914; it equals 0 otherwise. The dependent variable in cols. (3) and (6) equals 1 if the youth reported attending high school or college during 1914; it equals 0 otherwise. The base group for religion is "no church affiliation reported." Each regression also includes an intercept, three year-of-age dummies, and a dummy variable for "missing" family head's years of schooling. The regressions in cols. (2) and (3) also include seven dummy variables for counties. Those reported in cols. (5) and (6) include two dummy variables for cities. The numbers in parentheses are Huber–White robust standard errors that account for both correlated errors within households (because there can be more than one child in a household) and heterscedasticity. The regressions in cols. (5) and (6) are weighted by city sampling weights to reflect the different rates of our sampling Davenport, Des Moines, and Dubuque.

SOURCE   Iowa State Census of 1915 urban and rural samples. See Appendix.

graduates. Yet, even though those from more privileged backgrounds disproportionately attended high school, just 20 percent of high school students came from families in which the household head was a high school graduate. Similar results obtain in the rural counties (even excluding the farm population). That differences existed by parental background is understandable. The important point is that despite these differences, the vast majority of public high school students in Iowa had parents who did not have a high school diploma and were not white-collar workers. The non-elites were sufficiently numerous to have easily voted for the greater expenditures to support the high schools.[29]

WHAT WERE THE RETURNS TO HIGH SCHOOL IN IOWA, C.1915? At the outset of this article, we noted that many of the reasons for the expansion of secondary education could be traced to the pecuniary returns to attending high school. The problem for those researching the subject has been the lack of national data on education and earnings before the federal census of 1940. In a previous study comparing earnings for occupations that generally demanded secondary schooling with earnings for occupations that did not, we found a substantial wage premium at the start of the high school movement. The Iowa State Census sample enables a more direct estimation of the returns to high school for the population reporting occupational income for 1914. Table 5 reports results from estimating log (annual earnings) equations for three groups of non-farm workers—males eighteen to seventy years old, males eighteen to thirty-four years old, and unmarried females eighteen to thirty-four years old. The specifications include measures of schooling attainment, and controls for potential labor-market experience, nativity, and years in the United States for the foreign born.[30]

---

29 Educational differences by family background would also have been large if we had considered elite occupations rather than the schooling of the household head. George S. Counts, "The Selective Character of American Secondary Education," *The School Review and The Elementary School Journal,* XIX (May 1922), 40, made similar points about differences in school attendance by father's occupation in Mt. Vernon, N.Y. But in Count's data, by the senior year of high school, almost 88 percent of all students were the children of white-collar workers, whereas 49 percent were in sixth grade.
30 On earnings for different occupations and the educational wage premium, see Goldin and Katz, "Decline of Noncompeting Groups."

Table 5 Estimates of the Returns to Education by Type of Schooling for Non-Farm Occupations from Log(Annual Earnings) Regressions, Iowa State Census, 1915

	MALES, 18 TO 70 YEARS	MALES, 18 TO 34 YEARS	FEMALES, UNMARRIED, 18 TO 34 YEARS
Linear spline function in education			
Years of common school ≤ 9	.046	.070	.016
	(.004)	(.006)	(.012)
Years of common school ≥ 10	.007	.009	.022
	(.011)	(.018)	(.027)
Years of grammar school ≤ 9	.071	.101	.060
	(.004)	(.006)	(.011)
Years of grammar school ≥ 10	.032	.027	−.002
	(.019)	(.024)	(.062)
Years of high school	.104	.119	.125
	(.005)	(.006)	(.008)
Years of college × (years of high school > 0)	.098	.122	.145
	(.006)	(.009)	(.014)
Years of college × (years of high school = 0)	.047	.102	.026
	(.017)	(.035)	(.047)
College but no high school, dummy	.281	.172	.414
	(.053)	(.085)	(.113)
Business school, dummy	.403	.281	.474
	(.074)	(.088)	(.100)
Native-born	.206	.129	−.011
	(.027)	(.035)	(.081)
(Years in U.S. × 10^{-2}) × foreign-born	.488	.261	−.004
	(.095)	(.258)	(.006)
R^2	.233	.270	.310
Standard error (root mean-squared error)	.580	.526	.554
Number of observations	10,734	5,169	1,897

NOTES   The dependent variable in each regression is log (total annual earnings for 1914 from occupation). Each regression also includes an intercept, a quartic in potential experience (age − total years of schooling − 6), a non-white dummy, and a dummy for whether years in the United States is missing. The samples consist of all individuals in the appropriate age–sex–marital-status group in non-farm occupations reporting positive 1914 earnings, without missing data for age, schooling, race, or nativity. The regression pools the sample containing counties without large cities and that with the three large cities (Davenport, Des Moines, and Dubuque). Observations are weighted to reflect the different sampling rates in the two samples to make the regressions representative for the entire population of Iowa (except for individuals in the rural areas of counties containing large cities).

SOURCE   Iowa State Census of 1915 urban and rural samples. See Appendix.

The schooling-attainment measures given in the Iowa State Census allow us to differentiate among various types of schools. Most Iowans living in the open country would have attended a common school for their elementary years, whereas their urban counterparts would have gone to a grammar (or graded) school. Members of either group could have continued to high school, college, business school, or any other type of school. Early in this century, many individuals went to common and grammar schools for more than eight years. In some cases, as discussed earlier, common schools took up the task of educating rural teenagers who did not have high schools to attend. In other cases, however, common-school attendance beyond eight years meant that the student had been "retained," or held back. We can compute the returns to years of common- and grammar-school education beyond the usual number to see whether the added years substituted for secondary school or were simply remedial by entering the schooling variables as a linear spline function.[31]

Most important to our understanding of the high school movement is that the return to a year of secondary school is substantial in all three estimations. It is 10 percent for males of all ages, 12 percent for the younger group, and 12.5 percent for the younger group of females. The returns per year of high school are about equal to those for each year of college.[32]

Since it was not unusual in the nineteenth and early twentieth centuries for individuals to have attended college without having gone to high school—either because they went to a preparatory department of a college or because they were tutored at home—we must include variables accounting for returns to years of college when years of high school were zero. Three college variables are entered: One interacts years of college with a dummy variable when years of high school are greater than zero; one interacts years of college with a dummy variable when there is no

31 See Goldin, "America's Graduation from High School," on the importance of figuring out whether the added years should be considered as secondary or grammar school. Older Americans in 1940—the first year when the federal census inquired about educational attainment—appear to have vastly overstated their years of education in comparison with data from secondary schools, contemporaneous with their possible attendance. One possibility is that many Americans attended grades nine through twelve in common schools.
32 The estimated returns to high school are similar in specifications that also include controls for church affiliation, county, city, and parents' nativity.

high school; and one is a dummy variable for college when there is no high school. The results suggest that the returns to a year of college in the absence of high school, for the younger group, are about the same as those to a year of high school. That is, young men who did not list any high school but who went on to college most likely attended the preparatory department of their college or university. The business school dummy is substantial for both men and women.[33]

The returns to the lower grades show that extra years of either common- or grammar-school education had scant returns, if any. That is, extra years at the elementary school level do not appear to have substituted in any way for years in high school. The return to a year of high school was considerably higher than for the extra years at the lower grades. Only for the older men in the sample did the return to more than ten years of grammar school amount to a nontrivial magnitude, but even then, it was one-third of that earned for a year of high school.

In sum, the returns to education by type of schooling for non-farm occupations show that secondary education had a substantial payoff in Iowa c. 1915. A return on the order of 12 percent per year is one-and-one-half times the return to a year of college in 1980, and about the same as that to a year of college in 1995, a time when returns are considered to have been notably high.[34]

The high school movement, which picked up steam around 1910 in the Great Plains, Far West, and parts of New England and the Midwest, was an enormous undertaking for local government. The cost of moving a generation of young people through four years of high school was equal to, if not more than, the value of

33   The returns that we calculate do *not* net out the direct costs of education, which would have been substantial for many business schools but close to zero for public high schools. Most individuals who stated that they attended a business school went for few years, if that. Thus the returns to business school, even netting out the costs, are enormously high. Many of the younger males with business-school training were bookkeepers, and many of the females were stenographers. The high returns in 1915 indicate why high schools began to offer commercial courses and why young people flocked to commercial schools in the 1910s and 1920s.

34   David H. Autor, Lawrence F. Katz, and Alan B. Krueger, "Computing Inequality: Have Computers Changed the Labor Market?" NBER working paper 5956 (Cambridge, Mass., 1997), Table 1, report that a year of college in 1995 had a 12 percent return but only an 8 percent return in 1980.

the resources used to educate them to the eighth grade. Yet, community after community swiftly built high schools and hired qualified teachers.

The reasons why parents wanted their children educated and why their teenagers readily flocked to the schools are clear. First and foremost, secondary schooling brought extremely high returns for both males and females c. 1915. Some of the returns were garnered by those who left their rural homes and moved to towns and cities. But even in Iowa the returns were substantial. Young people did not have to leave even this largely rural and small-town state to profit from the human capital acquired in high school c. 1915. Our estimates, derived from a unique set of manuscripts— the Iowa State Census of 1915—reveal that the return to a year of high school was about 12 percent. But why did the public take up this expensive provision of a relatively private good?

Analysis of a cross section of states in 1910 and 1928 reveals that homogeneity of residents—in the form of ethnicity, religion, and income—a high level of wealth or income, and a community made stable by a strong presence of older people increase the apparent support for high schools in the early to middle years of the movement. Smaller towns and villages in the United States were the locus of the movement's activity; high school attendance there was the greatest. We suspect that these small towns and villages were reservoirs of social capital that helped to fuel the high school movement. The only consistent rationale for the public provision of this essentially private good was that it was an intergenerational loan from one generation to the next. Although we cannot fully disassociate the roles of alternative activities for teenagers from the existence of social capital, our evidence is more consistent with the latter than the former. The areas of the country with the greatest tangible wealth and seemingly the greatest intangible wealth, or social capital, witnessed the earliest and the most rapid diffusion of the high school movement.

Many of the leading states of the high school movement continue to score high on various social-capital indicators today. The state-level correlation of the 1928 high school graduation rate with a current social-capital index combining five factors (measuring associational activity, social trust, and political/civic participation) is 0.64 (see Figure 4, upper panel). In the absence of two outliers (North Dakota and Nevada, two of the least populous states), the correlation is 0.81. Current measures of social capital are more highly correlated with various economic indicators of the early twentieth century than with more recent ones. For example, the correlation with the log of per capita wealth in 1912 is 0.73 (excluding Nevada); the correlation with the log of agricultural income per farm worker in 1900 is 0.71 (0.86 without California and Nevada); and the correlation with per capita income in 1900 is 0.61 (0.72 without California and Nevada). In contrast, the correlation with a current income measure—the log of per capita income in 1994—is 0.22.[35]

States that led in the high school movement continue to lead in educational quality indicators, as shown in the lower panel of Figure 4. The correlation between a current index of educational performance and the high school graduation rate in 1928 is 0.60 (0.73 without California and Nevada). The social capital assembled in the early part of this century, which apparently helped to drive the high school movement, appears to survive today in some form and to contribute to human capital formation even today.[36]

APPENDIX: THE 1915 IOWA STATE CENSUS PROJECT

The 1915 State Census of Iowa was the first state or federal census to include information about education and income prior to the federal census of 1940, and it contains considerable detail about other aspects of individuals and households—for example, church affiliation, which was never solicited in a federal census; wealth; and years in the United States and in Iowa. It is a complete sample of the residents of the state.

35 We thank Putnam for providing us with his indices of social capital and educational performance. See Jay Braatz and Putnam, "Families, Communities, and Education in America: Exploring the Evidence," Harvard University working paper (Cambridge, Mass., 1997). The social-capital index is defined in the notes to Figure 4. The reported correlation coefficients in this paragraph and that following cover the "lower forty-eight" states except where indicated. State per capita income data in 1900, and state agricultural income per farm worker data in 1900, are from Simon Kuznets, Ann Ratner Miller, and Richard A. Easterlin, *Population Redistribution and Economic Growth: United States, 1870–1950. II. Analyses of Economic Change* (Philadelphia, 1960). State per capita wealth data for 1912 are from U.S. Department of Commerce, *Statistical Abstract of the United States* (Washington, D.C., 1925). State per capita income data in 1994 are from U.S. Department of Commerce, *Statistical Abstract of the United States* (Washington, D.C., 1996).
36 The state educational-performance index combines three factors. See Braatz and Putnam, "Families, Communities, and Education in America." The educational-performance index is defined in the notes to Figure 4.

Fig. 4 Recent Social-Capital and Educational-Performance Indices, and the 1928 High School Graduation Rate

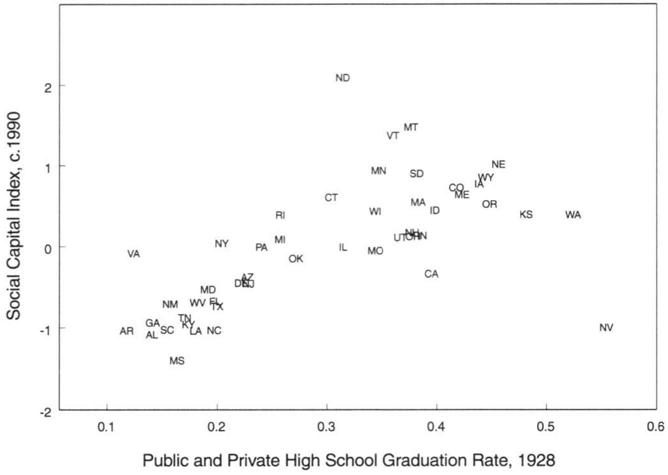

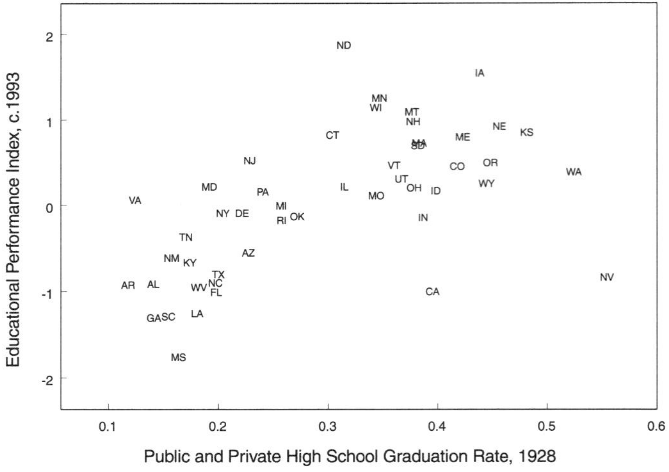

SOURCES   For the social-capital index, see Jay Braatz and Robert D. Putnam, "Families, Communities, and Education in America: Exploring the Evidence," Harvard University working paper (Cambridge, Mass., 1997). The index is an unweighted mean of the Z-scores of five components: (1) 501 (c)(3), that is, non-profit, organizations per capita in 1989; (2) daily newspaper circulation per capita in 1991, capped for three states (Massachusetts, New York, and Virginia) to avoid bias from nationally circulated newspapers; (3) mean voter turnout in the presidential elections of 1988 and 1992; (4) the average number of associational memberships per capita from the General Social Survey—Inter-university Consortium for Political and Social Research (ICPSR) electronic data—all available years from 1974 to 1994; and (5) the social-trust measure from the General Social Survey, all available years from 1972 to 1996. For the educational-performance index, see Braatz and Putnam, "Families, Communities, and Education." The index averages three components: (1) a combination of seven National Assessment of Educational Progress scores for 1990, 1992, and 1996; (2) the average Scholastic Aptitude Test score in 1993, adjusted for participation-rate differences among states; and (3) a measure of the high school dropout rate for 1990 to 1995 that combines four factors. For the 1928 high school graduation rate, see Goldin, Appendix to "How America Graduated from High School: An Exploratory Study, 1910 to 1960," National Bureau of Economic Research–Development of the American Economy working paper 57 (Cambridge, Mass., 1994). The rate is computed as the ratio of public and private graduates to the number of seventeen-year-olds in the state.

The returns—written by census takers (assessors) on index cards, one for each individual—were deposited in the Iowa state archives in Des Moines and microfilmed by the Genealogical Society of the Church of Jesus Christ of Latter-day Saints (Mormons) in 1986.

The census cards, now on microfilm, are grouped by county, although the large cities (those having more than 25,000 residents) are grouped separately. Within each county or large city, all records are alphabetized by last name and within last name by first name (notwithstanding occasional errors). The current project has sampled the records for three of the largest Iowa cities—Davenport, Des Moines, and Dubuque. We planned to sample Sioux City, but the microfilms are too light. Counties that did not contain a city of more than 25,000 people in 1910 have also been sampled. The counties were chosen by grouping the ninety-nine counties in Iowa in four equal-sized units by education and then randomly taking three from each of the four groups. This procedure produced twelve counties, eight of which (Adair, Buchanan, Carroll, Clay, Johnson, Lyon, Marshall, and Wayne) have been sampled thus far. They conveniently span much of the geography of the state: Clay and Lyon in the northwest, Johnson and Buchanan in the east, Wayne in the south central, Marshall in the central, Carroll in the west central, and Adair in the southwest.

SAMPLING STRATEGY FOR THE URBAN AND RURAL SAMPLES

Urban Sample. For each of the cities, about one-fourth of the films, distributed throughout the alphabet, were purchased. We took every other name on each roll of microfilm chosen for the sample and entered only completed last names; for example, the first name on a roll was not taken. If the cards did not go in alphabetical order, we attempted to reorder them.

Rural Sample. For each of the counties, one film (from a total of four to seven, depending on the county) was purchased. We sampled all names on each roll of microfilm chosen for Buchanan, Carroll, Lyon and Marshall, and one-half of the names for Adair, Clay, Johnson, and Wayne.

VARIABLES INCLUDED   All variables on the census cards were taken for the data collection (in order of recording): card number, sex, color, marital status, months of schooling in 1914 by type of school (public elementary, private elementary, high school, or college), ability to read and/or write, handicaps (blind, insane, deaf, idiot), naturalization status (if foreign-born), years in Iowa and years in the United States, full name, age, address (county, post office, town or township, and ward), occupation, months unemployed and total earnings from occupation for 1914, extent of education (years in common, grammar, high school, college), birthplace, home or farm ownership, incumbrance on and value of the same, military service, church affiliation, father's and mother's birthplaces, assessor's name, and any remarks on the card.

FAMILY RECONSTITUTION   Entire households were surveyed, but because the cards were boxed alphabetically, we can reconstitute only nuclear families in which all members have the same last name. Our interest was in grouping parents with their dependent children. The assessors numbered each of the cards, almost always in sequential order within a household. Additional information was provided by address (particularly important for the cities, although P.O. address was not given in Davenport), parents' places of birth, and the assessor's name. We used all these pieces of information to reconstitute the families, although we primarily used card number, last name, and address. Of those aged fifteen to eighteen in the rural-county sample, we matched 89.1 percent to an adult household head; we matched 78.7 percent in the large-city sample.

For several reasons, we could not match all teenaged children to parents or guardians. First, children and their guardians did not always have the same last name. Some children had been orphaned; some boarded with relatives to advance their education; and others boarded for reasons of work. Second, cards of parents were sometimes alphabetized incorrectly or the last names misspelled. Since two of the cities provided complete addresses, misspelling would have been less of a problem. But because we skipped every other name, we could have missed parents whose last names were alphabetized differently from that of their children. There are many reasons, some pertaining to early twentieth-century life and others having to do with late twentieth-century data collecting, why all families could not be reconstituted.

DUPLICATE CARDS   Because the census was taken over a period of time (we do not know how long), we term individuals who appear more than once in the sample the "duplicates." In some cases, the origin of the "duplicate" is clear: The individual was in an asylum or a school and was counted in both places. In other cases, the individual apparently moved or went through some other life transition, such as marriage. Certain ethnic groups (Russian Jews, for example) and blacks were more apt to be counted twice, probably because of their greater frequency of moving. We coded one record as the original and one as the duplicate; we do not use the duplicated information in our sample. About 2 percent of the urban sample were duplicates; practically none of the rural sample was.

Myron P. Gutmann and Sara M. Pullum

From Local to National Political Cultures: Social Capital and Civic Organization in the Great Plains

It is exciting to think about Putnam's concept of social capital in the context of the semi-arid American Great Plains. Will his theorem hold in an environment so different—in every social and physical sense—from that of urban Italy? Putnam finds that people who form voluntary associations based on common activities or concerns experience greater levels of social integration and political involvement. He calls this civic engagement "social capital" because the power of the group transcends potential individual productivity. Benefits of these reciprocal networks include better community institutions; the building of neighborhood trust, resulting in lower crime rates; and political activism to further local needs. In his work on Italy, Putnam focuses on the overtly political ramifications of social capital. He shows that as regional measures of social capital became stronger in Italy from 1970 to 1989, politicians responded by placing greater emphasis on compromise and efficiency. By pooling resources, citizens were able to alter the prevailing beliefs about government's role and its relationship to the community, which Putnam terms "political culture." As a result of the active application of social capital, politicians viewed regional loyalty as more important than party affiliation, and citizen satisfaction as a concrete and achievable goal.[1]

Although the title of this article refers to civic organizations, our investigation initially focuses on political participation in gen-

Myron P. Gutmann is Director of the Population Research Center and Professor of History, University of Texas, Austin. He is the author of *Towards the Modern Economy: Early Industry in Europe, 1500–1800* (New York, 1988); co-author, with Kenneth H. Fliess, of "The Social Context of Infant and Childhood Mortality in the American Southwest, 1850–1910," *Journal of Interdisciplinary History,* XXVI (1996), 589–618.

Sara M. Pullum is a Ph.D. candidate, University of Texas, Austin.

The research for this article was supported by grant number 1R01 HD33554 from the National Institute of Child Health and Human Development of the National Institutes of Health. The authors are grateful to Geoff Cunfer and the rest of the Great Plains Population and Environmental team in Austin, as well as to the administrative offices of the United States National Grasslands, for advice and assistance.

1 Robert D. Putnam, "Bowling Alone: America's Declining Social Capital," *Journal of Democracy,* VI (1995), 65–78; *idem,* with Roberto Leonardi and Raffaella Y. Nanetti, *Making Democracy Work: Civic Traditions in Modern Italy* (Princeton, 1993).

eral elections. When we extend it later to local institutions, we turn not to civic institutions (having to do with cities) but to rural institutions—specifically, fifteen publicly owned grasslands, administered in a variety of ways along the communal and democratic spectrum. We ask how differences in the administration of the grasslands reflect on longer traditions of public participation.

The most dramatic changes that we find do not reflect a loss of social capital so much as a change in political culture from a local to a national perspective. Although the voter-participation index that we use cannot detect all the elements of social capital, it is an adequate way to gauge the differences between counties and the changing nature of public life over time. Considerable evidence suggests that local political cultures were extremely important until the 1952 presidential election, as indicated by the differences between states in voter participation. After 1951, local identification—through states—played less of a role, and religion and ethnic origin played more of one. This new political culture is more diverse but still vibrant. The new national media—especially television—might have been responsible for bringing it about by giving people multiple sources of identity that go beyond their local or state community.

The Great Plains are part of the great natural grassland that stretches across the central part of North America eastward from the Rocky Mountains. We define the boundary of the Great Plains on the east by the line of 700 mm average annual precipitation, on the west by 5,000 feet of elevation, on the north by the Canadian border, and on the south by the thirty-second parallel in Texas and New Mexico. Counties are our units of analysis—450 of them in ten states throughout the area that we define as the Great Plains.

In many ways, the social history of the Great Plains, like that of much of the United States, does not conform to Putnam's analyses. European-Americans began to settle the region only in the second half of the nineteenth century; white farmers and ranchers made a significant appearance in some areas only after World War I. Moreover, many of the people who settled in the region did not stay long. High rates of immigration and emigration are consistent themes in the settlement of the United States. Many people came not to establish their families as long-term farmers, like European peasants, but to profit in the short term from land speculation. However, whether they profited or not, they departed. That tradition continued as the region became more urbanized.[2]

In the absence of a population that stayed in the same place over a long period of time, it is difficult to see how the kind of cultural stability encapsulated in Putnam's concept of social capital could have existed in the Great Plains. Not only did people there not recall 500 years of public participation; many of them could not have known a pattern of public participation that was a generation old. Moreover, the history of the European-settled Great Plains does not include the kind of cultural and political autonomy that Putnam asserts for certain Italian regions. The governing structure of the United States has always been federal, with no large-scale introduction of regional autonomies to parallel the Italian model. Hence, we seem to be searching for something that could not have existed.

There is another side to the story, however. The Great Plains region, as we define it, is not so homogeneous that all its residents behaved in the same ways. Differences between groups of Great Plains counties might well translate into variations in levels of social capital, just as Putnam hypothesized about differences in Italy. Our conceptualization of the social, economic, and environmental history of the Great Plains suggests that some groups of people, in certain counties, were more likely than others to participate in a political or civic process.

Our search for evidence of different levels of social capital in the Great Plains counties begins with environmental and locational effects and then turns to patterns of land use. The Great Plains area is large enough to be divided into a grid of environmental sub-regions by temperature (from low temperatures at the north to high temperatures to the south) and precipitation (from low levels in the east to very low levels in the west). The

---

2   Gutmann et al., "Staying Put or Moving On? Ethnicity, Migration and Persistence in Nineteenth-Century Texas," Texas Population Research Center Papers (Austin, 1990); Terry G. Jordan, *German Seed in Texas Soil: Immigrant Farmers in Nineteenth-Century Texas* (Austin, 1996); Jon Gjerde, "The Effect of Community on Migration: Three Minnesota Townships 1885–1905," *Journal of Historical Geography*, V (1979), 403–422; Sonya Salamon, *Prairie Patrimony: Family, Farming, and Community in the Midwest* (Chapel Hill, 1992).

temperature gradient is not associated with any particular way of life beyond adaptations to cold or heat, but the east–west aridity gradient is associated with different forms of agriculture. Precipitation, soil texture, and soil depth largely determine whether the land is better-suited for crops or livestock; most crops grow in areas of high precipitation and rich, deep soils. Due to greater population density, cropping regions probably were more likely to show patterns of community participation than ranching regions were, despite the traditions of group action in ranching, such as roundups. Figures 1 and 2 present maps of precipitation and cropping.[3]

Our second way of looking at political participation focuses on the likelihood of groups to participate in the political process. European settlers came to the region in a series of migratory waves. Many of the immigrants were British, but a significant number of them were German, Scandinavian, other Western European, Spanish, and, more recently, Mexican. Ethnic groups organized their lives in their own manner, at least in terms of agriculture and community. Some were more inclined than others to stay in one place. Germans and Scandinavians, for example, were more geographically persistent than the British or the Irish. Spanish settlers, or Hispanos, who came to New Mexico in the sixteenth century, were remarkably resistant to migration, developing and maintaining distinctive cultural patterns. The ethnic composition of counties should reflect political participation, especially in those counties with strong clusters of one group or another. Figure 3 presents maps of the distribution of people with German, Scandinavian, and British/Irish origins in the Great Plains in 1910.[4]

3 Gutmann et al., "Farm Programs, Environment, and Land Use Decisions in the Great Plains, 1969–1992," unpub. paper presented at the biennial meeting of the American Society for Environmental History, Baltimore, 1997; Ingrid C. Burke et al., "Interactions of Land Use and Ecosystem Function: A Case Study in the Central Great Plains," in Peter M. Groffman and Gene E. Likens (eds.), *Integrated Regional Models: Interactions Between Humans and Their Environment* (New York, 1994), 79–95.

4 Gutmann, Susan Gonzalez Baker, and Pullum, "Ethnicity and Land Use in a Changing Environment: The Great Plains in the Twentieth Century," paper presented at the annual meeting of the Population Association of America, Washington, D.C., March, 1997, and at the conference, "New Immigration History," Texas A&M University, 1997; Jordan, *German Seed;* D. Aidan McQuillan, *Prevailing Over Time: Ethnic Adjustments on the Kansas Prairies, 1875–1925* (Lincoln, 1990); Salamon, *Prairie Patrimony;* Gjerde, *From Peasants to Farmers: The Migration from Balestrand, Norway, to the Upper Middle West* (Cambridge, 1985); James C. Malin,

Fig. 1 Cropland as a Percentage of Total Farmland, Great Plains Counties, 1974

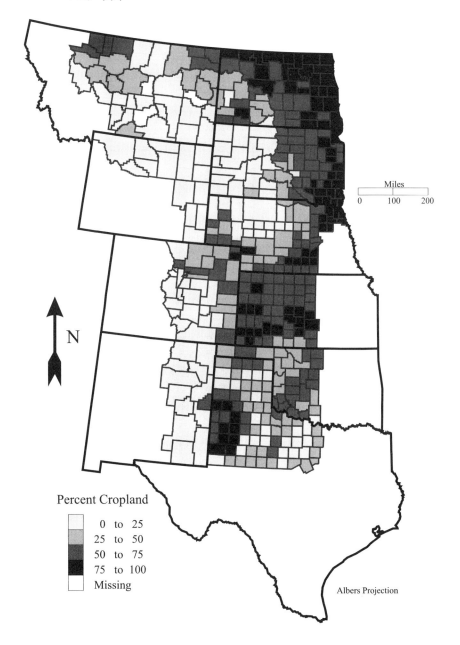

Miles

0   100   200

N

Percent Cropland

0   to   25
25   to   50
50   to   75
75   to   100
Missing

Albers Projection

Fig. 2 Average Monthly Growing-Season Precipitation (April–September)

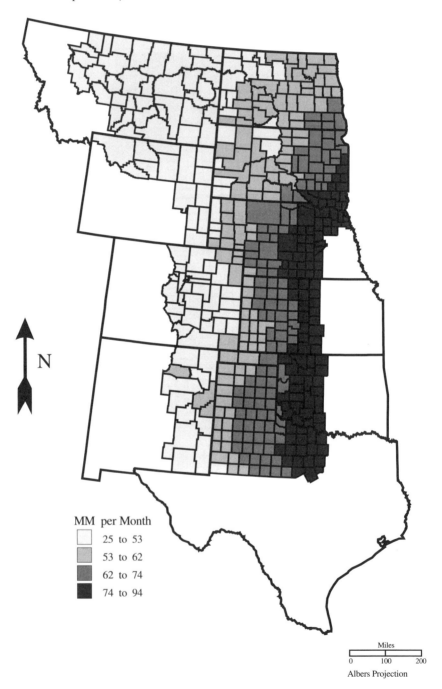

N

MM per Month
25 to 53
53 to 62
62 to 74
74 to 94

Miles
0   100   200
Albers Projection

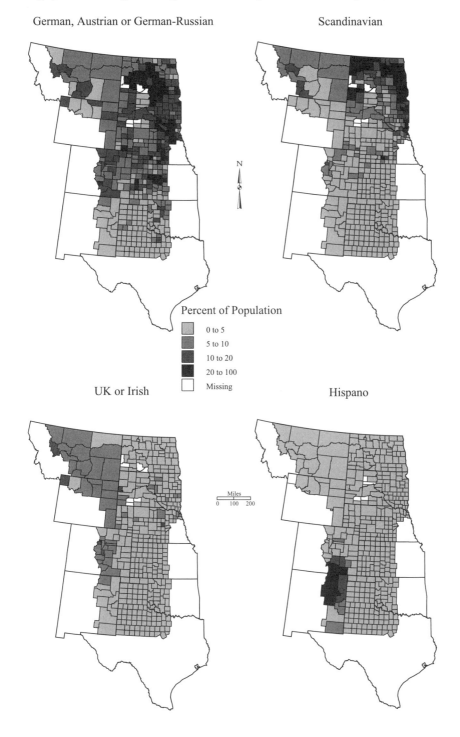

Fig. 3 Percentage of Population in Major Ethnic Groups, 1910

German, Austrian or German-Russian

Scandinavian

Percent of Population

- 0 to 5
- 5 to 10
- 10 to 20
- 20 to 100
- Missing

UK or Irish

Hispano

Religion is related to ethnic origin, but is not exactly the same thing. Religious participation seems likely to be associated with civic participation; religious groups with a commitment to local control might show greater religious participation. Although the United States census usually has not included religion in the main enumeration, the size of religious groups can be estimated from existing data. The maps in Figure 4 show the proportion of residents reported in the four largest religious groups in 1916.[5]

Although agricultural traditions, ethnicity, and religion seem most analogous to the Italian patterns in Putnam's model, other aspects of cultural and social life in the United States inform our research—the first two being schooling and educational attainment. We hypothesize that certain populations within the Great Plains were more disposed than others to send their children to school, and to have attained a high level of education, and we assume these variables to be correlated with political participation. The other elements in this final group of hypotheses are related to each county's population size, its age distribution, its proportion of urban inhabitants, and its overall population density. Smaller and more isolated communities are more likely to demonstrate high levels of participation than urban areas are. In recent years, older populations are more likely to participate, too.

Political culture also has a geographical basis. The particular state in which one lived mattered as much as anything else in determining political culture, especially during the early and mid-twentieth century. Most dramatically, Texans have been less likely to participate in general elections than most other voters in the Great Plains.

POLITICAL PARTICIPATION IN THE TWENTIETH-CENTURY UNITED STATES: LOOKING FOR EVIDENCE OF SOCIAL CAPITAL   In this article, voter participation in twelve general elections between 1880 and 1988 is the dependent variable to measure social capital (see Figure 5). The assumption is that national political institutions

---

History and Ecology: Studies of the Grassland (Lincoln, 1984); Gutmann et al., "Staying Put"; Malin, *Winter Wheat in the Golden Belt of Kansas* (Lawrence, 1944); Richard Nostrand, *The Hispano Homeland* (Norman, 1992).

5 The Census Bureau collected data about religious adherence in 1890, 1906, 1916, 1926, and 1936. Private groups took surveys of religious participation in 1951, 1972, 1981, and 1991. See the Appendix for a list of the sources for these data.

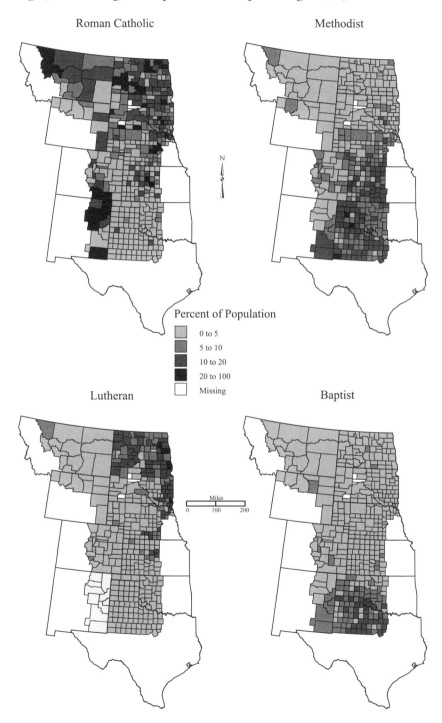

Fig. 4   Percentage of Population in Major Religions, 1916

Roman Catholic

Methodist

N

Percent of Population

0 to 5
5 to 10
10 to 20
20 to 100
Missing

Lutheran

Baptist

Miles
0   100   200

might reflect both differences in social capital among Great Plains subregions, and the changing relationship of the Great Plains to the rest of the nation as a whole. Although the kind of local "institution building" to which Putnam refers is not measurable, changes in the identification of the voters of this region with national institutions are. Our data about presidential-election turnout suggests that the people of the Great Plains did not always perceive themselves as having a stake in national government. Yet, some groups displayed active participation in these elections, even when national turnout was low. We attempt to explain why different groups within this population chose to vote, even when others notably did not. Although we looked at congressional elections, for reasons of economy, we do not report the results; they corroborate those derived from the presidential elections.

A major question of this research is whether an increased sense of community translated into active participation in political life. Several historians have argued that local community cohesion leads to greater attention to legislative control. But is the long-term goal of such legislative activism the separation of the community from national politics? That is, do small cohesive communities vote in national elections only to protect specific freedoms? If so, does a decrease in the subregional effects on voter turnout reflect the cultural homogenization that derives from increased communications and higher education?[6]

The United States has witnessed four major eras in voter behavior since 1840. Voter-turnout percentages increased from 1840 to 1900 but declined from 1900 to 1928, partially as a result of woman suffrage. In the Great Plains, women attained the vote in Wyoming, Colorado, and Kansas decades before the Nineteenth Amendment passed in August 1920. Nationally, voter participation increased slightly from 1930 to 1960, due to New Deal party realignment, but fell again from 1960 to 1980. Figure 5 shows the contrast between national voter turnout for selected presidential elections and that of the Great Plains counties. Voter participation was higher nationally than in the Great Plains until 1920; it has been higher in the Great Plains ever since.[7]

6 Thomas A. Woods, *Knights of the Plow: Oliver H. Kelly and the Origins of the Grange in Republican Ideology* (Ames, Iowa, 1991); Richard Hogan, *Class and Community in Frontier Colorado* (Lawrence, 1990).
7 Several states enfranchised women before the passage of the Nineteenth Amendment. The following cases of early woman suffrage are relevant to our analysis: Wyoming, in 1869;

Fig. 5 Percentage of Adult Population Voting for President, Great Plains and the United States as a Whole

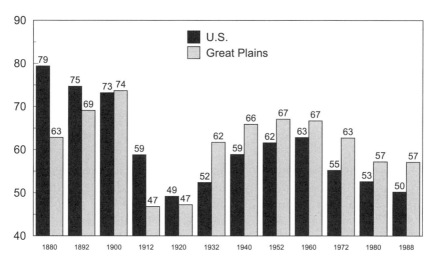

At some point in time, the voting behavior of the tightly knit communities of the Great Plains became less controlled by a local political culture and more responsive to national trends. As late as the 1930s, rural communities across the nation still enjoyed a sense of distinction from the new urban order. Urbanization might be the reason for the change in voting patterns; the region certainly became more urban over time. When did such factors as education and urbanization begin to have a greater effect on voting behavior than such indicators of cultural isolation as high religious participation?[8]

Colorado, in 1893; and Kansas, in 1912. By the 1920 election, women in all states could vote. The National American Woman Suffrage Association, *Victory: How Women Won It: A Centennial Symposium, 1840–1940* (New York, 1940); Paul Kleppner, *Who Voted? The Dynamics of Electoral Turnout, 1870–1980* (New York, 1982); Joel H. Silbey (ed.), *Voters, Parties, and Elections* (Lexington, 1972). We are unable to get election data for Nebraska in 1920, 1932, and 1940, and North Dakota in 1892, 1900, 1912, and 1920. The Inter-University Consortium for Political and Social Research (ICPSR) has withdrawn these data from public availability while revising them. For the national data, we use tables in the U.S. Bureau of the Census, *Historical Statistics of the United States* (Washington, D.C., 1976), for years up through 1920. For 1932 to 1988, we use data from the U.S. Bureau of the Census, *Statistical Abstract of the United States, 1990* (Washington, D.C., 1990). These two series diverge in how they calculate the denominator. For years covered by both sources, the rate is about 2 percent higher in *Historical Statistics* than in *Statistical Abstract*.

8   Hal S. Barron, *Mixed Harvest: The Second Great Transformation in the Rural North* (Chapel Hill, 1997); Walter Dean Burnham, "The Changing Shape of the American Political Universe," in Silbey (ed.), *Voters, Parties, and Elections,* 205–234.

Our analysis is ecological, that is, not so much about the behavior of individuals as about the behavior of groups. Putnam's theory is about historical communes. Ours, by necessity as much as anything else, is about counties, based on data about a range of independent variables that capture pertinent concepts. Table 1 presents the main independent variables, together with definitions, sources, problems, and issues about the timing of availability. In some cases, the years of availability are irregular; we do our best to work around them. We have chosen not to interpolate data, with the exception of total population, for which we assume linear growth. (See the Appendix for a description of the sources.)

Our initial method is to estimate the coefficients of regression equations in which the dependent variable is the percentage of the voting-age population in a county that voted for president in a given general election. The independent variables represent our choices of factors that might differentiate the political behavior of voting-age residents in the Great Plains.[9]

VOTER PARTICIPATION AND SOCIAL CAPITAL IN THE GREAT PLAINS, 1880 TO 1988   We have estimated the coefficients of forty-eight different regression models. Because of the quantity and complexity of those results, we do not report all of the regression coefficients. We explain the differences between counties by the percentage of total eligible voters who went to the polls. The substantial differences in the extent of voter participation reveal a strong geographical pattern. Figure 6 presents levels of voter participation in presidential elections in three representative years—1920, 1940, and 1988. In the first half of the century, large proportions of voters turned out in some of the northern states, and small proportions in Texas and Oklahoma. The pattern partly diminished over time.[10]

In constructing our regression models, we followed a conventional additive approach, beginning with a smaller model that

9   We do not make use of Gary King, *A Solution to the Ecological Inference Problem: Reconstructing Individual Behavior from Aggregate Data* (Princeton, 1997), in this context. We think that the ecological approach is more appropriate. For our approach to autocorrelation, which we also do not use herein, see Gutmann, Andres Peri, and Glenn D. Deane, "Migration, Environment, and Economic Change in the U.S. Great Plains, 1930–1990," unpub. paper presented at the annual meeting of the Social Science History Association, Washington, D.C., 1997.

10   The authors will be pleased to provide the detailed regression results upon request.

Fig. 6 Percentage of Adult Population Voting for President

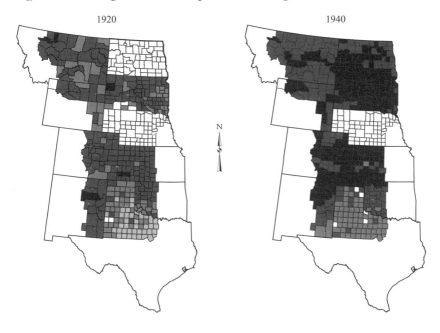

1920   1940

N

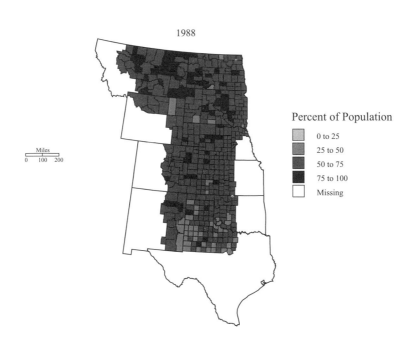

1988

Miles
0   100   200

Percent of Population

	0 to 25
	25 to 50
	50 to 75
	75 to 100
	Missing

incorporates some of the interesting effects and adding others to see how much the model improves. The model starts with the characteristics listed in Table 1—largest party vote, population, education, and climate and land use. The second stage adds dummy variables representing the states, and the third, the percentage of the county population belonging to major religious groups. In the fourth stage of the analysis, we substitute the percentage of the population belonging to major ethnic groups for the religious-group variables. Because ethnicity data is limited to a few years only, we use the 1910 ethnicity data for all election years from 1880 through 1940, and the 1990 data for all election years from 1952 through 1988, assuming that the ethnic characteristics of counties changed slowly. We do not try a fifth regression model for each year with religion *and* ethnicity, because exploratory analyses showed that the percentage of Lutherans was highly correlated with people of Scandinavian (and to a lesser extent German) origin, and the percentage of Catholics was highly correlated with people with German, Mexican, and Hispano origins.

Table 2 presents the adjusted R^2 values for our regression models in all years. The four columns represent the four models just described. Tables 3, 4, and 5 present, in simplified form, the regression results for three of the four models. The strategy is to show the direction of the effect, and the statistical significance (from the p-value) associated with the effect. Table 3, for example, reveals that counties in Texas had higher participation than those in Wyoming (the reference category) in 1900, and lower participation in 1912 through 1960, and in 1980. The coefficient was significant in all years except 1952 and 1980; no significant effect is evident in 1892, 1972, and 1988. Table 3 also reveals that a higher average county temperature in a decade is associated with lower county participation in presidential elections, beginning in 1920. This temperature effect is interesting, but the fact that temperature rises along a north-to-south gradient should warn against any blanket causal assertion that hot weather reduces voter participation.

The R^2 values in Table 2 begin to tell a chronological story. From 1880 to 1900, the variables predict relatively little of the variation between counties in voter participation. From 1912 through 1940, however, the story changes dramatically, and even our "basic" model explains a minimum of 45 percent of the variation in county voter participation. Although the basic model is remarkably successful in explaining variation in voter participation between counties, adding the states improves it significantly, at least between 1912 and 1972. The addition of variables that tell us the percentage of membership in major religious groups is an improvement over the basic model, but not so much as the model that adds variables of race and ethnicity. At best, we can explain almost 92 percent of the variation in voter participation, for 1940.

Largest Party Vote. We include the variable, largest party vote (the percentage of all votes cast for the party that received the most votes for president), in order to make sense of a preliminary result that showed low participation for Texas. In order to determine whether all the electoral action in Texas took place in the primary rather than in the general election, we included a variable that measured the percentage of votes cast for the majority party, on the grounds that a party landslide (as often happened in Texas) would discourage general election voting. The results confirmed our hypothesis, but only weakly. Between 1900 and 1940, counties with a large majority-party vote had lower participation. Only in 1980 was the result significantly different.

Population Characteristics. In general, the larger the population—and the larger the urban population—the lower was voter participation. In the early years—and again in 1980—however, a denser population meant a higher turnout. As we expected, if community mattered, rural voters and voters in smaller counties went to the polls.

Age Distribution. Our hypothesis is that counties with large older populations—aged fifty-five or more—were likely to show high voter participation. We base this theory on two different ideas: first, that this age group developed its attitude toward voting during a period that Putnam describes as having comparatively high social capital; and second, that this age group tends to vote in response to its own interests. As Goldin and Katz suggest, the older generation of a community has a significant personal investment in the protection offered by civic organizations. Because many older community members benefitted from social networks, such as educational programs, early in their lives, they often vote to perpetuate them. Our analysis shows that the percentage of the population aged fifty-five and over correlates well with high voter

Table 1 Independent Variables Used and Their Sources (and Problems)

VARIABLE	DEFINITION	SOURCE	MISSING DATA & PROBLEMS	INTERPOLATION RULES
Largest Party Vote	percent of population voting for county's most successful party in presidential election	ICPSR county-election data		
Population characteristics				
Log of Population	mathematical log of county population	population census		Population is a linear interpolation.
Population density	population per square mile	population census	only used for 1880, 1890, 1920	Data are for closest decennial year—not interpolated.
Rural population density	total population less urban population, per square mile	population census	no data for 1880, 1890, 1920	Data are for closest decennial year—not interpolated.
Percent urban	percent of population in places with 2,500 or more persons	population census	no data for 1880, 1890, 1920	Data are for closest decennial year—not interpolated.
Percent age 55 and over	percent of population aged 55 and over	population census		Data are for closest decennial year—not interpolated.
Race and ethnicity				
Percent African-American	percent of population that is African-American	population census		Data are for closest decennial year—not interpolated.
Percent UK and Ireland	percent of population of British or Irish ethnicity	population census	ethnicity data existing for 1910 and 1990 only	Ethnicity data are not interpolated. 1900, 1912, 1930, 1932, and 1940 use 1910 data; 1980 and 1988 use 1990 data.
Percent German	percent of population of German ethnicity			
Percent Scandinavian	percent of population of Scandinavian ethnicity			
Percent Eastern European	percent of population of Eastern European ethnicity			
Percent Mexican	percent of population of Mexican ethnicity			
Percent Hispano	percent of population of Hispano ethnicity			

Religion			
Percent Baptist	percent of population that is Baptist	U.S. Census, National Council of Churches of Christ, Roper surveys	religion data existing for irregular years only	Religion data are not interpolated. 1880 and 1892 use 1890 data; 1900 and 1912 use 1906 data; 1920 uses 1916 data; 1932 uses 1926 data; 1940 uses 1936 data; 1960 uses 1952 data; 1972 uses 1971 data; 1988 uses 1990 data.
Percent Roman Catholic	percent of population that is Roman Catholic			
Percent Episcopalian	percent of population that is Episcopalian			
Percent Lutheran	percent of population that is Lutheran			
Percent Methodist	percent of population that is Methodist			
Percent Presbyterian	percent of population that is Presbyterian			
Education				
Percent in school	percent of population aged 5–18 enrolled in school	population census	no data for 1880 or 1900	Data are for closest decennial year—not interpolated.
Percent with college	percent of population aged 25+ with college education	population census	no data for years prior to 1940	Data are for closest decennial year—not interpolated.
Climate, land use and location				
Percent cropland	percent of farmland in crops	agriculture census	no data for years prior to 1930	Data are for closest decennial year—not interpolated.
Mean precipitation	mean precipitation (monthly in mm) across the decade	computed from U.S. Historical Climatology Network (USHCN) station data		
Mean temperature	mean of maximum and minimum temperatures (monthly in C)	Computed from USHCN station data		
State dummy variables	county in a given state			

Table 2a   Adjusted R^2 Values for Forty-Eight Regression Models, Dependent Variable the Percentage of Adult Population Voting for President

YEAR	"BASIC" MODEL	ADD STATES	ADD RELIGION	ADD RACE AND ETHNICITY
1880	0.112	0.107	0.170	0.208
1892	0.295	0.335	0.519	0.324
1900	0.242	0.331	0.356	0.397
1912	0.529	0.713	0.748	0.732
1920	0.531	0.802	0.813	0.836
1932	0.719	0.872	0.881	0.909
1940	0.707	0.878	0.887	0.918
1952	0.629	0.777	0.791	0.812
1960	0.649	0.798	0.816	0.829
1972	0.585	0.695	0.718	0.755
1980	0.669	0.745	0.770	0.799
1988	0.666	0.696	0.725	0.766

Table 2b   Contents of Models (Independent Variables)

"BASIC" MODEL	ADD STATE VARIABLES TO THE "BASIC" MODEL	ADD RELIGION VARIABLES TO THE "ADD STATES" MODEL	ADD RACE AND ETHNICITY VARIABLES TO THE ADD STATES MODEL
Largest party vote	Colorado	percent Baptist	percent African-American
Log of population	Kansas	percent Episcopalian	percent UK and Ireland
Density or rural density	Montana	percent Lutheran	percent Germany
Percent urban	Nebraska	percent Methodist	percent Scandinavia
Percent age 55 and over	New Mexico	percent Presbyterian	percent East Europe/Russia
Percent school attendance	North Dakota	percent Roman Catholic	percent Mexico
Percent college attainment	Oklahoma		percent Hispano
Percent cropland	South Dakota		
Mean precipitation	Texas		
Mean temperature			

Table 3 Simplified Presidential-Election Regression Results, with States

	1880	1892	1900	1912	1920	1932	1940	1952	1960	1972	1980	1988	
Largest party vote	+	—	---	---	---	-	---	+		---	+++	+	Largest party vote
Log of population		+++	---	---	---	-	---	---	---	---	---	---	Log of population
Density													Density
Rural density				++			-	-		+	+		Rural density
Percent urban							-				-		Percent urban
Percent aged 55 and over		---	--		++	+++	+++	+++		+	+++	+++	Percent aged 55 and over
Percent school attendance									++	++	+++	+++	Percent school attendance
Percent college attainment									+++	++	+++	+++	Percent college attainment
Percent cropland											+		Percent cropland
Mean precipitation				++						++	++		Mean precipitation
Mean temperature											-	---	Mean temperature
Colorado		++	+++	+	+++	---	+++	+++	+	++	++	+++	Colorado
Kansas		+		-	+++	+++	+++	++					Kansas
Montana		+				-		---	-	+	---	+++	Montana
Nebraska		+			+++	-	+++		-	-	---		Nebraska
New Mexico					+++	+++	+++	++	++	+++	+++	++	New Mexico
North Dakota							+					+	North Dakota
Oklahoma			+++		++	++	+++	+++		++	-		Oklahoma
South Dakota		++	+++		++	++	+++				++	+	South Dakota
Texas				---	---		---	-	---				Texas
Wyoming				---	Reference Category for States								Wyoming
Adjusted R^2	0.107	0.335	0.331	0.713	0.802	0.872	0.878	0.777	0.798	0.695	0.745	0.696	Adjusted R^2

NOTES   Gray areas are variables that are not included in the models. Plus and minus signs indicate the sign of the coefficient. The significance of the effect is indicated as follows: 1 symbol (+) <= .05; 2 symbols (++) <= .01; 3 symbols (+++) <= .001.

turnout after 1920, suggesting a period effect similar to Putnam's. The positive coefficient increases greatly in 1980 and 1988, probably reflecting republican party affiliations. Prior to 1920, the fifty-five and over age group correlates with low voter participation, which supports Goldin and Katz's notion of the gradual building of social capital within communities and the resulting sense of generational responsibility.[11]

Education. In recent elections, the highly educated have been more likely to vote than the less-well educated, although higher education also correlates with high income, another individual indicator of voter participation. Our measure of school attendance captures the likelihood of families to send their children to school; the findings confirm our hypotheses that the tendency was more telling in the past than more recently, because of universal schooling. The strong relationship between attendance and voting in 1988, however, is something of a curiosity.

Environment and Land Use. We suppose that precipitation and cropland represent essentially the same social and economic condition in our models, namely, the distinction between farming and ranching communities according to electoral participation. Cropland does not appear as a separate variable before 1930, but the general trend for the two variables taken together is similar. Cropland and precipitation are not always significant, but when the are, they have positive coefficients: We suspect that farm communities are more likely to participate than ranching communities, all other things being equal. We have already mentioned the observed temperature effect—a gradient of lower to higher participation running from south to north, at least between 1920 and 1972.

State. The state in which a county was located is significant in many years. Using Wyoming as the reference category, we see two groups of state patterns: Colorado counties almost always showed higher voter participation than Wyoming; Kansas and South Dakota sometimes did. New Mexico, North Dakota, and Oklahoma also had years of higher participation than Wyoming, but the patterns were less well developed. Counties in Texas had

11 Putnam, "The Strange Disappearance of Civic America," *American Prospect*, XXIV (1996), 34–48; Claudia Goldin and Lawrence F. Katz, "Human and Social Capital: The Rise of Secondary Schooling in America, 1910 to 1940," paper presented at the conference, "Patterns of Social Capital: Stability and Change in Comparative Perspective," Harvard University, December 4–6, 1997, revised and published in this issue, 683–723.

lower participation, at least in the first two-thirds of the century, possibly representing the extreme case of single-party loyalty for which general-election participation was not important. The emergence of a strong Republican party to compete with the Democrats in Texas beginning in the 1970s may account for the change in the state's patterns.

Religion. The religion results in Table 4 suggest further avenues for research. What is most striking is that the counties with large Roman Catholic populations had higher and more consistent voter participation than the others. Episcopalian populations showed lower participation. The results for Presbyterian, Methodist, and Lutheran turnout were infrequently significant, but when they were significant, they were associated with higher participation. Baptists were associated with lower participation, except in 1892.

Race and Ethnicity. Our last set of results, in Table 5, describe the role of ethnic groups in determining the level of voter participation in a county's presidential elections. To reiterate, between 1880 and 1940, the census asked questions about the birthplace of respondents and their parents. As late as 1910, these data give an accurate sense of the ethnic origin of a county's population, because the great wave of immigration was still recent. Moreover, in 1910, the census bureau published county tabulations of all persons born within each major migratory ethnic group, as well as of all native-born persons whose parents were born in the source countries. The weakness of these data is that they underestimate the proportion of people who were descended from early immigrants, especially those from the United Kingdom, and to a lesser extent those from Germany. At the end of the twentieth century, the United States census bureau has taken a different approach to learning about the ethnic and national origins of the population. The 1980 and 1990 questionnaires asked directly about each person's "ancestry." The data are published for counties, and the 1990 responses contributed to our analysis.[12]

---

12   For more detail, see Gutmann et al., "Ethnicity and Land Use." Reynolds Farley, "The New Census Question about Ancestry: What Did it Tell Us?" *Demography*, XXVIII (1991), 411–429; Michael Hout and Joshua R. Goldstein, "How 4.5 Million Irish Immigrants Became 40 Million Irish Americans: Demographic and Subjective Aspects of the Ethnic Composition of White Americans," *American Sociological Review*, LIX (1994), 64–82. Ira Rosenwaike, "Ancestry in the United States Census, 1980–1990," *Social Science Research*, XXII (1993), 383–390.

Table 4 Simplified Presidential-Election Regression Results, with Religion

	1880	1892	1900	1912	1920	1932	1940	1952	1960	1972	1980	1988
Largest party vote											+++	---
Log of population		---	---	---	-	---		---	---	---	---	---
Density	+	++				-		-			+	---
Rural density				+							+	-
Percent urban			-	-					-		-	
Percent aged 55 and over		-	-		+	+++	+++	+++	++		+++	+++
Percent school attendance					+	+++	+++		+++		-	+++
Percent college attainment									+++	++	+++	+++
Percent cropland				+								
Mean precipitation					-	---	---	---	---	---	+	
Mean temperature				++	+++	++	+++	++				
Colorado				++	+++	+++	+++	++		+	+	++
Kansas					+++	+++	+++					
Montana		+	++		++	++	-				+	++
Nebraska			+			---			---	---	---	
New Mexico				+	+++	+	++	+		+		++
North Dakota						+	++				+	+
Oklahoma			++		+	+	+++	+++		++		
South Dakota			+++			+	+++			++	+++	+
Texas				-	---	---			---	-		
Wyoming							Reference Category for States					
Baptist		+++				---	-	---	-	---	---	---
Episcopalian		-	-		---	---		-	--	---	---	---
Lutheran				+								
Methodist				+++				+		+++		
Presbyterian				+++								
Roman Catholic	++			+++	+	+++	+++	+++	+++	+++	+	
Adjusted R^2	0.170	0.519	0.356	0.748	0.813	0.881	0.887	0.791	0.816	0.718	0.770	0.725

NOTES   Gray areas are variables that are not included in the models. Plus and minus signs indicate the sign of the coefficient. The significance of the effect is indicated as follows: 1 symbol (+) <= .05; 2 symbols (++) <= .01; 3 symbols (+++) <= .001.

Table 5 Simplified Presidential-Election Regression Results, with Race and Ethnicity

	1880	1892	1900	1912	1920	1932	1940	1952	1960	1972	1980	1988
Largest party vote											+++	
Log of population			---	--	--	---	---	-	---	---	---	---
Density		++				-						
Rural density				++				-		-	+	
Percent urban						-			-			
Percent aged 55 and over			---		+++	+	+	+++		-	+++	++
Percent school attendance				---	+++	+++	+++				-	++
Percent college attainment				++		++	++	+	+++	++	+++	+++
Percent cropland									+		+	
Mean precipitation										++		
Mean temperature					-	---	---	---	-	-		
Colorado			+++	+	++	+++	+++	++		+	+++	+++
Kansas		++	++		+++	++	+++	+		+	+++	+++
Montana		+				-		-		+		
Nebraska			++	+	++	-					--	
New Mexico							++			+	+	+
North Dakota										+	+	
Oklahoma						+	+++	+++		+		
South Dakota		+	+++			+	+++			++	+++	++
Texas			+++	---		---			-			+
Wyoming						Reference Category for States						
Percent African-American				--				-	---	-	-	-
Percent UK and Ireland							+++	+++	+	+++	+++	+++
Percent Germany							+++	+++	+++	+++	+++	+++
Percent Scandinavia				--		--	--			+	+++	+++
Percent East Europe/Russia	--		+++			++		+		+++	++	++
Percent Mexico									+++	+++	+++	+++
Percent Hispano	+++		+++		++	+++	+++	+++	+++	+++	+++	+++
Adjusted R^2	0.208	0.324	0.397	0.732	0.836	0.909	0.918	0.812	0.829	0.755	0.799	0.766

NOTES   Gray areas are variables that are not included in the models. Plus and minus signs indicate the sign of the coefficient. The significance of the effect is indicated as follows: 1 symbol (+) <= .05; 2 symbols (++) <= .01; 3 symbols (+++) <= .001.

We identify six groups of racial and ethnic origin—African-Americans (the percentage identified as "Black" or "Negro"), Mexicans, British/Irish, Germans, Scandinavians, and East Europeans/Russians. We also include a category for the Spanish population in New Mexico called Hispanos, whose ancestors settled in northern New Mexico as early as the sixteenth century, and who claim an ethnic identity different from that of Mexicans or other Latinos. These people are difficult to identify through the nativity question in the 1910 census because they were all born in the United States to parents who were born in the United States. Thankfully, they can be located through the self-identification question in the 1990 census.[13]

Our results about race and ethnicity show that only one group, the Hispano population of New Mexico, was consistently associated with higher voter participation, especially since 1920. Other groups, except for African-Americans and people of Mexican origin, were associated with higher participation, but only occasionally before the 1952 presidential election. Beginning with 1952, the four groups of European origin display higher voter participation as their proportion of a county's population increased. Although we believe this pattern to be accurate, we must note that we make a jump between the data of 1940, for which we still use the nativity and parents' nativity data from 1910, and that of 1952, for which we begin using the self-identified ancestry from the 1990 census.

Our statistical models explain little of the variation between counties in voter participation between 1880 and 1900. The situation might be inexplicable; alternatively, our variables might be inadequate or too few. The basic variables, plus state influences, however, can explain a major part of the variance between 1912 and 1940 (and possibly 1952). Voter behavior tended to cluster along geographical lines, and distinct political cultures tended to follow the north–south gradient associated with temperature, or to be associated with states. During the first half of the twentieth

13 Since the counties in which the Hispano population lives have changed little between the beginning and the end of the twentieth century, we use the 1990 county data about Hispanos for all years. See Gutmann et al., "Ethnicity and Land Use," for details. Ernest Barksdale Fincher, *Spanish-Americans as a Political Factor in New Mexico, 1912–1950* (New York, 1974); Suzanne Forrest, *The Preservation of the Village: New Mexico's Hispanics and the New Deal* (Albuquerque, 1989); Richard L. Nostrand, *The Hispano Homeland* (Norman, 1992).

century, voters in Colorado, Kansas, South Dakota, and New Mexico (identified as Hispanos or Catholics) were more likely to vote, and those in Texas less likely to vote. Voters from the other states—Montana, North Dakota, Oklahoma, and Wyoming—fit somewhere in the middle. We have insufficient data to comment on Nebraska.

Beginning with 1952, and more clearly 1960, counties with greater percentages of people reporting the most common European ancestries had greater voter participation. This trend might be an indication that the large-scale out-migration, and other social changes, that have occurred in the rural Great Plains have weakened state-level political cultures, replacing them with, or at least supplementing them by, ethnic-group political cultures that sustain a larger proportion of voter participation.

Our analysis shows that most of the voting variation can be explained by a simple set of variables that include population characteristics, education, environment, land use, and geography (in its broadest north–south sense). We gain precision by adding the state in which a particular county was located (to get a sense of state-level political cultures) and by adding either religious affiliation or ethnic identity. The results suggest that political participation shifted from a greater association with general location (state) during the middle of the twentieth century, to a greater association with ethnic affiliation during the latter part of the century. If we look at the coefficients (standardized for variation in the independent variable), the population of German ancestry has the strongest effect, followed by that from the United Kingdom/Ireland, Scandinavia, and the Hispanos of New Mexico. Although we do not report them formally in this article, the congressional elections demonstrate this pattern even more definitively than the presidential-participation results.

SOCIAL CAPITAL AND GOVERNANCE OF GRAZING ON NATIONAL GRASSLANDS   To this point, we have examined social predictors of community building, and the impact of those ties on civic participation. Now we turn to a directly political manifestation of social capital. We suggest that where strong community networks existed, citizens were more likely to make formal efforts to influence government policy on land use. The National Grasslands, the product of federal legislation in the 1930s, were designed to protect submarginal land in the Great Plains from erosion, as well as control agricultural over-production. Originally under the jurisdiction of the Soil Conversation Service, they have been administered by the United States Forest Service since 1953. The National Land-Use Planning Committee, founded in 1932, originally intended to remove more than 6.5 million acres from cultivation in the Great Plains. Today, however, the National Grasslands of the Great Plains contain 3.7 million acres. Because the boundaries of the National Grasslands do not follow county outlines, this analysis includes any county that has a grassland within it, even if a large section of the county is not grassland. Our study area includes fifteen of the National Grasslands, partially covering thirty-seven counties (see Table 6).[14]

As early as 1935, the federal government re-opened some of these areas to grazing, setting out guidelines for land use and issuing permits to ranchers. The Forest Service often cedes most of its duties to privately run grazing associations, which are, in some regions, fully responsible for issuing permits, collecting grazing fees, and controlling fires and trespass. Grazing cooperatives developed at different times on the various grasslands; approximately half of them formed during the 1930s and 1940s, soon after the land became available to ranchers. Although ranchers belonging to grazing associations must conform to guidelines set by the National Forest Service, they are otherwise autonomous. This scenario suggests that rural communities, far from being alienated from the federal government, are involved in a relationship of mutual trust with it. Moreover, the extent to which local users governed the land might reflect levels of social capital in Great Plains communities. We can use our historical data to assess the demographic and social characteristics of the relevant counties during the formation of their grazing organizations.[15]

---

14 U.S. Department of Agriculture, *The National Grasslands by State* (Washington, D.C., 1997).
15 Terry West, "USDA Forest Service Management of the National Grasslands," unpub. paper presented at a conference about the United States Dept. of Agriculture, Iowa State University, Ames, 1989; Douglas R. Hurt, "Federal Land Reclamation in the Dust Bowl," *Great Plains Quarterly*, III (1983), 94–106; Cornelia Butler Flora, "Social Capital and Sustainability: Agriculture and Communities in the Great Plains and Corn Belt," journal paper J-16309, Iowa Agriculture and Home Economics Experiment Station, Ames, Iowa, 1995, summary in *Sustainable Agriculture/Technical Reviews*, VII (1995), 11–13.

Table 6 Counties Intersecting with National Grasslands, and Their
Grazing Associations

COUNTY	NATIONAL GRASSLAND	YEAR GRAZING ASSOCIATION(S) ESTABLISHED
Baca, CO	Comanche	1970s
Las Animas, CO	Comanche	1970s
Otero, CO	Comanche	1970s
Weld, CO	Pawnee	1939
Morton, KS	Cimarron	1944
Stevens, KS	Cimarron	None
Dawes, NE	Oglala	1960s
Sioux, NE	Oglala	1960s
Colfax, NM	Kiowa	None
Harding, NM	Kiowa	None
Union, NM	Kiowa	None
Billings, ND	Little Missouri	1937
Golden Valley, ND	Little Missouri	1937
Grant, ND	Cedar River	1981
McKenzie, ND	Little Missouri	1937
Ransom, ND	Sheyenne	1941
Richland, ND	Sheyenne	1941
Sioux, ND	Cedar River	1981
Slope, ND	Little Missouri	1937
Cimarron, OK	Rita Blanca	None
Roger Mills, OK	Black Kettle	None
Corson, SD	Grand River	1960s
Custer, SD	Buffalo Gap	1940s
Fall River, SD	Buffalo Gap	1940s
Jackson, SD	Buffalo Gap	1940s
Jones, SD	Fort Pierre	1930s
Lyman, SD	Fort Pierre	1930s
Pennington, SD	Buffalo Gap	1940s
Perkins, SD	Grand River	1960s
Stanley, SD	Fort Pierre	1930s
Dallam, TX	Rita Blanca	None
Gray, TX	Lake McClellan	None
Campbell, WY	Thunder Basin	1930s
Converse, WY	Thunder Basin	1930s
Crook, WY	Thunder Basin	1930s
Niobrara, WY	Thunder Basin	1930s
Weston, WY	Thunder Basin	1930s

Because we argue that the presence of these associations is an indicator of community involvement, we must examine those counties in which no grazing associations presently exist. Of the thirty-seven counties in our study that intersect with the National Grasslands, only seven do not maintain grazing associations. These seven, which are scattered in the panhandle area of New Mexico, Texas, and Oklahoma, contain the Kiowa, McClellan, and Black Kettle National Grasslands. All four of these National Grasslands were originally under the supervision of the Soil Conservation Service, and later the National Forest Service. Currently, they are part of Cibola National Forest, headquartered in Albuquerque, New Mexico. To understand why the ranchers in this region did not form cooperatives, we need to take into account both regional commonalities and their shared administration from a single source.

The seven counties that contain the Kiowa, Rita Blanca, McClellan, and Black Kettle National Grasslands reflect two dissimilar patterns of community. The counties in Texas and Oklahoma, which comprise approximately three-fourths of the grassland area, show low levels of community identity that are consistent with their lack of grazing associations. Dallam and Gray counties, in Texas, and Cimarron and Roger Mills counties, in Oklahoma, show little evidence of ethnic clustering in 1910: The foreign population was comparatively low, perhaps indicating an early settlement period. In general, early settlement correlates with high levels of social capital, but not here. Of these four counties, the highest religious concentration was in Gray County, where 10.1 percent of the population was Baptist. Not surprisingly, three of the four counties were below the median in participation for the 1940 presidential election; the low of 38.1 percent fell to Gray County. Given the lack of ethnic or religious communities, and the low voter turnout, the failure of these counties to form grazing associations supports our hypotheses about measuring social capital. Communities with existing social networks, based on common cultural values or identities, are most likely to generate social capital that is strong enough to translate into political activism, whether at the national or local level.[16]

---

16 Although Gray County, Texas, is within the boundaries of Black Kettle National Grassland, the area of intersection is largely water, relegated to recreation. According to Charles Milner of the Black Kettle National Grassland administration, the foremost reason for the lack of grazing associations in Gray County is its physical landscape.

The lack of grazing associations in the four New Mexico counties—Colfax, Harding, Union, and Gary—is more difficult to explain, because they have high levels of ethnic and religious clustering. They are among the most concentrated sites of Hispano presence on the Great Plains, hence heavily Roman Catholic. Since our regressions show that Roman Catholics throughout the region were more likely to vote than other groups, we might have expected them to be more involved in such organizations as the grazing associations; voting participation in these counties was extremely high during the years when the grazing associations came into being. In 1940, 91.2 percent of Harding County voters turned out for the presidential contest, compared with a median of 78.1 percent for the thirty-seven grassland counties as a whole.

Since the conjectured association of social capital with ethnic and religious characteristics and high voting participation does not hold in this instance, what explains the lack of grazing associations in New Mexico? One possibility is that the federal administration of these lands was unusually strict, discouraging the formation of such groups. Another possibility is that these counties interacted with the government in such a way that even without an official grazing association, ranchers managed to exert control over grazing practices. A third answer to this apparently contradictory situation is that our measures of social capital are simply not applicable to this case. The cultural motivators of voting participation might not translate into the formation of local organizations; a myriad of other factors might have intervened.

Be that as it may, we believe that special circumstances obtained in the three New Mexico counties, notably long-standing tensions between small ranchers and commercial farmers. In the 1930s, New Mexican ranchers distrusted the Soil Conservation Service and the commercial farm-oriented interests that it represented. These tensions surfaced often during the 1930s and 1940s, leading to such oppressive management practices as the widely protested 1939 firing of George Quesenberry, the state agricultural extension director, who fought for the committee representation of groups of small farmers and ranchers. Furthermore, the dynamic between smaller and larger agribusinesses included a significant racial component. The Hispanos, who owned only small tracts if any land at all, were the primary losers in the National Grasslands project, which increasingly devoted resources to larger operators. The lack of grazing associations in these counties undoubtedly owes something to the fact that United States Forest Rangers appeared to many small operators in New Mexico as "uniformed occupational troopers."[17]

Some grazing associations inaugurated in the 1930s and 1940s are still strong today—for example, Cimarron National Grassland, in Morton County, Kansas, where ranchers formed a grazing association in 1944, immediately after the government re-opened the land for private use. According to the local ranchers, it was able to flourish because it was free from government interference. Since Morton County had no county agent, the landowners appointed all officers, and made decisions about grazing practices, based on the sketchy requirements of the government. Although the government had set a grazing fee, the association increased it to pay for its own administrative costs. Among the approximately 100 members of the association, twenty-three have been active for over forty years; some of them are widows who joined after the death of their husbands, the original members.[18]

The characteristics of Morton County are only partially consistent with a high level of social capital. The county's population was almost entirely native-born in 1910 (94.2 percent), and no ethnic or religious clustering was apparent. However, the county's total population at that time was a mere 1,700, following a severe out-migration in response to poor weather and widespread homestead fires in the 1890s. Hence, we rely on the 1990 ethnicity data to give a clearer picture of the county's composition in 1944, when the grazing association was formed. By 1990, German ancestry (21.8 percent) and United Kingdom ancestry (24.4 percent) were the greatest self-reported ethnic identifications in the county. Yet, those ethnic percentages are near the median for all grassland counties; they do not fully explain the strong community ties in Morton County. With reference to religion, however, the county showed a greater tendency toward monolithic grouping. In 1940, the greatest religious group by far was the Methodists—19.7 percent of the population, compared with a median of 2.6 percent for all grassland counties. This relatively high concentration of one religion might have translated into stronger community organization. In support of this notion are the regression

17 Forrest, *Preservation of the Village.*
18 Myrna K. Barnes, *Fifty Years of Roundups,* privately published history of the Morton County Grazing Association (Elkhart, Kans., 1993).

results in Table 5, which show that Methodists were slightly and positively associated with voter participation from 1952 to 1960.[19]

Voter turnout was high in Morton County during the crucial period of grazing-association formation. The 1940 presidential race elicited a participation rate of 88.9 percent, compared with the median of 78.1 for grassland counties. We submit that the strong community ties evidenced by the Morton County grazing association are partially due to religious clustering and partially due to other forces unmeasured. In this particular case, the settlement history of the county escapes our ethnic measures because of the late arrival of most of the population. The out-migration in the 1890s might have left a sense of solidarity among the settlers who remained. Equally possible is that the rapid settlement after 1913, when a railroad was completed, followed a pattern of community building that we do not yet understand.

A second grassland area that successfully established grazing associations is Little Missouri, which intersects with four counties—Billings, Golden Valley, McKenzie, and Slope, in western North Dakota. Little Missouri is the largest of the grasslands, with more than 1 million acres. It contains four grazing associations, established in 1937, immediately after the government permitted private use of the land. These organizations vary considerably in size; memberships run from 200 to 9. The largest, in McKenzie County, has a set number of members, based on ownership of predetermined sections of land. The association issues additional permits for lesser privileges to non-members. The second largest of the grazing associations on Little Missouri, Medora District in Billings County, was, in 1997, fighting the United States Forest Service for the right to continue grazing in the area.[20]

Unlike Morton County in Kansas, the counties in Little Missouri exhibit distinct ethnic and religious clustering. McKenzie County had a 27 percent Scandinavian population in 1910, compared with a median of 2.3 percent for all thirty-seven grassland counties. By 1990, Scandinavians were 38.4 percent of the county population, representing the second highest concentration of that ethnicity in all grassland counties for that year. Not surprisingly,

19 Joe Hartman and Mechele MacDonald, "The Cornerstone of Kansas," *Kansas Wildlife and Parks,* XLV (1988), 9–13.
20 Personal interview of Katie Goldsberry of the Medora Grasslands Office by Pullum, October 1997.

given the high levels of Scandinavian ethnicity, Lutherans dominated the religious scene in the 1930s and 1940s, representing 41
percent of the population; the median for all grassland counties
was only 1.6 percent.

Billings County, the site of the second largest grazing association, had equally significant ethnic and religious clustering,
although those clusters consisted of different groups. In 1910, it
had a 20.2 percent German population, compared with a median
of 6.4 percent for all thirty-seven grassland counties. By 1990,
Germans comprised 38.8 percent of the total population. The
county's religious characteristics at the time of the 1940 election
were extremely concentrated. Roman Catholics represented 41.3
percent of the population; Lutherans, the next largest group,
equalled only 2.6 percent. The Roman Catholic population appears even more significant in comparison with the median of 8.3
percent for all grassland counties at that time.

Despite their strong ethnic and religious concentration, however, the voting turnout for the four Little Missouri counties in
1940 was only slightly higher than the median for all grassland
counties. Even McKenzie, which showed the highest turnout in
the 1940 presidential race, achieved only 83.2 percent participation—the median being 78.1—and Harding County, New
Mexico, with no grazing association, reached 91.2 percent participation in the same election. Again, ethnic and religious clustering and the formation of grazing associations do not necessarily
correlate well with high voter turnout. Nonetheless, community
members were willing to become active in politics in response to
a direct threat to their economic interest. To combat inefficiency
in the federal governance of the Little Missouri grassland, ranchers
voluntarily formed grazing associations. Ranchers believed that
their associations had more power over practical matters than did
the Forest Service. Political culture became more accommodating
toward prevailing local interests, as evidenced by the federal government's willingness to let grazing associations make decisions
about the land. The statements of a ranger on the Little Missouri
grassland suggest the local involvement and political pragmatism
that Putnam found in his study of social capital in Italy: "We felt
that the regular forest service misunderstood our actions or could
care less, thus we ran the national grasslands on our own . . . there
were not a lot of rules to bind [us] . . . instead in the northern

Plains we operated with the grazing associations who dealt with day-to-day operations."[21]

The formation of grazing associations on the National Grasslands offers an opportunity to apply Putnam's model of social capital to the Great Plains. Although we cannot fully explain the events described herein, we can begin to understand them, from the perspective of religion, ethnicity, and voter turnout. Most of the counties that did not develop grazing associations conform to our notion of low social capital: They had little ethnic and religious clustering and low voter turnout. The exceptions are the three counties in New Mexico, where ethnicity and religion were important community factors, and voter turnout extremely high. But these counties seem to have been hampered by tensions related to race and over-representation of large-scale agribusiness concerns.

Our two examples of grasslands that managed to form strong grazing associations offer varying fits with our model of social capital. Cimarron National Grassland in Morton County, Kansas, had unremarkable ethnic clustering, a somewhat notable Methodist presence, and high voting participation. The counties intersecting with Little Missouri National Grassland in North Dakota had the opposite imbalance of characteristics—strong ethnic and religious communities but a voting turnout only slightly above the median. Each of these factors contributes something to our understanding of the formation of grazing associations, and helps to test our ideas about social capital.

Ethnic and religious effects are among the building blocks of other community networks. People with these factors in common may be more likely to meet for the sake of unrelated activities and thereby generate social capital. We argue that once such civic involvement exists, it is only a small step to the political activism that Putnam describes. However, we find that national and local political activism are independent of each other. Counties that show high participation in national elections may not organize at a smaller scale because citizens do not perceive a direct local threat. Even though high levels of social capital might exist, they will not necessarily mobilize a community toward local government. We also observe the reverse situation, namely, a local government

21 West, "USDA Forest Service," 6–7.

that is stronger than participation in national elections, as a response to a direct need. The measures that we use in this study capture only some of the sufficient causes of the political manifestations of social capital. Other factors are less predictable, and more difficult to quantify. Further consideration of these issues will, we hope, elicit other methods by which we can measure and predict community involvement in local government.

Social capital existed everywhere in the Great Plains to some extent; what we measure in this article are differences in levels of social capital between counties within the Great Plains. Although it is difficult to judge from our measures what led to different levels of political participation during the late nineteenth and early twentieth century, we are increasingly able to predict the differences between voter participation at the county level from the 1920s until the middle of the twentieth century. The key element in that prediction is the state in which the county was located; the state represents the presence of a local political culture that added to—and probably partly overcame—the ethnic, religious, and economic differences within communities, and even within individual towns and counties. The social capital that underlay state political cultures might have included feelings of regional pride, identification with particular issues or candidates, or such common economic considerations as agricultural choices based on the environment. Although we cannot identify precisely why location at the state level influenced voting choices, the fact that it did suggests a sense of shared community beyond personal interaction. This factor reflected social capital of a deep and sustained sort, even if we cannot equate it with choral societies or parent–teacher associations.

A local political culture that matured at the end of the first half of the twentieth century was gradually replaced by a national, media-reliant political culture that allows more opportunities for choice. Our data capture this transformation imperfectly, but the strengthening of ethnicity effects, at the expense of state effects, is a key indication of it. Individuals identify themselves with far more variety now than they did fifty years ago. The effect of these new affiliations is evident in the diminution of major-party effects and the rise of age-group effects. The exact mechanisms by which this transformation occurred, and the precise ways in which people perceive their participation, require a different kind of research than we have done thus far. The future calls for an examination of how participation worked within individual communities.

Despite the need for further study, the importance of the transition from local to national political cultures is not to be underestimated. We use the plural here, because we believe that there were, and still are, many political cultures—with much social capital—in the Great Plains. Moreover, we stress the role of national media in shaping the diversity of the political cultures that have emerged during the previous half-century. Unitary local embodiments of social capital no longer shape public behavior so much as multiple and widely dispersed embodiments of it do. People are not simply North Dakotans or Swedish-Americans, but also Republicans, Christians, parents, senior citizens, members of organized labor, or liberals. Television might have encouraged passivity in some ways, but exposure to more ideas—from Pat Buchanan's to Jesse Jackson's—has allowed Americans more opportunity to choose.

The story of the national grasslands confirms the complexity of social capital in the Great Plains; it allows us to see how local institutions match up with national trends and national participation. Since their conception in the 1930s, the National Grasslands have had more or less democratic institutions for self-government, depending on choices made largely by local ranchers, within a context established by the federal government. Most of the grasslands have rancher-organized grazing associations that administer them together with representatives of the United States Forest Service. The few grassland areas without such grazing associations seem to have significantly different profiles. The largest of them— located in the Texas and Oklahoma panhandle—does not demonstrate the kind of religious or ethnic-group orientation that seems to issue in social capital. It hardly seems accidental that it turned out the lowest general-election vote in many years.

Like Putnam, we examined a large region with an eye toward understanding the differences between communities with regard to social capital, as manifested by their political participation, at both the local and national level. Counties with high levels of ethnic and religious cohesion are most likely to generate community sensibility and, in turn, civic organization. We do not systematically measure local institutions in this study, but there is evidence of social capital at the county and state level. A sense of community influences voting participation in presidential elections. In our study of grazing associations, we predict at least a tendency toward civic involvement, although we cannot predict its success. Further, community ties and sensibilities are important factors in national politics, and they provide people with enough power to recreate political culture to suit their needs.

APPENDIX: SOURCES FOR QUANTITATIVE DATA

ELECTION DATA

Inter-University Consortium for Political and Social Research. 1995. *United States Historical Election Returns, 1824–1968.* Machine-readable data file available as ICPSR file no. 1. Ann Arbor, Mich.

Inter-University Consortium for Political and Social Research. 1995. *Candidate Name and Constituency Totals, 1788–1988.* Machine-readable data file available as ICPSR file no. 2.

Inter-University Consortium for Political and Social Research. 1995. *General Election Data for the United States, 1970–1988.* Machine-readable data file available as ICPSR file no. 13.

AGRICULTURAL CENSUSES

Inter-University Consortium for Political and Social Research. 1972. *Historical Demographic, Economic, and Social Data: The United States, 1790–1970.* Machine-readable data file available as ICPSR file no. 3 (used for agricultural census data, 1930–1950).

Economic Research Service, U.S. Department of Agriculture. 1989. *Census of Agriculture County Profiles, 1949–82.* Electronic files on magnetic tape.

Bureau of the Census. U.S. Dept. of Commerce. 1990. *1987 Census of Agriculture.* Geographic Area Series: State and County Data Files. Electronic Files on CD-ROM (used for 1978).

Bureau of the Census, U.S. Dept. of Commerce. 1995. *1992 Census of Agriculture.* Geographic Area Series 1B: U.S. Summary and County Level Data. Electronic Files on CD-ROM (used for 1982, 1987, and 1992).

Bureau of the Census, U.S. Dept. of Commerce. 1997. *1969 and 1974 Census of Agriculture, Combined-Final, County and Misc. Data Files.* Electronic Files on CD-ROM, copied from original magnetic tapes.

POPULATION CENSUSES

U.S. Dept. of Commerce. Bureau of the Census, N.D. *County and City Data Book Consolidated File: County Data, 1947–1977.* ICPSR 7736 (used for 1940–1970 data). Washington, D.C.

U.S. Dept. of Commerce. Bureau of the Census. N.D. *County Statistics File 3 (CO-STAT3).* ICPSR 9168 (used for 1980 data). Washington, D.C.

U.S. Dept. of Commerce. Bureau of the Census. 1991. *Census of Population and Housing, 1990: Summary Tape File 3.* Machine-readable data files (used for 1990 data). Washington, D.C.

U.S. Dept. of Commerce. Bureau of the Census. 1996. *USA Counties 1996.* Machine-readable data files on CD-ROM (used for 1990 data). Washington, D.C.

RELIGION DATA

Inter-University Consortium for Political and Social Research. 1972. *Historical Demographic, Economic, and Social Data: The United States, 1790–1970.* Machine-readable data file available as ICPSR file no. 3 (used for U.S. Censuses of Religion, 1890).

U.S. Dept. of Commerce. Bureau of the Census. N.D. *Censuses of Religious Bodies, 1906–1936.* Machine-readable data file available from the Inter-University Consortium for Political and Social Research as ICPSR file no. 8 (sometimes also distributed as part of ICPSR file no. 3).

National Council of Churches of Christ in the U.S.A. 1952. *Survey of Churches and Church Membership by County, 1952.* Machine-readable data file available from the Inter-University Consortium for Political and Social Research as ICPSR file no. 14.

National Council of Churches of Christ in the U.S.A. 1971. *Survey of Church Membership, 1971.* Machine-readable data file available from the Inter-University Consortium for Political and Social Research as ICPSR file no. 7520.

Roper Center for Public Opinion Research. 1980. *Churches and Church Membership in the United States, 1980.* Storrs, Connecticut.

Roper Center for Public Opinion Research. 1990. *Churches and Church Membership in the United States, 1990.* Storrs, Connecticut.

CLIMATE DATA

T. R. Karl, C. N. Williams, Jr., F. T. Quinlan, and T. A. Boden, 1990. United States Historical Climatology Network (HCN) Serial Temperature and Precipitation Data, Environmental Science Division, Publication No. 3404. Carbon Dioxide Information and Analysis Center, Oak Ridge National Laboratory, Oak Ridge, Tenn. The historical climatology data are stored as point data for 1,221 stations in the United States at monthly intervals. We generalized these data for each month by interpolating from the point data to all points within the area, and then calculated an average for each county unit.

COUNTY BOUNDARIES

U.S. Historical County Boundary Files, 1790–1970. Available from the Department of Anthropology and Geography, Louisiana State University, Baton Rouge, Louisiana (for details, see Gutmann and Christie Sample, "Land, Climate, and Settlement on the Texas Frontier," *Southwestern Historical Quarterly,* xcix [1996], 136–175).

Lucian W. Pye

Civility, Social Capital, and Civil Society: Three Powerful Concepts for Explaining Asia

Many knowledgeable people believe that developments in East and Southeast Asia will vindicate the theory that successful economic growth can set the stage for political democracy. Two decades of rapid economic growth there hold out the promise that the arrival of democracy may not be far behind. First Japan and then South Korea and Taiwan broke from their one-party, authoritarian traditions to become plausible democracies. Their achievements have given hope that China and the economically developing Southeast Asian countries will follow the same path. Such, after all, was the implicit expectation in much of modernization theory, including the assumption that foreign economic aid would, by facilitating economic development, prepare the way for transitions to democracy.

Current practices from Singapore to Beijing, however, are a cause for concern. Not only have there been no smooth transitions from economic to political change in these countries, but numerous Asian leaders are now insisting that such a sequence is neither inevitable nor desirable. In contrast to the dominant thinking in Asia during the first two-thirds of the twentieth century that these societies had to take on new values in order to make both economic and political progress, voices there now are proclaiming that "Asian values" are different from Western ones, and that economic growth can occur without the individualism associated with pluralistic democracy.

In the light of these concerns, it becomes reasonable to reconsider judgments about the character of democracy in Japan, South Korea, and Taiwan since it is still seen as an exceptional event for an opposition party in even those supposedly democratic countries to come to power. Maybe Asian values are distinctive. Moreover, in the wake of the 1997/98 Asian financial crises, which brought into question the soundness of the widely proclaimed economic "miracles," the relationship between economics

Lucian W. Pye is Professor of Political Science, Emeritus, Massachusetts Institute of Technology. He is the author of *Asian Power and Politics: The Cultural Dimensions of Authority* (Cambridge, Mass., 1985); *The Spirit of Chinese Politics* (Cambridge, Mass., 1992).

and democracy in Asia has become even more murky and confused. Some who are anxious to be at the forefront in announcing new paradigms are already proclaiming that democracy in Asia might, paradoxically, arise as the result of economic troubles rather than successes.

Given all the uncertainties in the relationship between economic and political development in much of East and Southeast Asia, the time seems right to rethink the nature of social relations in Asia: Do they provide the basic essentials for stable, pluralistic democracy? The answer requires going beyond Putnam's conceptual framework, and to employ an approach based on three related and overlapping, but still distinct concepts: civility, social capital, and civil society.

Every society has its rules of *civility* that ensure social order, thereby forming an integrated functioning society and preventing confusion, disorder, and anarchy. *Social capital,* as defined by Putnam, testifies to the critical level of trust among the members of a society that makes collective action possible. Social capital builds upon the norms of civility; it is the next step up in the development of a democratic political culture. Finally, *civil society* consists of the diverse autonomous interest groups that can exert pressure on the state. The creation of a civil society is critical for the effective performance of democracy.[1]

These three concepts are the key building blocks for democratic theory. Civility involves the most general norms of personal interaction; social capital determines the potential for reaching community and national goals collectively, and civil society provides the critical basis for the articulation and aggregation of interests essential for pluralistic democracy. The particular civility norms of a country either facilitate or impede the accumulation of social capital. The amount of social capital amassed by a society sets the stage for the emergence of a healthy civil society, which in its turn provides the dynamics for democratic politics.

The ways in which these ideas fit together helps to illuminate such crucial developmental issues as the relationship between state and society, the boundaries between private and public activities, and the relative values of the individual and the community. These

---

1   Robert D. Putnam, with Roberto Leonardi and Raffaella Y. Nanetti, *Making Democracy Work: Civic Traditions in Modern Italy* (Princeton, 1993).

concepts serve as powerful tools for analysis, not as isolated variables but as patterns of interrelationships. We are dealing with clouds, not clocks.[2]

In trying to explain why Asia has developed the way it has, and in seeking to forecast likely future Asian developments, we must ask fundamental questions in terms of the three concepts: Do the standards of civility in the various countries encourage respect for differences in opinion and thereby allow constructive political competition to take place? Do they encourage withdrawal from politics and passivity toward authority? Is their brand of social capital consistent with the trust essential for a free society, or is it more in line with the culture of dependency common to stable autocracies? And what are the prospects for the growth of vibrant civil societies? Is the emergence of healthy establishments dedicated to the common good likely, or will the informal clustering of power produce corruption and rule by mafia? Will the agglutinative nature of power mean that the powerful and the rich will become as one, or will the political and the economic realms—the public and the private—diverge?

CIVILITY: THE RULES THAT FORM A SOCIETY   Shils maintained that civility is the most fundamental concept for understanding how societies are shaped and organized and, hence, the most basic concept for the discipline of sociology. Every society has distinctive rules of etiquette and standards of behavior that render the behavior of individuals more or less predictable and set the tone for public life. Civility is not to be confused with gentility or virtue; even a band of thieves and rogues has its stated and unstated rules of conduct. When civility totally breaks down, society ceases to exist. When civility is strong and widely upheld, the society will be integrated and coherent. Civility is critical not just for private, personal relationships, but also for relationships of power and authority. Since parliamentary democracy cannot operate without respect for rules of civility, civility is the measure of democratic political culture: High civility means smooth democ-

2   Gabriel Almond, building on Karl Popper's metaphor for understanding the continuum of determinacy to indeterminacy in physical systems, maintained that in spite of efforts by the more "scientifically" inclined to make the cause-effect relationship in the social sciences "clock-like," political causality still remains "cloud-like" ("Clouds, Clocks, and the Study of Politics," *World Politics,* XXIX [1977], 489–522).

racy; low civility means repressive rule to keep people in line. Pluralistic democracy, especially when it involves rival moral concepts, requires an exceptionally high level of civility.[3]

Three dimensions of civility are especially important for comparative political analysis. The first involves, on the one hand, differences in the standards of behavior with respect to personal, intimate relations, and, on the other, the norms for impersonal, public relationships. The second involves the standards governing status gradations—in particular, superior–inferior relationships. The third involves the norms controlling human aggression and managing conflict situations. The practices of a society in these three areas have significant consequences in facilitating or retarding democratic development.

All cultures recognize that norms of civility should differ in accordance with the relationship, establishing one set of standards for dealing with intimates—including family and personal relationships—a different set of norms for relations among acquaintances, and, finally, an outer ring of impersonal relations involving strangers. The rules in each sphere differ greatly from culture to culture; total reversals in the conventions are not without precedent. In American culture, the closer the relationship, the more informality obtains. Among family and friends, one can "relax"; among strangers, one exercises a certain propriety. In Chinese culture, however, the obligations of filial piety and the key Confucian relationships of father–son and brother–brother mean that in the heart of the family, high standards and ritual correctness are expected to be upheld. Yet, at the same time, rudeness is acceptable toward those foreigners who are thought to be mere "barbarians." This aspect of Chinese culture creates a problem of intimacy. People crave the presumed security of intimacy even as the standards of intimate relations have a distant, formal quality, and relations with strangers tend to be loaded with distrust and suspicion. In a partial attempt to overcome this difficulty, Chinese culture allows for the idea that people can become "old friends" almost instantaneously, thus pretending to change from strangers to intimates. Yet, Confucianism's lack of civility for all but face-

---

3   For a collection of some of his work on civility, see Edward Shils (ed. Steven Grosby), *The Virtue of Civility: Selected Essays on Liberalism, Tradition, and Civil Society* (Indianapolis, 1997). For an illuminating analysis of democracy's best strategy to cope with fundamental moral disagreements and, in particular, the need for reciprocity among citizens, see Amy Gutmann and Dennis Thompson, *Democracy and Disagreement* (Cambridge, 1996).

to-face encounters is hardly a favorable condition for participatory democracy.

For democratic development, the norms of civility must encourage positive rules for a wide range of impersonal relationships. The practices common in a traditional society, in which people are expected to be honest and helpful mainly with family and friends, and in which they can feel free to outwit and cheat outsiders, will not support a pluralistic democracy. Significantly, the five key Confucian relationships jump from father–son, brother–brother, and husband–wife to neighbor–neighbor and prince–subject, largely bypassing the huge realm of impersonal relationships. This lack of bonding at a more generalized level caused Sun Yet-sen to say that "China is a plate of sand." As he correctly saw it, Chinese society showed little social integration beyond family, clan, and personal relationships.

The Southeast Asian cultures tend to have elaborate rules for conducting impersonal relationships, but almost always in hierarchical terms, thus exemplifying the second key dimension of civility—the rules about how superiors and subordinates should conduct their relations. Cultures differ in how people are expected to show respect and deference to authority figures, and in how those in power should treat the weak. Americans learn early that the best way to cope with father's authority is either to play along with him or to challenge his standards of justice by accusing him of being "unfair." Such is the training ground for the exaggerated American concern about equality. Americans strive to get on friendly terms, even on a first-name basis, with authority figures in the hope of jollying them into becoming less threatening, and to exploit any suggestion of unfairness, especially in not applying rules equally. In all of the Asian cultures, exactly the opposite norms prevail. Formality and correctness is expected and only the innocently naive expect fairness and equal treatment. Asians assume that those with power will make the most of their advantages, whether to play favorites openly or to humiliate the weak in order to keep them in their places.[4]

---

4 In Asia, defense of the weak often amounted to little more than the hope of shaming officials who misbehaved. In traditional China, those who felt mistreated by an official would frequently make a spectacle by wailing their sorrows publicly. Extreme cases determined to get even might go so far as to commit suicide on a magistrate's doorstep. Rather than being shamed, many Chinese officials probably felt the act to be good riddance.

Moreover, all of the Asian cultures practice rituals of civility in superior–inferior relationships that glorify the dignity of the superior; in these cultures, dignity is the essence of power. The result is that those in authority tend to be hypersensitive to any hint of a slight or any implicit challenge to their status. The political effect is to reinforce authoritarian norms and complicate the development of the adversarial relationships essential for competitive democracy.

Superior–subordinate relations, particularly the all-important patron–client ties in Southeast Asia, have much to teach about the creation of social capital. Before turning to that subject, however, we need to examine the third dimension of civility—the management of aggression. Democracy requires strong norms about handling disagreements and controlling the instincts of aggression.

Because anxieties about aggression are particularly intense in Southeast Asia, the dominant rules for social conduct emphasize the suppression of any sign of aggressive sentiments. The Burmese and Thai societies harbor a strong presumption that since people can easily be provoked into violence, the exercise of infinite care and caution in the treatment of others is necessary at all times. One has only one's self to blame for someone else's violent reaction. For example, the Javanese attach tremendous value to the ideal of *alus,* that is, acting in a "pure," "exquisite," "subtle," or "civilized" manner. In the same spirit, conduct should never suggest the shame of *kasar,* which signifies "impoliteness," "coarseness," or "vulgarity." Such intense concern with conforming to refined and ritualized behavior and suppressing strong emotions can be inimical to democracy. It compels people to mask their real sentiments, practice conformity, and pretend to positions that they do not really hold. The need for such a high degree of suppression of aggression means that every now and then in Malay and Javanese society, explosive reactions occur. To run "amok" is, after all, a Malay word.

In Thailand and Burma, as well as in Indonesia and Malaysia, the conventional norms against any show of hostility are so strict that the extreme volatility of political antagonism seems almost inevitable. Since these societies recognize no legitimate display of political opposition, they make it difficult for dissidents to disagree without becoming disagreeable. It is an all-or-nothing predicament.

In sum, although civility is a broad concept that encompasses the social standards of an entire society, its norms can also be very precise, focusing on person-to-person relations, especially those based on power. Civility is thus a key ingredient in linking the general culture of a people to their political culture. The Asian cultures have elaborate standards of personal civility, but they are strikingly weak in the areas of impersonal interaction, which is most important for democratic political cultures. They have vivid standards for superior–inferior relations, but few guidelines for the behavior of equals, which are indispensable for democracy. Finally, their oversensitivity to any sign of antagonism is a serious obstacle to any legitimation of political competition.

Civility cannot be encouraged or produced by state policies; it cannot even be maintained by the coercive powers of the state. Rather, civility depends upon social pressure and the shame that comes with the sense of wrongdoing. Social change has created a moral vacuum in many Asian societies, eroding the potency of civility. Incivility exists in all cultures and at all times, not just in those undergoing dramatic change. Yet, in rapid social change, when old norms no longer apply, new ones might not be available to take their place.

Despite the problems that Asian cultures as a whole demonstrate with certain aspects of civility, many of their subgroups manifest appropriate norms for democratic development. Societies embody a host of established role relationships, each of which demands distinct standards of behavior. These relationships can be seen as either more specialized norms of civility or as providing the basic elements of social capital.

SOCIAL CAPITAL: NETWORKING AND LEARNING TO WORK TOGETHER ON THE BASIS OF TRUST   Social progress calls for the accumulation of binding sentiments of trust and reciprocity, which can provide the bases for effective collective behavior. When a society as a whole is deficient in such sentiments, it lacks the capacity for social mobilization and cannot achieve much economically or politically. The process of accumulating social capital is analogous to that of accumulating the financial capital necessary for economic development. When social capital is positive and constructive, it can produce establishments at either the local or national level, in which elites in different walks of life work together for the common good. When the networking is negative, the result can be a government of corrupt backdoor deals, which, in extreme cases, can end up as mafia rule.

The art of working together requires a significant degree of trust in others so that the benefits of reciprocity can flourish. Members of a society must feel instinctively that if they do a favor, they will in time receive some benefits in return. Trust alone, however, is not enough to further democracy; antisocial gangs can also have codes of honor and trust. Yet, distrust is an unqualified obstacle to positive social development.

Viewed from the perspective of the individual, trust emanates from two sources. The first relates to the basic personality of the individual that is established during infancy and early childhood. Some people have more trust than others; some are characterized by outright distrust. To greatly oversimplify a complex process, during the earliest phase when babies have not learned to differentiate themselves from their environment, they either experience a magical universe in which every cry somehow brings desired responses, or a disconnected, uncertain—even whimsical—universe. The former encourages an instinctive sense of trust in others, whereas the latter can foster a personality marked by distrust.[5]

The second source of trust comes at a later phase of socialization when children learn to distinguish between friends and enemies. Usually the map is quite simple: Family is the realm of security; then comes the circle of acquaintances, which children know on a face-to-face basis; and finally come strangers and, beyond them, foreigners. Trust is generally highest among those who are most like oneself physically and culturally; those most distrusted tend to look different and follow different practices.

Trust and distrust are also shaped by instruction about all kinds of unseen forces—from the idea of a kind and loving God to superstitions about evil spirits, ghosts, and demons. Hence, the universe becomes either predictable, just, and fair or deceptive and dangerous, unless these hidden powers can be harnessed for protection or good luck.

Cultures vary as to how elaborate and frightening these unseen worlds are, but they all include a magical element to explain

---

5 Erik H. Erikson analyzed the connection between trust/distrust and the Freudian oral stage of development in *Childhood and Society* (New York, 1950).

cause and effect in the political realm. Because nobody can see the political process in full operation, people have to create their own fantasies, that is, "theories" about the mysterious capabilities and operations of power and authority. The mystique of leadership depends upon a belief in the potency of unseen forces. When cynicism prevails and authority erodes, society becomes ungovernable. Democracy treads a thin line between respect for authority and the belief that no man is any better than another. The notion that respect should go to the office and not necessarily the man is subtle and not at all natural in tradition-oriented societies.

Such basic issues as the value of working hard, the prudence of saving or delaying gratification, and the reward for behaving correctly are all instinctive and largely settled during the formative socialization process. The Chinese, probably more than other Asians, develop a strong sense of basic trust early, especially with respect to family and clan ties. They also learn that by careful attention to rituals, they can increase their "luck" and reduce the likelihood of misadventure. Several Southeast Asian cultures, however, are noteworthy for treating infants in erratic ways—for not systematically relating effort to reward and for teaching that to delay gratification is to lose opportunity. These cultures carry elaborate spirit worlds filled with more evil than good.

Differences in cultures' levels of basic trust and rules about treating friends and strangers tend to show up in their various networking arrangements. The Chinese system of *quanxi,* or personal connections, is a firmly structured, institutionalized arrangement for ensuring mutual obligation. Family members owe each other support without question; nepotism is a positive practice in China. The connections of quanxi extend outward to those who share a certain identity, for example, those from the same village, town, or even the same province, those from the same class in school or even the same school in different years, and select acquaintances.[6]

Quanxi is not a form of emotional bonding but a formal one, defined largely by objective determinants. Neither personal affinity nor a strong sentiment of debt or obligation for favors rendered need be part of the relationship. Shared background

6   For discussions of quanxi, see Mayfair Mei-hui Yang, *Gifts, Favors and Banquets: The Art of Social Relationships in China* (Ithaca, 1994); Pye, *Asian Power and Politics: The Cultural Dimensions of Authority* (Cambridge, Mass., 1985), 293–299.

alone is enough to force one to recognize an obligation. More-over, payment for a favor need not be immediate or commensu-rate. Indeed, a poorer or weaker party can repay repeated favors with nothing more than a show of deference and respect to the more fortunate one. In this sense, quanxi is unlike the comparable Japanese personal ties of *on* and *giri,* which entail a powerful sense of obligation and indebtedness that cannot be alleviated without definite reciprocation. In Japan, one would not want to put someone under obligation who could not reciprocate effectively.

The Chinese never developed explicit rules of quanxi to distinguish between the virtuous and the dishonorable. The gen-eral feeling in China is that the practice of quanxi has something slightly shameful about it, despite an awareness that the culture could not operate without it. Thus, the domain of quanxi has an amoral quality, which allows it to slip easily from respectable reciprocity to skullduggery.

Although social capital in Southeast Asia varies with the rich cultural differences in the region, it is useful to look at it in terms of two paired cases—Indonesia and the Philippines, where elabo-rate patron–client networks mean that questions of social capital directly shape the civil society, and Burma and Thailand, where social capital barely involves more than the norms of civility.[7]

Political and social life in Indonesia is structured according to the elaborate binding system of *bapakism,* involving a *bapak,* father or patron, and his *anak buah,* children or clients. The relationship is like a family, since once someone has declared that he owes the incalculable debt of *hutang budi* to a bapak figure, the patron can no more dismiss him than a father can rid himself of a son. A rising star in Indonesia may find himself engulfed with lifelong clients who cannot be denied. Just like a natural father, a bapak can be stuck with miserable, no-good anak buaks, and there is little he can do about it.[8]

---

7 The analysis of the Southeast Asian cultures in the paragraphs to follow is based on more detailed treatment in Pye, *Asian Power and Politics,* 90–132.
8 When I once suggested to a distinguished Indonesian political scientist that traditional customs could be used for constructive purposes, he replied,

> You Americans are incorrigibly optimistic; you can always find a silver lining in every cloud. You don't really know what tradition is. You probably think that it is just superiors using one form of address to subordinates and subordinates using another in

In contrast to the Western attitude that patrons have all the advantages and clients are constantly exploited, in Indonesian politics, the anak buahs often force their bapaks to assume risks in order to gain more power and influence so that they might benefit from them. Americans tend to think of patron–client relations as analogous to a general of the infantry sending his troops into harm's way. For the Indonesians, the proper analogy is with the airforce, in which officers risk death by flying into combat while enlisted men remain behind at the base. Furthermore, since the enlisted men pack the officers' parachutes, the officers are well advised to stay on friendly terms with them.

The ease with which unbreakable bonds can be initiated with patrons means that those in favored positions are constantly under siege from people anxious to declare their loyalty to them. Geertz has described the terrible predicament of aspiring Javanese entrepreneurs who become so inundated with undeniable requests for jobs that their businesses soon collapse. The Javanese understandably tend to feel that the Chinese have an unfair advantage in business matters because they only have to look after their blood relatives; a good Javanese finds it impossible to say "no" to any unfortunate person.[9]

Since Indonesian culture makes no sharp division between the political and the economic realms, the traditional practices of bapakism generate relationships that Westerners would consider to be blatant corruption and cronyism. The dramatic financial turmoil of 1997/1998 in Southeast Asia exposed the extent to which President Suharto's six children had built up a $30 billion empire. The pattern was simple: Anyone with a hopeful entrepreneurial plan would ask one of the children to serve as patron; in return, the children became ever-more wealthy. It would have required an unnatural degree of self-restraint and a very un-Javanese independence of mind for the children to have stood aside and not become rich. The financial crisis also revealed the difficul-

---

return. Let me tell you what tradition is. If you are a superior, it means that you will have more money in your bank account at the end of the month than at the beginning. People just put it there, and there are no quid pro quos, because that would make it a materialistic society.

9   Clifford Geertz, *Agricultural Involution: The Process of Ecological Change in Indonesia* (Berkeley, 1963; reissued 1971).

ties of Indonesian bankers operating in a culture in which prying into other people's affairs and explicitly questioning their motives is unseemly. The requirements of alus demand that a great deal of make-believe must be taken as fact.

The nature of Indonesian social capital is also revealed in the customs of *gotong-rojong* and *musjawarah,* community mutual assistance and discussion leading to consensus, respectively. In principle, decisions should be made by consensus after extensive deliberations, but in practice, although the younger participants call for bold actions, and the middle-aged add their cautious wisdom, in the end, the senior figure usually declares what the "consensus" is, whether or not anybody ever articulated it. Since the power of consensus, like all power, involves invisible forces, only a leader with almost magical ability can discern where it lies and assert it authoritatively.

In contrast to the rigid enduring rules of Indonesian bapakism, patron–client ties in the Philippines are looser and less durable. To be a patron in the Philippines is decidedly less onerous and usually more openly profitable. Whereas in Indonesia, power is essentially status, in the Philippines, power, *lakas,* means privilege and exemption from regulation, sometimes to the extent of being totally above the law. Patron-client relations in the Philippines tend to be freewheeling; networks can form and disband as people move about seeking better patrons.

As Lande has noted, children in the Philippines get an early start in seeking out patron–client relations. Siblings often find themselves in different "families," since each child has his or her own set of special aunts, uncles, and godparents, or *compadres.* This fluid form of relations has convinced some scholars that patterns of "bossisms" rather than patron–client ties are the appropriate models of relationship in the Philippines. To keep their power bases, leaders have to go beyond patronage and rely upon coercion and intimidation. Social norms of reciprocity are not strong enough to sustain enduring power structures.[10]

Both Burma and Thailand have acute problems with social capital. The problem in Burma is especially severe because basic

10 Carl Lande, "Networks and Groups in Southeast Asia: Some Observations on the Group Theory of Politics," *American Political Science Review,* LXVII (1973), 103–127; John T. Sidel, "Philippine Politics in Town, District, and Province: Bossism in Cavite and Cebu," *Journal of Asian Studies,* LVI (1997), 947–966.

distrust is so widespread. It goes back to Burmese socialization practices: Infants are not given predictable security, and children are routinely subjected to fear. For example, putting children to bed with the warning that they might never wake up if they have certain dreams is considered not cruel but amusing.

Above all, Burmese culture evinces a deep ambivalence about power. Everyone wants it, but people are too timid to try for it. Nobody wants to be a subordinate, because inferiors are vulnerable and cannot trust anyone with power. Three Burmese concepts help to explain their outlook: Any Burmese, from a villager to a high official, wants to be recognized as possessing *pon,* that is, a person of quality, deserving of respect. Pon is a blend of charisma, commanding presence, grace, dignity, and holiness. Closely related is the concept of *awza,* or power, which is, in a sense, pon in a social context. Every group has someone who has the awza, and anyone can aspire to it. The common response to someone else in a favored position is, "Why him, why not me?"

This attitude would lead to endless power struggle and anarchy if not for the third concept, *ahnadeh,* which the Burmese insist is unique to their culture. It signifies a physical sensation that makes people hold back from asserting their interests and defer instead to the wishes of others. One cannot turn down the requests of others no matter how contrary they are to one's own. The Burmese contend that they have trouble competing in business with Chinese and Indians because the others are not bound by ahnadeh and the ideals of pon. In short, the Burmese believe that they have a higher level of civility than either the Chinese or the Indians. What we can say for sure, however, is that their development of social capital has not gone much beyond the realm of civility; they show little to no trust.

Unlike the Burmese, the Thais find it comfortable to accept gradations, and they take a positive view of the subordinate's role. Their ideal of leadership is *metta,* a form of kindness and compassion. A superior is also supposed to be endowed with *karuna*—a passion to be helpful and supportive of the self-esteem of lesser people. "Little people" feel vulnerable without the benefits of a superior's karuna. With it, they experience *kamulgjei*—an exhilarating sense of will, vital energy, and purposefulness. Subordinates are expected to reciprocate their leaders' kindness by displaying "awe." This exchange of "will" and "awe" is the glue of social relations; it results in more effective collective action than the Burmese pattern permits.[11]

This review of networking practices in East and Southeast Asia demonstrates that social capital differs greatly depending upon the purposes to which it is directed. The Chinese quanxi networks are powerful forces for economic relationships, but politically they tend to become liabilities, easily serving as the bases for corruption. In Indonesia, the bonding of bapakism can produce political stability but also stagnation. In the Philippines, the looser social ties are compatible with elements of democracy, but the struggle for power undermines effective governance. In Burma, trust is so low that there is little in the way of social capital, and in Thailand, leaders are caught between having to be kindly and considerate, on the one hand, and effective and bold, on the other hand.

CIVIL SOCIETY: AUTONOMOUS POWER GROUPINGS AND THE INTER-ESTS OF SOCIETY VERSUS STATE   The mystery in Asia is why societies with such pronounced norms of civility and respectable levels of social capital have had such weak civil societies and, hence, such a poor history of democracy. The question is particularly intriguing in the case of the Confucian cultures where much that is assumed to be associated with social capital—such as etiquette, a work ethic, a high valuation of education, and strong rules for mutual bonding—is in evidence.

Weber was not the only one to claim that Confucianism was incompatible with capitalism and liberal democracy. His argument was advanced more shrilly by the Chinese themselves in the May Fourth Movement when they called for the extermination of their traditions in favor of "Dr. Science and Mr. Democracy." During the 1920s and 1930s, the Chinese overwhelmingly believed that their traditional culture was a curse that had left China backward and weak. In the 1950s through the 1960s, Confucianism was regarded as fertile soil for Leninist Communism, with its emphasis upon authority and ideological conformity, and finally, during the 1980s and 1990s, in a great reversal, as supportive of economic growth and the pursuit of riches. For our purposes, we need only

11   The skill with which Thais are able to discern rankings in the pecking order is evident in the words of a young Thai who told me that he belonged to an informal group of twenty-four students, who had returned from studying abroad, among whom he ranked seventh.

focus on the peculiar nature of civil society in traditional China. The conventional wisdom is that China lacked a strong civil society. China did not develop strong, autonomous, informal political interest groups capable of imposing their will on the state. Nor did it give any signs of an emerging bourgeoisie, even during its periods of economic ascendancy during the twelfth and thirteenth centuries when it was the world's most advanced country.[12]

Confucian philosophy placed the merchant next to the bottom in the social scale. Both the mandarin and the peasant, who ranked above the merchant, agreed that the game of the merchant was to cheat the customer. Hence, merchants lacked true civility. In practice, however, merchants belonged to generally well-organized, functional guilds, which operated largely to discipline their members by setting standards and adjudicating disputes, not to exert pressure on the government about public policy. Merchants were content to leave such matters to the mandarins and the imperial court, modestly denying any interest in altering the dictates of officialdom. They sought special consideration only with respect to the application of the laws in their particular cases, and as a token of appreciation, they might slip officials a little something for their troubles. In short, the guilds operated not as pressure groups but as protective associations.

This formula has continued to operate to this day. Businessman and the now-growing middle class in China still passively accept government authority and still engage in various forms of corruption. The tycoons of Hong Kong sing the praises of Beijing's leaders most loudly and oppose any movement toward democracy most strenuously.

The story of the non-development of a civil society in China is, however, even more complicated than the conventional view

---

12 Max Weber (trans. Hans H. Gerth), *The Religion of China* (Glencoe, 1951). It would take us too far in the wrong direction to explore why each of these judgments about Confucianism was correct under the circumstances of its times. We can only hint at the answers: During the first period, since the Chinese state was pathetically weak, and the society lacked both large-scale institutions and the framework necessary for national economic growth, the focus of Confucian values operated only in the realm of family ties and personal relationships. During the second period, since the Communist state was all-powerful, the requirement of giving deference and obedience to political authority and the state ideology was seen as a new version of "Confucian" orthodoxy. During the third period, since the political environment was compatible with, and tolerant of, private entrepreneurial activities, the manifestations of frugality, hard work, and stress on education were seen as enduring features of "Confucianism."

can show. The Confucian rules of ethics applied to both the public and private realms but only in a way that reinforced the powers of the state, because, instead of the clear division of state and society that feudalism produced in Europe and Japan, China inclined toward a three-way division—state (*guan*), public (*gong*), and private (*si*) realms. The state comprised mandarin bureaucracy, with the emperor at the top and the local magistrate at the bottom. It monopolized all legitimate political authority. The private sphere contained the extremely powerful and disciplined Chinese family and clan system. Its influence was not supposed to extend outside its legitimate domain. In Chinese culture, the selfish assertion of private interest in the state or public realm was a gross social evil, one of the ultimate sins.[13]

Between the state and the private arenas lay the clearly defined public sphere, which consisted of the collective actions of the gentry in the countryside and the merchant guilds in the cities. Actions within this sphere help to explain in greater detail why the Chinese failed to develop a civic culture, even though they had a strong sense of civic virtue and public spiritedness (*gongzheng*).

In addition to the merchant guilds, the cities had a variety of societies and, more particularly, benevolent associations that looked after their members' welfare. In many cities, these organizations established schools, foundling homes, and community temples, and sometimes under the auspices of local elites, they assumed such civic responsibilities as water control, social welfare, famine relief, the building of roads, ferries, and bridges, and even public security through the formation of a local militia. Significantly, the public role of these local institutions became more active when the dynasties were in decline and the state was weak, as during the late Ming. Thus, the public sphere of action operated on behalf of the state even though it was not an agent of the state. The local elites complemented the state; they did not challenge the state with a different agenda of interests and concerns, as in Europe and Japan.

13 This analysis of the three spheres of traditional Chinese life is heavily indebted to the work of Mary Backus Rankin, particularly "The Origins of a Chinese Public Sphere: Local Elites and Community Affairs in the Late Imperial Period," *Etudes Chinoises,* IX (1990), 13–60; "Some Observations on a Chinese Public Sphere," *Modern China,* XII (1993), 158–182.

This tripartite division of the state, the public, and the private spheres helped establish in China a vivid sense of what the tasks of government should be, laying a positive foundation for subsequent political development. But it also produced a tradition that inhibited the development of a true civil society, because it worked to suppress the articulation of special interests and to deny legitimacy to a political process in which the society could balance the powers of the state.

The ending of the imperial era and the establishment of the Republican period brought an increase in the number of institutions that could have become the basis for a stronger civil society. In the Treaty Port cities during the 1920s and 1930s, for instance, labor unions, independent newspapers, and publishing houses sprang up, along with many kinds of business and professional associations. During the Mao Zedong era, most of these institutions fell into the hands of the state and the Party and lost their potential for being separate voices for society.

What has been slow in coming is the legitimization of individual and group interests. The traditional perspective of private interests as shameful expressions of selfishness and greed is still strong in China. If China is ever to develop a strong civil society, the public realm between the state and the private ones must go beyond its traditional view of government and champion the free and open expression of every social interest. The traditional Chinese faith in a benevolent government that can take care of society without any help from outside has outlived its usefulness. Such an arrangement might have been possible when China was a predominately agricultural society, but now that the country has become more modernized and industrialized, its legitimate competing and conflicting interests must be allowed to make public their cases for policy support, or they will have to operate in dishonorable ways, using the "back door," exploiting the powers of quanxi, and practicing outright corruption.

Behind the glitter of the recent "miracle" economy lies a pattern of sordid relationships between avaricious cadres and get-rich-quick entrepreneurs who straddle the line between government and business by arranging tax exemptions for themselves and imposing "management fees" and "voluntary donations" on third parties. The easy acceptance of corruption by the economically successful works against the introduction of democracy; cronyism is less demanding than transparency in the articulation and aggregation of interests.[14]

The experiences of all advanced industrialized countries indicate that the only way to manage the growth of interests is to permit a strong civil society. This system is fundamental to the operations of democracy, which, in spite of its faults, remains the best way to accommodate and reconcile social conflicts. Although China has started to take on the appearance of modernity, especially in its coastal cities, it still has a way to go before it will be compelled to give up its antidemocratic and anti-true-capitalist ways and create a vibrant civil society.

In Southeast Asia, the struggles for independence created the rudiments of civil society in the form of the various groupings that challenged the colonial rulers. Most of the first organizations involved young people and students—in Burma, the YMBA (Young Men's Buddhist Association) and in Indonesia, several Muslim organizations. But, in time, these movements were absorbed into the all-embracing nationalist parties, which, with independence, became the new governments. Although the transition from being an opponent of the state to being part of the state was generally quick and easy, the nationalist leaders subsequently made sure that no new groups would emerge to challenge their authority. Thus, the initial phase of nation building in Southeast Asia tended to stifle the creation of civil society by declaring any disagreement with the state to be a subversive act.

The East and Southeast Asian cultures are not deficient in norms of civility, in social capital, or even in some facets of civil society. But they have combined these elements in ways that diverge from the Western pattern during its evolution toward democracy. Confucian culture had powerful norms of civility, but it lacked the rules for impersonal dealings beyond the face-to-face level that are critical for the development of a pluralistic democracy. Similarly, the emphasis on civility and trust in Southeast Asia largely pertains to relations with familiars; those outside of one's network circle are to be distrusted. In other words, in Asian cultures role relations are of a particularistic nature and resistant to a universal-

---

14   For an excellent analysis of the people who combine business and government in today's China, see Margaret M. Pearson, *China's New Business Elite* (Berkeley, 1997).

istic outlook. That, of course, is exactly the language of modern-ization theory, which for some people means that we are on the right track.

Are there specifically "Asian values" that evade Western cate-gories? If so, they are not the ones advanced by Lee Kwan Yew of Singapore and by Mahathir Mohamed of Malaysia, who have argued that Asian values differ from Western ones in their em-phasis on the community rather than the individual. All societies require individual and collective rights and duties to be in balance. The question of what constitutes the ideal balance has been central in Western political theory. Moreover, the balance point in any dynamic society tends to shift back and forth over time.

Our analysis leads to a significantly different conclusion from this version of the "Asian values" argument in its definition of *community*. the Singapore-Malaysian view equates the "commu-nity" to the state, thereby interpreting any pressure from a civil society against state policy as an affront to the community and a subversive activity. Our analysis of the Asian cultures finds that the issue of the individual versus the community is played out at the much-lower level of family, clan, neighborhood, and imme-diate community. What is striking in Asian cultures is the huge gap between that level and the realm of the state. The world of the citizen and that of the government remain far apart in non-democratic Asia. To define the state as the only legitimate com-munity, and thus deprive citizens of individual rights, comes close to advancing a fascist ideology.

Our discovery of the great divide between the three con-cepts—civility, social capital, and civil society—and the domain of the state is, however, not as pessimistic about the prospects of democracy as it might at first seem. It does mean that merely accumulating civility and social capital will not in itself be enough to facilitate transitions to democracy. The void between the realm of social relationships and that of the state must be filled by a national political process in which diverse social interests can be articulated and aggregated to serve as the basis of public policy.

The key to this learning process is a collective effort to define the national identity of the country in terms of the modern nation-state. Society must lead in this quest for a modern national identity; if the state has a monopoly on the national ideals, the result can be a form of fascism. China faces a particularly acute problem in this regard, because at this juncture in its history, the ideals of nationhood that are going to replace the outmoded principles of Marxism–Leninism–Maoism are still undecided. The Chinese leaders speak about the need to build a new "spiritual civilization" and "socialism with Chinese characteristics," but they have not yet accepted the need for society as a whole to take a lead in this quest.

The prospects for democracy in the Southeast Asian countries are better where social capital seems to be strengthening the growth of civil society, especially in Thailand and the Philippines. Burma has the most intractable problems. Since its culture aggressively socializes distrust, it offers limited capabilities for collective action. Singapore and Malaysia would be at the forefront of the transition to democracy if not for their current fixation on the false concept of "Asian values." However, in another generation or two, new leaders might be able to make changes that bring political life more in line with the sophistication of their economies.

The fact that the norms of civility, the forms of social capital, and the structures of civil society differ from country to country in Asia, as well as from the Western countries, means that the evolution toward democracy in each country will have distinctive characteristics. The result will not be an "Asian" form of democracy but a rich variety of types, ranging from the Malaysian and Thai to the Korean and Taiwanese. Each country's culturally distinct qualities will produce mixes that will yield unique national systems.